New Social
Movements

New
Social
Movements
From Ideology
to Identity

**Edited by
Enrique Laraña,
Hank Johnston, and
Joseph R. Gusfield**

Temple University Press
Philadelphia

Temple University Press, Philadelphia 19122
Copyright © 1994 by Temple University. All rights reserved
Published 1994
Printed in the United States of America

The paper used in this publication meets the minimum requirements of American National
Standard for Information Sciences—Permanence of Paper for Printed Library Materials,
ANSI Z39.48-1984 ☉

Library of Congress Cataloging-in-Publication Data

New social movements : from ideology to identity / Enrique Laraña,
    Hank Johnston, and Joseph R. Gusfield.
        p.   cm.
    Includes index.
    ISBN 1-56639-186-5 (alk. paper). — ISBN 1-56639-187-3 (alk. paper:
    pbk.)
    1. Social movements. 2. Social history—1945– 3. Social
psychology. I. Laraña, Enrique. II. Johnston, Hank.
III. Gusfield, Joseph R., 1923– .
HN17.5.N4855   1994
303.48′4—dc20   93-37495

Contents

Part III
Collective Action and Identity in Changing Political Contexts

Part I

Culture and Identity in Contemporary Social Movements

Chapter I

Identities, Grievances, and New Social Movements

Hank Johnston
Enrique Laraña
Joseph R. Gusfield

In the last two decades, the emergence of new forms of collective action in advanced industrial societies stimulated a provocative and innovative reconceptualization of the meaning of social movements. Its relevance has been highlighted by the process of delegitimization of major political parties in Europe at the end of the 1980s, as shown in recent electoral results that have demonstrated considerable support for new or nontraditional parties in Germany, Austria, Italy, and France. In both Europe and North America, movements have arisen that stretch the explanatory capacities of older theoretical perspectives. Peace movements, student movements, the anti-nuclear energy protests, minority nationalism, gay rights, women's rights, animal rights, alternative medicine, fundamentalist religious movements, and New Age and ecology movements are but a sampling of the phenomena that have engaged the puzzled attention of sociologists, historians, and political scientists. What is significant for sociologists in such developments is the inability of these movements to be clearly understood within the European or American traditions of analysis. They constitute the anomalies of Kuhnian "normal science."

For much of this century sociological studies of social movements have been dominated first by theories of ideology and later by theories of organization and rationality. Especially in Western Europe, but also in the United States, sociologists have focused on the systems of ideas that movements have espoused. These have often been described in general terms, such as socialism, capitalism, conservatism, communism, fascism. The problem of the analyst has often been that of understanding the economic or class base of the movement or at least some set of discrete interests and sentiments, such as social status, that characterize a group in the social structure. The movement could then be seen as a response to a felt sense of injustice that the ideology specified and that provided the basis for mobilization. Partisanship and mobilization involved a commitment to the ideas and goals of the movement and its program.

The basic problem of many analysts was to understand the process of movement formation by analysis of the social structure that gave rise to the ideology and the problems to which it was addressed. The focus was directed toward groups that occupied specific places in the social structure from which derived objective interests and demands. The nineteenth-century emphasis on labor and capital fit well into this general paradigm, from which it was also derived. Labor movements and the rise of new political parties have long been the ideal-typical images of social movements and mobilization; through them, the revolutionary actions of communism and fascism were further examined.

Marxist-oriented scholars, as well as some others, have emphasized the class origins and interests of movements and the ideological programs accompanying them. This emphasis on elements of ideology, commitment, and partisanship led to the dominance of ideas as ideologies in understanding the emergence of social movements and collective action. It furthered a focus on the strains and conflicts in social structure as the sources of movement formation, dissent, and protest activity. What it ignored was the importance of organization and the consequences of organizing into group associations. It assumed that the existence of potential conflicts and strains would automatically generate associations of people to correct them.

An interest in the organizational aspects of movements tapped an existing vein of theoretical and empirical interests. Since Max Weber and Ernst Troeltsch there had been a keen interest in charisma and routinization through the functional and strategic considerations of organizational expansion. A series of studies of religious organizations focused on the pathos associated with loss of an original mission as sects became churches. Others, influenced by Weber's writings on bureaucratic organization, have emphasized the internal changes within the movement as an organization. In more recent years, guided in part by conceptions of rational choice, sociologists have gone well beyond Weberian insights into a focus on how collective action depended on the ability of associations to mobilize resources and to conduct the organization on the basis of planned and rational action.

As a corrective to the dominance of ideas and structural strain in the older theories, the resource mobilization perspective was a welcome addition and substitution. Sociologists, especially Charles Tilly and John McCarthy and Mayer Zald, pointed out that there was always strain in the society and that mobilization required both resources and a rational orientation to action. The actor in movements and in protest action was not under the sway of sentiments, emotions, and ideologies that guided his or her action, but rather should be understood in terms of the logic of costs and benefits as well as opportunities for action. When dealing with existent organized groups, as in labor unions or in the civil rights movement, the emphasis on organization could ignore the already existing ideologies. By treating the activities of collective actors as tactics and strategy, the analyst could examine movements and countermovements as engaged in a rational game to achieve specific interests, much like pluralist competition among interest groups in political analysis.

This broad canvas, theoretically spanning finer conceptual and empirical issues that have been debated for more than a century, nevertheless constitutes the painted backdrop for two fundamental questions about new social movements. Why did they create a theoretical problem for the sociologist? And what was lacking in either of the general perspectives outlined above? Such movements had certainly occurred in the past. Earlier this century, witness the Young Movements of Europe (Young Germany, Young Italy, etc.) and the temperance movements in the United States or suffrage movements and student movements on both sides of the Atlantic. In many ways, the student movements of the 1960s, by raising issues that were more than just "problems of interpretation," heralded the first challenges to these classic paradigms (Flacks 1967; Laraña 1982; Katsiaficas 1987).

The concept "new social movements" is a double-edged sword. On one side, it has contributed to the knowledge of contemporary movements by focusing attention to the meaning of morphological changes in their structure and action and by relating those changes with structural transformations in society as a whole. These changes are the source of these movements' "novelty" when compared with the model of collective action based in class conflict that prevailed in Europe since the industrial revolution (Melucci 1989, see also Chapter 5). On the other side, there is a tendency to "ontologize" new social movements (Melucci 1989). This means using the term broadly, as if it captures the "essence" of all new forms of collective action. There is also a tendency to give the concept more explanatory power than is empirically warranted, which no doubt derives from its popularization. The concept, however, refers to an approach rather than a theory; it is not a set of general propositions that have been verified empirically but just an attempt to identify certain common characteristics in contemporary social movements and develop analytical tools to study them (Melucci 1989; Laraña 1993b). The bundle of new social movements mentioned earlier were difficult to conceptualize with either the imagery of the ideological movements of the past or the rationally organized interest group.

Conceived as such, the analysis of new social movements (NSMs) can be advanced by cross-cultural research and by contrasting them with movements of the past that originated in class conflict. To this end, a good starting place is the specification of the fundamental characteristics of NSMs. By no means do all current movements display the following characteristics of new social movements, nor can all current movements be designated new. In many cases, their appearance among current movements leads us to conceptualize them along dimensions of differences from earlier cases of collective action and social movements.

First, NSMs do not bear a clear relation to structural roles of the participants. There is a tendency for the social base of new social movements to transcend class structure. The background of participants find their most frequent structural roots in rather diffuse social statuses such as youth, gender, sexual orientation, or professions that do not correspond with structural explanations (Klandermans and Oegema 1987). This has been striking in two especially strong movements: the Greens in Europe and the ecological movement in America. It is evident also in such other movements as the anti–nuclear energy movement in Europe and America or the animal and children's rights movements in the United States.

Second, the ideological characteristics of NSMs stand in sharp contrast to the working-class movement and to the Marxist conception of ideology as a unifying and totalizing element for collective action. Especially in Europe but also in the United States, movements were characteristically perceived in accordance with overarching ideologies: conservative or liberal; right or left; capitalist or socialist. Marxist thought, always more dominant in Europe than in America, provided the paradigm for perceptions of action, either bourgeois or proletarian. The new social movements are more difficult to characterize in such terms. They exhibit a pluralism of ideas and values, and they tend to have pragmatic orientations and search for institutional reforms that enlarge the systems of members' participation in decision making (Offe 1985; Cohen 1985; Laraña 1992, 1993a). These movements have an important political meaning in Western societies: They imply a "democratization dynamic" of everyday life and the expansion of civil versus political dimensions of society (Laraña 1993b).

Third, NSMs often involve the emergence of new or formerly weak dimensions of identity. The grievances and mobilizing factors tend to focus on cultural and symbolic issues that are linked with issues of identity rather than on economic grievances that characterized the working-class movement (Melucci 1985, 1989). They are associated with a set of beliefs, symbols, values, and meanings related to sentiments of belonging to a differentiated social group; with the members' image of themselves; and with new, socially constructed attributions about the meaning of everyday life. This is especially relevant to the ethnic, separatist, and nationalistic movements within existing states. The Catalan and Basque movements in Spain, the Asian and Hispanic movements in the United States, the ethnic movements in the former Soviet Union and even Palestinian nationalism are all examples of new identities emerging in the modern world. The women's movement and the gay rights movement also exemplify this trend. All of these new identities are formed as both private and public ones or old ones remade along new lines.

Fourth, the relation between the individual and the collective is blurred. Closely related to the above point, many contemporary movements are "acted out" in individual actions rather than through or among mobilized groups. The "hippie" movement is the most striking instance, but it is equally true of aspects of other movements where the collective and the individual are blurred, for example, in the gay rights and the women's movements. Another way of thinking about the same phenomena is that in and through movements that have no clear class or structural base, the movement becomes the focus for the individual's definition of himself or herself, and action within the movement is a complex mix of the collective and individual confirmations of identity. The student movements and various countercultural groups of the 1960s were among the earliest examples of this aspect of collective action.

Fifth, NSMs often involve personal and intimate aspects of human life. Movements focusing on gay rights or abortion, health movements such as alternative medicine or antismoking, New Age and self-transformation movements, and the women's movement all include efforts to change sexual and bodily behavior. They extend into arenas of daily life: what we eat, wear, and enjoy; how we make love, cope with personal problems, or plan or shun careers.

Sixth, another common feature of NSMs is the use of radical mobilization tactics of disruption and resistance that differ from those practiced by the working-class movement. New social movements employ new mobilization patterns characterized by nonviolence and civil disobedience that, while often challenging dominant norms of conduct through dramatic display, draw equally on strategies influenced by Gandhi, Thoreau, and Kropotkin that were successfully used in the past (Laraña 1979; McAdam 1988; Morris 1984; Klandermans and Tarrow 1988).

Seventh, the organization and proliferation of new social movement groups are related to the credibility crisis of the conventional channels for participation in Western democracies. This is especially true with regard to the traditional mass parties from which NSMs tend to have a considerable degree of autonomy — and even disdain. This crisis is a motivational factor for collective action in search of alternative forms of participation and decision making relating to issues of collective interest (Whalen and Flacks 1989; Melucci 1989).

Finally, in contrast to cadre-led and centralized bureaucracies of traditional mass parties, new social movement organizations tend to be segmented, diffuse, and decentralized. While there is considerable variation according to movement type, the tendency is toward considerable autonomy of local sections, where collective forms of debate and decision making often limit linkages with regional and national organizations. This has been called the "self-referential element" of the new movements, and it constitutes another sharp distinction with the hierarchical, centralized organization of the working-class movement and the role of the party organization in the Leninist model.

These characteristics of new social movements are not independent of links with the past. Nor is there an absence of continuity with the old, although that varies with each movement. The women's movement has its roots in the suffrage movement of the late nineteenth century in America. New Age movements can trace connections to earlier spiritualist teachings and Eastern philosophies; and contemporary health movements have roots in various quasi-medical orientations that proliferated earlier in this century. Even movements with old histories have emerged in new forms with more diffuse goals and different modes of mobilization and conversion. It is both the newness of expression and extension as well as the magnitude and saliency of such movements that constitutes the basis for needing revised frameworks of understanding.

The theoretical roots of social movement scholarship provide a backdrop to the contemporary discussion of new forms of social movements. Are the new movements as new as they seem? What social and cultural changes have led to the emergence of such movements? Are the ideologies of the past 150 years, with their general programs of reform and revolution, no longer operative in these movements? Has the fulcrum of social movement action shifted from a concern for large-scale societal change to narrower, more self-oriented goals of claiming and realizing new individual and group identities? As Alberto Melucci, one of the contributors to this book, has written elsewhere concerning the influence of a changed social structure on movements, "The freedom to have which characterized . . . industrial society has been replaced by the freedom to be" (Melucci 1989, 177–78).

This volume was conceived as an effort to provide some provisional answers to these questions. Many of its chapters share basic assumptions of the social constructionist approach and synthesize the classic and modern perspectives in order to better explain contemporary social movements in Western societies. Social constructionist insights into the way that meanings and collective beliefs arise as central to movement emergence help explain the nature of new grievances and from whence they came. This first chapter joins the theoretical debate by focusing on three of the themes mentioned above, all of which recur in the chapters that follow: the role of identity in social movements, the place of ideology and its relation to collective identity, and issues arising from ideational and structural continuity in contemporary forms of mobilization. Our goals are to identify the key issues, to point out provocative junctures of theory and research, and to reassess where this new conceptual apparatus might take us.

Dimensions of Identity in Social Movement Theory

About twenty-five years ago several American sociologists noted the growing popularity of social movements concerned with the identity of their members. Ralph Turner (1969; see also Chapter 4) observed that personal identity and personal transformation were increasingly themes of diffusely organized social movement organizations. Orrin Klapp (1969) also discussed the collective search for identity as a response to the impoverishment of interaction in modern society. He argued that modern, rationalized, social relations no longer provided reliable reference points from which to construct one's identity. The movements he observed—"identity seeking movements," such as religious and self-help groups, and less organized, trendy, collective behaviors—were attempts to reclaim a self robbed of its identity.

The new social movement perspective holds that the collective search for identity is a central aspect of movement formation. Mobilization factors tend to focus on cultural and symbolic issues that are associated with sentiments of belonging to a differentiated social group where members can feel powerful; they are likely to have subcultural orientations that challenge the dominant system. New social movements are said to arise "in defense of identity." They grow around relationships that are voluntarily conceived to empower members to "name themselves. "What individuals are claiming collectively is the right to realize their own identity: the possibility of disposing of their personal creativity, their affective life, and their biological and interpersonal existence" (Melucci 1980, 218).

Both approaches seem to assume that the pursuit of collective identity flows from an intrinsic need for an integrated and continuous social self, a self that is thwarted and assaulted in modern society. The link between the "morphological social changes" described by Melucci and identity-seeking behaviors seems to result from four factors that are characteristic of postmodernism: material affluence, information overload, confusion over the wide horizon of available cultural alternatives, and system inadequacies in providing institutionally based and culturally normative alternatives for self-identification (see Inglehart 1990, 347). The issues that NSM groups advocate reflect the expanded horizons of personal choice and point out cracks in the system, often in the form of newly defined global concerns. Individuals seek out new collectivities and produce "new social spaces" where novel life-styles and social identities can be experienced and defined. Much as Klapp's explanation of the collective search for identity implicitly criticized modern society, NSM research points out the need for system adjustments via movement formation and the cultural challenges that new movements pose (Habermas 1981, 36–37).

NSM thinking and research so far has produced important insights about the nature of these groups, but to date these insights have not taken the form of an overall theory. The four factors mentioned above are often left implicit; how they interrelate in the formation of new groups has not been developed. A cynosure of the new social movement perspective that needs further elaboration is the linkage between the broad structural changes that are said to characterize postindustrial society and identity problems for individuals. This task can begin with a systematic approach to the concept of identity itself. An understanding of who one is, in all its complexity, is fundamental to the formulation of goals, plans, assessments, accounts, and attributions that constitute making one's daily way. That it is so fundamental may explain why, from the new social movements approach, there is a tendency to refer to the concept of identity in a taken-for-granted way. There has been much written in sociology about various aspects of identity, and in the last decade, psychological research has increasingly examined the relationship between individual and group identity (Tajfel 1978; Tajfel and Turner 1985; Turner 1985; Turner et al. 1987). From this vast literature, three distinct dimensions of identity stand out as central for participation in social movements:

individual identity, collective identity, and public identity. A more theoretical approach requires clear conceptualizations about how they are related.

Individual Identity

For most sociologists, the term individual identity is inherently contradictory. Apart from the "hard wiring" of gender and kinship—which we are only beginning to understand—who a person is and what he or she becomes are thoroughly social processes. Yet, in several ways individual identity is important in understanding social movement participation. It relates to the wholly personal traits that, although constructed through the interaction of biological inheritance and social life, are internalized and imported to social movement participation as idiosyncratic biographies. Psychologists studying group formation (Tajfel 1978, 1981; Turner et al. 1987) clearly separate individual identity from its social aspects derived from group membership, but a sociology of social movements must recognize that individual identities are brought to movement participation and changed in the process.

The degree to which they are changed can be used as a means to classify movements—from totalizing cults of personal transformation, where the individual identity is taken over by the group, to checkbook quasi-movements like Greenpeace and Ross Perot's United We Stand America, where individual identification may not extend beyond a bumper sticker. Stephen Reicher has noted a parallel continuum regarding the degree to which group-based, socially constructed aspects of identity come to dominate the "imported" individual aspects (see Turner et al. 1987, 169–202).

The field of social movements has appropriated symbolic interactionist approaches to social roles and social location (Stryker 1980) as the conceptual foundation for thinking about individual identity. The social self of a movement adherent is made up of several social identities that are, in part, shaped as they are acted out, but also that correspond to institutional and organizational roles that proscribe normative behaviors (Merton 1957). These insights have influenced subsequent research in social psychology on role strain, role change, and role conflict. Another line of research has been directed at operationalizing and measuring individual identity in its various dimensions. A fundamental problem is that most people can describe "who they are" in only limited terms. The verbal articulation of identity is often limited to counseling psychology or self-help psychologizing of a popular nature. Outside these contexts, and outside life-cycle influences that bring identity issues to the foreground, expression of individual identity in all its facets is not usually necessary. In the ebb and flow of everyday life, identity only becomes an issue when one's status quo is threatened.

In most sociological fields that touch on identity issues— social movements, deviance, family studies, health and medicine—discussions of individual identity are based on the basic framework described above. Erving Goffman's insights into the managed and situational nature of self-image (1959, 1967) have important implications for a sociological approach to individual identity, as does recent work on the relation between self-concept and spoken discourse (Perinbanayagam 1991), but these ideas have proven difficult to reconcile with positivistic research strategies. Recently, feminist research has broken new ground in specifying male-female differences in thinking about oneself and others that derive from biology and culturally defined gender influences.

One of the problems with this key concept is also a source of strength: its interdisciplinary nature in both sociology and psychology. One aspect of a psychological focus emphasizes pathological and unconscious forces and the developmental progress toward adulthood. The work of Erik Erikson (1958, 1968) has focused on the meaning of psychosocial identity as a subjective sense of "continuity and being oneself," and as a fundamental step in personal development. This subjective sense does not arise in isolation but requires the existence of a community. Sociologists and social psychologists have pointed out that personal identity emerges through the mirror of social interaction, that is, by playing different roles and by interpreting how others see us. Although the degree to which a core identity is established and functions as an integrating concept will vary, the basic insight of Meadian social psychology also holds true: Individual identity is quintessentially social and its core—if it can be apprehended at all by a reflective self—is relativized according to interactive situations. If identity is difficult to grasp because so much of its content is locked away in the black box of mental life, then it is more difficult to specify because the contents are shifted and rearranged according to social context. The concept provides a tool to analyze a concrete set of facts and problems where the individual and the social realms intersect; this reinforces the need to integrate the biological and sociological models of human behavior.

The dichotomy of a core identity versus a malleable one—or individual versus social identity, to use Tajfel's terms (1981)—should be an important focus in future social movement research. A key question is the extent to which NSMs are disproportionately represented by a coming-of-age generation for whom questions of identity are paramount due to developmental psychological factors. In the three NSM groups studied by Melucci and his colleagues in *Altri Codici* (1984), in addition to the one that was characterized by Giovanni Lodi and Marco Grazioli (1984) as a "youth movement," all seem to be composed largely of people between the ages of eighteen and twenty-eight.

More than in other stages in one's life cycle, search for identity is a youthful activity. Erikson's (1968) fifth developmental stage occurs in late adolescence, when a process of solidification of a mature identity occurs through reconciliation of ascribed roles and new or emergent adult roles. He also pointed out that there is a intrinsic link between identity and ideology. An individual's identity becomes consistent when it is built in a common ideological orientation that renders it meaningful and gives it coherence. To take one example, in interviews with leftist and nationalist militants in Barcelona, Hank Johnston (1991) found that many spoke vividly of psychological dissonance that arose from reconciling a traditional, often religious, and middle-class upbringing with newfound Marxism. Identity reconciliation was the substance of interaction with dense interpersonal networks of young student and working-class militants. It forged a solidarity in these groups that imparted a resilience against state repression. It also provided for a unique flexibility and breadth that served to bridge different oppositional groups during mass mobilization. Sustained by intense discussions among friends, these networks were the functional equivalent of "new social spaces" discussed by Melucci.

It is our guess that among different social movements, the emphasis on identity quest results from the intersection of several factors, one of which is the coming of age of a cohort in an economic and social milieu that frees them from immediate material concerns and disposes them to intense introspection about who they are. Although research on new social movements recognizes that these factors are related to participation, identity search and temporariness of involvement are treated as something new, deriving from system changes in postindustrial society (Lodi and Grazioli 1984). To the extent that we are dealing primarily with youth movements, or at least movements that bear the imprint of a large youthful membership, then identity search cannot be explained exclusively by postindustrial changes.

Collective Identity

The concept of collective identity has recently been thrust into the foreground of social movement theory. Aldon Morris's and Carol Mueller's book, *Frontiers in Social Movement Theory* (1992), contains several chapters that either deal directly with this concept or have sections that discuss it. Taken together, these treatments point out the multifaceted and interrelated nature of the concept; the paradoxical result is that the theoretical spotlight simultaneously reveals many more angles, corners, niches, and shadows. Let us see if we can clarify the ways of talking about collective identity, and in particular point out the relationship between several closely related concepts like group boundaries, group membership, solidarity, and the organization of everyday life.

The concept of collective identity refers to the (often implicitly) agreed upon definition of membership, boundaries, and activities for the group. According to Melucci (forthcoming), "Collective identity is an interactive and shared definition produced by several individuals (or groups at a more complex level) and concerned with the orientations of action and the field of opportunities and constraints in which the actions take place." It is built through shared definitions of the situation by its members, and it is a result of a process of negotiation and "laborious adjustment" of different elements relating to the ends and means of collective action and its relation to the environment. By this process of interaction, negotiation and conflict over the definition of the situation, and the movement's reference frame, members construct the collective "we."

This social constructionist definition has three dimensions that make collective identity an especially difficult concept to pin down empirically. First, it is predicated on a continual interpenetration of—and mutual influence between—the individual identity of the participant and the collective identity of the group. Second, by the very nature of the phenomena we study, the collective identity of social movements is a "moving target," with different definitions predominating at different points in a movement career. Third, distinct processes in identity creation and maintenance are operative in different phases of the movement.

In the midst of all this change and flux, this concept is often employed as if it was frozen in time and space, neglecting its process-based nature and shifting boundaries. A related problem refers to the "facticity" of collective identity and the way it serves as a predicate of behavior. A frequent usage, although one that seems to occur more as a rhetorical device than a conscious analytical position, is to speak of collective identity as something that stands above and beyond the individual social actors and takes on a life of its own. Suggestive of Herbert Blumer's early conceptualization of esprit de corps (1955) and other early collective behavior theorists that emphasized group consciousness, this is a definition that directs attention away from individual contributions and attaches it to a movement organization defined in the aggregate as a collective actor. In this usage, both "collective identity" and "social movement" can be spoken of without reference to the processes that constitute them. Rather, like Émile Durkheim's *conscience collective*, collective identity is the repository of movement values and norms that define movement behavior from some epistemological point beyond the individual participant. It is a "social fact" that dictates prohibitions and appropriate behaviors.

Yet there is a grain of insight that can be winnowed from the Durkheimian position. We have in mind the notion that an identity is both cognitively real—that is, based on lived experience and knowledge stored in memory—and idealized in Goffman's sense of ideal notions of how a role behavior should be. To share a collective identity means not only to have had a part in constituting it but also, in some instances, "obeying" its normative proscriptions. Clearly, this is an aspect of collective identity that meets Durkheim's external and constraining criteria for social facts; and, from this perspective, to partake in a collective identity means also doing (and not doing) certain things. The key insight is that normative and valuational elements of external social relations are closely associated with how one thinks about oneself; these elements guide and channel behavior within—and without—the group. In this sense, doing (appropriate movement-related behaviors) and being (identity) are inextricably linked. This closely follows Stephen Reichter's treatment of identity and crowd behavior (see Turner et al. 1987, 169–202). He suggests that the more the individual identifies with the group, the more likely emergent group norms will constrain and shape behavior. The power of emergent norms works through the mechanism of collective identity and the intrinsic human tendency to affirm group identification (see Tajfel and Turner 1985).

Bearing this in mind, we can turn to the more common, constructionist usage that has been drawn on by NSM thinking. The constructionist view has been emphasized in current analyses of radical feminist, gay, and lesbian groups (Margolis 1985; Marshall 1991), as well as attempts to explain ethnic politics and nationalism (Johnston 1985; See 1986; Nagel and Olzak 1982; Anderson 1991). Characteristic of this approach, Melucci asserts that "collective identity is a product of conscious action and the outcome of self-reflection more than a set of given or 'structural' characteristics. [It] tends to coincide with conscious processes of 'organization' and it is experienced not so much as a situation as an action" (1992, 10–11). By stressing the "process-based, self-reflexive and constructed manner in which collective actors tend to define themselves today" (10), contemporary approaches to collective identity acknowledge a strong symbolic interactionist influence. This tradition points to interaction among social movement participants as the locus of research on identity processes. In Europe, one tendency has been to explore this avenue of investigation through "intervention research" (Touraine 1981; Melucci 1984). In North America, research has followed an identity-focused agenda via traditional interactionist issues: self-presentation, dramaturgical analysis, conversions, and gender and gender interaction. Regardless of research strategy, the global point is that collective actors define themselves in a social context, and any constructionist view of identity must make reference to both the interactive situations where identity is formed and shaped and to the other people who join in the task.

This raises inevitable questions about the relation between group membership and collective identity. Debra Friedman and Doug McAdam (1992, 169) have discussed how individual attachments to preexisting groups and interpersonal networks frequently function as sources of collective identity when these attachments are highly valued. The assumption of valued group attachments allows the authors to recast collective identity as a selective incentive, to use Mancur Olson's (1965) term, as a way of reconciling a microstructuralist focus with rational choice models. Collective identity becomes a valued commodity that is worth the commitment of time, resources the "capital" of individual autonomy and the risk of presentation of self because the group from which it is derived is also valued.

The issue goes to the core of social movement formation, and there are several answers, which, taken together, can help the student of social movements think more systematically about the creation of collective identities. First, following the argument of Friedman and McAdam, one can consider organizational strategy. In their analysis, the organization "provides an identity" and "shapes it for consumption." This might be called a "strategic constructionist perspective," to coin a term, that suggests, for some movements, there are leaders, committees, or cabals that plot the best collective identity for the movement, much like marketing executives strategizing the best way to present a product. It is a "top down" approach to collective identity that seems to be more useful in some movements than others. This approach would be especially useful in later stages of movement development when social movement organizations are established and likely to be thinking of these strategic terms. At earlier stages, however, when issues are being articulated and groups coalesce around issues, it makes sense that a more "bottom up" approach is, if not the entire answer, then at least deserving of a place in the theoretical equation. These issues are expanded in the next two sections.

Public Identity

While the two previous dimensions of identity involve self-assessments—either by an individual or by the group—the concept of public identity captures the influences that the external public have on the way social movement adherents think about themselves. Both individual identity and collective identity are affected by interaction with nonmembers and by definitions imposed on movements by state agencies, countermovements, and, especially in the contemporary movement environment, the media. There are different courses and different channels by which public definitions can influence movement identities, and it makes sense that, depending on the source, there can be different effects.

On the one hand, there is a long tradition of research on how impersonal influences affect movement identities. State repression can intensify we-them distinctions and fortify group identification and commitment (Trotsky 1957; Smelser 1962; Brinton 1965; Hierich 1971), especially in radical political movements (Knutson 1981; della Porta and Tarrow 1986; della Porta 1992; Pérez-Agote 1986). Particularly important in today's movement environment are the information media and the role of the media in shaping a movement's image (Gamson 1988; Gitlin 1980). Enrique Laraña (see Chapter 9) observes how a split in the internal and external images of a movement can result from journalists' tendency to focus on professionalized movement representatives and visible aspects of movement activities. Another element of media identity is the process of influencing the assignment of meaning through framing activities by leaders. This occurred in the Basque and Catalan movements in Spain and in Spanish student mobilizations during the 1980s.

On the other hand, a neglected aspect of research on public identity is personal influence and social impact. By this we refer to concrete interaction between members of a movement and non-members. Research in social psychology has demonstrated that the more intimate, local, and personally relevant an informational input, the greater the influence it has on opinion (Latané 1981). If media images of a movement can influence personal or collective identity, their influence carries more weight if it comes via people who are close to and who are valued by the movement participant. With the exception of totalizing groups such as cults and radical cells, the collective aspect of identity formation tends to be at best a part-time endeavor; and what others (especially primary relations) think about the movement can carry great weight in a developing collective identity. An individual's social life will include others outside the movement group. This is even more relevant for movement participants who are deeply associated in community life, especially in the early phases of the movement when the demands on time and resources characteristic of the increasing pace of mobilization are just beginning. Then the relation between the public identity and the emergent collective identity is critical.

As a movement mobilizes, committed members will progressively exclude extraneous ties in favor of movement-based interaction. Boundary maintenance, a term used in ecological theory to understand the creation of resource niches, is another way of thinking about increasingly exclusionary behavior. Verta Taylor and Nancy Whittier (1992) discuss how radical feminists engage in a species of boundary maintenance by building alternative loci of affiliation called "feminist counterinstitutions" to affirm their collective identity. There is a time-budgeting dimension to these actions in that the larger proportion of daily activities that movement-related roles occupy in a social actor's overall identity—that is, the sum total of his or her roles—the sharper the boundaries, the clearer the we-they distinctions, and the stronger the collective identity. Boundaries can be thought of as activities and definitions that reinforce collective definitions through we-they distinctions, which are often marked by differences in physical appearance, dress, speech, demeanor, and other behaviors. There is variation in the panorama of movements regarding the sharpness of boundary distinctions. Taylor and Whittier review the efforts at exclusion among lesbian feminist groups, while other movements are less exclusionary and even may wax inclusive in later stages of their careers, with negative effects on collective identity and commitment (Zald and Ash 1966; Gerlach and Hine 1970). It makes sense that the strength of boundary maintenance (which is an activity) and we-they distinctions (which is a cognition) are related to collective identity in terms of the relationship between time and effort dedicated to movement activities.

We know a great deal about the social processes by which collective identity gathers strength, but our thinking about the topic has not been able to explain starting mechanisms, that is, the initial kick that moves potential participants to choose one set of social ties above others. This brings us to the third approach to the issue of emergent collective identities, and to what we see as a forgotten theoretical issue: the relation between what a social movement is about—its substance in the form of grievances, demands, and a program for change—and the way its collective identity can be codified in an ideology.

Ideology, Grievances, and Collective Identity

"Old movements" coalesced around shared grievances and perceptions of injustice. Programs for amelioration of these grievances and attribution of cause constituted the ideological base for mobilization. In the movement context, the link between ideology and grievances was strong, as it was conceptually in early theories of social movements. Ideology as a codification of wrongs and injustices was seen as a necessary process for mobilization to occur (Smelser 1962). In deprivation theories, the link between grievances and action was fundamental to explanatory logic, but typically it was left implicit. Research in the symbolic interactionist tradition emphasized the definition of a situation as unjust and warranting action; the specification of collective solutions was understood as key to mobilization processes. William Gamson, Bruce Fireman, and Steven Rytina's research into the emergence of injustice frames offers decisive insights into the earliest mechanisms by which grievances become articulated (1982; see also Gamson 1992).

In the 1960s, several observers—Daniel Bell, Ralph Turner, Joseph Gusfield, Orrin Klapp, among others—noted that an increasing number of movements and conflicts articulated grievances that were not based on economic and class interests. These movements were based on less "objective" elements such as identity, status, humanism, and spirituality. In a sense, the link between mobilization and grievances became less compelling. While not without their own ideological base and in varying degrees among different groups, these movements were less characterized by the extensive ideological articulation usually found in socialist and communist organizations. Shortly thereafter, the link between grievances and mobilization was further deemphasized as factors relating to resources, organization, and strategy gained theoretical predominance in the field.

The year 1990 brought the collapse of Marxist-Leninist states, and with it the debilitation of the most highly developed oppositional ideologies of the twentieth century. Richard Flacks (see Chapter 14) points out that there is much more to the Left's vision than the way it was distorted by the communist parties of the socialist bloc. He argues that the grand tradition of the Left has both been an integral part of how generations of activists have thought about themselves and a transcendent view of what society could be. This tradition was internalized into one's social identity; it was lived in one's daily contacts and through the content of that interaction. Although ideology, grievances, and collective identity are analytically separate, there is a strong relationship between them, one that has been muted in the past but has been brought into the theoretical foreground by NSM research.

The traditional theories of social movements did not emphasize the link between grievances and identity as relevant to explaining movement formation, but it makes sense that the link was there. For laboring men and women, for peasants, and for anarchist militants, the substance of grievances, and their interpretation by ideologies, was embedded in everyday life. E. P. Thompson's (1963) study of the emergence of the English working class shows that identity as a tradesman permeated everyday life and that there were many instances when the collective identity deriving from a shared sense of injustice was particularly strong. In his study of protests of weavers in Rouen, France, William Reddy (1977) shows how structural changes outside village society threatened the way of life for seventeenth-century weavers. The forms of protest weavers instigated were closely linked with the defense of their traditional social statuses. Similarly, anarchist groups in nineteenth-century Spain first organized athenaeums where workers gathered at the end of the day to socialize, discuss issues, and take courses. Family activities such as picnics and choral groups were also organized (Esenwein 1989). In West Virginia, the identity of a united mine worker's organizer in the 1930s was closely linked to the injustices he and his compatriots faced in the mines, in the company towns, in company stores, and in seeing the ravages of poverty on their children. Although none of the militants would have characterized their involvement in terms of a quest for identity, through the newly ground lenses of NSM concepts, the degree to which close friends and everyday activities were linked with the movement becomes apparent. Collective identity and grievances are not the same, but their close association lies in the fact that the organization of how social movement adherents think about themselves is structured in important ways by how shared wrongs are experienced, interpreted, and reworked in the context of group interaction.

These observations are strikingly similar to recent work in

feminist theory and the women's movement about the politicization of everyday life. Because gender stereotyping and discrimination permeates most modern social relations, there is a fundamental injustice embedded at the level of quotidian interaction. An
important aspect of the feminist program has been to create new
social spaces, ones that are equally quotidian, where women can
respond to, and in the extreme, withdraw from, gender discrimination and interaction with men in order to nurture their own
identities (Taylor and Whittier 1992). These kinds of groups,
which are characteristic of the women's movement, are often considered prototypical of NSM organizations.

To understand how movements are distributed on the axis of
grievances and identity, we suggest that the following reckoning
is helpful. First, all movements, to some degree, are linked with
issues of individual and collective identity via the way that focal
grievances affect everyday life. In the United States, mobilizations
in response to economic crisis and rising unemployment during
the 1930s, often led by communist activists, followed the classic
pattern of European workers' movements (Piven and Cloward
1971, 62). People participated massively in collective action because they were hungry and without jobs. These were matters that
went to the core of their existence and collective identity was not
the focus of action. Yet, in the United States, status movements
are closely linked with identity issues (Gusfield 1963; Zurcher and
Kirkpatrick 1976; Luker 1984). Here the grievances are actuated
by perceived threats to how one defines oneself, such as the way
that the popularization of abortion threatens, for some women,
traditional conceptions of motherhood. Status movements take
action about "other people's business" because that business often
poses a threat to how the mobilizing group defines itself. They
might be seen as precursors of NSMs if we accept that identity
issues become a basic mobilizing factor.

New social movements display a paradoxical relationship between identity and grievances. First, the very nature of grievances
for NSMs merges them closely with the concept of identity. For
movements about gender or sexual identity, for example, the collective grievances are inextricably linked with issues of identity
quest in the group context. The support and identity-affirming
functions of feminist and gay rights groups are well known. Second, where grievances have a more important place in group for-

mation, such as in ecological groups, the NSM perspective tells us that identity quest co-occurs as a displaced (or unconscious) but nevertheless fundamental raison d'être of group formation. Third, for some NSM groups, such fundamental grievances as threats to the ozone level, nuclear proliferation, or saving whales are so distant from everyday life that they can only remain immediate through their ongoing social construction and reassertion in the group context. Indeed, one might speculate that in those instances when the goals of NSM groups are particularly global and distant from achievement, it is the intensely personal orientations and the close melding of the group with everyday life that provide the sustaining lifeblood of cohesion. In rational choice terms, identity defense and affirmation provide the necessary counterbalancing selective incentives where the more practical payoffs of the movement are small.

Continuity in New Social Movements

An important focus of recent research has been the informal organizational networks as the platform from which movement formation occurs. Joseph Gusfield (1981) emphasizes the role of "carry-ons and carry-overs" from one movement to another; Adrian Aveni (1977), Mark Granovetter (1983), and Doug McAdam (1982, 1988) all argue for the importance of preexisting networks of relations in collective action; and Aldon Morris (1984) looks at the role of established social organizations—"movement halfway houses"—in the growth of the civil rights movement. In a similar vein, Leila Rupp and Verta Taylor (1987) discuss "abeyance structures" during the recumbent periods of the women's movement in a hostile political climate. In the even more hostile setting of the authoritarian state, Hank Johnston examines the role of "oppositional subcultures" in several nationalist mobilizations (1991, 1992, 1993; see also Pérez-Agote 1990). These subcultures are comprised of well developed but, for the most part, private social networks that are built up in response to repression and the stilted discourse of public life in closed societies.

The theoretical import of this work on the "microstructural" factors prior to mobilization is that the temporal frame of analysis gets pushed back in order to focus on premobilization phases as partial explanations of the shape and course social movements take. This shift also tends to lay bare the role of cultural content since continuity arises not only through persistance of organizations but also through the shared meanings and beliefs of movement members. Its significance for current research on social movements might contribute to overcoming its structuralist bias and to framing research within the perspective of a "interpretative sociology" (see McAdam, Chapter 2; Gamson 1988). This "epistemological reframing" would permit a deeper approach to the study of social movement formation that draws on the latent, nonvisible, cognitive dimensions instead of visible and political aspects (Melucci 1989; see also Laraña, Chapter 9). Consideration of the historical preconditions of mobilization is of course nothing new—seeking causes in itself implies temporal priority—but the search for a movement's origins has, in the past, focused either on intellectual currents or preexisting resources rather than on the nonvisible networks that function in everyday life as premobilization structures.

Prior to this research, the analysis of social movements had taken a more "volcanic" approach: It is attracted to an event when it erupts through the surface of social life, and it focuses on the flow of human, organizational, and resource-related magma. Taylor (1989, 761) points out that NSM research tends to succumb to this tendency as well. Her research with Rupp (1987) chronicles how organizational and cultural continuities can shape highly noninstitutionalized NSM forms of organization. Their study reviews how the intense commitment, rich and variegated culture, and strong activist networks facilitated the resurgent women's movement in the mid 1960s. Although their emphasis is on continuity in repertoires of contention, there are several points where one sees continuities in the shape of everyday organization within the retrenched movement, especially the solidarity, cohesiveness, and commitment within the abeyance networks they describe. These characteristics were important sources of personal support in the difficult postwar years of the women's movement and suggest that in periods of quiescence factors related to personal and collective identity may be at work to establish links of continuity (Taylor 1989; see also Laraña, Chapter 9). One is led to speculate the degree to which the prior organization stimulated smaller support groups that, in contrast to lobbying organizations, characterize the newness of contemporary feminism.

In a similar vein, the roots of the New Left in the United States have been traced by several researchers (Whalen and Flacks 1984; Wood 1974; Isserman 1987) who have pointed out strong continuities with the Old Left. Taking the women's movement and the New Left together, the point is that while events of greater or lesser magnitude punctuate history, there is an important thread of organizational and cultural continuity for many NSMs in the United States insofar as the focus of analysis shifts to everyday activities. On the other hand, research in the European tradition has stressed the special significance of great historical events and the path-breaking influence of ideas and persons. From this perspective, as analysts of new social movements in Europe sifted through the soil of postmodernism, they have located the first sprouts of new social movements among the relatively recent mobilizations of students and the New Left in the late 1960s (Habermas 1981; Kriesi 1992).

The fact that the NSM perspective has generated wider enthusiasm in Europe than in the United States provides evidence about the nature of theory construction and its patterns of diffusion in sociology. As we pointed out earlier, the European tradition of social movement research, reflecting the influence of Marxist thought, emphasized structural backgrounds of class to a greater extent than the American studies. In the United States, the situation has been historically different and there has never been a strong party representing the working class. Flacks (see Chapter 14) attributes this fact to the peculiar characteristics of the American labor force, especially its multiethnic character, which is the result of waves of immigration. Instead of the unification of the people sharing the tradition of the Left, there has been a fragmentation of the working class in ethnic groups and trade unions based on ethnic solidarity. The growth of a unified working-class party was prevented by a system where the competition between ethnic groups created obstacles to class solidarity. The absence of strong leftist parties and socialist unions in the United States atomized working-class organization into local manifestations and decentralized civil society to a greater extent than in Europe.

If we search for cultural factors, there is a long tradition of individualism and self-help/self-improvement movements in the

United States (Meyer 1975). These have roots in the broader cultural templates discussed over 150 years ago by Alexis de Tocqueville in *Democracy in America* and more recently by Bellah et al. (1985). In the words of de Tocqueville, the American propensity to "self-interest properly understood" fomented a wide array of interest groups and voluntary associations that exercised influence at local levels of government early in the nation's history. These local forms of participation continued to characterize American society throughout the nineteenth and twentieth centuries. In Europe, despite wide variations between countries, there were two social forces that shaped civil participation differently: the institutional church and the Left. While European society today is more secularized than the United States, the Catholic church and other religious groups played important roles in the development of social movement organizations, especially in some countries like Belgium, Italy, and Spain. The church in Europe enjoyed a quasi-monopoly on the kinds of transcendental questions that sects and cults in the United States have regularly taken up. These observations must be taken as generalizations that gloss many factors, but they stress that the utility of the NSM perspective is intimately related to the cultural and intellectual soil in which it germinates.

A final point regarding continuity in NSM groups is often overlooked, but it is central to cultural and organizational continuity over long periods. We have in mind the relations between generational cohorts alluded to earlier (see Braungart and Braungart 1984). Intergenerational relations are a key aspect of how continuity in culture, ideology, and organizational form is achieved (Mannheim 1952). This is not to imply a one-way relation from the wizened older generation to the young. Rather, in many movements there are opportunities for reciprocity where the older members mitigate the radicalism of youth, and youthful members open new horizons to the older generation (Johnston 1991). These are processes that are not examined in depth by new social movement research, despite methodological strategies, for example, participant observation and "intervention," that would seem to lend themselves to such questions (Touraine 1981; Melucci 1984). To the extent that the quest for identity is a youthful activity, theoretical concern with intergenerational relations will become more relevant for the study of contemporary movements. Whittier's (1993) treatment of generational relations in the women's move-

ment may signal the beginning of a shift in interest in this area
of research.

Conclusions

This chapter opens with a review of European and North American traditions in so-
cial movement scholarship and two questions about new social
movements: Why have they posed such a challenge to traditional
theories? And, What was it about the traditional theories that
proved to be inadequate? From the NSM perspective, the answer
to the first question centers on the link between structural change
characteristic of postindustrial society and movements that emphasize identity in the context of a wide variety of grievances and
forms of organization embedded in the everyday life of participants. The answer to the second question is that traditions of the
past, perhaps colored by their particular ideological lenses, did not
grasp the everyday and identity dimensions of the "old movements" they sought to explain.

The heart of this chapter focuses on the idea that a more
systematic approach to NSMs requires stronger conceptual development regarding identity, especially if the linkages between the
social actor and structural changes characteristic of postmodern
society are to be specified. Identity has two central dimensions—
individual and collective—both of which are shaped by a third—
public identity. Both individual and collective identity are characterized by a dualistic epistemology in which continuity and change
coexist as alternative approaches. Individual identity is composed
of both its fixed aspects, which are "imported" by each participant
to social movement groups, and by its fundamentally malleable
quality, which is shaped in the course of interaction within the
collectivity. Similarly, collective identity can be conceptualized
at any point in time as a fixed content of meanings, frames of
interpretation, and normative and valuational proscriptions that
exercise influence over individual social actors. On the other hand,
collective identity is also an emergent quality of group interaction,
which is strengthened by group solidarity and boundary maintenance activities and shaped by public images of the group via
interaction with nonmembers.

Part of the task we face is to refine both conceptual and

methodological tools. Research strategies must permit the complexity of identity to unfold in the data-gathering process. This issue is echoed in Bert Klandermans's call for longitudinal research of movement activists (1992, 53–75, see also Chapter 7). Batteries of questions focused wholly on identity issues will be required for meaningful comparisons over time. But the complexity of identity is such that fixed choice questions can access only some dimensions of the concept. More often than not, the raw data of identity is expressed in halting and fragmented accounts, platitudes, and monologues—sometimes spontaneous, sometimes rehearsed—of "who we are" and "who I am." Moreover, aspects of identity can change in the course of data-gathering itself. In some instances, different aspects of identity are invoked for different behaviors being observed, or for different phases—and even responses—in the interview process. A woman may discuss issues of the environmental movement as an activist, as a mother, as a manager, as a spouse, or as a Latina. Sociological intervention, discourse analysis, informal interviewing, and qualitative research strategies, such as those suggested by Scott Hunt, Robert Benford, and David Snow (see Chapter 8) would be very helpful.

Our examination of continuity and change in individual and collective identities suggests further research. First, in examining the "imported" qualities of individual identity, we note a potential correlation between identity quest and youthful composition of NSM groups. The degree to which there is a mix between young adults, for whom identity questions are important, and older members is an important dimension on which NSM groups might be distributed. The processes of intergenerational relations, reflected in the cohort composition of new social movements, while traced in several studies of the New Left and the women's movements, has not been pursued elsewhere.

Second, we note that the emphasis of "identity quest" will differ among NSMs and, given the centrality of the concept, it makes sense that this is a dimension on which NSM groups should be categorized. Comparisons require reliable measures of both individual and collective identity orientations that, by freezing concepts that are also inherently malleable and emergent, violate the dual nature of identity concepts. Nevertheless, there is much to be gained by intermovement and cross-national comparisons. It may be necessary to shed prejudices about measures of individual identity deriving from susceptibility theories in order to establish a comparative data base about who joins NSMs.

Third, we also note that the link between grievances and everyday life of movement participants might vary between NSM groups. The extent to which grievances are tied to everyday concerns in contrast to more global issues that seem quite removed from mundane concerns is a provocative question, and it makes sense that there will be considerable variation in the panorama of NSM groups. A working hypothesis is that where global concerns are far removed from everyday life, movement cohesion requires the selective incentives of a strong identity component. Moreover, the relationship between identity and the immediacy/globalness of grievances may comprise another dimension on which NSMs can be analyzed.

A final observation arises from current events in Europe. The specter of violent skinheads and neofascist youth movements in Europe raises the question if these, too, somehow fit into the NSM equation of identity quest, everyday embeddedness, and broad structural change. When seen in the context of the crisis of credibility of the main traditional political actors, the emergence of xenophobic movements presents similarities with post–World War I Europe. In the past, NSMs have been discussed as a creative force of change, signifying directions for cultural and social innovation. Yet, there may be a darker side that parallels the dangers presented by collective identities in the mold of totalitarian movements of the past. Surely the rise of nationalist movements and ethnic hatred also go to the core of how social actors think about themselves. Unlike mass society theory, the NSMs represent alternative channels for participation in public life (see Flacks, Chapter 14). If this is so, the revival of violent racist groups in the same European countries that give birth to Nazism and fascism would confirm the Marxist dictum, "History repeats itself: the first time as a tragedy, the second as farce."

References

Anderson, Benedict. 1991. *Imagined Communities*. 2d ed. London: Verso.
Aveni, Adrian F. 1977. "The Not-So-Lonely Crowd: Friendship Groups in Collective Behavior." *Sociometry* 40:96–110.
Bellah, Robert N., Richard Madsen, William M. Sullivan, Ann Swidler, and

Steven M. Tipton. 1985. *Habits of the Heart*. Los Angeles: University of California Press.

Blumer, Herbert. 1955. "Collective Behavior." In *An Outline of the Principles of Sociology*, edited by Robert Park, pp. 68–121. New York: Barnes and Noble.

Braungart, Richard G. 1984. "Historical Generations and Generation Units: A Global Pattern of Youth Movements." *Journal of Political and Military Sociology* 12:113–35.

Braungart, Richard G., and M. M. Braungart, eds. 1984. Special issue, "Life Course and Generational Politics." *Journal of Political and Military Sociology* 12.

Brinton, Crane. 1965. *Anatomy of Revolution*. Rev. ed. New York: Knopf.

Cohen, Jean L. 1985. "Strategy or Identity: New Theoretical Paradigms and Contemporary Social Movements." *Social Research* 52, 4:663–716.

della Porta, Donatella. 1992. "Introduction: On Individual Motivations in Underground Political Organizations. In *Social Movements and Violence: Participation in Underground Organizations*, edited by Donatella della Porta, pp. 3–28. Vol. 4 of *International Social Movement Research*. Greenwich, Conn.: JAI Press.

della Porta, Donatella, and Sidney Tarrow. 1986. "Unwanted Children: Political Violence and the Cycle of Protest in Italy, 1966–1973." *European Journal of Political Research* 14:607–32.

Erikson, Erik. 1958. *Young Man Luther*. New York: Norton.

———. 1968. *Identity: Youth and Crisis*. New York: Norton.

Esenwein, George R. 1989. *Anarchist Ideology and the Working-Class Movement in Spain, 1869–1898*. Berkeley: University of California Press.

Flacks, Richard. 1967. "The Liberated Generation: An Exploration of the Roots of Student Protest." *Social Issues* 13, 3:52–75.

Friedman, Debra, and Doug McAdam. 1992. "Collective Identity and Activism: Networks, Choices, and the Life of a Social Movement. In *Frontiers in Social Movement Theory*, edited by Aldon D. Morris and Carol McClurg Mueller, pp. 156–72. New Haven: Yale University Press.

Gamson, William A. 1988. "Political Discourse and Collective Action." In *From Structure to Action*, edited by Bert Klandermans, Hanspeter Kriesi, and Sidney Tarrow, pp. 219–44. Vol. 1 of *International Social Movement Research*. Greenwich, Conn.: JAI Press.

———. 1992. "The Social Psychology of Collective Action." In *Frontiers in Social Movement Theory*, edited by Aldon D. Morris and Carol McClurg Mueller, pp. 53–76. New Haven: Yale University Press.

Gamson, William A., Bruce Fireman, and Steven Rytina. 1982. *Encounters with Unjust Authority*. Homewood, Ill.: Dorsey.

Gerlach, Luther P., and Virginia H. Hine. 1970. *People, Power, and Change: Movements of Social Transformation*. Indianapolis: Bobbs-Merrill.

Gitlin, Todd, 1980. *The Whole World Is Watching*. Berkeley: University of California Press.

Goffman, Erving. 1959. *The Presentation of Self in Everyday Life*. New York: Doubleday.

————. 1967. *Interaction Ritual*. New York: Doubleday.

Granovetter, Mark. 1983. "The Strength of Weak Ties: A Network Theory Revisited." In *Sociological Theory*, edited by Randall Collins, pp. 201–33. San Francisco: Jossey-Bass.

Gusfield, Joseph R. 1963. *Symbolic Crusade*. Urbana: University of Illinois Press.

————. 1981. "Social Movements and Social Change: Perspectives of Linearity and Fluidity." In *Research in Social Movements, Conflict, and Change*, edited by Louis Kreisberg, vol. 3. Greenwich, Conn.: JAI Press.

Habermas, Jürgen. 1981. "New Social Movements." *Telos* 49:33–37.

Hierich, Max. 1971. *The Spiral of Conflict: Berkeley 1964*. New York: Columbia University Press.

Inglehart, Ronald. 1990. *Culture Shift in Advanced Industrial Society*. Princeton: Princeton University Press.

Isserman, Maurice. 1987. *If I Had a Hammer . . . : The Death of the Old Left and the Birth of the New Left*. New York: Basic Books.

Johnston, Hank. 1985. "Catalan Ethnic Mobilization: Some 'Primordial' Modifications of the Ethnic Competition Model." In *Current Perspectives in Social Theory*, edited by Scott McNall, 6:129–47. Greenwich, Conn.: JAI Press.

————. 1989. "Toward an Explanation of Church Opposition to Authoritarian Regimes: Religio-oppositional Subcultures in Poland and Catalonia." *Journal for the Scientific Study of Religion* 28:493–508.

————. 1991. *Tales of Nationalism: Catalonia, 1939–1979*. New Brunswick, N.J.: Rutgers University Press.

————. 1992. "Religion and Nationalist Subcultures in the Baltics." *Journal of Baltic Studies* 24, 2 (Summer): 133–48.

————. 1993. "Religio-Nationalist Subcultures under the Communists: Comparisons and Conceptual Refinements." *Sociology of Religion* 54, 4:237–55.

Katsiaficas, George. 1987. *The Imagination of the New Left*. Boston: South End Press.

Klandermans, Bert. 1992. "The Case for Longitudinal Research on Movement Participation." In *Studying Collective Action*, edited by Mario Diani and Ron Eyerman, pp. 55–75. London: Sage.

Klandermans, Bert, and Dirk Oegema. 1987. "Potentials, Networks, Motivations, and Barriers: Steps toward Participation in Social Movements." *American Sociological Review* 52:519–31.

Klandermans, Bert, and Sidney Tarrow. 1988. "Mobilization into Social Movements: Synthesizing European and American Approaches." In *From Structure to Action*, edited by Bert Klandermans, Hanspeter Kriesi, and Sidney Tarrow, pp. 1–38. Vol. 1 of *International Social Movement Research*. Greenwich, Conn.: JAI Press.

Klapp, Orrin. 1969. *Collective Search for Identity*. New York: Holt, Rinehart, and Winston.

Knutson, Jeanne N. 1981. "Social and Psychological Pressures toward a Negative Identity: The Case of an American Revolutionary Terrorist. In *Behavioral and Quantitative Perspectives on Terrorism*, edited by Yanov Alexander and J. M. Gleason New York: Pergamon.

Kriesi, Hanspeter. 1992. "The Political Opportunity Structure of New Social

    Movements." Paper presented at the First European Conference on Social Movements, Wissenschaftszentrum Berlin für Socialforschung, Berlin, October 30.

Laraña, Enrique. 1979. "La Constitución y el derecho a la resistencia." In *Revista de la Facultad de Derecho de la Universidad Compultense de Madrid*. Monográfico sobre la Constitución Española, no. 2:183–203.

———. 1982. "La juventud contemporánea y el conflicto intergeneracional." *Revista de Juventud* 3:41–62.

———. 1992. "Student Movements in the U.S. and Spain: Ideology and the Crisis of Legitimacy in Post-Industrial Society." Paper presented at the International Conference on Culture and Social Movements, University of California, San Diego, June 17–20.

———. 1993a. "Ideología, conflicto social y movimientos sociales contemporáneos." In *Escritos de teoría sociológica en homenaje a Luis Rodríguez Zúñiga*. Madrid: Centro de Investigaciones Sociológicas.

———. 1993b. "Los movimientos sociales en España (1960–1990). Análisis de tendencias." In *Tendencias sociales en la España de hoy*, edited by Salustiano del Campo. Madrid: Centro de Investigaciones Sociológicas.

Latané, B. 1981. "The Psychology of Social Impact." *American Psychologist* 36:343–56.

Lodi, Giovanni, and Marco Grazioli. 1984. "Giovani sul territorio urbano: l'integrazione minimale." In *Altri Codici: Aree di movimento nella metropoli*, edited by Alberto Melucci, pp. 63–125. Bologna: Il Mulino.

Luker, Kristin. 1984. *Abortion and the Politics of Motherhood*. Berkeley: University of California Press.

McAdam, Doug. 1982. *Political Process and the Development of Black Insurgency, 1930–1970*. Chicago: University of Chicago Press.

———. 1988. *Freedom Summer*. New York: Oxford University Press.

Mannheim, Karl. 1946. *Ideology and Utopia: An Introduction to the Sociology of Knowledge*. Translated by Louis Wirth and Edward Shils. New York: Harcourt, Brace.

———. 1952. "The Problem of Generations." In *Essays on the Sociology of Knowledge*, edited by Karl Mannheim, pp. 276–320. London: Routledge and Kegan Paul.

Margolis, Diane Rothbard. 1985. "Redefining the Situation: Negotiations on the Meaning of 'Woman'." *Social Problems* 32:332–34.

Marshall, Barbara L. 1991. "Reproducing the Gendered Subject." In *Current Perspectives in Social Theory*, vol. 11. Greenwich, Conn.: JAI Press.

Melucci, Alberto. 1980. "The New Social Movements: A Theoretical Approach." *Social Science Information* 19:199–226.

———. 1985. "The Symbolic Challenge of Contemporary Movements." *Social Research* 52:789–816.

———. 1989. *Nomads of the Present: Social Movements and Individual Needs in Contemporary Society*. Philadelphia: Temple University Press.

———. Forthcoming. "The Process of Collective Identity." In *Social Movements and Culture*, edited by Hank Johnston and Bert Klandermans. Minneapolis: University of Minnesota Press.

————, ed. 1984. *Altri Codici: Aree di movimento nella metropoli.* Bologna: Il Mulino.

Merton, Robert K. 1957. *Social Theory and Social Structure.* Rev. ed. New York: Free Press.

Meyer, Donald. 1975. *The Positive Thinkers.* Garden City, N.Y.: Doubleday.

Morris, Aldon D. 1984. *The Origins of the Civil Rights Movement.* New York: Free Press.

Morris, Aldon D., and Carol McClurg Mueller, eds. 1992. *Frontiers in Social Movement Theory.* New Haven: Yale University Press.

Nagel, Joane. 1986. "The Political Construction of Ethnicity." In *Competitive Ethnic Relations,* edited by Susan Olzak and Joane Nagel, pp. 93–112. Orlando, Fla.: Academic Press.

Nagel, Joane, and Susan Olzak. 1982. "Ethnic Mobilization in New and Old States: An Extension of the Competition Model." *Social Problems* 30:127–43.

Offe, Claus. 1985. "New Social Movements: Challenging Boundaries of Institutional Politics." *Social Research* 52:817–68.

Olson, Mancur, Jr. 1965. *The Logic of Collective Action.* Cambridge, Mass.: Harvard University Press.

Pérez-Agote, Alfonso. 1986. *La reproducción del nacionalismo vasco.* Madrid: Centro de Investigaciones Sociologicas/Siglo XXI Editores.

————. 1990. "El nacionalismo radical vasco. Mecanismos sociales de su aparición y desarrollo." Paper presented at "New Social Movements and the End of Ideologies," a seminar held at Universidad Internacional Menendez Pelayo, Santander, Spain, July.

Perinbanayagam, R. S. 1991. *Discursive Acts.* New York: Aldine de Gruyter.

Piven, Frances Fox, and Richard Cloward. 1971. *Regulating the Poor.* New York: Vintage Books.

Reddy, William M. 1977. "The Textile Trade and the Language of the Crowd at Rouen." *Past and Present* 74 (February): 62–89.

Rupp, Leila, and Verta Taylor. 1987. *Survival in the Doldrums: The American Women's Rights Movement, 1945 to the 1960s.* New York: Oxford University Press.

See, Katherine O'Sullivan. 1986. *First World Nationalism.* Chicago: University of Chicago Press.

Sewell, William H., Jr. 1980. *Work and Revolution in France.* Cambridge: Cambridge University Press.

Smelser, Neil. 1962. *Theory of Collective Behavior.* New York: Free Press.

Stryker, Sheldon. 1980. *Symbolic Interactionism: A Social Structural Version.* Palo Alto, Calif.: Benjamin/Cummings.

Tajfel, Henri. 1978. *Differentiation between Social Groups: Studies in the Social Psychology of Intergroup Relations.* London: Academic Press.

————. 1981. *Human Groups and Social Categories.* Cambridge: Cambridge University Press.

Tajfel, Henri, and John C. Turner. 1985. "The Social Identity Theory of Intergroup Behavior." In *The Social Identity Theory of Intergroup Behavior,* edited by W. G. Austin and S. Worchel, pp. 7–24. Chicago: Nelson-Hall.

Taylor, Verta. 1989. "Social Movement Continuity: The Women's Movement in Abeyance." *American Sociological Review* 54, 5:761–75.

Taylor, Verta, and Nancy Whittier. 1992. "Collective Identity in Social Movement Communities: Lesbian Feminist Mobilization." In *Frontiers in Social Movement Theory,* edited by Aldon D. Morris and Carol McClurg Mueller, pp. 104–29. New Haven: Yale University Press.

Thompson, E. P. 1963. *The Making of the English Working Class.* New York: Pantheon Books.

Touraine, Alain. 1981. *The Voice and the Eye: An Analysis of Social Movements.* New York: Cambridge University Press.

Trotsky, Leon. 1957. *The History of the Russian Revolution.* Translated by Max Eastman. Vols. 1–3. Ann Arbor: University of Michigan Press.

Turner, John C. 1985. "Social Categorization and the Self-Concept: A Social-Cognitive Theory of Group Behavior. In *Advances in Group Processes,* edited by E. J. Lawler, pp. 77–122. Greenwich, Conn.: JAI Press.

Turner, John C, with Michael A. Hogg, Penelope J. Oakes, Stephen D. Reicher, and Margaret S. Wetherell. 1987. *Rediscovering the Social Group: A Self-Categorization Theory.* New York: Basil Blackwell.

Turner, Ralph H. 1969. "The Theme of Contemporary Social Movements." *British Journal of Sociology* 20:390–405.

Whalen, Jack, and Richard Flacks. 1984. "Echoes of Rebellion: The Liberated Generation Grows Up." *Journal of Political and Military Sociology* 12:61–78.

———. 1989. *Beyond the Barricades: The Sixties Generation Grows Up.* Philadelphia: Temple University Press.

Whittier, Nancy. 1993. "Feminists in the 'Post-Feminist' Age: Collective Identity and the Persistence of the Women's Movement." Unpublished paper.

Wood, James L. 1974. *The Sources of American Student Activism.* Lexington, Mass.: Lexington Books, Heath.

Zald, Mayer N., and Roberta Ash. 1966. "Social Movement Organizations: Growth, Decay, and Change." *Social Forces* 44 (March): 327–41.

Zurcher, Louis A., Jr., and R. George Kirkpatrick. 1976. *Citizens for Decency: Antipornography Crusades as Status Defense.* Austin: University of Texas Press.

Chapter 2

Culture and Social Movements

Doug McAdam

Over the past two decades, the study of social movements has been among the most productive and intellectually lively subfields within sociology. But, as with all emergent paradigms, the recent renaissance in social movement studies has highlighted certain aspects of the phenomenon while ignoring others. Specifically, the dominance, within the United States, of the "resource mobilization" and "political process" perspectives has privileged the political, organizational, and network/structural aspects of social movements while giving the more cultural or ideational dimensions of collective action short shrift.

From a sociology of knowledge perspective, the recent ignorance of the more cultural aspects of social movements is the result of the rejection of the classical collective behavior paradigm, which emphasized the role of shared beliefs and identities but whose hints of irrationality and pathology (Klapp 1969; Lang and Lang 1961; Smelser 1962) made it unattractive to a new generation of scholars whose own experiences led them to view social movements as a form of rational political action. Whatever the reason, the absence of any real emphasis on ideas, ideology, or identity has created, within the United States, a strong "rationalist" and "structural" bias in the current literature on social movements. At the most macro level of analysis, social movements are seen to emerge in response to the "expansion in political opportunities" that grant formal social movement organizations (SMOs) and movement entrepreneurs the opportunity to engage in successful "resource mobilization." At the micro level, individuals are drawn into participation not by the force of the ideas or even individual attitudes but as the result of their embeddedness in associational networks that render them "structurally available" for protest activity. Until recently, "culture," in all of its manifestations, was rarely invoked by American scholars as a force in the emergence and development of social movements. The renewed interest in the topic has been spurred, in part, by the European "new social movement" perspective, which has made cultural and cognitive factors central to the study of social movements (Brand 1990; Eyerman and Jamison 1991; Melucci 1985, 1989).

This chapter broadens the discourse among movement scholars by focusing on some of the links between culture and social movements. Specifically, I address three broad topics: the cultural roots of social movements, the emergence and development of distinctive "movement cultures," and the cultural consequences of social movements.

The Cultural Roots of Social Movements

The "structural bias" in movement studies is most evident in recent American work on the emergence of social movements and revolutions. With but a few exceptions, recent theorizing on the question has located the roots of social movements in some set of political, economic, or organizational factors. While acknowledging the importance of such factors, I add cultural factors and processes to this list as important constraints or facilitators of collective action. There are three distinct ways in which culture can be said to facilitate movement emergence.

Framing as an Act of Cultural Appropriation

Drawing on the work of Erving Goffman (1974), David Snow and various of his colleagues (Snow et al. 1986; Snow and Benford 1988) have developed the concept of "frame alignment processes" to describe the efforts by which organizers seek to join the cognitive orientations of individuals with those of social movement organizations. The task is to propound a view of the world that both legitimates and motivates protest activity. The success of such efforts is determined, in part, by the *cultural resonance* of the frames advanced by organizers. In this sense, framing efforts can be thought of as acts of cultural appropriation, with movement leaders seeking to tap highly resonant ideational strains in mainstream society (or in a particular target subculture) as a way of galvanizing activism.

Much has been made of Martin Luther King, Jr.'s use of Gandhian nonviolence as an ideological cornerstone of the civil rights movement. In fact, King's interest in and advocacy of Gandhi's philosophy was largely irrelevant to the rapid emergence and spread of the civil rights struggle. Far more significant was King's appropriation and powerful evocation of highly resonant cultural themes, not only in the southern black Baptist tradition, but in American political culture more generally.

> Consider King's "I have a Dream" speech. Juxtaposing the poetry of the scriptural prophets—"I have a dream that every valley shall be exalted, every hill and mountain shall be made low"—with the lyrics of patriotic anthems—"This will be the day when all of God's children will be able to sing with new meaning, 'My country 'tis of thee, sweet land of liberty, of thee I sing' "—King's oration reappropriated that classic strand of the American tradition that understands the true meaning of freedom to lie in the affirmation of responsibility for uniting all of the diverse members of society into a just social order. (Bellah et al. 1985, 249)

Indeed, this was King's unique genius: to frame civil rights activity in a way that resonated not only with the culture of the oppressed but with the culture of the oppressor as well. King successfully mobilized Southern blacks while he generated considerable sympathy and support for the movement among whites as well.

The student democracy movement in Beijing in the spring of 1989 also drew on deeply resonant cultural themes and traditions in the early days of the struggle. The initial march on April 27 that stimulated the movement was ostensibly organized to mark and mourn the death of former premier Yu Yaobang. Such public displays of respect and veneration for departed leaders (and the dead more generally) have deep roots in Chinese political culture. By framing the march as an act of public mourning, movement organizers appropriated long-standing cultural symbols in the service of the movement. This helps explain both the large size of the initial march and the surprising restraint exercised by Communist party leaders in dealing with the students. The cultural legitimacy that attached to the march encouraged participation while constraining official efforts at social control.

*Expanding Cultural Opportunities
as a Stimulus to Action*

Scholars such as Charles Tilly (1978), Sidney Tarrow (1994), Doug McAdam (1982), Theda Skocpol (1979), Jack Goldstone (1991), Hanspeter Kriesi (1990), and Herbert Kitschelt (1986), among others, have established the notion that social movements/revolutions often emerge in response to an expansion in the "political opportunities" available to a particular challenging group. The argument is that movements are less the product of meso level mobilization efforts than they are the beneficiaries of the increasing political vulnerability or receptivity of their opponents or of the political and economic system as a whole.

Although I generally concur with this view, I think it betrays a "structural" or "objectivist" bias in many of its specific formulations. It is extremely hard to separate these objective shifts in political opportunities from the subjective processes of social construction and collective attribution that render them meaningful. In other words, "expanding political opportunities . . . do not, in any simple sense, produce a social movement. . . . [Instead] they only offer insurgents a certain objective 'structural potential' for collective political action. Mediating between opportunity and action are people and the subjective meanings they attach to their situations" (McAdam 1982, 48).

The causal importance of expanding political opportunities, then, is inseparable from the collective definitional processes by which the meaning of these shifts is assigned and disseminated. Given this linkage, the movement analyst has two tasks: accounting for the structural factors that have objectively strengthened the challenger's hand, and analyzing the processes by which the meaning and attributed significance of shifting political conditions is assessed. This latter task prompts speculation about the existence and significance of expanding cultural opportunities in the emergence of collective action. By "expanding cultural opportunities" we have in mind specific events or processes that are likely to stimulate the kind of collective framing efforts mentioned above. A close reading of the historical literature on social movements suggests that framing efforts may be set in motion by at least four distinct types of expanding cultural opportunities.

Ideological or Cultural Contradictions. The first type of cultural opportunity involves any event or set of events that dramatize a glaring contradiction between a highly resonant cultural value and conventional social practices. Many such examples can be found in the social movement literature. For example, the contrast between the egalitarian rhetoric and the sexist practices of the early American abolitionist movement have long been regarded as an important impetus in the development of the nineteenth-century women's rights movement. As Sara Evans (1980) and others have argued, much the same thing happened in regard to the women's liberation movement of the 1960s and 1970s. In this case, it was the egalitarian rhetoric and forms of sexual discrimination evident within the civil rights movement and the white student Left that fueled the development of a radical feminist "frame" legitimating protest activity.

One final example of the facilitating effect of this kind of ideological or cultural contradiction can be seen in regard to the threatened 1940 march on Washington. A. Philip Randolph, the president of the American Association of Sleeping Car Porters, organized a mass march on Washington to protest discriminatory labor practices in the defense industries. The apparent spur to action in this case was the glaring contradiction between President Franklin D. Roosevelt's growing anti-Nazi rhetoric—especially its "master race" philosophy—and his own tactic acceptance of racial discrimination at home (Fishel and Quarles 1970; Sitkoff 1978).

Suddenly Imposed Grievances. Another cognitive stimulus to framing processes comes from what Edward Walsh (1981) has called "suddenly imposed grievances." The term describes those dramatic, highly publicized, and generally unexpected events—human-made disasters, major court decisions, official violence—that increase public awareness of and opposition to previously accepted societal conditions. As an example of this process, Walsh (1981) cites and analyzes the generation of anti–nuclear power activity in the area of Three Mile Island following a 1979 accident there. Bert Useem's (1980) analysis of a movement in Boston during the mid 1970s aimed at stopping the busing of school children to achieve school desegregation leaves little doubt that the resistance was set in motion by a highly publicized court order mandating busing. Harvey Molotch (1970) documents a similar rise in protest activity among residents of Santa Barbara, California, in the wake of a major oil spill that took place in 1969.

The initial verdict in the Rodney King beating case (Los Angeles, California, April 1992) is as another example of a highly dramatic event spurring protest activity.

Dramatizations of System Vulnerability. Another "cultural" or "cognitive opportunity" that may stimulate increased framing and other mobilization efforts are those events or processes that highlight the vulnerability of one's political opponents. For example, the unanimous 1954 U.S. Supreme Court decision in *Brown v. Board of Education* declaring racially segregated schools unconstitutional convinced many in the black community of the political and legal vulnerability of the southern system of segregation and, in turn, accelerated the pace of civil rights organizing nationwide (Gerber 1962; McAdam 1982).

The collapse of Communist party rule in Poland and the unwillingness of Mikhail Gorbachev to use military force to suppress the Solidarity movement was widely interpreted throughout Eastern Europe as a sign that all Communist regimes in the region were in trouble. This is not to deny the deep structural roots of the crisis in the Soviet Union (see Tarrow 1991), but a crisis needs to be transparent if it is to serve as a cue for collective action. The end of communist rule in Poland served as just such a cue. This pivotal event led, in turn, to increased framing and other mobilization activities by reformers in all of the Warsaw Pact countries.

Finally, the ineffectual 1991 coup attempt by Soviet hardliners made it clear just how weak and out of touch the once formidable Communist party bosses had become, thus emboldening citizens from across the USSR to step up demands for political independence and economic reform.

The Availability of Master Frames. Finally, one other cultural opportunity has the potential to set in motion framing efforts and mobilization more generally. This is the availability of what David Snow and Robert Benford (1988) term "master protest frames" legitimating collective action. Movement scholars continue to err in viewing social movements as discrete social phenomena. Instead, movements tend to cluster in time and space precisely because they are not independent of one another (McAdam and Rucht 1993). To illustrate, the major movements of the 1960s in the United States were not so much independent entities as offshoots of a single broad activist community with its roots squarely in the civil rights movement (McAdam 1988). One of the things that clearly linked the various struggles during this period was the existence of a "master protest frame" that was appropriated by each succeeding insurgent group. The source of this frame was the civil rights movement, but in short order the other major movements of the period used the ideological understandings and cultural symbols of the black struggle as the ideational basis for their efforts as well. Evans (1980) has documented the idealogical/cultural links between the women's liberation and civil rights movements, while Doug McAdam (1988) has done the same for the black struggle and the antiwar and student movements. The ideological imprint of the civil rights movement is also clear in regard to the gay rights, American Indian, farmworkers, and other leftist movements of the period. All of these groups, drawing heavily upon the "civil rights master frame," came to define themselves as victims of discrimination and, as such, deserving of expanded rights and protection under the law. They mapped their understandings of their own situations on the general framework first put forward by civil rights activists.

The same point applies with equal force to other periods of heightened movement activity. The rash of student movements that flourished around the globe (for example, in Spain, Mexico, Japan, France, Italy, Germany, and the United States) in 1968 were clearly attuned to and influenced by one another, resulting in the development and diffusion of a "student left master frame" (Caute 1988; Katsiaficas 1987).

In similar fashion, the success of Solidarity in finally breaking the Communist party's forty-four-year monopoly on power in Poland encouraged other Eastern European dissidents to adopt prodemocracy frames in their own countries. The same process can be seen in the former Soviet Union, with the success of independence movements in the Baltic states encouraging the rise of ideologically similar ethnic nationalist movements in many of the other former Soviet republics.

The more general theoretical point is that successful framing efforts are almost certain to inspire other groups to reinterpret their situation in light of the available master frame and to mobilize based on their new understanding of themselves and the world around them. Thus, the presence of such a frame constitutes yet another cultural or ideological resource that facilitates movement emergence.

The Role of Long-Standing Activist Subcultures in Movement Emergence

Movement scholars have focused a great deal of attention on the role of existing organizations or associational networks in the emergence of protest activity (Freeman 1973; Gould 1991; McAdam 1982, 1986; Morris 1984; Oberschall 1973; Rosenthal et al. 1985). This literature betrays the "structural bias" of the field as a whole. Virtually all of these authors attribute the importance of prior organization to the concrete organizational resources, that is, leaders, communication networks, and meeting places, that such groups provide. Established organizations, however, are the source of cultural resources as well.

In other words, what is too often overlooked in structural accounts of movement emergence is the extent to which these established organizations/networks are themselves embedded in long-standing activist subcultures capable of sustaining the ideational traditions needed to revitalize activism following a period of movement dormancy. These enduring activist subcultures function as repositories of cultural materials into which succeeding generations of activists can dip to fashion ideologically similar, but chronologically separate, movements. To use Ann Swidler's (1986) term, these subcultures represent the specialized "tool kits" of enduring activist traditions. The presence of these enduring cultural repertoires frees new generations of would-be activists from the necessity of constructing new movement frames from whole cloth. Instead, most new movements rest on the ideational and broader cultural base of ideologically similar past struggles. To assert such continuity is to take issue with certain new social movement theorists (Melucci 1989) who hold that the movements of the 1960s and 1970s represented a total break with past activism. That these movements extended and modified existing activist traditions is undeniable. At the same time, it seems clear that they were initially rooted in the very traditions they subsequently transcended. Examples of these kinds of cross-generational continuities in movement activity are numerous.

In all western industrial nations, for example, the tradition of labor activism has served as a broad cultural template available to succeeding generations of workers as a resource supporting mobilization. In similar fashion, several generations of American peace movements have drawn on a rich pacifist tradition, as nurtured and sustained by a combination of religious denominations (for example, Quakers and Unitarians) and secular-humanist organizations (for example, American Friends Service Committee and Fellowship of Reconciliation). At the other end of the political spectrum, an enduring tradition of antiimmigrant and white supremacist activism has served as a broad "tool kit" encouraging American right-wing movements over many generations. Finally, in Spain, long-standing separatist traditions in both Catalonia and the Basque region have served as the wellspring from which several cycles of nationalist movements have flowed (see Johnston, Chapter 11).

Although the role of such long-standing activist subcultures has received little attention in studies of movement emergence, their imprint seems apparent. In his definitive study of the structural origins of the American civil rights movement, Aldon Morris (1984) documents the critical contribution made by what he terms "movement halfway houses." These were such established organizations as the Highlander Folk School and the Fellowship of Reconciliation that, despite intense repression, sustained earlier traditions of civil rights activism. They were available to play the role of organizational and cultural "midwives" in the "birth" of the new movement.

Leila Rupp and Verta Taylor (1987) provide a rich, detailed portrait of the survival of another enduring activist subculture — that of American feminism — during the long hiatus between the decline of the suffrage movement and the emergence of the contemporary women's movement. Like Morris, Rupp and Taylor focus on the crucial role of organizations and specific individuals in nurturing and sustaining an activist subculture during a period of movement dormancy. The result was the survival of a set of ideas, organizational practices, and activist traditions that served as one of the important "tool kits" shaping the cultural contours of modern American feminism.

Enrique Laraña (see Chapter 9) offers another example of cultural continuity in activist traditions. He documents the historical persistence of Marxist discourse and images of struggle in one of the two wings of the Spanish student movement. Howard Kimmeldorf's (1989) comparative study of unionism among East and West Coast dockworkers has continued to shape the ideology and practices of the union to the present. Finally, the imprint of long-standing traditions of student activism are evident on a number of American college or university campuses. For example, one of the best predictors of which colleges and universities contributed student volunteers to the 1964 Mississippi Freedom Summer project was the presence of an active socialist or communist student organization on campus during the 1930s. It should come as no surprise that Berkeley and other colleges such as Antioch and Oberlin sent large contingents of volunteers to Mississippi in 1964. In doing so they were merely drawing on and perpetuating the localized activist subcultures that have long existed on and around those campuses.

Movement emergence, then, is never simply the result of some fortuitous combination of macropolitical opportunities and meso level organizational structures. While important, these factors only afford insurgents a certain structural potential for successful protest activity. Mediating between opportunities and concrete mobilization efforts are the shared meanings people bring to their lives. These meanings, in turn, are expected to be shaped by the cultural resources and opportunities mentioned above.

The Emergence and Development of a Movement Culture

An interest in the relationship between social movements and culture clearly transcends the emergent phase of collective action. Indeed, that relationship becomes more complicated and potentially more interesting as the movement develops because the direction of causal influence in the relationship can run both ways. Not only will the movement bear the imprint of the broader cultural context(s) in which it is embedded but insurgents are also likely to develop a distinctive movement culture capable of reshaping the broader cultural contours of mainstream society.

That such cultures do exist is intuitively clear to anyone who has participated in any but the most ephemeral of movements. Social movements tend to become worlds unto themselves that are characterized by distinctive ideologies, collective identities, behavioral routines, and material cultures. The more thoroughgoing the goals of the movement are, the more likely it is that a movement culture will develop. This is not surprising. Having dared to challenge a particular aspect of mainstream society, there is implicit pressure on insurgents to engage in a kind of social engineering to suggest remedies to the problem. The challenge is to actualize within the movement the kind of social arrangements deemed preferable to those the group is opposing. Again, the more thoroughgoing the changes proposed, the more the tendency to conceive of the movement as an oppositional subculture—a kind of idealized community embodying the movement's alternative vision of social life.

Movement cultures are not static over time. Having opened up the question of the restructuring of social arrangements, there is no guarantee that insurgents will confine their attention to the specific issues or institutions originally targeted. When this happens, movements can take on the character of hothouses of cultural innovation. Anything and everything is open to critical scrutiny. Change becomes the order of the day.

At the moment, we lack any real theoretical or empirical understanding of the processes that shape the ongoing development of distinctive movement cultures, and such an understanding is beyond the scope of this chapter. We can begin to move in that direction by calling attention to two factors that would seem to influence the shifting character of a movement's culture.

Shifts in the Social Locus of the Movement

Social movements typically develop within particular social and generational strata or geographic locations. The expectation is that the culture of the movement will, at least initially, reflect these social, generational, and geographic origins. Movements are hardly the property of those population segments who gave them life in the first place. On the contrary, it is not uncommon for the locus of protest activity to shift over the life of a movement. As such shifts occur, we should see a shift in the ideational and material culture of the movement that reflects the new class, regional, generational, or other social loci of the movement.

One example of this process comes from Lynn Hunt's (1984) definitive study, *Politics, Culture, and Class in the French Revolution.*

Hunt's work documents the dramatic shift in the dominant ideology and material symbols of the Revolution that accompanied the change in the class composition of the movement between 1789 and 1795. Dominated at the outset by the emerging bourgeoisie, intellectuals, and even elements of the aristocracy, by 1794–1795 control of the Revolution had passed to artisans, shopkeepers, lawyers, and other less class-privileged elements of French society.

An equally dramatic shift in the cultural content of a movement occurred in the American civil rights movement during the decade of the 1960s as a result of a fundamental shift in the class and geographic loci of protest activity. While the movement initially developed within the churches and other institutions of the Southern, urban, black middle class, by the late 1960s its "home" had shifted to the urban ghettos of a poorer and more secular Northern black community. Partly in response to this shift, the ideational and material culture of the movement became less religious in nature, more explicitly political, and more aggressively focused on the assertion of a shared and distinctive "cultural nationalism" among black Americans. This is not to say that these shifts were solely the product of the geographic and social changes, but they clearly played a part in the broader cultural transformation that occurred during these years.

Nancy Whittier (1993) provides a final example of the shifting cultural content of a movement in her analysis of generational replacement in the contemporary women's movement. Whittier argues persuasively that the very real differences in the cultural content and "tone" of the current movement have come about not because the pioneering feminists of the 1960s and 1970s have changed their collective identities but because new "activist cohorts" have entered the movement and brought distinctive cultural styles and identities to the struggle.

Perceived Effectiveness of the Movement's Dominant Core

Successful movements tend to be fairly heterogeneous, drawing adherents from a variety of subgroups within the population. These subgroups will vie for cultural as well as strategic political influence over the movement. At any one time, however, it is usually possible to identify a particular segment within the movement as dominant. To the extent that this segment is widely perceived as substantively effective, its cultural "package" will likely be privileged as well. To the extent it is seen as ineffective, strategic and organizational control of the movement will likely shift (often following a period of conflict) to some other contender, thereby enhancing the importance of its cultural package.

The contemporary women's movement in the United States affords a prime example of this phenomenon. Initially, the movement coalesced around radical feminists with roots in both the American "New Left" and the "counterculture" of the 1960s. Eschewing formal organization and leadership, this wing of the movement pioneered the use of consciousness-raising groups as a form of activism. As effective as these groups were in drawing new recruits into the movement, they came to be seen by many as ineffective vehicles for pursuing political and economic change (Freeman 1973). Partly as a result of this critique, influence over the movement gradually shifted to an older, more politically and organizationally conventional group of women who were affiliated with the National Organization for Women (NOW). The results of this shift were cultural as much as political and organizational, with the countercultural affinities of the radical wing gradually giving way to the more conventional, professionalized ethos of NOW loyalists.

The Cultural Consequences of Movements

In assessing the impact of social movements, scholars have tended to focus their attention narrowly on political or economic consequences. Given the central importance attached to political or economic change by most social movements, this is certainly an important topic for systematic investigation. At the same time, resistance to significant political or economic change is likely to be sufficiently intense as to mute the material effects of all but the most successful movements. As many commentators have noted, even a movement as broad based and widely supported as the American civil rights movement failed to effect the fundamental redistribution in political and economic power that it ultimately sought. The opposition of the political and economic establishment to such a redistribution was simply too strong and too united to permit its occurrence.

Given the entrenched political and economic opposition movements are likely to encounter, it is often true that their biggest impact is more cultural than narrowly political and economic. Although the topic has never been systematically studied, the examples of movement-based cultural change would seem to be numerous and extraordinarily diverse. What follows is an impressionistic survey of some of these many changes. It is not exhaustive; it merely reflects the richness and diversity of the forms of cultural innovation that may be the result of movement dynamics.

As Ralph Turner reminds us (see Chapter 4), social movements have been the source of some of the most transformative ideologies or belief systems the world has ever known. We would do well to remember that Christianity, Islam, the Protestant Reformation, and subsequent sectarianism began life as the organizing frames for specific social movements. In many other cases, movements served as the principal vehicles by which belief systems, derived elsewhere, were modified and extended. So, for example, Marxist thought was profoundly shaped and deepened by figures associated with both the Russian (Lenin, Trotsky), Chinese (Mao Zedong, Jou Enlai, Lin Biao), and Cuban (Castro, Che Guevara) Revolutions. Through such figures as Voltaire and Rousseau in France and Thomas Paine and Thomas Jefferson in the American colonies, the French and American Revolutions had a similar impact on Enlightenment thinking.

Specific social movements can also give rise to what Snow and his colleagues (1986) call "master protest frames"; that is, ideological accounts legitimating protest activity that come to be shared by a variety of social movements. So, as noted earlier, the civil rights movement advanced a "civil rights" master frame that was, in turn, adopted by other movements as the ideological grounding for their efforts. These movements include the women's, gay rights, handicapped rights, and animal rights movements. The various revolutions in Eastern Europe have appropriated the "democracy frame" first advanced by the Solidarity movement in Poland.

Social movements have also served historically as the source for new collective identities within society. For example, the identities Christian and Muslim emerged in the context of social movements. So, too, did that of the "working class" via the labor movement. In a more contemporary vein, the identity of "feminist" grew out of the modern women's movement. Indeed, many proponents of the new social movements perspective (Inglehart 1981, 1990; Melucci 1980, 1989; Offe 1985; Touraine 1981) argue that what is "new" about the new social movements—including the women's movement—is the central importance they attach to the creation of new collective identities as a fundamental goal of the movement. In fact, social movements have always served this function, whether it was an explicit goal of the movement or an unintended consequence of struggle.

Social movements have also been a force for innovation in strategic action forms. What began as emergent and often illegal tactics in yesterday's movements often become legitimate, institutionalized forms of politics in later years. The strike and the sit-in are two examples. Both tactics were pioneered in the labor movement, but later came to be recognized as legitimate forms of action by various groups. Elisabeth Clemens (1993) argues that the contemporary importance of lobbying owes historically to its successful and legitimating use by women activists in the period from 1880 to 1920.

Throughout history, social movements have also functioned as a source of new material cultural items. Hunt's (1984) cultural analysis of the French Revolution makes clear the extent to which popular symbols and the material culture of France were transformed during the Revolution. Virtually all political revolutions usher in cultural revolutions as well. The Chinese Revolution, for example, set in motion a thoroughgoing state effort to fashion a popular culture compatible with the ideals of the movement. The same thing has occured more recently in Iran, with the Islamic Revolution ushering in a period of intense anti-Western feeling leading to the wholesale rejection of Western-style consumer goods and other cultural items. Ironically, the reverse process is currently underway in the Soviet Union, with the popular rejection of the Communist party encouraging a simultaneous process of Western-style cultural liberalization and experimentation.

Revolutions are not the only force that exert a powerful transformative effect on the material culture of a society. For example, the 1964 Mississippi Freedom Summer Project gave early expression to a number of specific cultural items that came to be associated with the 1960s counterculture (McAdam 1988). In general, as authors such as Morris Dickstein (1989) have shown, the counterculture and the movements of the 1960s had a profound effect on American popular culture. Dress and hairstyles, popular music, movies, dance, and theater were powerfully affected by the political turbulence of the era. The roots of the "drug culture" can also be found in the political and cultural movements of the 1960s. Language was affected; "black English" made inroads into popular English, and the feminist critique of the traditional vernacular prompted efforts to fashion more gender-neutral modes of expression.

Similar linguistic "insurgencies" are currently under way elsewhere. In the Canadian province of Quebec, French-speaking separatists affiliated with the Parti québécois have succeeded in making French the official provincial language. In Catalonia, separatists continue to press for the same designation for Catalan, underscoring their resolve by painting over street signs in Castilian with the equivalent word or phrase in Catalan.

To round out this survey, mention should be made of the effect of social movements on the culture and practices of mainstream institutions in society. In his thorough study of the impact of liberation theology on the Latin American Catholic church, Christian Smith (1991) provides a fascinating example of this process. Inspired in part by the spread of communist movements in the region, the liberation theology movement spawned a kind of revolution within the church that is still being waged today. In the United States, the movements of the 1960s have had a dramatic effect on the structure and curricular content of higher education in the United States. Structurally, the political turbulence of the era led to the establishment of African American, Native American, Hispanic, and women's studies programs on many college and university campuses. In addition, the heightened awareness of minorities spawned by the movements has resulted in far more curricular attention to minority groups in social science and humanities courses.

The forms of cultural change that flow from social movements are many and varied, and we know little about which factors or characteristics of movements account for the extent of their cultural impact. As a first approach to the question, I would emphasize the role of four factors in mediating the cultural consequences of social movements. These factors are: the extensiveness of the movement's goals, the movement's success in attaining those goals, the extent to which the movement results in prolonged and meaningful contact between two previously segregated groups, and the extent of the movement's access to existing cultural elites in society.

Breadth of the Movement's Goals

All other things being equal, the more extensive its goals, the more likely that a movement will be a force for cultural change. Given this understanding, it is not surprising that all of the examples of cultural change mentioned in the previous section are the products of movements whose goals were very broad. Revolutionary movements have the broadest goals; they seek nothing less than the replacement of an existing political, economic, and social order. Accordingly, of all types of movements, revolutions typically have the greatest potential for stimulating significant cultural change. Given their fundamental interest in replacing the old regime, insurgents will almost invariably seek to destroy the cultural expressions of the old order and substitute a new revolutionary culture in its place (Gramsci 1971). At the other end of the revolution to reform continuum, movements of the narrow reform variety typically exert little cultural force. For example, the current anti–drunk driving movement has but a few if any cultural, as opposed to legal or political, implications. Its goals are simply so narrow and so specific as to rule out any broader cultural critique of American society.

The Degree of Success Achieved by the Movement

History, as the old saying goes, is written by the winners. The same is true for all major forms of cultural expression. A second determinant, therefore, of the cultural impact of a movement is the degree to which the movement is successful politically. Following Marx (1977), it would seem to be the case that cultural dominance rests, to a large extent, on a firm political and economic base. Accordingly, I hypothesize that the cultural impact of a movement will be commensurate with the substantive political and economic success it achieves. Again, this is most evident in the case of successful revolutions, wherein the victors move to eradicate the cultural, as well as political, vestiges of the old regime and to popularize cultural forms expressive of the new revolutionary order. At the other extreme, movements that fail to achieve any political leverage typically leave few cultural traces behind.

Contact between Previously Segregated Groups

Those movements that have been especially important as sources of cultural innovation would seem to be those that resulted in meaningful, that is, egalitarian, contact between previously segregated social strata. The significance of this kind of contact—the interaction between what Harrison White (1991) calls two "value streams"—is its potential to produce a new cultural hybrid based on the two subcultures present in the movement. Movements of this type have been among the most important in human history.

The early Christian movement represented a unique cultural hybrid based on a merger of a rural ascetic Jewish tradition with that of urban Hellenized Jews and Romans throughout the eastern Mediterranean. The Indian independence movement facilitated unprecedented contact between the untouchables and the most privileged Indian castes. The result was not simply political success but a period of unusual cultural ferment as well. Finally, for a brief period of time, the American civil rights movement encouraged egalitarian contact between black civil rights activists and the white student left. In large measure, the roots of the 1960s counterculture are found in the distinctive cultural hybrid that grew out of this contact (McAdam 1988).

Ties to Established Cultural Elites

The final factor that can be expected to shape the broader cultural impact of a movement is the extent to which it is linked to established cultural elites in society. One of the commonplace observations concerning the cultural ferment of the 1960s was that it represented "culture from the bottom up." Instead of cultural innovation flowing, as it normally does, from an established cultural elite downward through society, it seemed to emanate from groups whose impact on mainstream culture is ordinarily quite small. What this observation misses is the fact that the groups in question had unusually strong ties to established cultural elites, thus granting them more access to the means of cultural production than they ordinarily would have had. The ties forged in the early days of the movement between civil rights activists and segments of the Northern intellectual and cultural elite afforded blacks increased opportunities for cultural influence. The white student left, dominated as it was by middle- and upper-middle-class youth, enjoyed considerable access to the means of cultural expression via their parents and other influential adults to whom they were directly or indirectly linked. Generally, those movements that are either rooted in culturally privileged classes or that are able to forge such links are likely to have a greater impact on the cultural contours of mainstream society than those movements that remain fundamentally isolated from the established means of cultural production.

Conclusion

What I offer here is the most preliminary statement of the relationship between culture and social movements. The topic is complex and multifaceted. These are the beginnings of what I hope will be an ongoing discourse on the subject by both movement scholars and cultural analysts. Only by encouraging such a discourse can we hope to move toward a fuller understanding of this relationship and move beyond the current structural and rationalist biases evident in the contemporary movement literature.

Acknowledgments: This chapter was completed while I was a Fellow at the Center for Advanced Study in the Behavioral Sciences. Partial support for the year at the Center was provided by the National Science Foundation (BNS-8700864). I would also like to thank Dick Flacks, Hank Johnston, Enrique Laraña, Dieter Rucht, David Snow, and Sidney Tarrow for their extremely helpful comments on various drafts.

References

Bellah, Robert N., Richard Madsen, William M. Sullivan, Ann Swidler, and Steven M. Tipton. 1985. *Habits of the Heart.* New York: Harper and Row.
Brand, Karl-Werner. 1990. "Cyclical Aspects of New Social Movements: Waves of Cultural Criticism and Mobilization Cycles of New Middle-Class Radicalism." In *Challenging the Political Order: New Social and Political Movements*

in Western Democracies, edited by Russell J. Dalton and Manfred Kuechler, pp. 23–42. New York: Oxford University Press.

Caute, David. 1988. *The Year of the Barricades*. New York: Harper and Row.

Clemens, Elisabeth. 1993. "Organizational Repertoires of Institutional Change: Women's Groups and the Transformation of U.S. Politics, 1890–1920." *American Journal of Sociology* 98:755–98.

Dickstein, Morris. 1989. *Gates of Eden*. New York: Penguin Books.

Evans, Sara. 1980. *Personal Politics*. New York: Vintage Books.

Eyerman, Ron, and Andrew Jamison. 1991. *Social Movements: A Cognitive Approach*. University Park: Pennsylvania State University Press.

Fishel, Leslie H., Jr., and Benjamin Quarles. 1970. "In the New Deal's Wake." In *The Segregation Era, 1863–1954*, edited by Allen Weinstein and Frank F. Otto Gatell, pp. 218–32. New York: Oxford University Press.

Freeman, Jo. 1973. "The Origins of the Women's Liberation Movement." *American Journal of Sociology* 78:792–811.

Gerber, Irwin. 1962. "The Effects of the Supreme Court's Desegregation Decision on the Group Cohesion of New York City's Negroes." *Journal of Social Psychology* 58:295–303.

Gitlin, Todd. 1987. *The Sixties: Years of Hope, Days of Rage*. New York: Bantam Books.

Goffman, Erving. 1974. *Frame Analysis: An Essay on the Organization of Experience*. New York: Harper.

Goldstone, Jack. 1982. "The Comparative and Historical Study of Revolutions." *Annual Review of Sociology* 8:187–207.

———. 1991. *Revolution and Rebellion in the Early Modern World*. Berkeley: University of California Press.

Gould, Roger. 1991. "Multiple Networks and Mobilization in the Paris Commune, 1871." *American Sociological Review* 56:716–29.

Gramsci, Antonio. 1971. *Selection from the Prison Notebooks of Antonio Gramsci*. Edited by Q. Hoare and G. N. Smith. New York: International Publishers.

Hunt, Lynn. 1984. *Politics, Culture, and Class in the French Revolution*. Berkeley: University of California Press.

Inglehart, Ronald. 1981. "Post-Materialism in an Environment of Insecurity." *American Political Science Review* 75:880–900.

———. 1990. *Culture Shift in Advanced Industrial Society*. Princeton: Princeton University Press.

Katsiaficas, George. 1987. *The Imagination of the New Left*. Boston: South End Press.

Kimmeldorf, Howard. 1989. *From Reds to Rackets*. Berkeley: University of California Press.

Kitschelt, Herbert P. 1986. "Political Opportunity Structures and Political Protest." *British Journal of Political Science* 16:57–85.

Klapp, Orrin. 1969. *Collective Search for Identity*. New York: Holt, Rinehart, and Winston.

Kriesi, Hanspeter. 1989. "The Political Opportunity Structure of the Dutch Peace Movement." *West European Politics* 12:295–312.

———. 1990. "The Political Opportunity Structure of New Social Movements:

Its Impact on Their Mobilization," Paper presented at "Social Movements, Framing Processes, and Opportunity Structures," a conference held at Wissenschaftszentrum, Berlin, July.

Lang, Kurt, and Gladys Lang. 1961. *Collective Dynamics*. New York: Crowell.

Laraña, Enrique. 1975. "A Study of Student Political Activism at the University of California, Berkeley." Master's thesis, University of California, Santa Barbara.

McAdam, Doug. 1982. *Political Process and the Development of Black Insurgency, 1930–1970*. Chicago: University of Chicago Press.

———. 1986. "Recruitment to High-Risk Activism: The Case of Freedom Summer." *American Sociological Review* 92:64–90.

———. 1988. *Freedom Summer*. New York: Oxford University Press.

McAdam, Doug, and Dieter Rucht. 1993. "The Cross-National Diffusion of Movement Ideas." *Annals of the American Academy of Political and Social Science* 527 (May): 56–74.

Marx, Karl. 1977. *Selected Writings*. Edited by David McLelland. Oxford: Oxford University Press.

———. 1979. *The Essential Marx: The Non-Economic Writings*. Edited and Translated by Saul K. Padover. New York: New American Library.

Melucci, Alberto. 1980. "The New Social Movements: A Theoretical Approach." *Social Science Information* 19:199–226.

———. 1985. "The Symbolic Challenge of Contemporary Movements." *Social Research* 52:789–816.

———. 1989. *Nomads of the Present: Social Movements and Individual Needs in Contemporary Society*. Philadelphia: Temple University Press.

Molotch, Harvey. 1970. "Oil in Santa Barbara and Power in America." *Sociological Inquiry* 40:131–41.

Morris, Aldon. 1984. *The Origins of the Civil Rights Movement*. New York: Free Press.

Oberschall, Anthony. 1973. *Social Conflict and Social Movements*. Englewood Cliffs, N.J.: Prentice-Hall.

Offe, Claus. 1985. "New Social Movements: Challenging the Boundaries of Institutional Politics." *Social Research* 52:817–68.

Rosenthal, Naomi, Maryl Fingrutd, Michele Ethier, Roberta Karant, and David McDonald. 1985. "Social Movements and Network Analysis: A Case Study of Nineteenth-Century Women's Reform in New York State." *American Journal of Sociology* 90:1022–55.

Rucht, Dieter. 1990. "The Strategies and Action Repertoires of New Movements." In *Challenging the Political Order: New Social and Political Movements in Western Democracies*, edited by Russell J. Dalton and Manfred Kuechler, pp. 156–75. New York: Oxford University Press.

Rupp, Leila, and Verta Taylor. 1987. *Survival in the Doldrums: The American Women's Rights Movement, 1945 to the 1960s*. New York: Oxford University Press.

Sale, Kirkpatrick. 1973. *SDS*. New York: Random House.

Sitkoff, Harvard. 1978. *A New Deal for Blacks*. New York: Oxford University Press.

Skocpol, Theda. 1979. *States and Social Revolutions*. New York: Cambridge University Press.

Smelser, Neil. 1962. *Theory of Collective Behavior*. New York: Free Press.

Smith, Christian. 1991. *The Emergence of Liberation Theology: Radical Religion and Social Movement Theory*. Chicago: University of Chicago Press.

Snow, David A., and Robert D. Benford. 1988. "Ideology, Frame Resonance, and Participant Mobilization." In *From Structure to Action: Comparing Social Movement Research across Cultures*, edited by Bert Klandermans, Hanspeter Kriesi, and Sidney Tarrow, pp. 197–217. Vol. 1 of *International Social Movement Research*. Greenwich, Conn.: JAI Press.

Snow, David A., E. Burke Rochford, Jr., Steven K. Worden, and Robert D. Benford. 1986. "Frame Alignment Processes, Micromobilization, and Movement Participation." *American Sociological Review* 51:464–81.

Swidler, Ann. 1986. "Culture in Action: Symbols and Strategies." *American Sociological Review* 51:273–86.

Tarrow, Sidney. 1989. *Democracy and Disorder: Protest and Politics in Italy, 1965–1975*. Oxford: Clarendon Press.

———. 1991. " 'Aiming at a Moving Target': Social science and the Recent Rebellions in Eastern Europe." *Political Science and Politics* 29:12–20.

Tarrow, Sidney. 1994. *Power in Movement: Social Movements, Collective Action, and Mass Politics in the Modern State*. New York: Cambridge University Press.

Tilly, Charles. 1978. *From Mobilization to Revolution*. Reading, Mass.: Addison-Wesley.

Touraine, Alain. 1981. *The Voice and the Eye: An Analysis of Social Movements*. New York: Cambridge University Press.

Useem, Bert. 1980. "Solidarity Model, Breakdown Model, and the Boston Anti-Busing Movement." *American Sociological Review* 45:357–69.

Walsh, Edward J. 1981. "Resource Mobilization and Citizen Protest in Communities around Three Mile Island." *Social Problems* 29:1–21.

White, Harrison. 1991. "Values Come in Styles, Which Mate to Change." Paper presented at the interdisciplinary conference "Toward a Scientific Analysis of Values," Tucson, Arizona, February 1–4, 1989.

Whittier, Nancy. 1993. "Feminists in the 'Post-Feminist' Age: Collective Identity and the Persistence of the Women's Movement." Unpublished paper.

Chapter 3

The Reflexivity of Social Movements: Collective Behavior and Mass Society Theory Revisited

Joseph R. Gusfield

Concepts and theories in the social sciences are marked by a distinctive thriftiness. Few are wasted. Fashionable for a while, they are criticized, discarded, and then, sometime later, they are salvaged from the ash can of ideas and revived, often in new contexts and with new polish on them. In this chapter, I examine some characteristics of contemporary social movements. In my view, collective behavior and mass society theories, partially discredited in current thinking about social movements, can be very useful in examining certain movements and some aspects of many others. This is especially the case in the context of recent thinking about the "new social movements."

I do not suggest yet another totalizing paradigm that seeks to destroy the usefulness of all existing perspectives in an effort to enter a claim to a monopolistic ownership of the entire turf of "social movements." I have no theory for all seasons.

Definitions of social movements and theories about them abound in sociology. The textbooks are filled with the names of theories and theorists, each purporting to provide the definitive way of thinking about and of studying the subject matter of the field. But definitions and theories, especially in this area, bear a relation to the objects and historical contexts that elicit curiosity and attention (Gusfield 1978). In part, arguments about differing perspectives are reactions to the different questions that analysts are asking about different phenomena. In many respects all of us are a little like the famed six blind Asian Indians in the classic parable. Each places his hand on a different part of the elephant and each, as a consequence, describes a different kind of animal. Our arguments about theories are as much arguments about what is worth studying and in reference to what intellectual, social, or political problem as they are about the behavior of that which we study.

The interest in social movements has been occasioned in great degree by attention to reformist and dissident mobilization of partisans into organized attempts to change the institutional and political structure of a society. Studies of labor movements, of political movements and ideologies, and of religious dissidence and sectarian development have abounded in Europe and in the United States. Much attention has been given to major ideological partisanship, such as communism, fascism, liberalism, and socialism. Research has been fueled by the emergence of current events. The emergence of German fascism led to a generation occupied with the problem of the requisites for democracy and the decline of liberalism. The rise of student protest and civil violence in the 1960s prompted a concern for the problem of the conditions of protest and riot (Gusfield 1978).

It is not that social studies mirror historical events or that they are directed toward a particular resolution of political issues, rather, the development of historical actions poses problems of scholarly attention. Concern for understanding the roots of social violence became a major scholarly pursuit in the wake of the riots and demonstrations of the 1960s in the United States.[1]

The emergence in the 1970s and 1980s of movements concerned with such matters as the ecology of the planet, nuclear protest, gender equality, gay rights, animal rights, and new religions has seemed perplexing to older schemes of understanding, which have been directed toward relatively organized collectivities. Current scholarship focuses on efforts to understand the conditions of emergence, development, and disappearance of new social movements. They have constituted an anomaly, a puzzle for earlier formulations and paradigms. In this sense, there has been a Kuhnian motion in which a normal science has found it difficult to encompass new data in old theories (Kuhn 1962).

Social Movements as Associations and as Meanings

Collective behavior and mass society theories are criticized for their failure to consider the importance of the mobilization of partisans into organized, collective action. Such action is posited essential to the emergence and effectiveness of movements (Oberschall 1973; Tilly 1978; McAdam 1982; Morris 1984). This criticism has been especially striking in the development of rational choice and resource mobilization approaches (Tilly 1978; McCarthy and Zald 1973). It has also been central to my own past criticism of mass society perspectives (Gusfield 1962).

Collective behavior and mass society theories on one hand and resource mobilization theories on the other reflect two diverse images of the elephant we call social movements. The distinction has been nicely put by Alberto Melucci (1989, 17–20). He refers to collective behavior theories as "actors without action." He refers to resource mobilization theories as "actions without actors." I view these differences as those that emphasize movements as the emergence of new meanings and those that emphasize movements as collectively organized actions. The first places an emphasis on ideas; the second on organizations.

A great deal of the study of social movements has been the study of people organized into associations. The National Organization for Women, the American Federation of Labor, the Hare Krishnas, or the Southern Christian Leadership Conference have been central in social movement analysis in the United States. So conceived, the study of a movement is preeminently the study of the actions and reactiona to associations, of people organized into a coordinated structure. The resources mobilization theory has emphasized this image and focused analysis on the strategy of mobilization and action as rational means for attaining fixed goals (McCarthy and Zald 1973, 1977; Tilly 1978; Olson 1971).

The collective behavior approach, as developed by Herbert Blumer and later by Ralph Turner and Lewis Killian, focused on the emergence and construction of new norms of social relationships and new meanings of social life (Blumer 1939; Turner and Killian 1987; Turner 1981). These new meanings emerged from processes in which people, in interaction with each other, develop new conceptions of justice and injustice, or morality and immorality, or the real and the fictitious. So conceived, the subject matter of social movements is the appearance of new constructions of rights, of procedures, of norms, of beliefs. To speak of feminism or New Age movements is to place the stress of analysis on the growing adoption of an idea, an identity, a way of conceiving a situation. Associations and organizations are instances and embodiments of meanings.

Resource mobilization theorists critiqued this imagery. They sought to bring the image of association from the background into the light of the foreground. They emphasized the importance of the mobilization of partisans or others into the associational contexts without which the ideas would remain ineffective and unrealized. From the point of view of collective behavior theorists, what was important about a movement was its consequences for change. For resource mobilization theorists, the movement had to be studied as a form of organizational behavior, that is, gathering and utilizing resources (McCarthy and Zald 1973, 1977; Jenkins 1983). Complementing the approach of the resource mobilization paradigm, the economic analysis of Mancur Olson and the delineation of the "free rider" problem has had a major influence on thinking about social movements (Olson 1971). Whether analysts agreed with it or not, Olson's work focused attention on individual goals and rational considerations. It brought utilitarian considerations of costs and benefits into the picture (Handler 1978). In throwing the light of deductive economic logic on the inductive analyses of sociologists, it made the question of how and where movements obtain resources a major question (Tilly 1978).

These highly warranted criticisms of collective behavior theory have led to an implicit deemphasis on ideas and changing meanings as pivotal to the understanding of many movements. Yet, a focus on organizational and associational elements are insufficient tools for understanding diffuse and often apolitical new social movements. The recent movements that have piqued the interest and attention of many sociologists often have not displayed a clear relationship to utilitarian interests, formed organizational agents, created communal sects, or emerged as attempts to alter existing institutions. What have come to be known as "new social movements" are, in one or another of these features, distinguished from the model of the social movement as sociologists have portrayed them in the past (Cohen 1985; Eder 1985; Melucci 1985; Offe 1985). Others, using different designations, have presented similar conceptualizations stressing the class or other structural and cultural characteristics of contemporary movements (Gusfield 1979a; Turner 1969).

It is important to clarify the distinction between movements seen as associations and movements seen as ideas or meanings. The labor movement and its specific organizations are a model of associational units that comprise a movement. There are members and nonmembers, there are programmatically stated goals, and an internal organization that constitutes a hierarchy of office-holding leaders and a rank and file of members. In contrast, while there are organizations that are part of the women's movement, they are only a part of the diffuse goals, the process of mobilizing partisans, the locus of partisanship. Being a member or nonmember is not constituted by a specific act but refers to types of ideational commitment. The action of the movement has its locus in a multiplicity of events, often that of individuals. The movement thrives in everyday interaction as well as in the context of collective action in institutions and toward the state.

This typology of images is, like most, too definitive. Most movements do both: take an associational form and a form in the spread of new meanings. Some movements involve one form to a greater extent than the other. The civil rights movement, while emphasizing collective action of organizations, was also a movement that changed both white and black conceptions of what is just and what rights are legitimate and possible. Its major thrust was toward the reform of institutions, but it has significantly affected racial identities and self-conceptions. The women's movement has its organizational side but is even more saliently a movement toward a change in conceptions of women and female rights relative to men. As such, it exists both inside and outside associational or organizational phases. Some movements, notably the "hippie" movement or the physical fitness movement have no associational or organizational existence at all. Yet, they manifest a shared direction, a set of goals, and a shared conception of what is right and just as well as a procedure to obtain such goals.

Utopianism of Social Movements:
Back to the Future

Am I putting irreconcilables together? Why place the "hippie" movement, an unorganized phenomenon with little overt social conflict, in the same sociological bin as the abortion or antiabortion movement or the civil rights movement? Certainly, for many purposes, they are radically different. Yet all three are perceived and talked about as "movements." (That they are so perceived is important to my analysis below.) Two considerations prompt this procedure.

First, the quality of deliberateness, of a socially shared and conscious search for change has been the hallmark of phenomena labeled "social movements" (Gusfield 1970). The imagination of a future as a new way of behaving is common to both movements. It has distinguished the social movement, as an instrument for producing change, from those changes that occur without specific direction or plan. A changing birthrate is an example of unplanned, nondeliberative change; it arises from the consequences of multiple acts without mutual awareness of others. The sources of change through movements implies the imagination of the future and the attempt to realize imagined states. It is an imagination that is perceived as shared; it recognizes a solidarity of partisans against a defined opposition. Even without organizational affiliations, people can be "feminists," "women's libbers," "hippies," or "New Age freaks."

Imagining an alternative to the present is the utopian element in all social movements. Social movements become issues about change or the repelling of change in ways that are broader than individual, idiosyncratic choices. The movement produces a state of choice, of decision between what has been accepted and even enforced and what is now conceived as unacceptable. What may have been unthinkable is now thinkable and possible. Once set in motion, the "hippie" movement provided a socially shared and supported choice of life-style where such social support had not existed (Berger 1982). It is further distinguished from an individually chosen life-style where the knowledge and supportive example of others is absent or not influential. Even where action is not collective in the sense of organized and interactive, it nevertheless occurs with the knowledge that others are acting similarly. The "hippie" movement became such as individuals became aware, through reading and through personal accounts of others, that new styles of living and new opportunities for action were emerging.

Second, while associational structure and cultural meanings are typological distinctions, in practice, few movements are entirely one or the other. Even if a movement lacks overt conflict, it engenders contention about possibilities and choice between alternatives. It represents social relations and culture in possible transition. The gay rights movement, which has its organizational manifestation, also exists in daily judgments that pose new issues for homosexuals and heterosexuals as to how they are to identify themselves and others. Self-conscious and deliberate choice is being made against a background of awareness of movements. In this way they affect and influence more than their members and opponents (Greenberg 1988; D'Emilio 1983).

Social Movements: Linear and Fluid

It is useful to make a distinction between linear and fluid movements (Gusfield 1981b). Linear movements present the image of a straight line narrative. The movement is a means toward an end. The labor movement and individual labor unions are examples. The movement is perceived as associational. What is studied are careers. The effort to change brings the movement into overt conflict and extrainstitutionalized action. Being goal-directed, it is assessed in terms of achievement: Is it successful or not? Have new patterns of labor-management relations been achieved, or do the old continue? The arena of action is public. The movement seeks institutional or political change. The goals of the movement are fixed, and they are crafted into programmatic action.

Fluid movements are much more difficult to specify. Since they imply changes in how values and realities are conceived, they occur outside or in addition to organized and directed action. They may involve contention with others and with alternative meanings and constructions. Yet, they are less likely to be drawn into such collective actions as strikes, boycotts, pickets, or demonstrations. They occur in the myriad actions of everyday life; in micro and less public acts. It is harder to identify success or failure. The women's movement and feminism occur in more than the organized efforts at constitutional amendment, equal rights legislation, and affirmative action. They also involve relationships and interactions between men and women in micro and even intimate relations. The movement occurs in the multiplicity of events where a conception of women's rights and gender justice have become issues.

The distinction is important and has been conceptualized in different ways by different writers. There is much that is akin to, as well as different from, Richard Flacks's distinction between history and everyday life. "History is constituted by activity which influences the conditions and terms of everyday life of a collectivity" (1988, 3). Yet, by no means is all of everyday life in history; much of it also creates and is history. My image here is rather that of the locus of action than the content of ideas or institutions. The institutional level of a movement is found in the efforts to change the rules and procedures of organizations and institutions. Often the state is either the target of change or the instrument through which the linear movement hopes to gain change. The animal rights movement or the antinuclear movement are illustrations of linear movements where the effort is toward protest of current procedures at the levels of the state and such organizations as research laboratories. Changes in the institutional rules are the goals of the movement. The animal rights movement, for example, is an attempt to change procedures of medical research so that animals are no longer used for research purposes (Jaspers and Nelkin 1989).

The everyday or interactive level is more fluid. It may not even have an organizational base. The "hippie" movement is, perhaps, a model. Many health movements, such as holistic health care, are illustrative (Lowenberg 1989). Here there is no organizational base at all. The dissidence is not directed at changing the state or an institution. It is concerned with developing alternative styles of medicine. The movement is found in the set of ideas and the individual responses to those ideas as they affect life-styles. Such ideas are promoted through journals and through interaction. Holistic health movements will have little impact on the state, nor do they seek it. They are dissenting movements within medicine, but they do little to change professional medicine, develop new state laws, or protest current medical or hospital practices.

They become arenas of action with little direct conflict with institutions. They are alternatives to professional medicine; they are not movements to change the medical institutions. In a sense, then bypass rather than change institutions.

In what sense are fluid movements socially shared? I examine this aspect of analysis more carefully below in relation to mass society theories. For the present, what is involved is action taken with the recognition that it is not isolated and individualistic. "The train of thought and action in each individual is influenced more or less by the action of every other" (Park and Burgess 1967, 225). If we imagine the interaction between homosexual and heterosexual persons prior to the emergence of the gay rights movement, we posit a conventionalized set of norms to which people adhere or behave in idiosyncratic, individualistic forms. Once the movement is set in motion, behavior can no longer be conventionalized. Behaviors are undertaken with a recognition that alternatives are both possible and socially legitimated at some level. Homosexuals attempt to change discriminatory laws but also become open about their identity. Interaction between homosexuals and heterosexuals takes on a new tone. That interaction need not be direct or face-to-face. It may exist in the imaginative rehearsals of action that are fostered by vicarious experience, such as reading or watching news or dramatic presentations. What is happening is that the conventional norms of deviance that have guided both homosexuals and heterosexuals have come to be doubted and their acceptance made problematic. What was "taken for granted" has become an issue.

Microarenas and Macroarenas: Collective Behavior Theory Revisited

The distinction between public and everyday arenas is significant in two senses. First, it indicates the importance of the linear-fluid distinction. Second, it indicates aspects of contemporary society that accentuate the fluid elements of social movements. Here, aspects of collective behavior theory point to an important characteristic of modern societies that social movement analysis needs to consider.

Both in Park and Burgess (1967, chap. 15) and in Blumer (1939), the concept of collective behavior is used as a contrast to social organization. Social organization is conventionalized and recurrent and provides institutionalized definitions of situations and expected behavior. Collective behavior is postulated as elementary social behavior—what occurs when social organization breaks down: "those phenomena which exhibit in the most obvious and elementary ways the processes by which societies are disintegrated into their constituent elements and the processes by which these elements are brought together again into new relations to form new organizations and new societies" (Park and Burgess 1970, 440–41; quoted in Turner 1981, 3).

Where the Chicago School differed from the French sociologists, such as Gustav LeBon, was in their assessment of the potentialities of collective behavior for social organization. The French saw crowds through the model of irrational, blind, and savage actors (Barrows 1988). The Chicago School saw them as the source of new ideas and new social organizations, that is, as the basis for the emergence of new norms (Turner and Killian 1987). Rather than viewing collective behavior as deviant, fearful, and anomalous, the Chicago School saw it as the seedbed of new institutions. Thus, they could conceive of social movements and fashion as part of the same area called "collective behavior."

The image of society that the collective behaviorists shared with other sociologists was the classical conception of the integrated community versus the institutionalized society. It was in disorganization and "social unrest" (what today we might call "alienation") that movements emerged. Movements and the emergence of new constructions of reality were contrasts to everyday, recurrent, and organized social life. The appearance of collective behavior was something to be explained. The sociologists' job was to study how new patterns of thought and new institutions emerged from elementary nonorganized actions.

It is at this point that the collective behavior theorists need revision. The contrast between a normal, established pattern of routine and one of the creation or construction of new meanings and institutions is not adequate to the understanding of contemporary societies. As a number of sociologists (Gusfield 1979a; Touraine 1977; Melucci 1989) have indicated, social movements, heterogeneity, and the presence of alternatives and choices is as much a pattern of contemporary life as is the model of social organization. Collective behavior is not an abnormal aspect of social life, it is a part of modern life. The general increases in income and discretionary time as well as the improvements in communication and transportation effect large areas of life; everyday life operates with varying degrees of freedom from the constraints of institutional organization. Richard Flacks (see Chapter 14) suggests that in the United States political parties are diminishing as centers of political power and innovation. Increasingly, he argues, social movements are supplanting established political parties as the focus of political activity.

A rigid view of social organization as "social fact" is giving way to a view of social order as a product and subject of deliberate action by members in what Alain Touraine calls "the self-production of society."

> The sociology of social movements cannot be separated from a representation of society as a system of social forces competing for control of a cultural field. . . . This sociology of action ceases to believe that conduct must be a response to a situation, and claims rather than the situation is merely the changing and unstable result of relations between the actors who, through their social conflicts and via their cultural orientations, produce society. (Touraine 1981, 30)

Social Movements as Sign and Symbol: The Reflexivity of Social Movements

Such critical considerations imply a revision of the collective behavior approach. Collective behavior is not an island in a sea of organized, conventional, and static human behavior. Social choices and social movements are deeply embedded in daily interaction. Change, conflict, and reassessment are constant aspects of human societies.

The collective behavior image of movements has reappeared in recent years in the attention given to movements as forms of framing (Snow and Benford 1988, 1992; Gamson 1992). Attention is given to the cognitive force of movements in defining events and in the social construction of objects toward which the movement is oriented. "Frame" is a vernacular term generally associated with paintings and photographs. "Frame" applied to everyday conduct is a means of defining situations and objects. Except in Hindu meditation, experience is never "pure"; it is an experience of something. That something involves a definition or meaning given to phenomena. "Definitions of a situation are built up in accordance with principles of organization which govern events — at least social ones — and our subjective involvement in them: frame is the word I use to refer to such of these basic elements as I am able to identify" (Goffman 1974, 10–11; see also Bateson 1972). The concept of framing is a recognition that the meaning of events may make for differing experiences of the "same" data. What is centrally attended to by one kind of interest or audience may not be attended to at all by another. As Erving Goffman suggests, "There is a sense in which what is play for the golfer is work for the caddy" (1974, 8).

Social movements are involved in constructing the experience of partisans and would-be partisans through the ways in which they define and describe the arena of their interest. The current abortion and anti-abortion movements are examples of how the "same" actions are differently framed. The terms "pro-life" and "pro-choice" conjure up different images of the abortion issue and relate it to different clusters of other issues and movements (Luker 1984). In this form, change has a significant ideational component.

Awareness that norms and meanings are at issue and in contention is itself a step in the development of change. From this standpoint, social movements have a reflexive character. They are something members of a society reflect on, think about, and are aware of. In attending to movements, members of a society recognize that social rules are at issue (Gusfield 1981b). Even where no association exists, as in the "hippie" movement," the recognition that a similarity of actions is occurring creates the movement. The very existence of a movement is itself a model of framing: It presents an area of life as at issue where it had previously been accepted as the norm. Alternatives now exist where choice and contention were absent.

In one sense, a social movement exists when members of a society share the recognition that specific social rules are no longer taken for granted. In the United States, the movement connected with laws against child abuse, both sexual and physical, has made the treatment of children by parents or other family members a matter of issue. What constitutes the "proper" behavior of parents to children has taken on a variety of new meanings. Attention and notice is taken of behavior that in the past was either unnoticed or unmentioned. Degrees and content of affection and of physical discipline have become matters to think about and to calculate. The relations between parent and child that were less open to state intervention are now legitimately regulated by law as well as by community opinion.

What takes place in the organized activities of many movements is significant in its stated goals and as an indication of what has become public acceptance or rejection of alternative possibilities. Success is measured not only by victory or defeat in legislative, bargaining or legal arenas but also in how the movement has changed the rules that are admissible in public arenas. As such a movement may support or undermine action at the interactional level, at the level of everyday life (Gusfield 1981b). The struggle over abortion in the United States is symbolically a struggle about the place of women relative to men (Luker 1984). Even local movements, for example, efforts to change street names in some cities from an existing name to one honoring Martin Luther King, come to symbolize the relative place of blacks in the American social order. In a paradoxical sense, *social movements occur when they are perceived to be occurring.* The existence of organized movements or the monitoring of events to suggest a movement in action can create the recognition that some accepted pattern of social life is now in contention; it has become an issue.

Insofar as movements possess a fluid rather than a linear quality, the question of membership is also fluid. Movements can have consequences and influence behavior without the kind of commitment or ideological agreement that is often posited for them. Frequently, we develop labels to identify members, for example, "women's libbers" or "peaceniks." Movements may achieve stated, formal goals with little effect on the everyday behavior they seek to transform (Handler 1978), just as they may fail to achieve major political goals while deeply affecting everyday behavior.

The Communication of Social Movements: Monitoring the Society

Movements exist along at least two dimensions. On one level, they are events and processes seeking, in a more or less deliberate fashion, to produce change in the political or institutional character of the society. On another level, they are signs that a segment of social life is potentially under challenge and alternatives are possible (Melucci 1989). Something that may have been unthinkable is now thinkable. They have significance for those who engage in their activities, but they may have significance also for those who become aware of them. They symbolize the transformation of a fixed social organization into an issue. Whether they are perceived as "right" or "wrong," they are perceived as in flux and in contention.

"Society" is not only the result of face-to-face interaction or of institutionally organized rules. It also exists as an object of observation and reflection (Gusfield 1979b). In this fashion, it exists at a distance from most observers. To perceive it requires organization and specialized institutions and their functionaries. It has to be monitored and constructed in the process of being monitored.

It is difficult to overestimate the influence of major communications industries and widespread formal education in understanding contemporary social movements. While they monitor events they also construct a more general sense of how events coalesce. The "hippie" movement, for example, could not be perceived as a movement without an agency that framed a set of individual events as a movement. Mass media are significant sources of the process of framing movements; of interpreting individual events as movements of change (Snow et al. 1986). Television news, for example, puts together the separately occurring events and frames them as a unity, as a movement of a particular kind. Whether movements are relatively organized or not, their depiction by the mass media influence both their understandings and those of less partisan observers in the audiences.

In the process of constructing the reality of the society, mass media do more than monitor: They dramatize. They create vivid images, impute leadership, and heighten the sense of conflict between movements and the institutions of society (Gitlin 1980; Ericson, Baranek, and Chan 1987). They project a vocabulary with which to discuss the movement. Consider some of the social types that are conveyed by terms such as "women's libber," "peacenik," "gay rights." The framing process is deeply influenced by the ways in which vehicles of news and entertainment frame the movements and their objects.

Mass Society Theory Revisited:
Social Movements as Theater

Despite its considerable drawbacks as a theory of modern politics, mass society theory contains a perception of significant aspects of modern societies that needs restatement. Developed in the effort to explain the emergence and character of totalitarian and other extremist movements, mass society theorists stressed the breakdown of class- and interest-oriented groups and the importance of groups alienated from social institutions, that is, groups that were not controlled by elites and were open to leadership that projected emotive, expressive elements into public life (Mannheim 1940; Arendt 1951; Selznick 1952, chap. 7; Kornhauser, 1959).

Mass society theory emerged in an effort to understand totalitarian, nondemocratic movements in Western, industrialized societies. As William Kornhauser points out, aristocratic theorists focused their attention on the decline of the authority of established elites and institutional controls. Democratic theorists focused attention on the ways in which rank-and-file members of bureaucratized organizations were unable to effectuate participation and influence decisions and policies. Both, however, projected a view of modern societies as ones in which great distances now prevailed between the institutions of social control and influence: church, school, government, class, ethnicity, even family and the individual at the level of his or her everyday life. The social and cultural diversities through which social commitment and control were conducted were no longer operative. The result was an alienated and homogeneous mass available to project raw, unmediated, unsocialized feelings into public policies.

Karl Mannheim, in *Man and Society in an Age of Reconstruction*, was perhaps especially prescient (1940). In an era of fundamental democratization, he argued, social and economic organization were increasingly rationalized on a functional basis. The control and influence of cultural elites diminished and the mass were unable to achieve the kind of substantive rationality essential to the complex technology and political participation of modern social organization. In his view, "The average person surrenders part of his own cultural individuality with every new act of integration into a functionally rationalized complex of activities. . . . [and]

gradually gives up his own interpretation of events for those others have given him. When the rationalized mechanism of social life collapses in times of crisis, the individual cannot repair it by his own insight" (59). And, "In a society in which the masses tend to dominate, irrationalities which have been integrated into the social structure may force their way into political life" (63).

Akin to collective behavior theory, mass sociey theory was vulnerable to the criticism that alienated, unorganized people were unable to mobilize for collective action (Gusfield 1962). Further, it became obvious that modern life was by no means so devoid of social organization or so alienated and anarchic as mass society theorists described (Shils 1972, chaps. 11, 12).

Nevertheless, the insights of mass society theorists have relevance for the kinds of fluid movements that I have been describing. It is not necessary to a sociology of social movements that all movements be studied through the same theory or that contrasting images of modern life may not both be applicable, sometimes to the same movement. Three aspects of mass society theory retain importance. They catch the nature of "interaction" in a significant area. First, a great deal of human "interaction" takes place at a distance, apart from face-to-face interaction, in a form of "parasocial interaction" (Horton and Wohl 1956). I have stressed this in discussing the role of mass media. In this sense the image of society as an audience, which is implicit in mass society studies, is still viable. Second, such interaction is, at least to an important extent, unmediated by socially organized institutions and groups. In that sense, the mass is useful as a concept not so much as a collectivity but as an area of action. Third, the mass audience is thus more standardized and homogenized than given by concepts of class, status, and ethnicity. This is not to negate the importance of these concepts but to attempt to specify where and when they may be most useful as analytical instruments. The same aggregate of people may be divided into classes, ethnic groups, and the usual sociological distinctions yet at other times and in other arenas operate as masses where a differentiated identity is absent.

The conception of the mass audience as the observers of the monitoring of movements underlines the view taken here of social movements as theater. The theatrical component of movements is a central way in which new meanings are disseminated (Edelman 1989). This is especially the case where the movement is oriented toward changing behavior of everyday life rather than the rules of institutions. Again, the labor and suffrage movements are not useful models for more fluid movements, while the "hippie" movement or the women's movement are. The insistence of many women on redirecting conventional language to erase the dominance of male imagery is an effective form of theater, of dramatizing changed conceptions now brought into consciousness.

This dramaturgical character of modern movements is of crucial importance (Snow 1983). Both the interpretive work of the monitors and the actions of organized movements toward those interpretations become significant. They form the essential linkage between public arenas and everyday life. The disposition of movements to undertake actions in order to dramatize the movement is a facet well caught in the title of Todd Gitlin's account of the interaction between the world of news coverage and student movements of the 1960s, *The Whole World Is Watching* (1980). As others have pointed out, it often leads the monitors to depict movements by concentrating on images of extremes of greater dramatic content. This has been recently observed in accounts of the news coverage of the anti-abortion movement in the United States (*Los Angeles Times* 1990). This monitoring and dramatic framing of events makes alternative modes of behavior accessible to wide audiences. Movements can be transmitted in a short period of time and people can be made aware of what thoughts and actions are shared and acted on by others, even outside the orbit of their personal acquaintance. The movement thus becomes a "sign of the times."

The revision of mass society theory that I assert as useful is found in distinguishing the alienation thesis from the understanding of mass communications as imagining society as a homogeneous, mass audience. The former, the alienating character of mass society, is far less viable than the latter, the image of the mass as an audience. Both collective behavior and mass society theories focus attention on the less organized aspects of social life. As perspectives toward social movements, they face in opposite directions. Collective behavior restores the importance of the interactive order as a significant locus of movements, especially many of the new movements oriented toward personal change. Mass society theories heighten our sensitivity toward the homogenizing, standardizing aspects of modern life. Here, the impact of mass communications media provides monitoring and framing functions that enable audiences to share experiences despite large diversities in class, culture, gender, and nation.

The plenitude of social movements that exist and persist in modern societies makes any single scheme of analysis too partial for expansion to all or even most movements (Gamson 1992). The more abstract the perspective, the less helpful it is for empirical study. In this chapter I emphasize the more fluid quality of many contemporary movements. My view has been well presented by David Snow. He points out that new or differing theoretical perspectives have the virtue of calling attention to otherwise unnoticed phenomena.

> Theoretical perspectives, functioning much like metaphors, not only highlights; they also hide. By focussing attention on some phenomena, other equally relevant things may be hidden or glossed over. Thus, just as it is useful and illuminating to approach the world with a range of metaphors, so it is useful to explain with a range of theoretical perspectives. And this especially is the case of phenomena which are not well bounded and about which there is much taxonomic debate and confusion, as is the case with collective behavior. (1983, 9)

Some objections may be made that many of the movements to which I have alluded in this essay are either trivial or do not involve dissent and great conflict. I assert that social movements studies have shown an undue emphasis on the political and have understated the importance of movements that create changes in everyday living outside the institutional structures of modern life (1979a). As social historians have been telling us in recent years, these, too, are very much part of history.

Note

1. During the 1970s a rash of works emerged with attention to how, where, and when movements utilized violence. See, for example, Tilly 1978.

References

Arendt, Hannah. 1951. *The Origins of Totalitarianism*. New York: Harcourt, Brace.

Barrows, Susanna. 1988. *Distorting Mirrors*. New Haven: Yale University Press.

Bateson, Gregory. 1972. "A Theory of Play and Fantasy." In his *Steps to an Ecology of Mind*. New York: Ballantine Books.

Berger, Bennett. 1982. *Survival of a Counter-Culture*. Berkeley: University of California Press.

Blocker, Jack. 1989. *American Temperance Movements: Cycles of Reform*. Boston: Twayne.

Blumer, Herbert. 1939. "Collective Behavior" In *An Outline of the Principles of Sociology*, edited by Robert E. Park. New York: Barnes and Noble.

Castells, Manuel. 1983. *The City and the Grass Roots*. Berkeley: University of California Press.

Cohen, Jean. 1985. "Strategy or Identity: New Theoretical Paradigms and Contemporary Social Movements. *Social Research* 52 (Winter): 663–716.

D'Emilio, John. 1983. *Sexual Politics, Sexual Communities*. Chicago: University of Chicago Press.

Edelman, Murray. 1989. *Constructing the Public Spectacle*. Chicago: University of Chicago Press.

Eder, Klaus. 1985. "The 'New Social Movements': Moral Crusades, Political Protest Groups, or Social Movements?" *Social Research* 52 (Winter): 869–901.

Ericson, Richard, Patricia Baranek, and Janet Chan. 1987. *Visualizing Deviance: A Study of News Organization*. Toronto: University of Toronto Press.

Flacks, Richard. 1988. *Making History*. New York: Columbia University Press.

Friedman, Lawrence. 1985. *Total Justice*. New York: Russell Sage Foundation.

Gamson, William. 1992. "The Social Psychology of Collective Action." In *Frontiers in Social Movement Theory*, edited by Aldon Morris and Carol M. Mueller. New Haven: Yale University Press.

Gitlin, Todd. 1980. *The Whole World Is Watching*. Berkeley: University of California Press.

Goffman, Erving. 1974. *Frame Analysis: An Essay on the Organization of Experience*. Cambridge, Mass.: Harvard University Press.

Greenberg, David. 1988. *The Construction of Homosexuality*. Chicago: University of Chicago Press.

Gusfield, Joseph. 1962. "Mass Society and Extremist Politics." *American Sociological Review* 27:19–30.

———. 1970. *Protest, Reform, and Revolt*. New York: John Wiley and Sons.

———. 1978. "Historical Problematics and Sociological Fields: An American Liberalism and the Study of Social Movements." In *Research in Sociology of Knowledge, Sciences and Art*, edited by Robert Jones, vol. 1. Greenwich, Conn.: JAI Press.

———. 1979a. "The Modernity of Social Movements." In *Societal Growth*, edited by Amos Hawley. New York: Free Press.

———. 1979b. "The Sociological Reality of America." In *On the Making of Americans: Essays in Honor of David Riesman*. Edited by Herbert Gans, Nathan Glazer, Joseph Gusfield, and Christopher Jencks. Philadelphia: University of Pennsylvania Press.

———. 1981a. "Prevention: Rise, Decline, and Renaissance." In *Alcohol, Science, and Society Revisited*, edited by Edith Gomberg, Helene White, and John Carpenter. New Brunswick, N.J.: Rutgers School of Alcohol Studies.

———. 1981b. "Social Movements and Social Change: Perspectives of Linearity and Fluidity." In *Research in Social Movements, Conflict, and Change,* edited by Louis Kriesberg, vol. 4. Greenwich, Conn.: JAI Press.

————. 1988. "The Control of Drinking-Driving in the United States: A Period in Transition?" In *Social Control of the Drinking Driver,* edited by Michael Lawrence, John Snortum, and Franklin Zimring. Chicago: University of Chicago Press.

————. 1989. "Constructing the Ownership of Public Problems." *Social Problems* 36 (December): 431–41.

Handler, Joel. 1978. *Social Movements and the Legal System.* New York: Academic Press.

Horton, Donald, and Richard Wohl. 1956. "Observations on Intimacy at a Distance." *Psychiatry* 19:215–29.

Jaspers, James, and Dorothy Nelkin. 1989. "The Animal Rights Movement." Paper presented at the annual meeting of the Society for the Study of Social Problems, Berkeley, California, August.

Jenkins, J. Craig. 1983. "Resource Mobilization Theory." In *Annual Review of Sociology,* edited by Ralph Turner and James Short, Jr., vol. 9. Palo Alto, Calif.: Annual Reviews.

Kornhauser, William. 1959. *The Politics of Mass Society.* Glencoe, Ill.: Free Press.

Kuhn, Thomas. 1962. *The Structure of Scientific Revolutions.* Chicago: University of Chicago Press.

Los Angeles Times. 1990. "News Coverage of Abortion Conflicts: Are They Biased?" July 2, section A, p. 1.

Lowenberg, June. 1989. *Caring and Responsibility: The Crossroads between Holistic Practice and Traditional Medicine.* Philadelphia: University of Pennsylvania Press.

Luker, Kristin. 1984. *Abortion and the Politics of Motherhood.* Berkeley: University of California Press.

McAdam, Doug. 1982. *Political Process and the Development of Black Insurgency, 1930–1970.* Chicago: University of Chicago Press.

McCarthy, John D., and Mayer N. Zald. 1973. *The Trend of Social Movements in America.* Morristown, N.J.: General Learning Press.

————. 1977. "Resource Mobilization and Social Movements." *American Journal of Sociology* 82:1212–41.

Mannheim, Karl. 1940. *Man and Society in an Age of Reconstruction.* London: Routledge and Kegan Paul.

Melucci, Alberto. 1985. "The Symbolic Challenge of Contemporary Movements." *Social Research* 52 (Winter): 789–816.

————. 1989. *Nomads of the Present: Social Movements and Individual Needs in Contemporary Society.* Philadelphia: Temple University Press.

Morris, Aldon. 1984. *The Origins of the Civil Rights Movement.* New York: Free Press.

Nelson, Barbara. 1984. *Making an Issue of Child Abuse.* Chicago: University of Chicago Press.

Oberschall, Anthony. 1973. *Social Conflict and Social Movements.* Englewood Cliffs, N.J.: Prentice-Hall.

Offe, Claus. 1985. "New Social Movements: Challenging the Boundaries of Institutional Politics." *Social Research* 52 (Winter): 817–68.

Olson, Mancur. 1971. *The Logic of Collective Action.* Cambridge, Mass.: Harvard University Press.

Park, Robert, and Ernest Burgess. 1967. "Collective Behavior." In *Robert Park on Social Control and Collective Behavior,* edited by Ralph Turner. Chicago: University of Chicago Press.

Pfohl, Stephen. 1977. "The Discovery of Child Abuse." *Social Problems* 24:310–23.

Ross, H. Laurence. 1989. *The New Philadelphia Story: The Effects of Severe Punishment for Drunk Driving.* Washington, D.C.: AAA Foundation for Traffic Safety.

Selznick, Philip. 1952. *The Organizational Weapon.* New York: McGraw-Hill.

Shils, Edward. 1972. *The Intellectuals and the Powers and Other Essays.* Chicago: University of Chicago Press.

Snow, David A. 1983. "A Dramaturgical Approach to Collective Behavior." Paper presented to the American Sociological Association, Detroit, Michigan, August 31–September 4.

Snow, David A., and Robert D. Benford. 1988. "Ideology, Frame Resonance, and Participant Mobilization." In *From Structure to Action,* edited by Bert Klandermans, Hanspeter Kriesi, and Sidney Tarrow. Vol. 1 of *International Social Movement Research.* Greenwich, Conn.: JAI Press.

———. 1992. "Master Frames and Cycles of Protest." In *Frontiers in Social Movement Theory,* edited by Aldon Morris and Carol M. Mueller. New Haven: Yale University Press.

Snow, David A., E. Burke Rochford, Jr., Steven K. Worden, and Robert D. Benford. 1986. "Frame Alignment Processes, Micromobilization, and Movement Participation." *American Sociological Review* 51:464–81.

Tilly, Charles. 1978. *From Mobilization to Revolution.* Reading, Mass.: Addison-Wesley.

Touraine, Alain. 1977. *The Self-Production of Society.* Chicago: University of Chicago Press.

Turner, Ralph H. 1969. "The Theme of Contemporary Social Movements." *British Journal of Sociology* 20 (December): 390–405.

———. 1981. "Collective Behavior and Resource Mobilization as Approaches to Social Movements: Issues and Continuities." In *Research in Social Movements, Conflict, and Change,* edited by Louis Kriesberg, vol. 4. Greenwich, Conn.: JAI Press.

Turner, Ralph H., and Lewis Killian. 1987. *Collective Behavior.* 3d ed. Englewood Cliffs, N.J.: Prentice-Hall.

Chapter 4

Ideology and Utopia after Socialism

Ralph H. Turner

It has often been observed that social movements exist and rise and fall in clusters that are more or less unified by dedication to common underlying values and worldviews. During any given period in history and within a given sociocultural complex, a few basic themes tend to shape the goals and worldviews of the most significant social movements, even when their specific concerns are quite disparate. Herbert Blumer (1939) called attention to this principle by distinguishing between specific and general social movements. General movements are "rather formless in organization and inarticulate in expression" (201), reflecting the historic emergence of new values. A specific movement, in contrast, "has a well defined objective or goal . . . [and] develops a recognized and accepted leadership and a definite membership characterized by a 'we-consciousness' " (202). He illustrated the distinction by citing the American antislavery specific movement, which grew out of the widespread nineteenth-century humanitarian general movement. Just how broadly he meant this idea to be applied was never clear because he failed to elaborate it. It goes considerably beyond the contention of Amitai Etzioni (1970) and Charles Tilly (1979), however, that a distinctive selection of tactics prevails in any given historical period.

A somewhat similar idea underlies the more recent concept of social movement "master frames" (Snow et al. 1986; Snow and Benford 1988; Johnston 1991), although it places more emphasis on strategies than on movement value orientations. "The master frame can be thought of as a general formula for solving problems related to the opposition movement: what collective actions are appropriate, who might be acceptable allies, what demands can be voiced, which ones are better left unvoiced, and how to interpret the responses of the regime" (Johnston 1991, 139). Likewise, Sidney Tarrow's (1983) concept of "cycles of protest" incorporates some of the same assumptions as Blumer's concept of general movements.

Recent discussions of "new social movements" assume that a comprehensive pattern of values, specific goals, strategies, and tactics distinguishes the dominant contemporary social movements in Western Europe and the United States from movements in previous eras. These discussions may usefully be thought of as describing a new general movement, which has given impetus and shape to a wide variety of contemporary specific movements.

The most comprehensive historical application of the concept of general movements is still that of Karl Mannheim (1946), who sought to identify a pattern in the historical succession of such general movements. My objective in this chapter is to examine some of the implications and issues from Mannheim's analysis in order to see whether they help to shed light on the contemporary diversity of social movements and movement styles and the new social movement thesis.

Mannheim: Ideology and Utopia

The paired concepts of "ideology" and "utopia," with the special meanings he assigns to them, are central to Mannheim's analysis. Both refer to widely shared thought-systems that are not entirely congruent with reality. They consist of the categories into which people unconsciously organize their experience in order to make sense of it, and they reflect the fundamental assumptions about reality that people take for granted. When people share a common ideology or utopia, they can discuss and debate social issues with a reasonable degree of mutual understanding. When people hold different ideologies or when some people's thought is organized in terms of an ideology and others' thought is organized in terms of a utopia, they typically talk past each other, misunderstanding each other's statements and actions. Every social order depends on the general acceptance of certain myths and the use of certain thought categories for its effectiveness and stability. The comprehensive system of thought that undergirds any existing social order is called ideology. Ideologies are thus potent conservative forces, permitting even dissidents to work ultimately so as to maintain the existing social order. Under some circumstances, however, a system of thought that is wholly incongruous with the existing order may emerge and gain widespread acceptance. When that system of thought mobilizes a sufficient number of people into action to shatter the existing social order and render the prevalent ideology no longer meaningful, it is called a utopia. The utopia becomes the basis for a general social movement that fosters profound social change, leading ultimately to a different social order and a new ideology to support it.

The relationship between ideology and utopia is conceived in Hegelian terms as a dialectic. A dialectical process is one in which a set of ideas known as the thesis gives rise to an opposing set of ideas known as the antithesis. The ensuing struggle between thesis and antithesis eventually results in a synthesis, which combines ideas selectively from both thesis and antithesis into a harmonious whole. That synthesis then becomes the new thesis, and the cycle begins anew as a new antithesis develops. Mannheim (1946) writes:

> The relationship between utopia and the existing order turns out to be a "dialectical" one. By this is meant that every age allows to arise (in differently located social groups) those ideas and values in which are contained in condensed form the unrealized and the unfulfilled tendencies which represent the needs of each age. These intellectual elements then become the explosive material for bursting the limits of the existing order. The existing order gives birth to utopias which in turn break the bonds of the existing order, leaving it free to develop in the direction of the next order of existence. (179)

A Historical Sequence

In his ambitious analysis, Mannheim (1946) begins with the year 1520, when, under the leadership of Robert Munzer, the chiliasm of the Anabaptists "joined forces with the active demands of the oppressed strata of society" (190). Chiliasm was a religious doctrine forecasting the imminent return of Christ to rule on earth for one thousand years. The chiliastic utopia expressed the wish dreams of the peasantry in opposition to the ideology of feudalism. Peasant protest was not driven by ideas but by "ecstatic–orgiastic energies" (192), and not by "optimistic hopes for the future or romantic reminiscences" (195) but by expectation of a union with the immediate present. Because existing social structures were totally irrelevant to the imminent new order, peasant frustrations were frequently expressed in outbursts of unrestrained destructiveness and violence.

As the feudal system decayed, partly in response to chiliastic outbursts, the liberal–humanitarian utopia associated with the American and French Revolutions displaced chiliasm as the dominant force challenging the ideology of the period. Although chiliastic outbursts remained a significant element in these movements, "the fundamental attitude of the liberal is characterized by a positive acceptance of culture and the giving of an ethical tone to human affairs. He is most in his element in the role of critic rather than of creative destroyer" (198). Expressing the personal style and wish dreams of a rising bourgeois class, liberal–humanitarianism was driven by ideas, assumed free will, and saw freedom as the ultimate goal. The liberal–humanitarian mentality is closer to reality than chiliasm, but its ultimate reliance on ideas still preserves a gulf between its utopia and reality.

In conscious contrast to this liberal outlook, the succeeding conservative utopia "gave positive emphasis to the notion of determinateness of our outlook and behavior" (206). Continuing the existing trend toward greater realism and acknowledgment of existing social structures, the conservative mentality simply feels comfortable with things as they are. With none of the liberal–humanitarian predisposition toward theorizing, conservatives only formulated a utopia in defense against attacks on the existing order, particularly from surviving elements of liberalism and chiliasm.[1]

Completing the series, the succeeding socialist utopia was "a new creation based on an inner synthesis of the various forms of utopia which have arisen hitherto and which have struggled against one another in society" (215); it was "a peculiar assimilation of the conservative sense of determinism into the progressive utopia which strives to remake the world" (218). Determinism was embodied in the theory of class conflict and a materialistic philosophy of human motivation, which latter was borrowed from the conservative utopia. The idealism of liberal–humanitarianism found expression in the image of a harmonious and just socialist society in which the state would no longer be needed to regulate human affairs. The wish dreams of the proletariat are expressed in the socialist utopia.

Mannheim does not view the particular sequence of utopias in a pattern–deterministic fashion, but he sees each utopia as reflecting the social order that gives rise to it. He nevertheless describes the sequence as a "general subsidence of utopian intensity," as each succeeding stage "manifests a closer approximation to the historical–social process" (223). As the utopian force diminishes, life becomes less inspired and more matter-of-fact. Mannheim was plainly distressed by what he saw as the imminent end of both utopia and ideology.[2]

> It would require either a callousness which our generation could probably no longer acquire or the unsuspecting naivete of a generation newly born into the world to be able to live in absolute congruence with the realities of that world, utterly without any transcendent element, either in the form of a utopia or of an ideology. At our present stage of self-consciousness this is perhaps the only form of actual existence that is possible in a world which is no longer in the making. It is possible that the best that our ethical principles have to offer is "genuineness" and "frankness" in place of the old ideals. (230–31)

Mannheim saw two sources of tension to disrupt this condition of stagnation. One consisted of social strata whose aspirations were still unfulfilled, who would keep alive the socialist utopia, "and thus, to a certain extent, will always cause the counter-utopias to rekindle and flare up again, at least whenever this extreme left wing goes into action" (231). The other source consists of the "intellectual section of society, which is becoming more and more separated from the rest and thrown upon its own resources" (233).

This image of a world in which utopian energy and vision has almost altogether dissipated seems incredible half a century later. Yet, Mannheim's analysis is well rooted in historical fact and sufficiently suggestive of generally applicable principles to warrant a serious effort to essay application to the contemporary social movement scene. In addition, such observations as his comment about an ethics of genuineness and frankness, made sixty years ago, seem strikingly contemporary—at least in American society.[3] We are now in a position to ask whether the present cacophony of social movements and organized protest is a continuation of the processes Mannheim described, a new sequence paralleling the old, or a set of developments that are not susceptible of analysis in Mannheim's framework.

Issues

There is often a vagueness in Mannheim's writing that makes it difficult either to apply or test his model. For example, at times his reference to the chiliastic impulse that is transferred from cause to cause and that ebbs and occasionally flows over time borders on the mystical. In addition, many questions remain to be answered before we can apply Mannheim's model with precision.

Among the many questions left unanswered by Mannheim's exciting analysis, two sets are fundamental. One set of questions concerns the dynamics of the process by which succeeding utopias are generated. The other has to do with what has and will follow the early twentieth century, when the sequence he describes came to an apparent close. Mannheim was quite explicit in denying the possibility of predicting future developments because of the decisive part played by human choice in shaping history. He did, however, suggest possibilities that are indicated on the basis of his scheme. At least some answers to the first set of questions are essential before we can address the second set in anything but a grossly empirical fashion.

Perhaps the most critical question is to what extent the process that Mannheim describes is incremental, in the sense that the direction of change is determined by the idiosyncracies of development at each stage in the process. If unpredictable developments and externally caused events contribute toward shaping the utopia that is spawned by a given ideology, outcomes will always remain unpredictable. Alternatively, to what extent is there an overall directive principle, such that the last stage should be predictable from a thorough understanding of the first stage? Although Mannheim's use of the dialectic seems to imply the former, his proposal that there is a steady decline in energy or optimism about the prospects for the human condition in the sequence from the chiliastic to the socialist utopia clearly implies the latter. If we accept this latter interpretation as at least partly correct, we must approach the question of recent and future utopias by searching for a new organizing principle based on a major system change. If we accept the former interpretation, we must look for appropriate antitheses to the postsocialist ideology. If, as seems the case, both interpretations are partially correct, we must look for even more complicatedly determined outcomes.

Closely related is the question of exactly how Mannheim means the dialectical principle to apply. While the utopia is ideology's antithesis, there is not just one logically conceivable antithesis but there are many, and the antithesis is far from absolute. What, then, determines the character of the utopia that becomes the dominant critique of any given ideology? In his analysis, Mannheim strangely neglects any reference to the stage of synthesis, which becomes the new ideology, as coming between successive utopias. While utopias oppose ideologies, both of which are at the cultural level, Mannheim speaks more of the distinctive conditions of social structure than of ideology in explaining the focus of each new utopia. It is clear, then, that Mannheim's implicit model incorporates social structure as well as culture. Perhaps the model might best be described as one in which each major utopia induces or contributes to significant changes in social structure, which synthesize utopian elements with surviving features from the prior stage of social structure. The functioning of the modified social structure then has identifiable consequences that are different for the members of different classes. Certain of these consequences, particularly in relation to the aspirations introduced or raised by the recent utopia, become salient and constitute the basis for the next utopia. The consequences consist of both constraints and opportunities. New opportunities view as intolerable conditions that were once taken for granted as misfortunes; they become injustices (Turner 1969). The particular way in which the cognitive side of the new utopia is formulated reflects the dialectical principle of logical opposition to the justificatory ideology. The main thrust or direction of the utopia is better explained as an emotional response to the direct impact of social structure on members of the general movement's principal constituency. Since the ideology is not an accurate but a justificatory representation of the social structural condition, no amount of understanding of ideologies and prior utopias would allow one either to explain or predict the nature of ensuing utopias.

Also unclear in Mannheim's analysis is the function of constituency in shaping the dominant utopia. The content of each utopia reflects the wish dreams (or interests?) of a class in society. Mannheim never describes a principle to explain or predict what particular class will be the constituency for the dominant utopia in any given era. For the chiliasts and the socialists, he seems to be identifying a class that was particularly oppressed or at least by-passed by the benefits accruing to other strata; for the liberal-humanitarians, the significant fact was that they were the rising class; for the conservatives, the important observation is that they did not feel deprived but feared burgeoning attacks on the legitimacy of their existing privileges; and for the socialists, the debate still rages over whether the working classes were increasingly oppressed or slowly gaining during the early stages of industrialization.

A closely related ambiguity concerns the relationship between the constituent class and the broader sociocultural dialectical process whereby each new utopia is indirectly a reaction to the prior utopia. The implied principle seems to be that the critical constituency assimilated ideas selectively from the then-current ideology and prior utopias—especially the most recent—for consistency with their own structurally based perspective. One might think of the fashioning of a utopian worldview as the culmination of a learning process in which ideological and cultural-affective resources are selectively adopted, adapted, rejected, and reversed according to how they harmonize with the constituencies' situationally induced feelings.

A third realm of ambiguity concerns the relationship between the dominant value, goal, or object espoused by a movement and the mode of thought and action that characterizes the movement. Mannheim describes the utopian mentality as permeating all aspects of behavior and thought. He points out, for example, the compatibility of dominant art forms with the prevailing utopian mentality. He stresses especially the time orientation characteristic of each utopia as affecting both patterns of thought and modes of action. One wonders whether, for example, the pursuit of freedom as a crucial value necessarily requires the accommodating mentality and mode of action Mannheim ascribes to the liberal-humanitarian movement. And, attributing violent outbursts and extremist declarations in contemporary movements to surviving chiliastic survivals seems arbitrary.[4] As we look at contemporary social movements, we should probably treat the linkage between particular movement values and modes of thought and action as an open question.

A fourth set of ambiguities revolves about the empirical diversity and multiplicity of movements during any historical era.

Mannheim wrote as if there were but a single movement during a given historical period and throughout Western Europe, or that history was shaped by only one movement at a time. This seems a gross oversimplification. What, then, determines the range over which a given utopia holds sway? To what extent can major contending utopias coexist? To what extent can the processes described by Mannheim proceed at different rates in different sectors of society, so that contentions based on different utopia–ideology pairs are taking place simultaneously? To what extent are key elements from one dominant utopia diffused into the worldviews of social movements promoting quite diverse causes? More profoundly, can there be different social movement systems, each with its own sequence of utopias, proceeding in parallel during the same extended historical period?

Movements of the 1960s

In 1969, I looked at the themes of contemporary social movements, and I attempted to relate them to Mannheim's paradigm. I suggested that every new movement era was heralded by the redefinition of a condition heretofore viewed as a misfortune, now newly viewed and deeply felt as an injustice. The condition so redefined in the 1960s was the lack of a sense of personal dignity or a clear sense of identity. The new utopia was a demand that society provide people with a sense of personal worth—something that had been, and for many people still is, regarded as a strictly individual and private problem. At that time, alienation of the individual (in its social psychological meaning as a feeling of estrangement in interpersonal relations and from the organizations and communities in which one participates) and depersonalization of society were leading symbols in the new utopia, and existentialism was the compatible philosophy. In the United States, the most prominent and organized movement embodying the new utopia became known as the New Left.

Departing from Mannheim's formula, I proposed that the primary constituency for the new utopia was not an economic class but an age cohort, namely, youth. This change occurred because the major adjustments being made in social structure at that time had more to do with the relative privileges and obligations of age groups than of economic classes. Proposing that the constituencies for Mannheim's utopias could all be seen as classes that were rising economically or confronted with new opportunities,[5] I argued that revised patterns of childrearing and international reaction against authoritarianism, symbolized by Adolf Hitler, coupled with the demographic fact of swelling numbers in the age cohort gave youth power and privilege that the age group had not previously experienced. I suggested that "The problem of alienation and the sense of worth is most poignantly the problem of a youthful generation with unparalleled freedom and capability but without an institutional structure in which this capability can be appropriately realized" (Turner 1969, 399). The spread of this theme to prominence in other movements was illustrated with reference to the "Black is beautiful" theme in the American "black power" movement and similar applications in other movements. As a slogan, "Black is beautiful" represented a new strategy in the long struggle to overcome discrimination and inequality, a strategy whose inspiration came at least in part from the currently prevailing social movement theme.[6]

In subsequent work, not specifically addressed to social movements, I proposed that there had been shift throughout the Western world in the criteria people used in identifying their "real selves" from institution to impulse (Turner 1976). Traditionally, people have thought of themselves in terms of their institutional roles and group memberships. One's occupation, gender, age group, family membership and role, religious affiliation, educational attainment, political affiliation, and publicly acknowledged achievements and recognitions were among the typical components in one's self-conception. The impulse self represented a struggle to find one's true self by separating oneself from institutional labels and constraints. The corresponding self-conception consists of personality traits and dispositions, personal likes and dislikes, and other characteristics that transcend any particular institutional role or group affiliation. "Institutionals" recognize their real selves in their achievements, in their pursuit of ideals, and, for many, in altruistic self-sacrifice. "Impulsers" find themselves in freeing their behavior from the constraints of reason and social norms so as to act strictly upon impulse, and in establishing relationships with others within which they can safely speak and act on impulse. Comparison between survey data from a probability sample of adults in the United States and questionnaire data from student samples in one U.S., one British, and two Australian universities documented the prevalence of the often proclaimed "quest for identity" among university students in the three countries; it also revealed the very low incidence of such a quest among other segments of the population in the U.S. sample[7] (Turner 1975; Turner and Gordon 1981).

Attempting to place this analysis in a larger context, I noted that movements or movement series typically begin with a pattern of rather chaotic, poorly focused protest, without benefit of a clear and constructive program for implementing their values. This may have been the proper interpretation of chiliasm, rather than its being seen as comparable to the liberal-humanitarian and socialist utopias. The assumption was that the worldwide student disruptions of the 1960s might correspond to the chiliastic phase in Mannheim's sequence of economic class–based movements. They might then be followed by movements with more clearly defined programs designed to implement the value of human worth and mitigate the depersonalization of social institutions. These subsequent movements might not be carried by youth but by other common-interest segments of society, especially other age cohorts.

Contemporary Social Movements

Now that two decades have elapsed since the original publication, and the disturbances of the 1960s have become ancient and not particularly relevant history to a new generation of college youth, how well does the preceding analysis stand up, and what linkage can be made to Mannheim's sequence? Following the analogy to chiliasm, can the New Left and the more loosely coordinated worldwide youth activism of the 1960s be conceived as the beginning stage in a new, differently constituted sequence, but still amenable to Mannheim's type of dialectical analysis? Alternatively, can they be better understood now as a next stage after socialism in Mannheim's original sequence? In either case, has the movement's impact lasted? Has it persisted as a movement or have essential elements of its utopia been incorporated into the utopias of more recent social movements? Or, is it to be dismissed as a "flash in the pan," an idiosyncratic episode caused by a unique coincidence of several historic events, with little long-range impact on contemporary social movements?

Let us consider first the possibility, that the New Left was a fifth or sixth stage in Mannheim's original sequence. The movement was clearly a reaction against a social order that had extensively accommodated to demands and values from the liberal-humanitarian, conservative, and socialist utopias. The politico-industrial system and the welfare state together were blamed for many of the world's ills. Furthermore, borrowings from socialist and liberal-humanitarian utopias were abundant in New Left ideology. In these two important respects, the New Left fits the pattern of a further stage in Mannheim's sequence. Nevertheless, the movement clearly does not fit on the trajectory toward increasing realism and pessimism about human nature that Mannheim found in the four utopias he examined. In addition, it never evolved a clear image of a program to rectify the twin evils of the politicoindustrial system and the welfare state. Also, the movement rests on a fundamental shift in the basis upon which the principal constituency was differentiated from the rest of the population, that is, from economic class to age group. Hence, it remains, in retrospect, more like chiliasm, as the enthusiastic and largely unrealistic early expression of a new utopian pattern than the continuation of a sequence that moves toward greater and greater realism. Like the chiliastic utopia that borrowed fundamental elements from early Christianity and a variety of medieval movements, it drew selectively from prior utopias while adding unique features. The discontinuity is too great for it to be conceived as an additional stage in the original sequence.

If youthful protest of the 1960s is therefore to be conceived as the start of a new sequence, there must be evidence that important elements of its utopia have become embedded in contemporary culture, that lasting social structural changes occurred in society in response to its demands, and that new utopias incorporate both themes from the 1960s' movements and critiques of a society that has accommodated to demands from the earlier movement.

A search for clues to this puzzle might begin by asking whether a distinctive mental frame of reference associated with the 1960s has survived. One such clue is evidence that, in spite of external appearances, the impulsive conception of the true self has persisted and perhaps become even more prevalent among college youth. This frame of reference has been documented by David Snow and Cynthia Phillips (1982). This finding lends further confirmation to the original thesis that this was a long-term trend, predating the 1960s decade, a thesis that was also supported by James Benton's (1981) content analysis of leading American magazines from 1920 to 1978. Like each of the utopian uprisings of the past, and like the sudden worldwide eruption of "democracy" movements in 1989 and 1990, youthful protest in the 1960s constituted the crystallization of previously accumulating changes in worldviews, either provoked or facilitated by the conjunction of critical historic events.

While the most salient theme of the 1960s movements in the United States was peace, the peace theme was neither new nor distinctive to the New Left movement. It was strong enough during the early years of World War II that it might well have kept the United States out of active combat except for the Japanese attack on Pearl Harbor and the stigma of anti-Semitism.[8] Merle Curti (1929) impressively documented the importance of peace movements in American history throughout the nineteenth century. The ebb and flow of American peace movements has reflected the changing threat and costs of war. Consequently, I do not think that the prevalence of peace themes in current movements can serve as evidence for the start of a new movement sequence. Rather, we must look for new ways of thinking about the issue of peace and war that are more in harmony with the new utopian trend—if there is one.

Other prominent themes in the New Left movement included opposition to large-scale organization of all kinds, the antigrowth and antitechnology theme that "less is better," and a stress on participatory rather than representative democracy. In California, the movement remained strong enough to elect and reelect a leading exponent of these values, Jerry Brown, to eight years as governor. Many changes have been made, nationwide, in the directions of decentralization, monitoring of new technology in terms of human values, and openness of government and business decision making to public view.

The distrust of large government, large business, and large labor has been documented for the United States by Seymour Lipset and William Schneider (1987). There is abundant evidence to the present day of declining public identification with government in the United States. While it may be less clearly embodied in organized social movements, it finds frequent expression in grass-roots protests such as wildcat strikes and local protests of all kinds. Symptomatic of the longing for participatory democracy are the continuing insistence on open meetings of decision-making and advisory bodies, the almost ritualistic use of public demonstrations in all causes, and the widespread experimentation with Japanese participatory work organization in American and European factories (Cole 1989; Turner 1991).

The theme of "less is better," with a suspicious attitude toward technology, growth, and so-called progress, may be the most distinctive legacy of the movement. Slow growth and antidevelopment movements have proliferated in communities all over the United States; they have an impressive record of success. While the environmental movement is divided between an "appropriate technology" and a changed life-style wing, the cautiousness about accepting technological solutions to problems; the opposition to nuclear energy; the resistence to urban expansion; the concern about environmental exploitation and pollution; and the preservationist attitude toward natural environments, historically significant structures, and ecological balance are all significant expressions of the general theme.

If the Green movement is the quintessential "new movement," its continuity with New Left themes is striking. The following words by the modern environmentalist Lester Milbrath (1984) could easily have been transplanted with minor adaptations from the New Left's Port Huron Statement of 1962.

> In modern society, we have developed a socio-technical-economic system that can dominate and destroy nature. Alongside it, we have retained a normative and ethical system based on 2000-year-old religions. The lack of congruence between these two systems threatens the continued existence of our civilization. Our science tells us how our world works physically but provides no moral guidance for our behavior within it. The normative prescriptions from inherited religions do not address the power and exuberance of modern human activities. The environmental modern-day prophets are trying to unite a sophisticated understanding of how the world works with a new normative ethical system that recognizes and addresses those realities. (101)

The concept of alienation, introduced by Marx and used by the socialist utopia to refer strictly to the worker's relationship to work, and given central meaning in the 1960s with a changed, more psychological meaning, is once more given altered meaning to fit the values of the Green movement. Jonathon Porritt, a leader of the British environmental movement, writes that "alienation has become a part of our lives." He defines alienation as "that sense of estrangement people experience between themselves and their work, their own health, their environment, and the workings of their democracy" (1985, 77). Thus he broadens the referent for alienation and the meaning of ecology to subsume all aspects of people's relationship to their daily experience.

It seems fair to conclude that important themes from the New Left utopia have diffused and found expression in a wide variety of contemporary movements. As they have done so, however, the constituency has broadened. As many scholars have already observed, the constituencies for most of these "new movements" are the educated middle classes (Cohen 1985). Indeed, the prominence of the middle classes in recent movements has often been noted. The student protesters of the 1960s were disproportionately of middle-class origin. Frank Parkin (1968) early called attention to the dominantly middle-class constituency of the British movement for nuclear disarmament. But, in most cases, the movements have not defined either the problem or their goals primarily in terms of broad economic class oppositions or age-group conflicts. In a survey of middle-class campaigns in Britain in the 1970s, Roger King and Neill Nugent (1979) conclude that "neither the middle classes as a whole, nor our particular activists, display a unity of purpose warranting the description 'middle class revolt' *per se*" (184). Some of the campaigns they examined were addressed to issues that particularly impacted the self-interests of a segment of the middle class, while others had a classless reference to general issues of culture and morality. One might say that they defined their enemies primarily in value terms. Frank Parkin (1968) makes the point sharply:

> It will be suggested that whereas working class radicalism could be said to be geared largely to reforms of an economic or material kind, the radicalism of the middle class is directed mainly to social reforms which are basically moral in content. Again, whereas the former holds out the promise of benefits to one particular section of society (the working class) from which its own supporters are drawn, the latter envisages no rewards which will accrue to the

middle class specifically, but only to society at large, or to some underprivileged groups. It is argued in fact that the main pay-off for middle class radicals is that of a psychological or emotional kind—in satisfactions derived from expressing personal values in action. (2)

The most critical question remains: Is the conviction that a sense of personal worth, of meaning in life, is a fundamental human right that must be protected and promoted by our social institutions germane to these new movements? Or, was the establishment of a sense of personal worth and meaning in life a distinctively adolescent problem, with no counterpart among the middle-class adults who are the newer movements' principal constituents? In fact, a somewhat more sophisticated version of the same theme recurs in more recent utopian pronouncements. The ecologists in particular stress the need for humankind to understand their proper place as a part—variously significant or insignificant—of the natural order, rather than as a race apart from and above nature. Peace and antinuclear movements and the variety of "slow-growth" movements call for a reexamination of self in relation to the world or the universe. The women's movement pursues opportunities for self-fulfilment and human dignity. Clearly the problem of who we really are has persisted and spread even as it has broadened to encompass the concerns of a variety of more specific movements.

It is highly plausible, therefore, to think of the youthful protest of the 1960s as a forerunner in the historical process that has precipitated a new movement pattern that seems characteristic of the contemporary era. This pattern is in contrast to the post–Middle Ages sequence of more class-based and class interest–oriented social movements. Only history written in future decades or centuries can establish securely whether this is the correct interpretation of social movements in the second half of the twentieth century. For now, this seems the most reasonable interpretation.

Further Questions

While this essay has thus far dealt more in questions than in answers, still further questions are stimulated by the foregoing incomplete analysis. One question arises from a more comprehensive look at American history. The nineteenth-century social movements that were taken as prototypes for theory building from the perspective of collective behavior resemble in some ways the "new social movements" more than the economic class-oriented movements on which Mannheim and many traditional European scholars focus. The movement for the abolition of slavery, the movement for public education, the temperance movement, the movement for women's suffrage, the children's movement, the foreign missions movement (religious), prison reform, and others had largely middle-class constituencies and promoted objectives that did not benefit the middle class exclusively or even primarily. Charles Beard (1913) advanced a class struggle interpretation of the writing of the American Constitution (adopted in 1789), but subsequent historical research has generally discredited or greatly moderated that view.[9] The public education movement in the United States was once interpreted as a working-class movement, but that interpretation, too, is hardly credited by contemporary educational historians. Similarly, Joseph Gusfield (1963) demonstrated a class element in the temperance movement, but he would not place it in the same category of class interest-based movements as Mannheim's examples.

The foregoing list reminds us that the American movements were often counterparts to European movements. Yet these do not seem to figure in Mannheim's analysis, unless they can be seen as expressions of the liberal-humanitarian utopia. Hence, we are prodded into asking whether the new social movements are really new with respect to type of constituency and their value orientation or whether they represent a continuation and further evolution of a very significant, but overlooked, movement segment that never fit the "old" pattern of class-oriented movements.

Another question concerns another important set of contemporary movements often neglected in discussions of new movements. Raising the question "What next?" in the 1950s, I suspected then that nationalistic, ethnic, and racial movements might be to the twentieth century what Mannheim's great movements were to earlier centuries. As we near the end of the century, the impression becomes even stronger that the most prevalent and powerful movements worldwide have been of this type. Furthermore, nationalistic/ethnic movements have a history antedating the current century. In a classic analysis, Carlton J. H. Hayes

(1931) traced the history of modern nationalism back to the break up of the "old internationalism" in eighteenth-century Europe. While these movements have varying degrees of class involvement, their constituencies and the interests involved transcend class boundaries. It has even been suggested that prior to the accession of Franklin Roosevelt to the U.S. presidency in 1933, politics and political movements were more sectionally based than class based (Bell 1955, 10). Sectionalism bears a close relationship to nationalism. Because of their long history, these nationalistic and ethnic movements are ripe for a longitudinal analysis paralleling Mannheim's analysis of class-based movements. Have there been stages in the development of ethnic and nationalistic utopias that have been linked through a dialectical process, with each new version of ethnonationalism constituting a reaction against a sociocultural system that incorporated elements from an earlier version? Alternatively, have there been changing meanings and styles of nationalism that correspond to the patterns of concurrently evolving class-interest movements? To what extent are ethnic and nationalistic aspirations expressed in the language of class-based issues, so that one finds distinctively chiliastic, liberal-humanitarian, conservative, and socialistic images of the ethnic community or nation? One would then expect to see new conceptions of the ethnic community and nation corresponding to the themes of today's "new" social movements.

It is probably much too early to sort out the themes in the current Eastern European transitions. Indeed, the unseating of established power in these countries may have come too easily and too quickly to facilitate the focusing and elaboration of utopian goals and worldviews. However, if we accept the premise that these are largely nationalistic movements, the evolving utopias can be analyzed from two points of view. First, to what extent can they be explained as antitheses to the existing ideologies that synthesize socialist and earlier worldviews? Second, to what extent can they be explained as a next stage or continuation of the historic evolution of nationalistic worldviews? A comparison of the analytic power of these two approaches, or discovery that neither contributed much to understanding, would have significant theoretical implications.

The 1960s witnessed black power, then weaker Chicano power, "Native American"[10] power, and all-Asia movements in the United States; they were clearly linked to nationalistic-ethnic movements in other parts of the world. Ethnic revival movements have usually been explained in either anthropological or political terms, rather than treated as part of the general social movement phenomenon. For example, a prominent review of studies generalizes: "Ethnicity is mobilized by features of modern states that legitimate ethnic politics, and rationalized market systems raise the utility of ethnic organization over other forms of social organization" (Olzak 1983, 356). But viewing the ethnic revival and nationalism together in terms of a Mannheimian style of analysis could shed valuable light on both the ethnic revival and the broader field of social movements.

In the 1970s the resurgence of the women's movement brought still another constituency to the fore. This, too, is the revival of a movement that got under way in both Europe and the United States in the nineteenth century. It is clear that the movement's major discourse employed successively the language of the liberal-humanitarian, the socialist, and the 1960s movements. An interesting question is, then, to what extent was the transmission of utopian visions a one-way or a reciprocal exchange between the class-interest movements and the women's movements, and to what extent are the two sets of movements susceptible of parallel analysis?

Finally, one must ask where religious movements fit into the scheme for social movement analysis. New religious movements, revivals of old religious movements, and religious themes in political organizations seem to have intensified in recent years (Beckford 1986). If it is the nature of major social movement utopias to permeate the society's patterns of behavior, expression, and thought, then religious movements cannot be left out of the analysis.

In conclusion, I have raised many questions and answered few. I propose simply that the analytic framework used by Karl Mannheim in *Ideology and Utopia,* with suitable updating and other modifications, be employed to shed new light on the genesis, character, and dynamics of today's major social movements, including nationalist, ethnic revivalist, gender, and religious movements. Such analyses may help clarify the meaning and the validity of the concept of "new social movements."

Notes

1. I have never been able to understand why Mannheim designated the postrevolutionary conservative thought of the nineteenth century as a utopia rather than as ideology.

2. See "end of ideology" discussions: Aron 1957; Bell 1960; Rejai 1971; and Shils 1955. For a more recent view that major ideological dispute has ended with the final victory of the liberal-humanitarian worldview, see Fukuyama 1989.

3. See Bellah et al. 1985 for one characterization of values in contemporary American society.

4. Explaining America's "Boston Tea Party" or Patrick Henry's "Liberty or Death" pronouncement (my illustration) on the basis of surviving chiliastic elements has a hollow ring.

5. This formulation bears some resemblance to status politics theory. Status politics is contrasted to class or economic interest group politics; it was introduced initially to explain the proliferation of conservative social movements during periods of prosperity. While class politics explained movements during periods of economic depression as reactions against economic loss and hardship, status politics explained movements of economically secure or rising classes as efforts to protect or impose their traditional values and preserve their social status. (See especially essays by Daniel Bell, Richard Hofstadter, and Seymour M. Lipset in Bell 1955.) Subsequently, a variety of conservative movements have been explained as status politics, such as the American temperance movement (Gusfield 1963) and the antipornography movement (Zurcher and Kirkpatrick 1976). My formulation differs, however, in proposing that constituencies need not be economic classes but that they should be categories of people whose privileges have been rising.

6. Lest I be misunderstood, I did not attribute choice of the "Black is beautiful" theme to "unparalleled freedom" for black youth. Rather, I saw a process of cultural diffusion, whereby a theme that evolved principally among white youth supplied a frame of reference that other groups then assimilated to their concerns.

7. Comparable general population data were not available for Australia and Britain.

8. The "America First" movement, as the movement to keep the United States out of World War II was called, was accused of being insensitive to the plight of Jews in Germany and occupied Europe under Hitler. The suspicion that America Firsters were anti-Semitic was accentuated when the national hero and prominent movement spokesman Charles Lindberg declared publicly that American Jews were behind the effort to involve the United States in the war.

9. The Beard thesis held that the Constitution was written and adopted by wealthy property owners in a successful attempt to subvert the benefits gained by less wealthy classes through the American Revolution of 1776 and instituted in the Articles of Confederation (adopted as the law of the original thirteen states in 1781). The classic attack on the Beard thesis was by Forrest McDonald (1958). A more moderate critique was offered by Lee Benson (1960). The debate is summarized pro and con in a collection of papers edited by Leonard Levy (1969).

10. "Native American" is the term employed polemically to refer to persons of American Indian ancestry.

References

Aron, Raymond. 1957 *The Opium of the Intellectuals*. Garden City, N.Y.: Doubleday.

Beard, Charles A. (1913) 1941. *An Economic Interpretation of the Constitution of the United States*. New York: Macmillan.

Beckford, James A., ed. 1986. *New Religious Movements and Rapid Social Change*. Paris and London: UNESCO and Sage.

Bell, Daniel, 1960. *The End of Ideology*. New York: Free Press.

———, ed. 1955. *The New American Right*. New York: Criterion Books.

Bellah, Robert N., Richard Madsen, William M. Sullivan, Ann Swidler, and Steven M. Tipton. 1985. *Habits of the Heart*. Berkeley: University of California Press.

Benson, Lee. 1960. *Turner and Beard: American Historical Writing Reconsidered*. New York: Free Press.

Benton, James S. 1981. "The New Sensibility: Self and Society in the Post-Industrial Age." Ph.D. diss., University of California, Los Angeles.

Blumer, Herbert. 1939. "Collective Behavior." In *An Outline of the Principles of Sociology*, edited by Robert E. Park, pp. 221–80. New York: Barnes and Noble.

Cohen, Jean L. 1985. "Strategy or Identity: New Theoretical Paradigms and Contemporary Social Movements." *Social Research* 52:663–713.

Cole, Robert E. 1989. *Strategies for Learning: Small Group Activities in American, Japanese, and Swedish Industry*. Berkeley: University of California Press.

Curti, Merle E. 1929. *The American Peace Crusade: 1815–1860*. Durham, N.C.: Duke University Press.

Etzioni, Amitai. 1970. *Demonstration Democracy*. New York: Gordon and Breach.

Fukuyama, Francis. 1989. "Have We Reached the End of History?" *National Interest* 16:3–18.

Gusfield, Joseph R. 1963. *Symbolic Crusade: Status Politics and the American Temperance Movement*. Urbana, Ill.: University of Illinois.

Hayes, Carlton, J. H. 1931. *The Historical Evolution of Modern Nationalism*. New York: Richard R. Smith.

Johnston, Hank. 1991. *Tales of Nationalism: Catalonia, 1939–1979*. New Brunswick, N.J.: Rutgers University Press.

King, Roger, and Neill Nugent, eds. 1979. *Respectable Rebels: Middle Class Campaigns in Britain in the 1970s*. London: Hodder and Stoughton.

Levy, Leonard W., ed. 1969. *Essays on the Making of the Constitution*. New York: Oxford Press.

Lipset, Seymour M., and William Schneider. 1987. *The Confidence Gap: Business, Labor, and Government in the Public Mind*. Baltimore: Johns Hopkins University Press.

McDonald, Forrest. 1958. *We the People: The Economic Origins of the Constitution*. Chicago: University of Chicago Press.

Mannheim, Karl. 1946. *Ideology and Utopia: An Introduction to the Sociology of Knowledge.* Translated by Louis Wirth and Edward Shils. New York: Harcourt, Brace.

Milbrath, Lester W. 1984. *Environmentalists: Vanguard for a New Society.* Albany: State University of New York Press.

Olzak, Susan. 1983. "Contemporary Ethnic Mobilization." *Annual Review of Sociology* 9:355–74.

Parkin, Frank. 1968. *Middle Class Radicalism: The Social Bases of the British Campaign for Nuclear Disarmament.* Manchester: Manchester University Press.

Porritt, Jonathon. 1985. *Seeing Green: The Politics of Ecology Explained.* Oxford: Basil Blackwell.

Rejai, Mostafa, ed. 1971. *Decline of Ideology?* Chicago: Aldine.

Shils, Edward. 1955. "The End of Ideology?" *Encounter* 5:52–58.

Snow, David A., and Robert D. Benford. 1988. "Ideology, Frame Resonance, and Participant Mobilization." In *From Structure to Action,* edited by Bert Klandermans, Hanspeter Kriesi, and Sidney Tarrow. Vol. 1 of *International Social Movement Research.* Greenwich, Conn.: JAI Press.

Snow, David A., and Cynthia Phillips. 1982. "The Changing Self-Orientations of College Students: From Institution to Impulse." *Social Science Quarterly* 63:462–76.

Snow, David A., E. Burke Rochford, Jr., Steven K. Worden, and Robert D. Benford. 1986. "Frame Alignment Processes, Micromobilization, and Movement Participation." *American Sociological Review* 51: 464–81.

Tarrow, Sidney. 1983. *Struggling to Reform: Social Movements and Policy Change during Cycles of Protest.* Ithaca: Cornell University Press.

Tilly, Charles. 1979. "Repertoires of Contention in America and Britain: 1750–1830." In *The Dynamics of Social Movements,* edited by Mayer N. Zald and John D. McCarthy, pp. 126–55. Cambridge, Mass.: Winthrop.

Turner, Lowell R. 1991. *Democracy at Work: Changing World Markets and the Future of Labor Unions.* Ithaca: Cornell University Press.

Turner, Ralph H. 1969. "The Theme of Contemporary Social Movements." *British Journal of Sociology* 20:390–405.

———. 1975. "Is There A Quest for Identity?" *Sociological Quarterly* 16:148–61.

———. 1976. "The Real Self: From Institution to Impulse." *American Journal of Sociology* 81:989–1016.

Turner, Ralph H., and Steven Gordon. 1981. "The Boundaries of the Self: The Relationship of Authenticity to Inauthenticity in the Self-Conception." In *The Self-Concept: Advances in Theory and Research,* edited by Mervin D. Lynch, Ardyth A. Norem-Hebeisen, and Kenneth Gergen, pp. 39–57. Cambridge, Mass.: Ballinger.

Zurcher, Louis A., Jr., and R. George Kirkpatrick. 1976. *Citizens for Decency: Antipornography Crusades as Status Defense.* Austin: University of Texas Press.

Chapter 5

A Strange Kind of Newness: What's "New" in New Social Movements?

Alberto Melucci

In systems of high information density, individuals and groups must possess a certain degree of autonomy and formal capacities for learning and acting that enable them to function as reliable, self-regulating units. Simultaneously, highly differentiated systems exert strong pressure for integration. They shift social control from the content of action to its languages, from the external regulation of behavior to interference in the cognitive and motivational preconditions for it. Conflicts tend to arise in those areas of the system that are most directly involved in the production of information and communicative resources but at the same time subjected to intense pressures for integration. Today, the crucial dimensions of daily life (time and space, interpersonal relations, birth and death), the satisfying of individual needs within welfare systems, and the shaping of personal and social identity in educational systems are constructed through the production and processing of information.

Individuals and groups are allocated increasing amounts of information resources with which to define themselves and to construct their life spaces. At the same time, however, these same processes are regulated by a diffuse social control that passes beyond the public sphere to invade the very domain where the sense of individual action takes shape. Dimensions that were traditionally regarded as private (the body, sexuality, affective relations), or subjective (cognitive and emotional processes, motives, desires), or even biological (the structure of the brain, the genetic code, reproductive capacity) now undergo social control and manipulation. The technoscientific apparatus, the agencies of information and communication, and the decision-making centers that determine policies wield their power over these domains. Yet, these are precisely the areas where individuals and groups lay claim to their autonomy, where they conduct their search for identity by transforming them into a space where they reappropriate, self-realize, and construct the meaning of what they are and what they do.

Conflicts are carried forward by temporary actors who bring to light the crucial dilemmas of a society. The conflicts I describe here, which do not exhaust the range of social conflicts, concern the production and the appropriation of resources that are crucial for a global society based on information. These same processes generate both new forms of power and new forms of opposition: Conflict only emerges insofar as actors fight for control and the allocation of socially produced potential for action. This potential is no longer exclusively based on material resources or on forms of social organization; to an increasing extent, it is based on the ability to produce information.

Conflicts do not chiefly express themselves through action designed to achieve outcomes in the political system. Rather, they raise a challenge that recasts the language and cultural codes that organize information. The ceaseless flow of messages only acquires meaning through the codes that order the flux and allow its meanings to be read. The forms of power now emerging in contemporary societies are grounded in an ability to "inform" that is, to "give form." The action of movements occupies the same terrain and is in itself a message broadcast to society conveying symbolic forms and relational patterns that cast light on "the dark side of the moon"—a system of meanings that runs counter to the sense that the apparatuses seek to impose on individual and collective events. This type of action affects institutions because it selects new elites, it modernizes organizational forms, and it creates new goals and new languages.

At the same time, however, this action challenges the apparatuses that govern the production of information, and it prevents the channels of representation and decision making in pluralist societies from adopting instrumental rationality as the only logic with which to govern complexity. Such rationality applies solely to procedures, and it imposes the criterion of efficiency and effectiveness as the only measure of sense. The action of movements reveals that the neutral rationality of means masks interests and forms of power; it makes clear that it is impossible to confront the massive challenge of living together on a planet, by now become a global society, without openly discussing the ends and values that make such cohabitation possible. Movements highlight the insuperable dilemmas facing complex societies, and by doing so force them openly to assume responsibility for their choices, their conflicts, and their limitations.

By drawing on forms of action that relate to daily life and individual identity, contemporary movements detach themselves from the traditional model of political organization, and they increasingly distance themselves from political systems. They move in to occupy an intermediate space of social life where individual needs and the pressures of political innovation mesh. Because of the particular features of movements, social conflicts can become effective only through the mediation of political actors, even though they will never restrict themselves to only this. The innovative thrust of movments, therefore, does not exhaust itself in changes to the political system brought about by institutional actors. Nevertheless, the ability of collective demands to expand and to find expression depends on the way in which political actors are able to translate them into democratic guarantees.

As my thinking in this area has developed, I have gradually abandoned the concept of class relationships. This concept is inseparably linked with capitalist industrial society, but I used it as an analytical tool to define a system of conflictual relationships within which social resources are produced and appropriated. The notion of class relationships has been a tool with which to analyze systemic conflicts and forms of domination in complex societies. It is a traditional category that I employed to focus on the relational and conflictual dimension of the production of the basic orientations of a society. In systems like contemporary ones, where classes as real social groups are withering away, more appropriate concepts are required. This must be accomplished without ignoring the theoretical problem that the category of class relationships has left behind as its legacy. That problem can be defined as knowing what relations and what conflicts are involved in the production of the crucial resources of a particular system. Addressing this question is essential to an understanding of the dual articulation of autonomy and dependence that characterizes the political system and the relationship between movements and processes of representation and decision making.

The theoretical problem is therefore whether there are forms of conflict that engage the constitutive logic of a system. The notion of mode of production is too closely associated with economic reductionism. Production cannot be restricted solely to the economic-material sphere; it embraces the entirety of social relationships and cultural orientations. The problem is thus whether one can still talk of antagonist conflicts, that is, conflicts that involve the social relationships that produce the constitutive resource of complex systems: information. Analysis of exchanges internal to the political market, or the knowledge we have acquired concerning strategic behavior in organizations and political systems, shows that many contemporary conflicts, sometimes even violent ones, are the expression of social categories or groups claiming access to representation. A demand for inclusion in an institutional system of benefits may even be radical, but it implies not so much antagonism toward the logic of the system as pressure for redistribution.

If no analytical space is left open for asking the question about antagonist conflicts, then we have not only erased such a question and failed to resolve the problem it raises but we have failed to demonstrate its futility. The European Left now seems to be replacing the Marxist model with a model of the exchange or the rationality of decision-making choices. In the past, I have analyzed class conflicts from within a constructivist and systemic framework already very far from the Marxist model, but explanation of contemporary conflicts solely in terms of exchange strikes me as inadequate. I believe that the question of the systemic nature of conflicts should be kept open: What does the term "system logic" mean in highly differentiated systems? Is it possible to identify antagonist conflicts without their actors being characterized by a stable social condition? Can the arenas of conflict change? These questions become stimulating working hypotheses if the analytic space for their formulation is kept open. These questions may serve to guide analysis of contemporary movements.

New Movements?

This analytical framework helps to clarify a recurrent issue in the debate of the last ten years (Cohen 1985; Offe 1985; Klandermans, Kriesi, and Tarrow 1988; Tarrow 1989), which concerns the "newness" of contemporary conflicts. What is new about the new social movements? As one of those who introduced the term "new social movements" into sociological literature, I have watched with dismay as the category has been progressively reified. Newness is by definition a relative concept, which here has the temporary function of signaling a number of comparative differences between the historical forms of class conflict and today's emergent forms of collective action. If analysis and research fail to specify the distinctive features of the new movements, we are trapped in arid debate between the supporters and critics of newness. On one hand, there are those who claim that many aspects of contemporary forms of action can be found in previous phenomena of history and that their alleged newness derives only from the myopia of the present from which so many sociologists suffer, especially when they are emotionally involved with their subject of study. On the other hand, the defenders of the newness of contemporary movements endeavor to show that these similarities are only formal and that phenomena change their meanings when set in different systems.

Both the critics of the newness of new movements and the proponents of the paradigm commit the same epistemological mistake: They consider contemporary phenomena to constitute a unitary empirical object, and on this basis either seek to define their newness or deny or dispute it. When faced with the women's movement rather than the peace movement, one side in the debate tries to mark out differences with respect to the past, the other stresses continuity and comparability with previous events.

The controversy strikes me as futile. Contemporary phenomena, in their empirical unity, are made up of a variety of components, and if these elements are not separated out, comparison between forms of action belonging to mutually distinct historical periods is based on an epistemological misunderstanding. It is not a question of deciding whether the empirical data observed are equivalent or comparable, instead, the question is whether their meaning and the place they occupy in the system of social relations can be considered to be the same. Thus, it becomes extremely difficult to decide, for example, how far the modern women's movement, as a global empirical phenomenon, is new compared with the first feminist movements of the nineteenth century.

In order to make this kind of comparison we must distinguish, within the overall empirical object, among different orientations of action (for example, the presence or absence of a conflictual attitude, dimensions of solidarity or of aggregateness, a breach or otherwise of the system's compatibility limits). We must distinguish also among the various systems of social relationships comprising the action. Seen in these terms, the women's movement of the nineteenth century, like its contemporary counterpart, is a composite and heterogeneous phenomenon. Thus, rather than compare two ethical objects in their entirety, one can relate certain, analytically defined aspects of the former with aspects of the latter and discern similarities and differences (Melucci 1984, 1989, 1991). Paradoxically, the result of the debate on new movements has been that the idea of movements-as-personages has faded. Contemporary movements, like all collective phenomena, bring together forms of action that involve various levels of the social structure. They entail different points of view. They belong to different historical periods. We must seek to understand, therefore, this multiplicity of synchronic and diachronic elements. Then we can explain how they combine into the concrete unit of a collective actor. Every empirical phenomenon offers us a cross section of a social structure, rather like a split in a rock reveals its inner composition and strata. Just as a photograph of the rock as a whole cannot be confused with the minerals and strata that compose it, so collective phenomena do not disclose their meaning to us if we only consider them in their totality. Instead, we must inspect the different orientations present in them (conflictual, non-conflictual, solidary, atomized), the different levels of society affected by the action (for example, modes of production, political systems, life worlds), and the different historial periods condensed into that particular phenomenon. Just as one must explain how the minerals and strata of the rock have combined to create that particular geological formation, so we must consider collective action as a result and not as a point of departure. The task of the analyst is to explain how this outcome has been collectively constructed, how it is maintained, and, perhaps, how it alters over time.

Having clarified this epistemological premise, we may still ask ourselves whether a new paradigm of collective action is taking shape. We do not ask this in an empirical sense, that is, in terms of the observed phenomenon as a whole, but analytically, that is, in terms of certain levels or elements of action. We must ask ourselves, therefore, if there are dimensions to the new forms of action that we should assign to a systemic context other than that of industrial capitalism. This question is dismissed by critics of new movements, like Charles Tilly or Sidney Tarrow, who place these phenomena on an exclusively political level. This kind of reductionism eliminates from the field of scientific inquiry the question of the appearance of a new paradigm of collective action: Do contemporary movements reveal systemic conflicts that are unrelated to those of industrial capitalism? This question disappears from the scene without any detailed or well-argued answer in the negative. Moreover, those specifically social dimensions of action that are so significant for the new movements are ignored. This gives rise to a myopia of the visible that concentrates exclusively on the measurable features of collective action—that is, their relationships with political systems and their effects on policies—while it neglects or undervalues all those aspects of the action of movements that consist in the production of cultural codes. This myopia ignores the reality that the elaboration in daily life of alternative meanings for individual and collective behavior is the principal activity of the hidden networks of contemporary movements and the condition for their visible action. In fact, when a movement publicly confronts the political apparatus on specific issues, it does so in the name of new cultural models created at a less noisy and less easily measurable level of hidden action.

Do contemporary collective phenomena comprise antagonist conflicts that are systemic in nature, or are these phenomena of social margination, of aggregate behavior, of adjustment by the political market? This general question can only be answered by first exploring alternative explanations for collective action, for example, in terms of dysfunctions or crisis (Alberoni 1977; Moscovici 1981; Turner and Killian 1987), or in terms of political exchange (Pizzorno 1978, 1985). Many contemporary conflicts can be explained on the basis of the workings of the political market, as the expression of excluded social groups or categories pressing for representation (Tilly 1978, 1986; Tarrow 1989). Here there is no antagonistic dimension to the conflict, there is only pressure to join a system of benefits and rules from which one has been excluded. If political boundaries are rigid, the conflict may even be violent (Gamson, Fireman, and Rytina 1982; Gamson 1990). However, it need not necessarily entail antagonism against the logic of the system but may, instead, express a demand for the different distribution of resources or for new rules (McCarthy and Zald 1977, 1981; Jenkins 1983). Similarly, a poorly functioning organization may be subject to even intense conflict, the aim of which, however, is to reestablish the proper functioning of the organization itself. The student movements of the late 1960s and more recent ones in various European countries (Spain 1987, France and Italy 1990) contained a common rejection of the authoritarian behavior of the educational system and a demand for greater efficiency and relevance.

Having exhausted the explanatory capacity of these dimensions, we still need to ask ourselves whether everything has been accounted for. We must preserve sufficient theoretical space in which the question of systemic conflicts can be formulated. Otherwise, the issue will have been glossed over without being given an answer or proved to be useless.

Social scientists are still heirs to a tradition that attributes this logic to "structures," regardless of the day-to-day relations entered into by actors as they construct the meaning of their action. The logic of a system is not necessarily to be looked for in large-scale interests or in the more visible forms of power; it is also to be found at the more simple levels of social life, where actors interact to define the possibilities and constraints of their action. Today, as overarching explanations (for example, global explanations of the logic of capitalism) begin to disappear, their place is taken by a kind of theoretical retreat into explanation of social relationships couched solely in terms of exchange, or into a purely terminological rearrangement of previous theories. Thus, the change under way in contemporary systems is now only referred to in allusive terms (complex, postindustrial, late capitalist society). The assumption is that these define a logic significantly different from that of industrial capitalism. This move neglects or suppresses the theoretical problems that this assumption incurs. The question of the existence of antagonistic conflicts with systemic scope, however, keeps open a number of questions that theoretical analysis must now address. For instance, a theoretical question of major importance is whether one can conceive of a dominant logic that does not necessarily manifest itself in a global and overarching form, but which instead distributes itself among various areas of the system to produce a wide variety of arenas and actors of conflict. This is a logic to be identified not just in the functional workings of the great apparatuses but, as the ethno-methodologists have taught us, in daily interaction.

Facing these questions forces us to leave behind the dualistic legacy of the nineteenth century that opposed, for example, structures and representations, or systems and actors (Giddens 1984; Crozier and Friedberg 1977). We must rethink social action into the process by which meaning is constructed through interaction (Neisser 1976; Von Foerster 1973; Watzlawick 1984; Von Glazers-feld 1985). It is actors who, through their relations, produce and recognize the sense of what they are doing. But interaction is never an entirely overt process. It lies within the field of possibilities and constraints that actors observe and utilize. Domination and power are not metaphysical realities lying outside the games that actors play; they are the most solid, permanent, and unbalanced forms of such games. Conflicts, therefore, act as signals of both the constructed nature of social action and its tendency to crystallize into structures and systems.

Information Societies

Where, then, can we locate the action of contemporary movements? Through an ever-growing interlacement of economic structures, complex societies produce apparatuses of political regulation and cultural agencies. Material goods are produced by information systems and symbolic universes controlled by huge organizations. They incorporate information and become signs circulating through markets of worldwide proportions (Touraine 1971, 1978, 1984; Habermas 1984). Conflicts move from the economic–industrial system to the cultural sphere. They focus on personal identity, the time and space of life, and the motivation and codes of daily behavior. Conflicts lay bare the logic now gaining its sway over highly differentiated systems. These systems allocate increasing amounts of resources to individuals, who use them to become autonomous loci of action; but the systems also exact increasing integration. In order to maintain themselves, they must extend their control by regulating the deep-lying sources of action and by interfering with the construction of its meaning. Contemporary conflicts reveal the contradictions in this process and bring to the fore actors and forms of action that cannot be fitted into the conventional categories of industrial conflict or competition among interest groups. The production and reappropriation of meaning seem to lie at the core of contemporary conflicts; this understanding requires a careful redefinition of what a social movement is and what forms of action display its presence.

In the course of history, societies have run through the gamut of the resources that drive every living system (matter, energy, information). There have been societies structured on material resources and societies that have depended on energy for their growth (steam and electricity as the engines of industrialization). Now, societies exist that rely on information for their survival, control of the environment, expansion into space, and the delicate equilibrium that preserves them from total war.

The microelectronic revolution has made it possible to concentrate enormous quantities of circuits into spaces that were unthinkably small twenty-five years ago. This has not only transformed the size of computers but has brought a staggering increase in the speed at which information can be processed and an enormous expansion in the amount of data that can be stored. Parallel advances in communication technologies mean that information can be collected, processed, and transmitted in fractions of a second and through limitless space.

What are the features of an information society? First, the transformations mentioned above have accentuated the reflexive, artificial, and constructed character of social life. Most experiences of life in complex societies are experiences "to the nth degree." In other words, they take place in contexts that are produced by social action, broadcast by the media, and internalized and enacted in a sort of involute spiral that turns reality into a memory or a dream. Most of the trivial activities of daily life are already marked by and depend on the impact of transformations in the sphere of information. New technologies incorporate an increasing quantity of information and contribute in turn to the massive expansion of information output. Here, too, a spiral process seems to multiply the reflexiveness of social action.

Another feature of an information society is the planetarization of the system. The circulation of information ties the world system together and raises new transnational problems over the control, circulation, and exchange of information. At the same time, it inflates the issues and arenas of conflict into worldwide proportions. The geographical localization of a problem is of secondary importance compared with its symbolic impact on the planetary system. The processes of globalization reactivate ethnic- and national-based forms of action that seek to give a stable and recognizable basis to identity. Old national questions, processes that were interrupted or historically repressed by the rise of the nation-state are, paradoxically, revitalized by the formation of a global space. Ethnic symbolism and concrete reference to a motherland lay a foundation for the development of a culture and a language for the identity of individuals and groups in a space that has lost its traditional boundaries. Ethnic-national movements are both the last residues of the process of modernization and the signal that modernism is being left behind.

In a system whose most advanced sectors employ over 50 percent of the population in activities involving the production, processing, and circulation of information, this basic resource structures social life. Information is a symbolic and therefore reflexive resource. It is not a thing; it is a good which to be produced and exchanged presupposes a capacity for symbolization and decodification. It is a resource that becomes such for the society as a whole only when other needs have been satisfied and when the capacity for symbolic production has been sufficiently freed from the constraints of reproduction. The notion of "post-material society" captures, at least in part, these transformations in progress. Systems that increasingly rely on information resources presume the acquisition of a material base and the ability to build symbolic universes endowed with autonomy (which, in turn, become conditions for the reproduction or the broadening of the material base itself).

Information does not exist for a society independently of the human capacity to perceive it. Being able to use a reflexive resource of this kind depends on the biological and motivational structure of humans as transmitters and receivers of information. The massive investment that complex societies make in biological research, in research into the brain and the motivational and relational mechanisms of behavior, demonstrates that the role of information as a decisive resource entails greater human intervention in inner nature. It requires an increased capacity for self-reflection, which reaches the point of the production of reproduction, the point at which interference in the deep biological structure of the species begins.

If information is characterized by the speed of its circulation and its rapid obsolescence, it becomes crucially important to control the codes by which mutable information is organized and interpreted. Increasingly, knowledge is less a knowledge of contents and more an ability to codify and to decode messages. Information is linear and cumulative; it constitutes the quantitative base of the cognitive process. Knowledge structures; it establishes relations, links, and hierarchies. There is a terrifying widening of the gap between these two levels of experience and what used to be called wisdom. Wisdom has to do with the perception of meaning and its integration into individual existence. Wisdom is the ability to maintain an integral core of experience in one's relations with oneself, with others, and with the world.

As information becomes the crucial resource for complex systems, these three levels progressively separate. Control over the production, accumulation, and circulation of information depends on control over codes. This control is not equally distributed, however, and access to knowledge becomes the terrain where new forms of power, discrimination, and conflict come into being. Simultaneously, the sense of individual experience, that is, the ability to incorporate the increasing quantity of information transmitted and received into an interior principle of unity, becomes increasingly fragile. A split opens between the realm of instrumental knowledge, which efficiently manipulates the symbolic codes that select, order, and direct information, and wisdom as the integration of meaning into personal experience.

The result is the search for identity, the quest for self that addresses the fundamental regions of human action: the body, the emotions, the dimensions of experience irreducible to instrumental rationality. This search allows the rediscovery of an irremediable otherness (other people, the Other, the sacred), a silent void that escapes the ceaseless flux of encoded messages. In this closedness and emptiness, we seek to fit back together the scattered fragments of a human experience that is constantly aware that it stands on the brink between life and death. To encounter the power of human action that transforms the world and that intervenes even in inner nature is simultaneously to encounter its limits. This awareness may take the form of a return to organized religion (the resurgence of sects and fundamentalisms), but it may open the way for a desacralized experience of the sacred and a new search for identity.

Information is difficult to control because it spreads through many different channels: language or interpersonal communication, the objects that incorporate information, or a more elaborate corpus of symbolic kind. Unlike other physical goods, information can be divided without losing its quality. It can be multiplied and divided among various actors without affecting its specific content. If power in complex societies is based on the control of information, it is potentially a very fragile kind of power, because the simple acquisition of information puts the actors in a communicative relation on the same level.

Power cannot be exercised, therefore, solely over the content of communications and over the manifest expressions of action. To be effective, power must shift its basis and take control of codes. Codes become formal rules, the organizers of knowledge, the new foundation of power. Wisdom fades away and a search for meaning seems senseless. Its place is taken by self-justifying, operational expertise. The codes on which the new forms of power build and develop themselves are invisible; the possibility itself of speaking and communicating is already organized within them. The risk is that there is no discourse other than that which privileged areas and groups in the system control through their power of naming and the monopoly that they seek to impose on language. Information is no longer a resource circulating among all actors; they cannot exchange it and they cannot cumulatively build their potential for knowledge. Instead, information becomes a system of empty signs, the key to which has been lost or hidden. The signs no longer concern themselves with their meaning.

Simultaneously, the potentially limitless extension of information increases the margins of uncertainty for the entire system. Uncertainty derives first from the difficulty of establishing nexuses in the enormous mass of information that we transmit and receive. This difficulty derives from the fact that the passage from information to knowledge is not guaranteed; indeed, sometimes the deluge of information actually impedes knowledge. Uncertainty affects the meaning of individual action because the disproportionate growth of information increases the options but also makes the decision difficult. The individual answer to the question, Who am I? becomes problematic.

As a result, complex systems are required to produce decisions in order to reduce uncertainty. An information system expands its decision-making capacity to keep pace with this requirement to cope with uncertainty. It assumes the features of a decisional, contractual system: decisional because reducing uncertainty means assuming the risk of the decision; contractual because, in order to decide, agreement must be reached over the rules of the game.

Uncertainty cannot be reduced except by making decisions and by agreeing on the framework within which these decisions are to be reached. The level of uncertainty constantly renews itself and expands, in part because the decisions create new problems even as they resolve the old ones. The decisional and contractual dimensions become central to the social life of complex systems. In other words, contemporary societies must continually establish and renew the pacts that bind them together and guide their action.

This applies both to society as a whole and to individuals and groups. Individually and socially produced identity must constantly cope with the uncertainty created by the ceaseless flow of information, by the fact that individuals belong simultaneously to a plurality of systems, by the variety of their spatiotemporal frames of reference. Identity must be forever reestablished and renegotiated. The search for identity becomes a remedy against the opacity of the system, against the uncertainty that constantly constrains action (Pizzorno 1987). Producing identity means stepping up the flow of information from the system and making it more stable and coherent. Producing identity contributes to the stabilization or modernization of the system itself. It is not only to the requirement of security and continuity that this search for identity responds. It also provides resources for individuation and enables individuals to perceive themselves as distinct from others. In the depth of this separateness, individuals discover the capacity to reject the dominant codes and to reveal their questionable power. They recognize themselves as producers of meaning and they are enabled to challenge the manipulation of meaning by the apparatus.

In systems of this kind, can we still talk of a dominant logic?

Certainly the spatial metaphors that characterized industrial culture (base/superstructure, centrality/marginality) are increasingly inadequate to describe the workings of centerless, and by now headless, complex societies. The decentralization of the loci of power and conflict makes it more difficult to identify central processes and actors. Does this mean that we must renounce any attempt to identify dominant logic? Does this mean that in complexity everything becomes the same as everything else?

A logic of dominance is not in contradiction with the idea of complexity. Contemporary societies have a dominant logic, but the site of this logic changes constantly. The areas and levels of a system that insure its continuity may change in time, just as the loci of conflict vary. Power does not inhere once and for all in certain structures; its concrete manifestations in the form of actors and relations are not definitive. Conflicts, too, may involve different actors and different sectors of the system. This is not to imply, however, that all forms of malcontent are equivalent, or that every form of social agitation expresses conflicts that have systemic scope. There are conflicts that strike at the logic of the system. Although addressing a circumscribed area, they bring to the surface the crucial dilemmas of complexity, and the power forms that such complexity produces, and render them visible to society as a whole.

Symbolic Challenges

Contemporary movements have passed from sequence to coexistence. Slices of experience, past history, and memory coexist within the same empirical phenomena. They become working components in the single action system of the movement. The traces of the past that persist in contemporary phenomena are not simply legacies of history or residues on which new accretions build themselves; they help to shape patterns of collective action in which historical and cultural elements coexist or blend. In what has been called the ecological movement, for example, we find traditional forms of resistance to the impact of modernization coexisting with a religious fundamentalism that draws its renewed energy from the appeal to Nature, pressures for a new ethical code regulating humanity's relationship with Nature, and political demands for the democratic control of energy policies. All these elements are blended together, perhaps temporarily, in that concrete actor of mobilization that we call a movement.

Because of their composite nature—a synchronous arrangement of different epochs and different stages of societal development—modern movements hold up a mirror to the system as a whole. In fact, in the great scenario of the media everything becomes simultaneous: the last remnants of the archaeology of societies mix with the most sensational images of the future. Amazon Indians being chased from their forest by bulldozers are as much part of the entertainment as films of outer space. As we watch from the comfort of our armchairs, our television screens transport us through time and space from prehistory to science fiction. Remote and unrelated experiences are juxtaposed; interchangeable signs stream past us in a pure sequence of images without the leaps in space and time that any reality would require.

Second, movements are not occasional emergencies in social life located on the margins of the great institutions; nor are they residual elements of the social order. In complex societies, movements are a permanent reality. They may be more or less visible and they may emerge as political mobilization in cyclical form (as Tarrow 1989 has done well to point out), but their existence and their effects on social relationships are neither sporadic nor transitory.

In contemporary societies, a specific sector or subsystem for collective action is becoming a differentiated and stable component in the working of the system. Movements acquire a certain independence from both the daily life of individuals and from political action by creating a specific space for their actions. The differentiation of complex systems is so extensive that collective action can acquire autonomous status. Noninstitutionalized, collective action separates from those other forms of action with which it was formerly confused (political action, in particular). In the industrial age, social conflicts were incorporated into struggles for citizenship, just as in the history of the workers' movement anticapitalistic social struggle and the fight against the bourgeois state coincided. When these two levels separate, as they do in contemporary societies, movements lose their character as personages engaged in a confrontation-clash with a state for citizenship rights. Instead, they form themselves into social networks, where a collective identity is negotiated and given shape.

Two features of these networks can be identified. First, a movement network is a field of social relationships where, through negotiation among various groups, a collective identity is structured. In this social field, the orientations and constraints of action are defined and redefined within the solidarity networks that link individuals together in their daily lives. Second, a movement network is a terrain in which identity is recomposed and unified. Networks within the movement insure a certain degree of continuity and stability in the identities of individuals and groups in a social system where this identity is constantly fragmented or destructured. The movement provides individuals and groups with a relatively stable point of reference from which to rebuild identities split among the various memberships, roles, and time scales of social experience.

The inevitable theoretical question at this point is whether contemporary movements are conflictual in character. Are there elements of antagonistic conflict in phenomena so distant from the image of the revolutionary, collective actor that we have inherited from the past? Is conflict found in phenomena so fragmented, dispersed, and interwoven that they are more like subcultures than political actors, more inclined towards expressive action than instrumental effectiveness? The answer lies at two different levels. The first level is the orientations of the movement's action. Such orientations constitute the basis on which its collective identity is negotiated. For the reasons set out above, a movement combines various orientations of action, and analysis must establish whether any of them are antagonistic in nature. If so, this does not exhaust the features of the movement but indicates the presence of an antagonism that cannot be reduced to political exchange or functional adaptation. The second level reflects the concrete operation of the movement's networks. This is the level where relations structure themselves and where organization and action express a conflictual message.

Let us consider the first point. Drawing on my empirical work (Melucci 1984), I have found that orientations of action are both general and specific in character. They are, in fact, the point of union between a particular actor and the field of opportunities-constraints to which its action refers. A particular social condition encourages conflict because it provides certain groups of people with access to central resources of the system. At the same time, it exposes this group to pressures that affect the formation of identity and meaning. This is the case, for example, of women or young people. In other cases, the factors that encourage conflict are not associated with a stable condition but nevertheless delimit a social space (for example, geographical location for certain sections of the environmentalist movement, or previous political and cultural history for certain sections of ecologist or pacifist militancy, or certain areas of the feminist movement). The conflict is provoked by these particular conditions, but it simultaneously brings into play problems that concern the system's overall logic and its dilemmas. The actor is always a specific entity, but the social field it addresses and the issues it raises comprise the entire system. This is the paradox of contemporary movements: they address the whole of society in the name of a category or a group, or on the basis of a particular place within the social structure.

Being young in contemporary society ceases to be a biological condition and is increasingly defined in cultural terms. People are young not because they have a certain age, but because they participate in a culture or life-style, because they live in a state of suspended animation relative to the duties, schedules, and rules of adult life. Youth as a symbolic condition engages the possibility and right to redefine, to change, and to reverse choices. This problem concerns not only young people but also society at large.

For systems that make change the condition of their existence, predictability is an essential requirement. The system promises and induces change, but it strives to keep it measurable and therefore controllable. Because of this condition of social suspension, young people oppose this logic by appealing the reversibility of choices; their actions take the form of an absence of planning, living for the present, and claiming the right to belong by choice not by allocation. Youth, the age par excellence of indeterminateness, openness, and discontinuity, becomes the metaphor for a right to change and to self-determination that challenges the social rules that impose continuity, conformity, and predictability. By seeking to appropriate the present and the right to be able to change things, young people embody a general cultural need and they question the roots of the logic of rational instrumentality.

For women, the profound memory of subordination and entrapment in a body "other" than that of the dominant culture make a struggle for emancipation an important, and quantitatively perhaps the most significant, component of the movement's action. Collective action by women, however, is structured not only on the campaign for equal rights but also for the right to be different. The struggle against discrimination and for access to the economic and political market interweaves with, but is nevertheless distinct from, the struggle for difference. Being recognized as different is perhaps one of the most crucial rights at stake in postindustrial systems. Granting recognition to women entails accepting a different outlook on reality, existence in a different body, and a specific way of relating to others and to the world. In societies that exert strong pressures toward conformity, the appeal to difference has an explosive impact on the dominant logic. By claiming difference, the movement addresses women and society as a whole. At the same time, the movement's action gives women access to political and cultural markets and helps to renew them. Success in the market transforms the movement into a pressure group, segments the network, bureaucratizes some groups, and dissipates others. The movement's professionalization, however, does not affect its antagonistic nucleus but makes it more difficult to locate.

This nucleus shifts toward the form of communication. The self-reflective form of the small group—which was the core of the women's movement and preceded and fostered its public mobilization—already expresses its intention not to separate doing from meaning, or action from awareness of its significance and its emotional content. The work done by the women in the movement speaks for all of us. It shows that one cannot act publicly and effectively without a stable component of reflectiveness that constantly questions the meaning of what is being done. Communication must find room not only for the instrumental logic of efficiency but also for the feelings, uncertainties, and affective conflicts that always nourish human action. What does this privileged communication of the women's movement, which has been engaged for so long and with such difficulty, actually express? Power and difference. Women's confrontation with male power has taught them to recognize that difference becomes power (Gilligan 1981). Female communication contains a demand and a challenge: it asks society whether a difference without power is possible; it tries to establish forms of communication that preserve difference.

Women rely on the female form of communication. They know it is different from male communication. They also recognize that it is not internally homogeneous and that it contains differences among women. When they use this form of communication, women interrogate the whole of society concerning the roots of communication. They raise the question of how diversity can be reconciled, whether unity in separateness is feasible, whether, in sum, humans can communicate without oppressing each other. In what sense is this message antagonistic? It is antagonistic in the sense that the system, which multiplies communication and lives by it, knows only two kinds of communication: identification, that is, incorporation into dominant codes, fusion with a power that denies diversity; or separateness, that is, difference as exclusion from all communication.

Other features of female communication reveal its antagonistic nature. The requirement not to lose sight of the particular—the value assigned to the details of experience, to memories of the day-to-day, to small gestures, to events without history—all these are features that have been dismissed as female narcissism but that have, in fact, a profoundly subversive significance. They challenge the standardization of experience and the homogenization of time that an information society exacts in order to make its procedures generally applicable.

Not all women mobilize themselves, however. The actors in the movement are those women who have experienced the contradiction between, on the one hand, promises of inclusion in the labor market, in the arena of political rights and equality, and, on the other, the social costs of being a woman restricted to the immutable roles of mother, wife, and mistress. Women who mobilize, therefore, are those who have experienced a surplus of resources within the narrow confines of the female condition. They are those with higher levels of schooling; they are those exposed to the contradictions of welfare systems (education, health, social security), of which they are often agents and recipients. The reaction by these women takes the form of cultural overproduction within the movement, a symbolic wastefulness that contains a profound ambivalence. "Female" activities within the movement consist of pointless meetings, writing for its own sake not for the market, apparently aimless communication, and time spent in ways incoherent with utility and efficiency. The cultivation of memory; the search for the margins, nuances, and seams of experience; and the duplication of the same activities by a myriad of groups, with complete disregard for economies of scale, are all aspects that the dominant masculine culture judges as "senseless." Nevertheless, it is this waste that breeds innovation, as recent years have shown.

In fact, on one hand, these activities comprise one way in which the system controls uncertainty; they form a sort of enclave where haphazard experiments in innovation are conducted. The system absorbs the results of these experiments by sifting out their essence in a kind of natural selection process. But, on the other hand, this symbolic wastefulness is also the expression of an irreducible difference; it is an expression of what is "valueless" because it is too minute or partial to enter the standardized circuits of the mass cultural market. The symbolic extravagance of female output introduces the value of the useless into the system, the inalienable right of the particular to exist, the irreducible significance of inner life that no history is able to record but by virtue of which individual experience becomes the ultimate core of experience.

The women's movement is hazardously balanced between its role as a modernizing force, a role which it cannot refuse but which makes it into a pressure group, and its function as a symbolic appeal that goes beyond the female condition. In its modernizing role, the movement helps to spread the political and cultural contents of feminism, by now professionalized. Small, residual fundamentalist groups resist institutionalization while groups of intellectuals cultivate the memory of the movement. As regards its symbolic appeal, the women's movement seems destined to deny itself as a specific actor. By giving everyone the chance to be different, it cancels its own separateness. The dichotomy "being yourself/being for others" seems to constitute the drama and the symbol of femaleness; it seems to define the collective action of women as well.

Environmentalist mobilizations are more visibly channels for the formation of new elites than the movements considered so far. Because of their lack of a common condition, environmentalist groups have a solidarity that is wholly symbolic in character. Here, too, the antagonistic level is hard to pin down because the movement's identity is largely structured by its role in institutional pressure and the presence of potential new elites. This movement directly confronts public policies and decisions in an external arena of action. In doing so, it has fulfilled a crucial function in applying pressure that has not only influenced policies but altered the criteria for innovation; it has redefined priorities and recalibrated the yardstick with which alternatives are measured.

There is, however, a strictly cultural dimension to the structuring of the environmentalist movement. In an artificial world, which is created by the proliferation of the instrumental capacity for social intervention, there still remain areas of shadow. That which escapes the artificial, society's construction of itself, speaks of missed chances or of possible dreams. The "Nature" to which the movement appeals symbolizes this frontier; it reminds the societies that take efficiency and effectiveness as their operational credo of the limits to their omnipotence. In the ecological practice of the movement's base groups, Nature is lived, acted, and experienced by upsetting the operational codes of destructive production.

This minuscule, almost invisible action reminds society that the power that enables it to produce is also the power that may destroy it; this respect for the shade, for the limit, for the secret rhythms of the cosmos within and without us is the other, inseparable side to humanity's urge to discover and to create (Bateson 1972, 1979). In this appeal to the shadow, to the unsaid and the unsayable, lies the most profound meaning of the new spiritual urgency that drives the collective action of many groups. Where it is not a renewal of the message of religion, where it is not a specialized sector of the market in emotions, spiritual experience in information societies is an appeal to wisdom; it is a call to that encounter with the self that is never entirely expressible in operational codes. The reintegration of human experience and the recomposition of otherness and its limit within a unity of some kind may be the most significant activity of these collective phenomena.

If acting as the transmitter and receiver of information according to codified procedures and criteria of efficiency has become the rule in information societies, closedness, silence, and the retreat into the void where the only words are those spoken to oneself constitute behavior of extraordinary subversive impact.

The orientations of the action of contemporary movements therefore reveal an antagonistic nucleus. If, in information societies, power is exercised in the control of codes, antagonism lies in the ability to resist and, even more so, to overturn dominant codes. Antagonism lies in the ability to give a different name to space and time by developing new languages that change or replace the words used by the social order to organize our daily experience. It lies in the ability to make room for wisdom beyond knowledge, to adopt an affective rather than an instrumental reflectiveness. These are the ways movements shape and interpret the flux of information, the ways they give another name to the world. Antagonism expresses itself in the structuring of the collective actor, that is, in the way that it organizes its own solidarity. As it structures itself, the action of movements is already a challenge to the system.

We can now turn our attention to the second dimension of movements, namely, the forms of organization and action as modalities of conflict expressed not in the content but in the form and in the process of collective action. The structure of mobilization is provisional and reversible; it is based on direct participation, which is considered a good to be used regardless of the results it achieves; it is designed to meet the needs of individuals who no longer distinguish between work time and leisure time. This structure broadcasts to the system beyond the concrete contents of the mobilization other codes that concern the definition of the individual in the collectivity. Predictable time is opposed by a reversible time that follows individual rhythms that are based on the plurality of memberships and on the requirement to experience change at first hand. Participation is seen as commitment and not as duty; it has sectorial and not global implications, but with a global concern; provisional and not life-long commitment, the circulation of individuals in different groups and organizations, are also indicators of this upsetting of codes.

The features that render the challenge to the system most visible are organizational structure and internal power relations. Movements function as open spaces where constantly negotiable contracts are made. The organization must insure this negotiation; it must make sure that collective action is the outcome of a contractual and reflective process. Concern for the quality of inner relations entails recognition of power relations, that is, a recognition of differences and the risks connected with them. The attempt to keep this dimension under control by intensifying self-reflective activity runs the risk that groups will close in on themselves. At the same time, however, it provides evidence of the contractual and reflective character of the relation. People are not what they are but who they choose to be. They do not belong to a group or to a project because they share an objective condition or because they have made a definitive, irreversible choice. They do so because they continue to choose and to assume responsibility for that choice.

This implicit contractuality is also the basis for the relation between more professionalized groupings and the rest of the movement. Although the former help to structure the collective identity and to nurture it, they also know that only by providing certain kinds of symbolic goods, and only by respecting the model of relations described above, will they be able to maintain their role.

The organizational structure of the networks and relations of power stand in opposition to the dominant codes. They say, in fact, that making power visible does not mean nullifying it, but it does place it under control. They also remind us that pacts with an invisible power are always false. They reject a logic of exchange that does not make its asymmetry explicit. This challenge is profoundly significant in systems that hide and neutralize the loci of power.

The antagonistic nucleus that I have described is flanked by other meanings. The search for antagonistic meanings of action is a product of analysis, and it is conducted once other explanatory criteria have been employed. It is used to explain those elements of behavior that have resisted explanation in terms of, for example, exchange relations or relationships based on strategic calculation. There are dimensions to the action of contemporary movements that cannot be explained by these paradigms. In particular, it is impossible to reduce the increasingly more formal and self-reflective character of group action, which seems to free itself of the contents that it may assume at any particular moment, to an explanation in terms of exchange relations. Such a deep concern with the form of action, with its character as a code, with its nature as a process, is difficult to reduce to analysis in terms of cost-benefit calculation. It requires other explanatory criteria. A fruitful approach here might be analysis of the antagonistic meanings of the action. The hypothesis is that conflict arises over the criteria themselves by which meaning is created. What is at issue in a conflict is not the terms of the exchange, or the best way to conduct it, but the actual meaning of the exchange itself.

At the same time, the antagonistic nucleus that engages formal codes is not a separate entity from the concrete contents that action assumes. The more the action coincides with its contents, that is, the more the group coincides with what it does and not how it does it, the more the challenge declines in strength and the more the group is institutionalized. The spiritual quest becomes a church; youth culture becomes a fashion that the media market appropriates and rapidly consumes; the issues of feminism become a renewal of customs and morals; ecology becomes a good traded on the political market. Institutionalization shifts the arena of conflicts to other issues and other actors. Questions and social groups that once stood at the center of the conflict find a few years later that they have become new elites, modernizers of the market, or reformers of the political system. In the meantime, in other areas of the system, other conflictual issues come to the fore which, in different ways and by mobilizing new actors, restate the fundamental dilemmas of complexity amid the conflicts inherent to high-density information systems. The field of conflict, in fact, comprises a number of central issues that have a certain permanence and stability, whereas the actors who give voice to these issues change quite rapidly. We can assume that a high degree of variability in the action of a group will favor autonomy between the forms and contents of action and a greater capacity to utilize the antagonistic impact of codes.

The antagonism of movements is eminently communicative in character. It offers other symbolic codes to the rest of society, codes that subvert the logic of the dominant ones. It is possible to identify three models of communicative action.

1. Prophecy: The message is that the possible is already real in the direct experience of those proclaiming it. The struggle for change is already incarnate in the life and in the structure of the group. Prophecy is a striking example of the contradiction be-

tween the form and the content of action I spoke of above. Prophets always speak in the name of someone else, but they cannot help but present themselves as the model of the message they are proclaiming. Thus, as movements battle to upset the codes, they spread cultures and life-styles that enter the market or are institutionalized.

2. Paradox. The authority of the dominant code appears through its exasperation or its overturning.

3. Representation. The message takes the form of a symbolic reproduction that separates the codes from the contents that habitually mask them. It may combine with the above two forms. Contemporary movements make use of such forms of representation as theater, video, and the media.

Using these three models, movements function for the rest of society as a specific kind of medium, the chief function of which is to reveal what a system does not say of itself, the kernel of silence, of violence, or of arbitrary power that dominant codes always comprise. Movements are media that speak through action. It is not that they do not say words, that they do not use slogans or send out messages; but their function as intermediaries between the dilemmas of the system and people's daily lives is mainly manifest in what they do. Their primary message is the simple fact that they exist and act. This tells society at large that there is a problem that involves everyone and around which new forms of power are being exercised. The power structure says that their solution to the problem is the only one possible while it hides its specific interests and its core of arbitrary power and oppression. Movements, doing what they do and in the way that they do it, announce that other avenues are open, that there is always another horn to the dilemma, and that the needs of individuals or of groups cannot be reduced to the definition that power gives them. The action of movements can be seen as symbol and as communication. This does away with the old distinction between the instrumental and the expressive meaning of action, for in contemporary movements the results of action and the individual experience of new codes tend to coincide. Action, over and above producing calculable outcomes, changes the rules of communication.

Hidden Networks and Visible Action

Contemporary movements display a two-pole pattern of functioning. The normal situation is a network of small groups submerged in daily life that require personal involvement in the creation and experimentation of cultural models. These networks only come into the open over specific problems, for example, mobilizations for peace. Although the hidden network is composed of small, separate groups, it is a circuit of exchanges. Individuals and information circulate through the network, and there are specific agencies (the professionalized nuclei) that insure a certain amount of unity. The hidden network allows multiple membership; is part-time with respect to both the life course and to the amount of time it absorbs; and requires the personal commitment and affective solidarity of those who belong to it.

The bipolar model shows clearly that latency and visibility have different functions and that they are reciprocally linked. Latency makes the direct experience of new cultural models possible, and it encourages change by constructing meanings and producing codes. Its cultural output often challenges dominant social pressures. Latency is a sort of underground laboratory for antagonism and innovation. When the small groups come out into the open, they do so in order to confront political authority on specific grounds. Mobilization has a multilayered symbolic function. It proclaims opposition against the logic that guides decision making with regard to a specific public policy. At the same time, it acts as a medium that reveals to the rest of society the connection between a specific problem and the logic dominating the system. Third, it proclaims that alternative cultural models are possible, specifically those that its collective action already practices and displays. The mobilization unifies the thrust of cultural innovation, antagonistic demands, and other levels that comprise the movement's action.

These two poles are reciprocally linked to each other. Latency makes visible action possible because it provides the solidarity resources it needs and builds the cultural framework within which mobilization takes place. Visible action strengthens the hidden networks, boosts solidarity, creates further groups, and recruits new militants who, attracted by the movement's public action, join its hidden networks. Mobilization also encourages the institutionalization of certain fringe elements in the movement and of new elites that have formed in the area.

For this model to persist and to operate effectively, certain conditions have to be fulfilled. These include:

1. A high degree of variability in the environment that prevents the groups in the hidden network from closing in on themselves.

2. High elasticity in the political system, which does not obstruct the delicate phases of passage from one pole to the other.

3. Area agencies and umbrella organizations, or temporary organizations, able to insure internal communications (during latency, mainly the former) and external communications (during mobilization, mainly the latter). These forms of leadership are compatible with a multifaceted structuring of groups and does not impede the typical structuring of the area.

The two-poles model seems to indicate that public mobilization is the moment of direct contact with political systems. In latency phases, only the professionalized nuclei maintain chiefly instrumental contacts with some sector of the political system. If the goal of the movement is mainly symbolic in nature, why should it engage in exchange relations with the political system, which are always part of a logic of representation? The main reason seems to be that collective actors must preserve areas of autonomy from the system, areas in which they can undertake change. This is the laboratory where formal models are created and which the movement fills with content addressed to specific goals. Thus, a relationship with the political system, in the form of some kind of exchange, is a condition for the safeguarding or the extension of this autonomy (Keane 1988).

A relationship of this kind can only come about by establishing a pact; this pact is not the basis of the exchange but only a condition for its furtherance. This logic is first delineated in the action of umbrella organizations and agencies as the mobilization proceeds. The pact—a circumscribed and reversible exchange with the institutions—simultaneously makes power visible. Power that is usually neutralized by procedures comes out into the open to take responsibility, that is, to exercise authority, in a pact. Thus, it becomes possible for movements to measure the distance that separates them from power, as well as to accept, disenchanted, the confrontation. Through these means it becomes possible for society to openly address the dilemmas that social movements have uncovered through their action, as well as to create or adapt the political institutions best suited to cope with those dilemmas.

References

Alberoni, Francesco. 1977. *Movimento e istituzione*. Bologna: Il Mulino.

Bateson, Gregory. 1972. *Steps to an Ecology of Mind*. New York: Ballantine Books.

———. 1979. *Mind and Nature*. New York: Dutton.

Cohen, Jean L. 1985. "Strategy or Identity: New Theoretical Paradigms and Contemporary Social Movements." *Social Research* 52, 4:663–716.

Crozier, Michel, and Erhard Friedberg. 1977. *L'acteur et le système*. Paris: Seuil.

Gamson, William A. 1990. *The Strategy of Social Protest*. 2d ed. Belmont, Calif.: Wadsworth.

Gamson, William A., B. Fireman, and S. Rytina. 1982. *Encounters with Unjust Authority*. Homewood, Ill.: Dorsey Press.

Giddens, Anthony. 1984. *The Constitution of Society*. Berkeley: University of California Press.

Gilligan, Carol. 1981. *In a Different Voice*. Cambridge, Mass.: Harvard University Press.

Habermas, Jürgen. 1984. *The Theory of Communicative Action*. Boston: Beacon Press.

Jenkins, J. Craig. 1983. "Resource Mobilization Theory and the Study of Social Movements." *Annual Review of Sociology* 9:527–53.

Keane, John, ed. 1988. *Civil Society and the State*. London: Verso.

Klandermans, Bert, Hanspeter Kriesi, and Sidney Tarrow, eds. 1988. *From Structure to Action*. Vol. 1 of *International Social Movement Research*. Greenwich, Conn.: JAI Press.

McCarthy, John D., and Mayer N. Zald. 1977. "Resource Mobilization and Social Movements: A Partial Theory." *American Journal of Sociology* 82, 6:1212–41.

———. 1981. *Social Movements in Organizational Society*. New Brunswick, N.J.: Transaction Books.

Melucci, Alberto. 1984. *Altri Codici*. Bologna: Il Mulino.

———. 1989. *Nomads of the Present*. Philadelphia: Temple University Press.

———. 1991. *L'Invenzione del presente*. 2d ed. Bologna: Il Mulino.

Moscovici, Serge. 1981. *L'Age des foules*. Paris: Fayard.

Neisser, Ulric. 1976. *Cognition and Reality*. San Francisco: Freeman.

Offe, Claus. 1985. "New Social Movements: Challenging the Boundaries of Institutional Politics." *Social Research* 52, 4:817–68.

Pizzorno, Allessandro. 1978. "Political Exchange and Collective Identity in Industrial Conflict." In *The Resurgence of Class Conflict in Western Europe since 1968,* edited by C. Crouch and A. Pizzorno. London: Macmillan.

——. 1985. "On the Rationality of the Democratic Choice." *Telos* 63 (Spring): 41–69.

——. 1987. "Considerazioni sulle teorie dei movimenti sociali." *Problemi del Socialismo,* n.s. 12:11–27.

Tarrow, Sidney. 1989. *Democracy and Disorder.* Oxford: Clarendon.

Tilly, Charles. 1978. *From Mobilization to Revolution.* Reading, Mass.: Addison-Wesley.

——. 1986. *The Contentious French.* Cambridge, Mass.: Harvard University Press.

Touraine, Alain. 1971. *La Production de la société.* Paris: Seuil.

——. 1978. *La Voix et le regard.* Paris: Seuil.

——. 1984. *Le Retour de l'acteur.* Paris: Fayard.

Turner, Ralph H., and Lewis M. Killian. 1987. *Collective Behavior.* 3d ed. Englewood Cliffs, N.J.: Prentice Hall.

Von Foerster, Heinz. 1973. "On Constructing Reality." In *Environmental Design Research,* edited by W.F.E. Preiser. Stroudsbourg, Penn.: Dowden, Hutchinson, and Ross.

Von Glasersfeld, Ernst. 1985. "Reconstructing the Concept of Knowledge." *Cahiers de la Fondation Archives Jean Piaget* 6.

Watzlawick, Paul, ed. 1984. *The Invented Reality.* New York: Norton.

Part II

Collective Actors in New Social Movements

Chapter 6

Activists, Authorities, and Media Framing of Drunk Driving

John D. McCarthy

Even protest movements in the United States tend to follow issue-specialized and geographically fissiparous patterns. State structures, established interest groups and oppositional groups all may mirror one another's forms of organization and scopes of purpose.

—Theda Skocpol

Death caused by drunk drivers is the only socially acceptable form of homicide.

—Candy Lightner

The Drunk Driver has turned his car into a weapon, a weapon that threatens the lives of the innocent.

—Ronald Reagan

With the rise of nearly universal use of automobiles during the past fifty years, deaths and serious injuries associated with automobiles have escalated rapidly. Highway fatalities are chronic in all rich nations simply because the automobile is central to the everyday lives of most citizens. Driving crash deaths in the United States have totaled between forty thousand and fifty thousand a year during the last several decades. Close to one-half of these deaths are thought to be alcohol related. Each of them has left behind grieving relatives and friends. A recent estimate of people who believe that they are victims of the "alcohol-related vehicular homicide" of a close relative or friend puts the number of immediate family members at 2.2 million people, the number of other relatives at 4.0 million, and the number of close friends at 3.6 million (Kilpatrick, Amick, and Resnick 1990, 79). Yet despite this pool of people that has existed for some time with the potential to initiate a collective search for a solution to this problem, no movement emerged, nor did the issue receive much media attention, until the late 1970s.

If the loss of a child to a drunk driver were enough to motivate a collective search for a solution to this problem, Marilyn Sugg would have founded MADD (Mothers Against Drunk Driving) in North Carolina in the late 1960s. When her son was killed by a drunk driver, Sugg tried to organize a collective response to protect others exposed to the threat of drunk drivers. But events like auto fatalities must be properly interpreted to be motivating, and proper interpretations must resonate with existing communities of discourse before they can effectively orient collective action. In 1968, automobile crashes were still generally understood as accidents, largely beyond any serious measure of control. Within this interpretive context, Sugg's outrage was channeled by local officials and community leaders into auto safety activities popular at the time.

The Marilyn Sugg case lacked the elements necessary to motivate collective action: an effective frame and organized constituencies to whom that frame is accessible and resonant. According to Gamson (1990), an effective frame "has three elements: (a) it defines the root of the problem and its solution collectively rather than individually; (b) it defines the antagonists—'us' and 'them'; and (c) it defines an injustice that can be corrected through the challenger's action" (155). More specifically, Snow et al. (1986) point out that creating an effective frame requires "fairly self-contained but substantial changes in the way a particular domain of social life is framed, such that a domain previously taken for granted is reframed as problematic and in need of repair, or a domain seen as normative or acceptable is reframed as an injustice that warrants change." A frame must resonate with the experience of a collectivity and be accessible with its mix of crosscutting identities. In 1968, Marilyn Sugg had available neither the cultural template of an effective frame for reinterpreting the dominant traffic accident frame nor resonant constituencies with whom she could create one.[1]

By the late 1970s, however, Candy Lightner's outrage when her daughter was killed by a drunk driver found both an existing template for an effective "killer drunk" collective action frame and a series of interlinked constituencies receptive to helping build a movement. The process of change that had so favorably transformed both the political and cultural opportunities confronting these two mothers concerned with drunk driving began with a group of American public health researchers in the late 1950s who disseminated the idea that accidents of many kinds are preventable and hence not accidents at all (Haddon, Suchman, and Klein 1964). As this idea began to be taken more seriously, public debate commenced over how to understand the potentially remediable causes of the deaths and injuries resulting from crashes involving automobiles. Several relatively coherent perspectives emerged during the several decades of claims-making that ensued. Two of them — auto safety and drunk driving — provided the cultural backdrop for interpretations of automobile crashes that were widely available to the surviving victims of crashes, some of whom became the activists of the citizens' movement against drunk driving. The citizen activists concerned with automobile crashes overwhelmingly adopted and, by and large, have continued to embrace, the drunk driving perspective. And, since each perspective frames the causes of the problem differently, thereby leading its proponents to offer quite distinct remedies for reducing crashes, the one adopted by the activists strongly shaped their goals and strategies.

As the first citizen activists began to organize, they entered a public arena dense with competing understandings of the causes of and solutions to automobile crashes and their consequences. In this essay I explain the principal origins of the auto safety and drunk driving frames, why the drunk driving frame became so powerfully appealing, and why it subsequently achieved such wide public attention. I begin by examining elements of the competing frames themselves. Frames may vary in their resonance, coherence, and sophistication. Recent thinking provides clues to the relative importance of these dimensions in understanding the differing appeal of public frames (Snow et al. 1986; Gamson 1990; Gusfield 1988b). The relative legitimacy, power, and access to resources of those who create and publicly advocate frames should be important in explaining success in having one's chosen frame prevail over others in the public imagination (Gamson 1988). Finally, the processes of newsmaking by media actors shape attention curves; our knowledge of many of the standard operating procedures of media actors will inform the analyses as they are unfolded.

The Creation of Dominant
Auto Fatality Frames

The frames advanced to explain automobile crash–related injuries and fatalities that have achieved a wide degree of public acceptance in the United States are "auto safety," "drunk driving," and, very recently, "public health" (Gusfield 1988a).[2] Each emphasizes different aspects and makes very different "sense" of a similar set of "facts." Each targets culprits in emotive language. And, each has been advanced by a more or less organized group of advocates. For a brief period in the mid 1960s the auto safety frame received the most public attention. Embedded in a widespread federal regulatory effort, it threatened to become the dominant frame for years to come. But toward the end of the 1970s drunk driving began to achieve wide attention and by the early 1980s had emerged as the dominant frame judging by public attention.

Auto Safety

Before 1960 in the United States, if any common public understanding of automobile accidents prevailed at all, driver error was the dominant account of crashes (Nader 1972). "The nut behind the wheel" was a widely known image implying unskilled, unbalanced drivers responsible for killing and injuring themselves and others. In the early 1960s, a loosely connected cadre of professional reformers and guerrilla bureaucrats promulgated a very different understanding of the causes of highway injuries and fatalities. Ralph Nader (1972) expressed their position: "The highway toll is neither in dispute nor obscure. The tragedy is known. How it is interpreted is another matter and one which has remained the principal obstacle to a rational selection of safety strategies and their implementation" (xiii).

Nader summarized the policy agenda of the new frame: "The aim should be to have the automobile industry produce an automobile that would be safe under the assumption that fools and drunks would drive it" (Gusfield 1988a, 115). In the same vein, Daniel P. Moynihan, then an employee of the federal Department of Labor, and before becoming senator from the state of New York, contended:

> There is not much evidence that the number of accidents can be
> substantially reduced simply by altering the behavior of drivers

while maintaining a near universal driver population. . . . This leads to the basic strategy of crash protection: it is assumed that a great many automobile accidents will continue to occur. That being the case, the most efficient way to minimize the overall cost of accidents is to design the interior of the vehicles so that the *injuries* that follow the *accidents* are relatively mild. An attraction of this approach is that it could be put into effect by changing the behavior of a tiny population—the forty or fifty executives who run the automobile industry. (Moynihan 1966, 12)

Animated by a new approach to the reduction of automobile-related injuries and deaths, a small band of reformers coalescing around Ralph Nader was crucial in bringing it to wide public attention. Their efforts rode the coattails of President Lyndon Johnson's Great Society initiatives that began to gain stream after 1964, as the Congress and the president undertook an aggressive program of domestic reform. In this climate, their activities proved instrumental in creating a new federal agency in 1966 that later became known as the National Highway Traffic Safety Administration (NHTSA). They hoped this agency would carry out a program of auto safety reform. The goals of that reform emphasized improvement in vehicle design rather than driver performance as the appropriate strategy to ameliorate the consequences of automobile crashes.

The essence of the frame was and is that improvements in automobile design can reduce the likelihood of death and injury by either making crashes less likely or, in the event of crashes, minimizing their consequences. In practice, a variety of automobile manufacturing standards were advocated to make crashes less likely, including ones to improve tire and brake quality. Seat belts, air bags, and safety glass would minimize the effects of the "second collision," that is, the collision between the driver and passengers and the interior of the vehicle.

The content of this frame is dense and sophisticated. Extensive research accumulated to support it and was widely disseminated. The frame resonated with a highly educated, technocratic elite who viewed public policy as a lever to improve the lot of the masses. Yet it was and is highly abstract and the framing language typically used by its advocates is unemotional. Finally, its logic was structural. Gusfield (1981) in accounting the most emotionally charged and popularly accessible versions of this frame says, "dramatic attributes occur as well in the personification of automobile design as 'villain.' . . . A possible drama of scene, of environment, is converted into one of agent, of auto industry directors as villains" (82).

The advocates sought a federal agency to create and enforce safety standards and enforce them on vehicle manufacturers. "The legislative history of the act [establishing the agency] indicates that Congress intended the federal government to emphasize standards that would mitigate injuries arising from the so-called 'second collision' between motorists and the vehicle interior" (Graham 1989, 219).[3] In practice, the professional reformers focused much attention on changing the behavior of vehicle manufacturers who had been notoriously uninterested in safety design concerns. They did so by bringing pressure to bear on the newly created agency that was empowered to establish minimum safety standards for newly manufactured automobiles.

In the professional reform tradition typical of U.S. policy making (Lowi 1969), a federal regulatory agency was created to guard the public interest in auto safety.[4] The agency's efforts to create and enforce auto safety standards, centered at the national level,[5] have been strongly resisted by auto manufacturers. Agency encouragement has come from three sources: the Center for Auto Safety, a Nader-inspired but now independent, professional reform organization; Public Citizen, the central fundraising and coordinating organization of the Nader professional reform empire; and the Insurance Institute for Auto Safety, a coalition of automobile insurance firms. The conflict around this frame has generated almost no organized grass-roots citizen involvement.

The Drunk Driver

The legislation that established NHTSA focused almost exclusively on auto safety but asked, incidentally, for a "thorough and complete study of the relationship between the consumption of alcohol and its effect upon highway safety and drivers of motor vehicles" (*Highway Safety Act of 1966*, 6). In 1968, the Alcohol and Highway Safety Report was delivered to Congress. Based on a body of "accident" research carried out by university researchers that showed wide alcohol involvement in automobile crashes, the report concluded, "The use of alcohol by drivers and pedestrians leads to some 25,000 deaths and a total of at least 800,000 crashes in the United States each year. Especially tragic is the fact that much of the loss in life, limb and property damage involves completely innocent parties" (U.S. Senate 1968, 1). It continued by assessing potential means for remedying the problem within the frame it offered. These were heavily weighted toward "legal means," later to be more commonly known as law enforcement approaches.

By defining the issue, attributing blame to the drinking driver, and embracing a law enforcement strategy, the report became the template for an effective drunk driving frame. It laid the groundwork for the extensive future activities of NHTSA and others, especially the National Safety Council, in disseminating the frame and in generating widespread state and local efforts based on its assumptions about how to best solve the problem. During the 1970s, NHTSA became the major institutional advocate of the drunk driving frame and, through its state and local programs, created a vast interlinked constituency of supporters for it.

The main dimensions of the frame were well in place by the time the citizens' movement against drunk driving emerged. Gusfield (1981), assessing the frame then, described its main elements:

> First, the drinking-driver is portrayed as "drunk." The "sin" of drinking and driving is almost a microcosmic and symbolic enactment of the sources of disorder, the unwillingness to respect controls and boundaries in social life. . . . The second aspect . . . is the term "drunken driver." Not the event "drinking-driving" but the person "drunken driver" is described. The personalization of the event keeps alive the sense of a drama of conflict against disordered persons, a performance of deviance. It is a drama of agents in which the individual is prime mover. (82)

The clear focus on personal responsibility embedded in the frame made the detection and punishment of drunk drivers an obvious solution to the problem for those who adopted the frame. Further, the broader consequences of increased levels of punishment were seen to be the reduction of drunk driving through its deterrence effects. Battlefield imagery was common among proponents, as in the phrase "waging war against drunk driving." Emotive language reviled "the scourge of drunk driving" and "the killer drunk."

As NHTSA developed a commitment to the drunk driving frame along with its originally mandated one to auto safety, budgetary commitment expanded in ways that were consistent with the new frame's implicit lines of action. A series of policies, including grants to state and local jurisdictions, an expanded research and development program, and an important series of enforcement demonstration programs, created broad institutional and professional support for the drunk driving frame. Support was particularly strong among state and local functionaries, state and local police, and an expanding research community. All three of these groups had a large stake in disseminating and institutionalizing the new frame; this was most true for local law enforcement officials.

Demonstration Programs. Between 1970 and 1974, thirty-five communities were provided large grants for Alcohol Safety Action Programs (ASAPs). The central theoretical mechanism of the programs entailed both general and specific deterrence, which was to be achieved through law enforcement. More than one-half of the ASAP funds were allocated to enforcement programs. As stated by NHTSA, "Enforcement of DUI laws constitutes the input factor of the ASAP system concept. Its goals are: (1) to identify, apprehend, and channel offenders into the judicial system, and (2) to optimize the level of effort directed at this activity in order to instill a high perception of risk of being apprehended in potential drinking drivers" (U.S. Department of Transportation 1974, 1). Rates of arrest for DUI/DWI (driving under the influence/driving while intoxicated) increased by more than 100 percent in these demonstration communities during the first two years of the programs as the police were provided support for stepping up their enforcement efforts. The rate of DUI/DWI arrests more than doubled during the 1970s across the United States, importantly as a result of these and other efforts of NHTSA. This stepped-up enforcement provided local police agencies an important stake in the drunk driving frame.

The ASAPs also supported extensive public information efforts designed to bring the drunk driver frame to wide local attention. Reasoning from the premise "that only a third of the public was aware that drunk driving is the major cause of fatal crashes, the ASAPs undertook public education campaigns on two levels. The first was to inform the community of the extent of the drunk driving problem, particularly the disproportionate role of the problem drinker in alcohol related crashes, and second, to inform specific target audiences about their opportunities to join a systematic effort to control and rehabilitate drunk drivers" (U.S. Department of Transportation 1974, 1).

Drunk Driving Research. From the beginning, NHTSA supported research efforts related to its concerns. Consistent with the drunk driving frame, it funded research on the detection of drunk drivers, especially breath testing to measure blood alcohol concentration (BAC). This technology, along with the legal changes allowing its implementation, aided police enforcement. Extensive research on the relation between alcohol and automobile crashes was also supported, buttressing the earlier work that had been summarized in U.S. Senate 1968. And, NHTSA launched an effort to create a reporting system in all states to test persons involved in fatal crashes for BAC. Known as the Fatal Alcohol Reporting System (FARS), this data base was designed to provide epidemiological evidence of the involvement of alcohol in fatal automobile crashes as well as a monitoring device to track the success of efforts to control drunk driving.

State and Local Grants. From 1967 to 1985 more than 1.8 billion dollars was allocated directly to local governments for community auto safety activities. These grants were shaped by the broader emphases of NHTSA so that many of them flowed to projects, such as driver education, pedestrian performance, traffic control, and emergency medical services, that were not central to the drunk driver frame. But more than 28 percent was for police traffic services, a significant proportion of which went to DUI/DWI enforcement activities, and more than 15 percent was allocated directly for what the agency called "alcohol counter-measures." These were programs derived directly from the drunk driving frame for understanding automobile crash fatalities and injuries.

Public Attention to Auto Safety and Drunk Driving: 1962–1979

The frames of auto safety and drunk driving and the vigorous efforts of their proponents to bring them to public attention prior to 1980 have been briefly described. I do not mean to imply that these two frames are necessarily mutually exclusive of one another. A reasonable observer might conclude that there is an element of truth in both frames and that policies based on each should be simultaneously pursued. But they do compete with one another for public attention (Hilgartner and Bosk 1988) because there is a limited amount of available space for mediated attention to public issues in general. And, multicausal explanations of problems generally lack the intrinsic appeal of more simplified accounts that target specific groups as responsible for them (Gusfield 1981; Snow and Benford 1988).

Evidence developed from *The Reader's Guide to Periodical Literature* chronicles the public attention focused on these two frames in the period just preceding the burst of attention to drunk driving. This source indexes the substantive articles in most mass circulation periodicals published in the United States.[6] Efforts of the proponents of the auto safety frame were very successful, it would seem, in bringing it to public attention during the mid 1960s. There are almost no stories indexed on auto safety issues in the early 1960s, but a major increase in public attention to auto safety during the period 1965 to 1967 coincided with the establishment of NHTSA. After waning in the late 1960s, attention to auto safety held steady at moderate levels into the late 1970s. Despite the widespread efforts by NHSTA and its local allies to promote the drunk driving frame and publicizing the issue, the media paid almost no attention during this entire period. A close observer believed that, "A public consensus existed about the evil of DUI . . . for several decades [but it was] . . . muted and immobilized" (Gusfield 1988, 126). But public attention to the drunk driving frame escalated rapidly after 1980.[7]

The Citizens' Movement Against Drunk Driving

The rise in public attention to the drinking and driving issue and the growth of the citizens' movement concerned about it followed similar trajectories.[8] Before assessing the substantive and biographical content of the public attention, I briefly describe the movement and demonstrate its impact on the likelihood of media coverage.

Beginning in the late 1970s a widespread movement of citizen advocate groups emerged in the United States whose members, many of whom are victims of drunk driving crashes, began working to reduce the level and consequences of drunk driving. Their efforts are widely seen by a variety of observers as having had some success. For instance, Senator John Danforth (1988) said of MADD, "This organization has made the public realize that drunk driving is not a victimless crime. This change in public attitude has made it possible for those of us in Congress and in state legislatures to pass stronger drunk driving laws." In discussing these local advocacy groups, Franklin Zimring (1988), a consistently skeptical social observer, says, "the mobilization [by the groups] of public opinion has been partially responsible for the increased prominence of drunk driving as a public policy issue" (374). He goes on to say, "My guess is that citizen action groups are a more important explanation [than others] of the passage of legislation in the 1980s" (380). Finally, Mark Wolfson (1988) concludes, in his systematic evaluation of the effects of local advocacy, that the efforts of these groups positively affected several state legislative initiatives and "may have [had] some influence on fatalities" (9).

The movement consists of a number of national and local organizations. At the national level, there are two umbrella groups, Mothers Against Drunk Driving (MADD), with headquarters in Hurst, Texas, and Remove Intoxicated Drivers-USA (RID), with headquarters in Schenectady, New York. Each of these groups has a large number of local chapters spread across many states. In addition to MADD and RID, there are a few groups that are not affiliated with either of the national umbrella groups. In 1985, there were about 450 local groups devoting themselves exclusively to the issue. The first local groups began in the

late 1970s in upstate New York. These groups later became affiliated with RID, which was started by Doris Aiken in 1979. By
1985 there were seventy active RID chapters in twenty-three states.
MADD was started by Candy Lightner in California in 1980 after
her daughter was killed by a drunk driver. MADD was quick to
diversify geographically, and it accelerated at a breathtaking pace
over the next few years. By 1985 more than 375 MADD chapters
existed.

By 1985, the movement had become truly national in scope,
with more than 450 local groups with at least one in every state
but Montana.[9] By then the majority of large American communities had a local group, and 55 percent of the American population
lived in a county in which one of the groups resided, 67 percent
lived in a county in which such a group recruited members, and
95 percent lived in a media market that included such a group
(McCarthy, Wolfson, and Harvey 1987). By 1985, local groups of
the movement had come close to saturating local communities
across the United States.

Local Groups and Activists

The constituent elements of the anti–
drunk driving movement are emblematic of many similar local
groups seeking a wide variety of changes in their communities
that have emerged during the last several decades. They include a
variety of victims' groups (Gibbs 1982) and many women's groups
(Mansbridge 1983). Distinctive in their size and shape, in the scope
of their goals, and the range of their tactics, the groups usually
operate out of a leader's home and are typically quite small, labor
intensive, and leader-centered projects. To think of the "communal activism" (Dalton 1988) of these "minimalist organizations"
(Weed 1991; Halliday, Powell, and Granfors 1987) as we do large,
complex organizations distorts their essential structural features.
Groups like these typically seek narrow, issue-specific reforms
that are seldom even partisan much less regime threatening. They
prefer ruly tactics in their change-seeking efforts; they concentrate
mainly on community outreach and advocacy. When they do employ unconventional tactics, they tend toward what Joyce Mushaben (1985) calls "soft protest," for example, candlelight vigils
honoring victims.

Information was gathered from local groups in order to describe their typical dimensions and the characteristics of their leaders. While a few of the groups are very large and resource rich, the typical group is small, with an average of thirty-five members and a mailing list of one hundred names. About six people beyond the leaders do volunteer work for the group during an average month. Seventy percent of the groups had annual revenue of $2,500 or less in 1985, with the median revenue being $1,229. Most local groups rely primarily on leaders, volunteers, and donations of money and other resources (for example, telephones, postage, and supplies) to carry on their work. Despite wide support by their communities (McCarthy, Wolfson, and Harvey 1987; Ungerleider, Bloch, and Conner 1987), the groups depend primarily on their members for both labor and financial support. This adds up to about 2,250 leaders, 2,700 regular volunteers, 15,750 group members, and 45,000 people on local mailing lists among the 450 plus groups existing in 1985.

Activists in this movement closely resemble the profile of activists in other advocacy movements (Verba and Nie 1972; Dalton 1988). Not surprisingly, the typical chapter officer is a woman, who either does not work outside of the home or works part-time. Often she is married with school-age children at home. Although all officers tend to be highly involved (Weed 1987), the chapter president is usually the most active (McCarthy, Wolfson, and Harvey 1987). About forty-three years old, she has had some college education. Weed (1987), in a survey of the MADD chapters, notes that "presidents were less apt to be in the labor force than other officers, and when they were employed they tended to hold slightly higher status jobs" (265). The officers on average contribute the greatest labor to the efforts of their groups.

Victim members comprise about one-fourth of the typical local group and fill most leadership positions. Among leaders, presidents are most likely to come from the ranks of those responsible for founding the organization. This description corresponds with the reports by Weed (1987) and Ungerleider, Bloch, and Conner (1987) on the leaders of MADD chapters.

Group Activities

While all the groups aim to reduce drunk driving, their efforts reflect different approaches, including varying emphasis on promoting public awareness, pursuing legislative strategies, and providing direct victim services. The leaders, typically, make many public appearances in a year on behalf of their groups and in the process recruit members and volunteers who help carry out group projects. Projects might include preparing and mailing newsletters, organizing nonalcoholic "proms" and "red ribbon" campaigns, monitoring court proceedings involving drunk drivers, running legislative campaigns, and the like. Groups usually organize some task committees in order to decentralize work on such projects.

Drunk Driving Attention: 1979–1987

As the movement emerged, public attention to the issue of drinking and driving escalated rapidly. A comparison of the amount of attention given to the issue of drunk driving in three different media sources reveals similar attention patterns for coverage on national network news programs, in 5 national circulation newspapers, and in locally originated stories appearing in 112 local newspapers.[10] In the peak years of coverage the national newspapers devoted an average of more than 30 stories to the issue, the networks close to 10 stories, and the local papers close to 5 stories to the issue. A noticeable increase in attention occurred between 1980 and 1981, with attention peaking during the period 1983 to 1984, and a noticeable decline in attention beginning thereafter. While the patterns are similar, the varying attention is attributable to the varying amounts of space/time that the three media sources have available for the coverage of issues. The contrast in attention to the drunk driving issue here compared to that before 1979 is striking. During the peak years of coverage attention to drunk driving outstripped attention to auto safety in each of these media sources.

Recall that there were extensive efforts by powerful federal and local actors to bring the drinking and driving issue to public attention long before the citizen activists arrived on the scene. Their emergence coincided almost perfectly with the increasing media attention to the issue. James R. Nichols,[11] long-time liaison between NHTSA and the citizen activists, has termed them the "missing link" in bringing the problem of drinking and driving to wide public attention in the United States. Gusfield (1988a) echoes this observation when he says MADD and other organizations "created a new movement that has given a dramatic form to an issue that had been dormant in American life" (125). He continues, "The developments of the 1970's had built a research and policy community that, even though relatively limited in power, could be utilized in the new atmosphere of public concern. Nevertheless, the ability of the movement to provide a symbolism, an imagery, and a dramatic focus was a potent catalyst" (126).

The movement's raw emotive power was thought by many to be its central avenue of impact on the public imagination. "The very name, MADD, presents the symbols that carry an expressive imagery. 'Mothers' puts the issue in a framework of violence against children. 'Against' provides an emotional sense of battle and enemies. 'Drunk drivers' provides an image of the DUI as asocially irresponsible and out of self-control. This is the 'killer drunk' who constitutes the villain of the story. MADD has brought to the public arena the emotional and dramatic expression of the public as victim" (Gusfield 1988a, 125). Andrew McGuire (1989), one of the earliest executive directors of MADD believes that one of its keys to success has been "literally the name of the organization. . . . It says what the organization does to you when you are into blaming perpetrators. You are mad about it." The recollections of Marinelle Timmons (1989), founder of the first MADD chapter in Texas and later Texas state coordinator of MADD, reinforce the image of the media as highly receptive to the anti–drunk driving message when delivered by the activists. "The media was there every time we moved and they loved it. We got tremendous print media. But, we did radio shows . . . we did television shows at least weekly. . . . It was incredible, the support. It really grew." Is there any reason to believe that the anti–drunk driving activists had any direct impact on the production of the drunk driving media attention cycle, or did they just "surf" the issue, that is, take advantage of a cresting wave of media attention to the issue they had little, directly, to do with generating?

The Role of Activists in Generating Media Coverage

Most social movement activists in general, and the anti–drunk driving activists in particular, attempt to bring their grievance as well as their interpretation of its sources to public attention. They do so in the belief that such attention will facilitate the social change they espouse. Wide agreement among activists regarding the difficulty in getting media coverage yields to broad debate about the best ways of going about achieving it on terms most advantageous to activists' causes (see Ryan 1991). There is little systematic evaluation of the independent role of varying activist efforts in achieving coverage. The simplest test of the impact of activists would assess whether their mere presence increases media coverage of their primary grievances. A more complex test would evaluate the variable importance of their efforts and differences in how they go about attaining media coverage.

Two sources of evidence offer an opportunity to estimate each kind of activist effect across local communities for the drunk driving media cycle. The first body of evidence relates the existence of a group in a local community to whether the local newspaper covered the drunk driving issue. The second, based on surveys of more than three hundred local groups, relates variations in group agency, strategy, and structure to variable local media coverage outcomes.

Group Presence and Newspaper Coverage

There exists an extensive research literature on how "news" is created by media institutions (Kielbowicz and Scherer 1986) suggesting that many factors beyond the efforts of activists and the objective nature of events shape what will be reported. Simply how much space is available (Fowler 1979), known among journalists as the size of the "news hole," the range of available news possibilities (Hilgartner and Bosk 1988), and the dramatic appeal of the potential material (Molotch 1979; Gitlin 1980) provide parts of the context within which activists attempt to get their story told.

The independent impact of the mere presence of activists in a community for achieving media coverage was assessed using evidence that was developed by selecting those local newspapers whose locally produced stories were indexed by *Newsbank* for each of the years 1979 to 1987 (McCarthy and Harvey 1989). An estimate of the presence or absence of an anti–drunk driving group on the likelihood of the drunk driving issue being the subject of *any* newspaper story during each year for the period 1979 to 1987 in 111 local communities was developed.[12] Then the presence or absence of an anti–drunk driving group in a community for each year was estimated from a census of these groups (McCarthy, Wolfson, and Harvey 1987). Finally, secondary data characterizing the community and the local newspaper was developed from various sources.

The impact of the size of the "news hole" was estimated by the size of the newspaper's circulation—the more subscribers, the more the advertising, and, therefore, the larger the news hole, and whether it was published daily or weekly. Both estimates of news hole size were significant predictors, in a logit regression analysis, of the likelihood of any coverage of drunk driving. The previous presence of an Alcohol Safety Action Program (ASAP) in a community had a significant impact on the likelihood of coverage of the issue. This suggests that having had a local program aimed at creating interest in drunk driving has a long-term effect on the likelihood of coverage in a community. The mere presence of a group had a strong and significant impact on whether the issue received coverage during the year; community income and population size had no effect on coverage. Apparently, no matter what they did, the presence of an activist group noticeably increased coverage of the drunk driving issue in a community.

Group Agency, Strategy, and Structure and Local Media Coverage

There is little systematic comparative evidence across groups that evaluates how the variable efforts of activists affect their ability to mobilize community resources, including media coverage of their own efforts.[13] But it seems plausible that the harder they try and how they go about attempting to mobilize resources should affect their success. In order to evaluate this expectation for the anti–drunk driving activists, data from a survey of local anti–drunk driving groups carried out in 1985 (McCarthy, Wolfson, and Harvey 1987) was used to assess the impact of several measures of individual leader effort, group emphasis, and organizational structure on a summary estimate of the group's success in gaining local media coverage of its efforts. The group's president reported on the group's goals, activities, leaders, and membership and also estimated the level of media coverage of the group's efforts provided by the major television stations and daily newspapers in the community.

The results of a multivariate analysis aimed at predicting media coverage with a variety of measures of leadership effort, program emphasis, and group structure shows, at best, modest effects of leadership effort on levels of self-reported local media coverage. However, groups that emphasize drunk driving victim issues and services report gaining substantially higher levels of coverage: victim emphasis exhibits the strongest effect in the model. This analysis suggests that, beyond a mere presence in a community, the most important thing that activists can do to attain media coverage of their own activities is to stress victimization.

Actors and Themes in the Content of Media Coverage

An analysis of the content of the media stories that make up the drunk driving media attention cycle chronicled above illuminate the interacting roles of state functionaries, activists, and media institutions in the production of the media cycle. Media—especially newspaper—records have been increasingly used by analysts of collective behavior (see Franzoni 1987; Olzak 1989). Yet that research has been focused almost exclusively on collective *events* of which the media—usually newspaper—reports are thought to be a more or less adequate representation (for exceptions see Gamson 1988; Gamson and Modigliani 1989). Here I focus not on events but on the substantive coverage of the drunk driving issue.[14] I regard this record as one index of what Gamson has called an "issue culture." An issue culture shapes the perceptions of activists and potential activists while it may also be shaped, to some extent, by their efforts. I attend to the actors who are part of the coverage, the main subjects and themes of the stories, and some dimensions of the framing of drinking and driving as it is portrayed in that coverage.

Sources

Three sources are used to create the population of media stories on drinking and driving that form the basis of the following content analyses. The first source is the *National Newspaper Index* (1979–1987), which indexes the substantive content of five major daily newspapers, the *New York Times*, the *Christian Science Monitor*, the *Los Angeles Times*, the *Washington Post*, and the *Wall Street Journal*, each of which purports to provide national coverage of issues and each has a substantial readership beyond its local community. All of the substantive content included in these papers is indexed, including editorials and letters to the editor.

The second source is *Newsbank* (1979–1987), which in 1989 indexed 118 newspapers that had been continuously indexed for the 1979–1987 period of interest. Stories originating in these newspapers provide the basis for the local coverage analyses. The papers range from very small circulation weeklies to large circulation dailies. News reports and feature stories make up a larger proportion of this record than for the five national newspapers. As a result, editorial coverage is rarer and wire service coverage of the issue is totally excluded from the population of articles coded.

The Vanderbilt *Network News Index and Abstracts* (1979–1987) is the third content source. It records the national nightly news broadcasts by ABC, CBS, and NBC, creates summary descriptions of story content, and indexes the content of the descriptions. These serve as the basis of the content coding. Since the story descriptions are not verbatim accounts of their texts, the analyses of television media records are not strictly comparable to the parallel analyses of the newspaper records, if for no other reason, because they leave out large portions of the text.

Coding Coverage Content

A systematic cross-referencing system was created for each index in order to locate all stories that focused primarily on the drinking and driving issue. The obvious key phrases such as "drunk driving," "alcohol," and "automobiles" were consulted, and a strategy of searching each index for articles was developed. The *National Newspaper Index* is an online index that produces a list of articles in response to a list of keyword designations. The strategy for developing this list of articles was to continue to provide keywords progressively distant from the substance of drunk driving until no more new articles were uncovered. The Newsbank hard-copy index was treated in the same way until no new articles were being uncovered for each year. A similar process was developed for the Vanderbilt abstracts. These procedures provided a list of stories for each source.

The national data set consists of 614 articles. The local data set consists of 2,696 articles. Only the 1980 and 1985 articles, about 16 percent of the total local newspaper articles, are analyzed here. The network data set consists of 182 stories. These records provided the raw material for content coding. The unit of analysis is the story.

A series of coding dimensions was developed. Some of these depended on earlier efforts to code this issue arena (Estep and Wallack 1985). They included: (1) characteristics of the article beyond its substance such as the date it appeared, whether it appeared on the front page, and its length; (2) the major substantive themes and subjects treated in the article such as passing new laws, law enforcement, alcohol-related crashes, and the rise of the citizens' movement; (3) the major corporate actors mentioned (up to five), such as state and local governmental officials, industrial representatives, and movement activists; and (4) evaluations of such frame dimensions as doubts about the drinking and driving frame itself, the use of extreme semantics, and suggestions for the need for tougher law enforcement efforts.[15]

Actors

The actor category scheme was developed deductively and was aimed at capturing the major clusters of corporate groups involved in creating and tending the drunk driving frame.[16] The first five corporate actors mentioned in each story were coded. The variable size of the news hole across the three sources resulted in more total mentions of actors in the national newspapers than the other two sources. The dominance of governmental officials among the actors mentioned is striking, but it should come as little surprise after knowing the extent of federal, state, and local governmental involvement in the drinking and driving issue prior to this period. Officials are more likely to be mentioned in national sources (both print and electronic) than local, primarily because the local papers are substantially less likely to attend to federal officials of any kind. Surprisingly, local stories are least likely to mention the activists.

There are some important trends in the notice of actors over the cycle. The spread of the movement is indicated in its representatives being mentioned more often as they become active in more communities. As the drunk driving issue became more widely publicized, more diversity develops among the actors mentioned, for example, mentions of corporate actors from the voluntary sector, such as church groups, professional associations, and non-profit groups, and among the "other" category (for example, schools, victims, and drunk drivers themselves) become more prominent. These patterns suggest that governmental actors were the dominant sources in the shaping of the issue culture surrounding drinking and driving during the cycle. While anti–drunk driving activists may have been a "catalyst" to this attention, they were far less likely to be mentioned, or seen as authoritative, than were governmental officials.

Themes

The theme category scheme was created by another research group attempting to inductively map the subject content of a large but haphazard sample of news coverage of this issue (Estep and Wallack 1985).[17] An important reason why governmental actors are so extensively noticed in the news coverage of the issue is revealed in this evidence: there is extensive governmental activity on drunk driving during the period, and that activity dominates the substantive coverage. Through the cycle, mention of legislative activity expands and contracts pretty much along the lines of the expansion of the movement and coverage of the issue in general. Law enforcement activity generally declines as a theme over the period, as widespread enforcement becomes more routine. Particular drunk driving crashes as a central theme declines throughout the cycle. Groups opposing drunk driving become less newsworthy later in the cycle as coverage of the issue declines. Legislative activity is more prominent as a theme in the local press than in either the print or electronic national press.

Frame Attributes

Several attributes of the drunk driving frame were coded in an attempt to grasp its dominance and appeal. The first aimed to capture its emotional appeal. Was "hot" rhetoric—references to killer drunks, ravaged victims, and the like—a part of the story? The second and third attributes focused on challenges to the frame itself. Was there any general doubt about the frame expressed in the story or were civil liberties questions raised about enforcement of drunk driving laws? And, finally, was the issue of alcohol availability, a key element of the most subversive counterframe, raised?[18]

Doubt about the drunk driving frame is very rare in any source and it is concentrated early in the cycle of coverage when it does appear. Doubt about the frame is nonexistent at the local level and in the national electronic coverage. The appearance of debate about the availability of alcohol increases as the national debate about a twenty-one-year-old drinking age escalates; it subsides after the law takes effect. Focus on alcohol availability, however, is greatest at the local level, and it retains attention late in the cycle there. There is a strong copresence of activists and the alcohol availability issue in stories in all media across the cycle. The difference in aggregate attention levels to alcohol availability between the national and local media sources is striking: the networks tend to ignore it.

The use of extreme semantics, rarer than might have been expected given the "focus-upon-the-victim" activists, is more common early in the cycle; it becomes very rare in any source by 1986. It is more common in national sources than local ones. In general, officials are more likely than other actors to be mentioned in articles that also include extreme semantics. Surprisingly, in neither the national nor the local coverage is there a significant copresence of activists and the kind of "hot" rhetoric in stories.

Actors and Themes

The analyses of national and local press coverage of the issue shows the dominance of state actors in publicly promulgating the drunk driving frame, even after the movement became strong. The active legislative, judicial, and executive agendas surrounding the issue as the activists took center stage meant that a large pool of knowledgeable "experts" in the problem and its solutions was available to be tapped by the media as "sources" who could speak authoritatively about it. The evidence suggests, as well, that the activists were far less directly responsible for the emotional presentation of the issue than has been the common perception. Yet, there is no question that the activists were important in helping to bring the media attention to it, as the evidence linking their presence and efforts in local communities to the likelihood of increased coverage has shown. What broader sense can we make of the emergence of modern social movements and their role in media attention cycles from the diverse evidence I have assembled here on the activists, sympathetic state actors, and the drunk driving media attention cycle itself?

Implications

Until recently, social movements were commonly conceived as purely independent manifestations of civil society. Accordingly, their main lines of challenge to structures of power, accepted ways of doing things, and ways of imagining the social world were seen to originate wholly among citizens who could seek redress in actions of the state (Tilly 1984) or through the redefinition of social reality (Melucci 1989). In these formulations, the state was seen either as an adversary or, at best, a passive actor (Gamson 1990). Yet, as I have shown, the movement against drunk driving was only possible through the earlier efforts of federal, state, and local functionaries. It emerged without direct assistance from the state, but it could not have emerged when it did had the federal functionaries not worked so diligently and successfully in framing the issue and mobilizing a collectivity of diverse state advocates in support of it. Only with the movement's emergence, however, were the many state functionaries able to bring their framing of the issue to wide public attention through the mass media. The movement was, indeed, the missing link. The movement's independent character, however, may yet make it a fickle proponent of the frame that enabled its emergence in the first place.

Independent State Actors

Traditional characterizations of the origins of state agency/citizen group partnerships portray a standard mobilization sequence: outraged, oppressed, excluded groups mobilize and draw attention to their plight, which results in the creation of a state agency that outlasts their outrage and which remains more or less committed to their concerns (Baumgartner and Jones 1993). The sequence is also embedded in common analyses of the transformation of social movements into interest groups (Lowi 1971).

The sequence of events encompassing the media attention, state efforts, and activist mobilization preceding the emergence of the drunk driving issue does not fit the standard mobilization sequence. Instead, the many state functionaries first actively created the opportunities for movement mobilization and then, once it emerged, took advantage of that mobilization to communicate their program through the media. The activist mobilization and subsequent media attention also allowed them to expand the scope and intensity of their efforts, for example, by increasing budgetary allocations and fielding new programs at the local as well as the federal level. The apparent anomaly presented by the case raises several questions about the nature of the modern state and has implications about the relationship between state segments and social movements that can extend our unfolding comprehension of their links (McCarthy and Zald 1977; Skocpol 1985; Costain 1992).

The first is the relative autonomy of state actors.[19] The state initiative on drunk driving is best described as a "policy project" conceived and fielded by an interlinked network of state actors. They crafted the drunk driving frame; they created a knowledge base that legitimated it, disseminated it, and embedded it in law enforcement and judicial practices; and, by doing so, they mobilized a wide "collectivity of state actors" (Skocpol 1985) who had interests in its hegemony. All of this preceded the emergence of the activist movement and reveals an independent band of state functionaries succeeding in promulgating change prior to any grass-roots citizen pressure. Their policy project is not inconsistent with the assumption that "state managers collectively are self-interested maximizers, interested in maximizing their power, prestige and wealth" (Block 1987, 84). The project was not motivated to any great extent, however, by organized capitalist interests, although it threatened, to some extent, and was, subsequently, constrained by the alcohol industry.

Once we have acknowledged the possibility of independent agency on the part of state segments, we must ask how their efforts can affect grass-roots citizen mobilization. Direct state facilitation of activist mobilization through the provision of material resources has been stressed by resource mobilization analysts (McCarthy and Zald 1977) and journalists (Bennett and DiLorenzo 1985). Although both federal and local material facilitation of the drunk driving activist's efforts has been important to their ongoing mobilization, its first appearance followed, rather than created, the local activism. The pattern is the same as that seen in the civil rights movement (McAdam 1982; Jenkins and Eckert 1986).

The facilitation most crucial to the emergence of this movement was indirect. The mechanism was the creation and reinforcement of "identity opportunities" for victims. Once the drunk driving frame was widely available, aggrieved individuals could conceive of themselves as victims of drunk drivers. Constructing such collective identities was directly facilitated in communities by the strong likelihood that local police and prosecutors would participate in helping the activists to cocreate the victim identity. The success of the drunk driving policy project had resulted in local governmental actors who responded positively to their efforts, which reflected legitimacy on their newly adopted victim activist selves.

Recall the experience of Marilyn Sugg, whose son was killed by a drunk driver in 1968 (Moose 1974), well before the hegemony of the frame was established. It demonstrates the importance of both the mobilizing frame and local state facilitators. Sugg tried to mobilize but was soon channeled into the North Carolina chapter of the National Association of Women's Highway Safety Leaders, a group struggling at the time to act on the consequences of the auto safety frame. As a result, her individual effort to adopt and act on a drunk driving victim identity was unsuccessful.

Media Processes

Media organizations proceed on their own logics of newsmaking, always dominated by profit making.

> What is newsworthy depends upon what is already newsworthy if the issue has not worn out its welcome, if importance as measured by governmental or other major institutional involvement is guaranteed, if the conflict is big but not so big as to stymie resolution, if the issue's sponsors manage to create an event or interaction with a public official that provides a good news peg, if the conflict involves appealing characters, if there's a good story line with a fresh angle, an unusual twist, or something moving or funny. (Ryan 1991, 51)

As the 1980s began, drunk driving was perfectly suited to the needs of media institutions, with diverse groups of well-informed officials prepared to speak about it, emotional victims capable of articulating the grief that resulted from it, and no vested interests seriously threatened by the initial framing of it.

Media institutions commonly display a heavy reliance on "official" sources in their stories (Gamson 1988), but the dominance of official actors shown here appears more excessive than usual. It results, in some part, from the lack of a credible counterframe advocated by organized groups—seen in the almost total lack of dispute about the core elements of the frame itself in the stories. When frames are in some dispute, the media's concern for "balance" seems to lead to more diversity in their choice of sources. Evidence from network news coverage of environmental risk, where dispute is more typical, shows far more use of activists as sources than has been seen here for the drunk driving issue (Greenberg et al. 1989). Ironically, the activists who appear to be importantly responsible for spurring this media attention cycle are given scant notice in it, and this is most true in their own community newspapers.

Independent Local Activist Projects

I characterize the anti–drunk driving activists as empowered by the groundwork accomplished by a coterie of state functionaries. My emphasis, however, should not devalue their heroic efforts or their own contributions to rethinking the problem of automobile fatalities. Their struggles have been marked by deep dedication and widespread tactical innovation. Their efforts have shown a characteristic geographical diversity in goals and tactics, mapping the decentralized nature of the political system they confronted. They came to their activism with few preconceptions, no consistent ideological baggage, and almost no prior political experience. Although there is no question that they shaped the public debate about automobile fatalities after they became engaged, tilting the public attention toward the drunk driving frame, they remained incredibly pragmatic in their search for solutions to reducing the likelihood of automobile crashes and the associated consequences in human suffering. Since they are, typically, nonideological, pragmatic problem solvers who betray no structural critique of the state or societal arrangements, they have been open to solutions to the problem from outside of the drunk driving frame. They were not adverse, right from the start, to trying to limit alcohol availability (exemplified by their heavy engagement in efforts to raise the drinking age and to promote server liability) or to fight for social changes that made automobiles safer for "fools and drunks" (for example, their wide involvement in laws requiring that seat belts be fastened).[20]

Developments in the last several years suggest that advocates of the "public health" frame—the central goal of which is to limit alcohol availability—may be successful in wooing the activists toward their alternative frame despite its serious threat to the alcohol industry. The state functionaries who advocate this frame succeeded in convening the Surgeon General's Workshop on Drunk Driving in 1988 that led to the creation of the National Coalition Against Drunk Driving, a coalition of organizations with direct state subsidy that is seriously committed to advocating the public health frame. Federal officials in the Office of Substance Abuse Prevention (OSAP) and many university-based public health programs have also become more actively involved in advocating the public health frame. Many local activist groups have adopted this frame, and significant conflict has developed within and among local groups about the appropriateness of more completely adopting it as the basis for future action. The weak association between the state actors whose efforts indirectly spawned the movement against drunken driving and its constituent local groups suggests that new waves of victim activists may yet be alienated from the frame that originally motivated their crusade.

Successfully establishing frame hegemony for an issue like this one has broad social control implications. As a dominant frame orients grass-roots action into centrain substantive channels, it diverts it from others. Templates of meaning probably place greater short-run constraints on grass-roots activists like these than does their relative access to material resources, since, for the most part, they depend primarily on volunteer labor. As some of the activists have begun to imagine changes that threaten the alcohol and automobile industries, their understanding of entrenched economic interests—retarded by the wide consensus surrounding the killer drunk frame—has begun to develop. But, thus far, its manifestations resemble the typically American primitive, populist reproaches to "big business."

Notes

Acknowledgments: An earlier version of this chapter was prepared for the Workshop on Social Movements, Counter-forces and Bystanders (Wissenschaftszentrum Berlin für Sozialforschung), Berlin, July 5–7, 1990. The critical assistance of Bob Edwards, Joe Gusfield, Hank Johnston, Doug McAdam, Frank Weed, and, especially, Jürgen Gerhards as well as the other participants in the WZB Conference is much appreciated.

1. I attend to the development of available frames in what follows. Potential activists, however, must undergo what Doug McAdam (1982) calls "cognitive liberation" before they can begin to act themselves. They must take the available frame (or create a new one) as their own in a dialectical process of making sense of their own personal circumstances—basically, inventing activist identities. I focus my attention primarily on the development of mobilizing frames themselves and ignore, for the most part, the individual processes of cognitive liberation.

2. These three frames by no means exhaust those that have been elaborated to account for automobile crash–related death and injury. One of them stresses the radically disproportionate involvement of young males in automobile crashes of all kinds, paralleling very closely the involvement of young males in serious crime. Such a "wild boys" frame has received little attention outside of the expert research community.

3. Another frame for understanding automobile accidents, akin to that of auto safety, is that of road design. As the idea that automobile crashes were preventable became more widespread, belief that better roads could reduce the likelihood of crashes also spread. For example, in 1965 the federal highway administrator Rex Whitton said in articulating the "road design" version of the auto safety frame, "I think the majority of drivers, most of the time, are performing as well as we can reasonably expect. . . . The danger in pursuing the phantom of the bad driver problem is that undue concentration on the supposed bad drivers too often takes our attention and energy away from what we can and should be doing to make our roads and streets safer for drivers" (U.S. Senate 1968, 4). While this frame was and is widely known among policy experts, it has not become widely known among the general public.

4. The articulation and institutionalization of the auto safety frame is a classic example of the professionalization of reform (see Moynihan 1969; McCarthy and Zald 1977).

5. Crucial to grasping the policy arena surrounding the public control of automobiles and drivers in the United States is the continuing locus of authority at the local level. While the federal role has grown during the last several decades, driver licensure, automobile registration, traffic enforcement, and criminal court jurisdiction remain local governmental functions (see Laurence 1988). The creation of frames of understanding has taken place within this context of scattered authority. In general, auto safety advocates have concentrated their attention more at the national level and those attempting to control drunk driving more at the state and local levels.

6. This index has been widely used as a source for showing trends in the coverage of public issues in the United States (for example, see Troyer and Markle 1983; Nelson 1984). It is probably more glacial in its reaction to short-term trends than are daily, or even weekly, newspapers.

7. I ignore the public health frame in what follows. The essence of the

frame is described by Gusfield (1988a): "From the perspective of an interest in public health, DUI is a facet of the problems produced by beverage alcohol. The countermeasures associated with the consumption and distribution of alcohol are central in this concern. . . . It is just as logical to control the institutions that sell alcohol, to treat chronic alcoholics or 'alcohol abusers,' and to maintain high prices on alcohol as it is to prohibit and punish DUI as a way of promoting automobile safety" (116–17). In this frame, the alcohol industry is the villain as it pursues profits at the expense of public health. In the same way that tobacco firms are portrayed as attempting to hook young smokers in order to create a continuous market for their products, alcohol producers, especially brewers, are seen as targeting young people in an attempt to create a lifelong clientele of heavy drinkers. It is argued that their ability to do so should be curtailed by making alcohol more difficult to get (e.g., limiting sales, increasing price) and reducing the demand for it (e.g., restricting advertising).

8. This section depends heavily on McCarthy, Wolfson, and Harvey 1987; and McCarthy and Harvey 1989.

9. We have not included certain kinds of groups that devote extensive efforts to the issue of drunk driving in our analysis of advocacy groups. Such groups include locals of Students Against Driving Drunk (SADD) and Boost Alcohol Consciousness Concerning the Health of University Students (BAC-CHUS), which are, respectively, high school and college student groups. These other local groups have never reached the prominence or sustained level of advocacy of the adult community-based groups.

10. The evidence on which these attention curves are based is described in more detail below.

11. Dr. Nichols was instrumental in making the earliest activists aware of one another's efforts in the late 1970s; he was the NHTSA project officer for a series of small grants that the agency made to the earliest groups.

12. The unit of analysis here is community year—111 communities over 9 years. The presence or absence of any newspaper coverage for each year is the dependent variable.

13. The following analyses as well as detailed descriptions of the measures are reported in McCarthy and Wolfson 1992.

14. There is an extensive literature that assesses the content of media stories for a variety of other purposes, however.

15. A subsample of the national data set, consisting of one hundred articles, was coded by pairs of coders. On average they agreed in 86 percent of their coding choices. This ranged from a high of 100 percent agreement for the year in which the article appeared to 78 percent for main actors mentioned, and 72 percent of major themes mentioned, and varying from 77 percent to 99 percent for the various frame dimensions. These interrater reliability results are similar to those achieved by other researchers who have focused on this issue arena (Estep and Wallack 1985), and they are consistent with levels of reliability in other studies of collective behavior. It is typical that the more complex the substantive category to be coded, the lower the interrater reliability. These levels of reliability are well within acceptable limits.

16. Actors (actors included in general categories)

A. State and local officials: state departments of transportation, state legislators, governors, state attorneys general, mayors, local judges, local prosecutors, local legislators, state police, local police, state appeals courts

B. Federal officials: U.S. representatives, U.S. senators, U.S. General Accounting Office, U.S. Department of Transportation, U.S. Supreme Court, U.S. National Transportation Safety Board, U.S. President, U.S. Justice Department, U.S. military, Centers for Disease Control, U.S. courts of appeal

C. Federal drunk driving programs: Alcohol Safety Action Programs, NHTSA, President's Commission on Drunk Driving, National Conference on Youth and Drinking and Driving

D. Alcohol industry: bar and restaurant owners, alcohol beverage distributors, alcohol beverage retailers, national licensed beverage association, TIPS (Training for Intervention Procedures for Servers of Alcohol), Distilled Spirits Council

E. Corporations: insurance companies, National Association of Broadcasters, National Association of Independent Insurers, Alliance of American Insurers, Smith and Wesson (manufacturer of breath-testing equipment), local radio stations

F. Voluntary sector: victims groups, private agencies dealing with alcohol abuse, church groups, fraternal organizations, trial lawyers bar, hospitals, National Safety Council, American Automobile Association, ACLU, American Psychiatric Association, American Bar Association, Boat Operators Association, SMART (Stop Marketing Alcohol on Radio and Television), Highway Safety Institute, National Charities Information Bureau, sports arena owners

G. Anti–drunk driving citizens groups: RID-USA, local RID chapters, national MADD, local MADD chapters, specific leaders, SADD, Citizens for Safe Driving, Football Players Against Drunk Driving (FADD), Truckers Against Drunk Driving (TADD), Physicians Against Drunk Driving, Dealers [auto] Against Drunk Driving

H. Other: high schools (officials, teachers, students), colleges and universities (officials, teachers, students), international actors, specific victims, drunk drivers

17. Themes (examples of specific themes included in general theme categories; after Estep and Wallack 1985)

A. Legislative activity: law/policy passed; law/policy defeated; bill/law/policy discussed, explained; impact of law discussed; historical background of law/policy explained

B. Judicial activity: reviews of judges' behavior/of courts' processing of DUI cases; constitutionality of law passed; constitutionality of enforcement practices of DUI; reports of specific convictions; general trends in convictions; reports on jail/prison conditions resulting from DUI offenders

   C. Law enforcement activity: law enforcement strategies (e.g., road-blocks, breathalyzers); general trends in arrests; reports of specific arrests

   D. Drunk driving programs: prevention/education programs; treatment issues of sentenced DUIs; community campaigns against DUI; new ideas for combatting drunk driving

   E. Public reactions to drunk driving: trends in public opinion; avoiding arrest and avoiding jail; reports on groups advocating changed laws (e.g., MADD, RID)

   F. Social costs of DUI: loss of lives; loss of property; individual costs (e.g., victims, personal burdens of injury); task force investigations of social costs

18. Framing questions (answered yes/no by coders)

   A. Rim talk: Is there any doubt of the "killer drunk" frame? (If anyone or anything besides a drunk driver is implicated as a cause of alcohol-related crashes in general or specifically, the answer is yes). Record quotations of doubting instances.

   B. Killer drunk: Does the article contain extreme semantics? For example, is drunk driving described as killing, murder, carnage, and/or drunk drivers as killers? Record quotations.

   C. Alcohol availability: Is there any statement made by any actor mentioned or the writer of the article that, in any way, alcohol availability needs to change (e.g., sale hours restricted, sale age increased)?

   D. Enforcement doubt: Is there any statement made by any actor mentioned or the writer of the article that an enforcement technique is oppressive or unconstitutional (e.g., that it violates the rights of individuals)?

19. There is extensive debate on the issue of the relative autonomy of state actors. See Carnoy 1984 for a summary of earlier lines of contention, and Block 1987 and Skocpol 1985 for more recent discussions.

20. There is good reason to believe (Ross 1985, 1992) that the drunk driving frame mis-specifies the problem of automobile fatalities. It does so in that the solutions that it implies have not been and cannot be very effective. The lack of much reduction in highway fatalities as the result of all of the legislative, judicial, and law enforcement activity that has transpired has led some local activists to seek other directions for solutions to the problem that motivates them.

References

Baumgartner, Frank R., and Bryan D. Jones. 1993. *Agendas and Instability in American Politics*. Chicago: University of Chicago Press.

Bennett, James T., and Thomas J. DiLorenzo. 1985. *Destroying Democracy: How Government Funds Partisan Politics*. Washington, D.C.: Cato Institute.

Block, Fred. 1987. *Revising State Theory: Essays in Politics and Postindustrialism*. Philadelphia: Temple University Press.

Carnoy, Martin, 1984. *The State and Political Theory*. Princeton: Princeton University Press.

Costain, Anne N. 1992. "Social Movements as Interest Groups: The Case of the Women's Movement." In *The Politics of Interests: Interest Groups Transformed*, edited by Mark P. Patracca, pp. 285–307. Boulder, Colo.: Westview.

Dalton, Russell J. 1988. *Citizen Politics in Western Democracies*. Chatham, N.J.: Chatham House.

Danforth, J. C. 1988. "Hearing on S. 2549, The Drunk Driving Prevention Act of 1988." Statement presented at the Senate Committee on Commerce, Science, and Transportation, Consumer Subcommittee, August 2.

Estep, Rhoda, and Lawrence Wallack. 1985. "The Message from the Media: Drinking and Driving in Newspapers." Washington, D.C.: U.S. Department of Transportation, National Highway Traffic Safety Administration.

Fowler, Glen L. 1979. "Predicting Political News Coverage by Newspaper Characteristics." *Journalism Quarterly* 56:172–75.

Franzoni, Roberto. 1987. "The Press as a Source of Socio-Historical Data: Issues in the Methodology of Data Collection from Newspapers." *Historical Methods* 20 (Winter):5–16.

Gallup Poll. 1984. "Support 21-year Drinking Age Law, Seat Belt Usage on the Increase." *Gallup Poll* 226 (July): 2–8.

Gamson, William. 1988. "Political Discourse and Collective Action." In *From Structure to Action*, edited by Bert Klandermans, Hanspeter Kriesi, and Sidney Tarrow. Vol. 1 of *International Social Movement Research*. Greenwich, Conn.: JAI Press.

———. 1990. *The Strategy of Social Protest*. 2d ed. Belmont, Calif.: Wadsworth.

Gamson, William, and Andre Modigliani. 1989. "Media Discourse and Public Opinion on Nuclear Power." *American Journal of Sociology* 95 (July): 1–37.

Gibbs, Lois. 1982. *Love Canal: My Story*. Albany: State University of New York Press.

Gitlin, Todd. 1980. *The Whole World Is Watching*. Berkeley: University of California Press.

Graham, John D. 1989. *Auto Safety: Assessing America's Performance*. Dover, Mass.: Auburn House.

Greenberg, Michael R., Peter M. Sandman, David B. Sachsman, and Kandice L. Salomone. 1989. "Network Television News Coverage of Environmental Risks." *Environment* 31 (March): 16–43.

Gusfield, Joseph. 1981. *The Culture of Public Problems: Drinking-Driving and the Symbolic Order*. Chicago: University of Chicago Press.

———. 1988a. "The Control of Drinking and Driving in the United States: A Period of Transition?" In *Social Control of the Drinking Driver*, edited by Michael D. Laurence, John R. Snortum, and Franklin E. Zimring, pp. 109–35. Chicago: University of Chicago Press.

———. 1988b. "Constructing the Ownership of Social Problems: Fun and Profit in the Welfare State." *Social Problems* 36:331–41.

Haddon, William, Jr., Edward A. Suchman, and David Klein, eds. 1964. *Accident Research: Methods and Approaches*. New York: Harper and Row.

Halliday, Terence C., Michael J. Powell, and Mark W. Granfors. 1987. "Minimalist Organizations: Vital Events in State Bar Associations, 1870–1930." *American Sociological Review* 52:456–71.

Highway Safety Act of 1966. U.S. Public Law 564. 89th Cong. 2d sess.

Hilgartner, Stephen, and Charles L. Bosk. 1988. "The Rise and Fall of Social Problems: A Public Arenas Model." *American Journal of Sociology* 94:53–78.

Jacobs, James B. 1989. *Drunk Driving: An American Dilemma.* Chicago: University of Chicago Press.

Jenkins, J. Craig, and Craig M. Eckert. 1986. "Channeling Black Insurgency: Elite Patronage and Professional Social Movement Organizations in the Development of the Black Movement." *American Sociological Review* 51:812–29.

Kielbowicz, Richard B., and Clifford Scherer. 1986. "The Role of the Press in the Dynamics of Social Movements." *Research in Social Movements, Conflicts, and Change* 9:71–96.

Kilpatrick, Dean G., Angelynne Amick, and Heidi S. Resnick. 1990. *The Impact of Homocide on Surviving Family Members.* Charleston: Crime Victims Research and Treatment Center, Medical University of South Carolina.

Kingdon, John W. 1984. *Agendas, Alternatives, and Public Policies.* Boston: Little, Brown.

Klandermans, Bert. 1984. "Mobilization and Participation: Social-Psychological Expansions of Resource Mobilization Theory." *American Sociological Review* 49:583–600.

Laurence, Michael D. 1988. "The Legal Context in the United States." In *Social Control of the Drinking Driver,* edited by Michael D. Laurence, John R. Snortum, and Franklin E. Zimring, pp. 136–66. Chicago: University of Chicago Press.

Lowi, Theodore J. 1969. *The End of Liberalism.* New York: Norton.

———. 1971. *The Politics of Disorder.* New York: Basic Books.

Luckey, James W., D. Jolly, K. C. Mills, K. McGuaghey, D. Horn, and E. Richichi. 1985. *Role of Media and Public Attention in Drinking Driver Countermeasures.* Washington, D.C.: U.S. Department of Transportation.

McAdam, Doug. 1982. *Political Process and the Development of Black Insurgency, 1930–1970.* Chicago: University of Chicago Press.

McCarthy, John D. Forthcoming. *Crashes, Not Accidents: The Emergence and Growth of the Citizens' Movement Against Drunk Driving.*

McCarthy, John D., and Debra Harvey. 1989. "The Impact of Local Collective Action on a Media Cycle: The Case of the Citizens' Movement Against Drunken Driving." Paper presented at the annual meeting of the American Sociological Association, San Francisco, August.

McCarthy, John D., and Mark Wolfson. 1992. "Resource Mobilization by Local Social Movement Organizations: Agency, Organization, and Strategy in the Movement Against Drinking and Driving." Unpublished paper. Life Cycle Institute, Catholic University of America, Washington, D.C.

McCarthy, John D., Mark Wolfson, David P. Baker, and Elaine Mosakowski. 1988. "The Founding of Social Movement Organizations: Local Citizens' Groups Opposing Drunken Driving." In *Ecological Models of Organizations,* edited by Glenn R. Carroll, pp. 71–84. Cambridge, Mass.: Ballinger.

McCarthy, John D., Mark Wolfson, and Debra Harvey. 1987. *Chapter Survey Report on the Citizens' Movement Against Drunken Driving*. Washington, D.C.: Center for the Study of Youth Development, Catholic University.

McCarthy, John D., and Mayer N. Zald. 1977. "Resource Mobilization and Social Movements: A Partial Theory." *American Journal of Sociology* 82, 6:1212–41.

McCombs, Maxwell E., and Donald L. Shaw. 1972. "The Agenda-Setting Function of Mass Media." *Public Opinion Quarterly* 36:176–87.

McGuire, Andrew. 1989. Interview. March 5.

Mansbridge, Jane J. 1983. *Beyond Adversary Democracy*. Chicago: University of Chicago Press.

Melucci, Alberto. 1989. *Nomads of the Present: Social Movements and Individual Needs in Contemporary Society*. Philadelphia: Temple University Press.

Molotch, Harvey. 1979. "Media and Movements." In *The Dynamics of Social Movements,* edited by Mayer N. Zald and John D. McCarthy, pp. 71–93. Cambridge, Mass.: Winthrop.

Moose, Ruth. 1974. "One Woman's War against Drunk Driving." *Good Housekeeping* 178:54–64.

Moynihan, Daniel P. 1966. "The War against the Automobile." *Public Interest* 3:10–26.

———. 1969. *Maximum Feasible Misunderstanding: Community Action in the War on Poverty*. New York: Free Press.

Mushaben, Joyce. 1985. "Grassroots and *Gewaltfreie Acktionen:* A Study of Mass Mobilization Strategies in the West German Peace Movement." *Journal of Peace Research* 23:109–22.

Nader, Ralph. 1972. *Unsafe at Any Speed: The Designed-in Dangers of the American Automobile*. Updated ed. New York: Grossman Books.

National Newspaper Index. 1979–1987. Menlo Park, Calif.: Information Access Corporation.

Nelson, Barbara J. 1984. *Making an Issue of Child Abuse*. Chicago: University of Chicago Press.

Network News Index and Abstracts. 1979–1987. Nashville, Tenn.: Vanderbilt University.

Newsbank. 1979–1987. New Canaan, Conn.: Newsbank.

Olzak, Susan. 1989. "Labor Unrest, Immigration, and Ethnic Conflict: Urban America, 1880–1915. *American Journal of Sociology* 94:1303–33.

Ross, H. Laurence. 1985. "Deterring Drunken Driving: An Analysis of Current Efforts." *Journal of Studies on Alcohol*. Supplement no. 10:122–28.

———. 1992. *Confronting Drunk Driving: Social Policy for Saving Lives*. New Haven, Conn.: Yale University Press.

Ryan, Charlotte. 1991. *Prime Time Activism: Media Strategies for Grassroots Organizing*. Boston: South End Press.

Skocpol, Theda. 1985. "Bring the State Back In: Strategies of Analysis in Current Research." In *Bringing the State Back In,* edited by Peter B. Evans, Dietrich Ruechemeyer, and Theda Skocpol, pp. 3–37. Cambridge, Mass.: Harvard University Press.

Snow, David A., and Robert D. Benford. 1988. "Ideology, Frame Resonance, and Participant Mobilization." In *From Structure to Action: Comparing Social Movement Research across Cultures,* edited by Bert Klandermans, Hanspeter Kriesi, and Sidney Tarrow, pp. 197–217. Vol. 1 of *International Social Movement Research.* Greenwich, Conn.: JAI Press.

Snow, David A., E. Burke Rochford, Jr., Steven K. Worden, and Robert D. Benford. 1986. "Frame Alignment Processes, Micromobilization, and Movement Participation." *American Sociological Review* 51 (August): 464–81.

Tarrow, Sidney. 1990. *Democracy and Disorder: Protest and Politics in Italy, 1965–1975.* New York: Oxford University Press.

Tilly, Charles. 1984. "Social Movements and National Politics." In *Statemaking and Social Movementss,* edited by Charles Bright and Susan Harding, pp. 297–317. Ann Arbor: University of Michigan Press.

Timmons, Marinelle. 1989. Interview. January 16.

Troyer, Ronald J., and Gerald E. Markle. 1983. *Cigarettes: The Battle over Smoking.* New Brunswick, N.J.: Rutgers University Press.

Ungerleider, Steven, Steven A. Bloch, and Ross F. Conner. 1987. "Report from the Drunk Driving Prevention Project." Integrated Research Services, Eugene, Ore.

U.S. Department of Transportation. National Highway Traffic Safety Administration, Office of Alcohol Countermeasures. 1974. *Alcohol Safety Action Projects.* Chap. 3, *Evaluation of the Enforcement Countermeasures Activities.* Washington, D.C.

U.S. Senate. 1968. Committee on Government Operations. Subcommittee on Executive Reorganization. *Federal Role in Traffic Safety.* 90th Cong. 2d sess.

Verba, S., and N. H. Nie. 1972. *Participation in America: Political Democracy and Social Equality.* New York: Harper and Row.

Wallack, Lawrence. 1984. "Drinking and Driving: Toward a Broader Understanding of the Role of Mass Media." *Journal of Public Health Policy* 5:471–96.

Weed, Frank J. 1987. "Grass-Roots Activism and the Drunk Driving Issue: A Survey of MADD Chapters." *Law and Policy* 90:259–78.

———. 1991. "Organizational Mortality in the Anti–Drunk Driving Movement: Failure among Local MADD Chapters. *Social Forces* 63:851–68.

Wilhelm, Maria. 1981. "A Grieving, Angry Mother Charges that Drunken Drivers Are Getting Away with Murder." *People Weekly* 15 (June 29): 24–26.

Wilson, John. 1983. "Corporatism and the Professionalization of Reform." *Journal of Political and Military Sociology* 11 (Spring): 53–68.

Wolfson, Mark. 1988. "The Consequences of a Social Movement: An Organizational Analysis of the Impact of the Citizens' Movement against Drunken Driving." Ph.D. diss., Catholic University, Washington, D.C.

Zimring, Franklin E. 1988. "Law, Society, and the Drinking Driver: Some Concluding Reflections." In *Social Control of the Drinking Driver,* edited by Michael D. Laurence, John R. Snortum, and Franklin E. Zimring, pp. 371–84. Chicago: University of Chicago Press.

Chapter 7

Transient Identities? Membership Patterns in the Dutch Peace Movement

Bert Klandermans

Among social movement scholars there is a growing awareness that movement participants share a number of beliefs that make it possible for them to act collectively (Morris and Mueller 1992). Alberto Melucci introduced the term "collective identity" to refer to these shared beliefs. He defines collective identity as "a shared definition of the field of opportunities and constraints offered to collective action" (1985, 793). These shared definitions are developed in interactions between individuals. Collective identity, according to Melucci, provides actors with the "common cognitive frameworks that enable them to assess their environment and to calculate the costs and benefits of their action" (1989, 35). Verta Taylor and Nancy Whittier suggest a slightly different definition that stresses "we"-feeling. For them, collective identity is "the shared definition of a group that derives from members' common interests and solidarity" (1991, 1). Both Melucci and Taylor and Whittier emphasize the significance of collective identity for collective action to occur. Whereas Melucci is rather vague about collective identity, Taylor and Whittier elaborate the concept more precisely. They distinguish three factors that contribute to the formation of collective identity: "1) the creation of socially constructed boundaries that insulate and differentiate a category of persons from the dominant society; 2) the development of consciousness that presumes the existence of socially constituted criteria that account for a group's structural position; and 3) the valorization of a group's 'essential differences' through the politicization of everyday life" (1991, 28). Although these factors may be too specific to the movement Taylor and Whittier are studying—the lesbian movement—no doubt the basic principles of creating boundaries, raising consciousness, and changing the symbolic meanings of everyday life are relevant for collective identity to evolve.

I carry this argument one step further. Where Melucci emphasizes the significance of collective identity as a prerequisite of collective action, and Taylor and Whittier explore the formation of collective identity, I argue that there is no such phenomenon as a stable collective identity which, once formed, governs collective action. Instead, I suggest that collective identities are transient phenomena. Studies that demonstrate that social movements change their character over time abound. There is every reason to assume that the collective identity of movement participants changes over time as the life cycle of a movement evolves. This, by the way, is not in contrast to Melucci and Taylor and Whittier, who both emphasize that collective identity formation is an ongoing affair. In fact, Taylor and Whittier's argument could be read as an account of the reformulation of the collective identity of radical feminists into a lesbian identity.

One of the vehicles for the transformation of collective identity is the changing composition of the body of activists within a movement. As a movement wanders through different stages in its existence, the profile of activists who enter the movement changes accordingly. There are numerous accounts of transient membership: Todd Gitlin's (1980) study of Students for a Democratic Society, Doug McAdam's (1988) account of the Freedom Summer are only two examples. Because collective identity is generated and maintained in interaction among participants, the influx of new categories of activists may change the collective identity of the people in the movement. To be sure, as long as new activists enter gradually it is more likely for them to adapt to those who are already active in the movement without changing collective identities too much, but if they enter in large numbers, a transition in collective identity is more likely to occur. With a new wave of activists entering a new configuration of shared beliefs evolves. The result may be a transformed collective identity or a division of labor along identity lines. This process of the changing composition of a body of activists and its consequences in terms of collective identity is the focus of this chapter.

The movement from which I draw my evidence is the peace movement in the Netherlands as it developed between 1967 and 1989. During this period, the Dutch peace movement went through a major protest cycle in four stages. It was quiescent in the early 1960s before organizing a successful petition against the production and deployment of neutron bombs; then it staged the largest demonstrations the country has ever seen and collected 3.75 million signatures in campaigns against the deployment of cruise missiles in the first half of the 1980s. It ended in a period of decline in the second half of the 1980s. Different categories of activists entered the movement during this cycle. In the meantime, many of them left the movement. Activists did not quit randomly; they left in groups, just as they had entered a number of years before.

The Data

The data stem from four different sources: (1) a study conducted by Ben Schennink (1988) among the 1970-generation of activists of the Interdenominational Peace Council (IKV), the core organization of the Dutch the peace movement; (2) a study by Hanspeter Kriesi and Philip van Praag (1988) among 149 core activists of the peace movement in 1985; (3) a panel study a colleague and I conducted among 119 activists from ten different local IKV groups, which was conducted at three different times (August 1985 before the petition campaign, December 1985 after the petition campaign, and June 1987 when the movement began to decline); and (4) in-depth interviews we conducted in the summer of 1989 with three categories of activists: nine who were at that time still active in the peace movement (persisters), six former activists who shifted toward another movement (shifters), and six former activists who were no longer politically active (terminators).

The Movement

A brief overview of two decades of peace movement in the Netherlands will help put the data in perspective. (See Rochon 1988 and Oegema 1991 for more extended descriptions.) Hanspeter Kriesi (1988) distinguishes four currents within the Dutch peace movement: a Christian current with the IKV as the core organization; a socialist current, which was established during the petition against the neutron bomb; Women for Peace; and a radical antimilitaristic tendency. Of the peace organizations involved in this cycle of the

Dutch peace movement, the IKV is the oldest. It is not unusual to split the twenty years into two periods. The first—consciousness-raising—period lasted from 1967 through 1976. In this period, IKV, a consciousness-raising organization founded in 1966 by the churches, tried to mobilize public opinion. The second—action—period lasted from 1977 through 1986. In this period, the three currents that were more action-oriented gained prominence.

The IKV was the logical outgrowth of the increasing concern within the Dutch churches about the threat posed by nuclear weapons. As early as in 1962, the General Synod of the Netherlands Reformed Church passed a resolution against nuclear armament. In the course of the 1960s, other denominations followed and became increasingly explicit in their denunciation of nuclear arms. In that same period, Pax Christi—a peace organization within the Catholic church founded shortly after the Second World War—replaced its spiritual, contemplative orientation with a more practical, organizing approach (Schennink, Becker, Bos, and Arends 1988). In 1965, Pax Christi took the initiative to approach the Protestant churches and suggest the establishment of an inter-denominational peace organization. The result was the formation of the IKV, a council consisting of representatives of affiliated churches. The council aimed at stimulating discussion of the nuclear arms issue within the Dutch churches. The two largest Protestant denominations, the Catholic church, and six smaller denominations participated in the council. They financed a small national secretariat to initiate and coordinate activities around the theme of peace with an emphasis on information and consciousness-raising.

Beginning in 1967, the IKV organized an annual event known as Peace Week. During Peace Week church parishes focused on themes related to peace and disarmament. The themes of the events indicate that the IKV placed the issue of war and peace in a broad context: "Spread wealth, not nuclear weapons" (1967); "Away with hunger and violence" (1975). Church members who showed an interest in the issue were asked to help organize the annual event, and those who helped organize were asked to become a more permanent local group. In this way IKV built up its network of core activists. During this period IKV demonstrated a lack of interest in political action.

In 1977, after ten annual Peace Weeks, IKV changed its strategy. The Peace Weeks had lost impetus. Their objectives had become vague and too general, the target group was undefined, and there was insufficient interest in pursuing concrete action. The collapse of the Peace Weeks was one of the reasons to look for a new strategy (Oegema 1991). Another reason was that moral appeals proved unsuccessful in deterring nuclear armament. Concerned about the decreasing significance of nuclear weapons as an issue, the council decided in 1977 to start a long-term campaign to force the Dutch government to abandon nuclear weapons as a stimulus to the process of global nuclear disarmament. This campaign marked IKV's departure from its strategy of abstaining from political action. The Peace Week groups were asked to commit themselves to a ten-year campaign with the slogan "Help Rid the World of Nuclear Weapons. Let It Begin in the Netherlands." To many, the surprise of the campaign became an enormous success. In 1970 there were 220 local groups; by 1985 the number had grown to 450. The number of core activists also grew from 4,500 in 1969 to about 20,000 in the 1980s. Certainly, IKV alone would not have been able to spur such enthusiasm. Two events sparked mass mobilization: the decision by the U.S. government to deploy neutron bombs in Europe, and NATO's decision to deploy cruise missiles. Both decisions brought the nuclear arms issue home to the Netherlands. This was no longer an issue between super powers; now the Dutch government itself had to decide on deployment in the Netherlands. The events that followed are well documented (Rochon 1988; Oegema 1991): 1.2 million signatures against the neutron bomb were collected in 1977; large-scale demonstrations against the deployment of cruise missiles took place in Amsterdam in 1981 and The Hague in 1983, with 450,000 and 500,000 participants, respectively; and 3.75 million signatures against the deployment of cruise missiles in the Netherlands were collected in 1985. Numerous activities took place on a smaller scale all over the country. Nevertheless, to the activists' dismay, the government decided in November 1985 to deploy cruise missiles. (The INF treaty between the United States and the Soviet Union prevented the deployment of the cruise missiles.) In the year that followed the movement rapidly declined. With some simplification, one could say that two years later, one-third of the groups had collapsed; of those groups that were still alive, one-third of the members had left; and the activity level of the remaining groups was less than one-third of what it had been before.

This cycle, and more precisely, the core activists who helped to shape the cycle and engaged in the social construction and reconstruction of collective identity, are the focus of the rest of this chapter. The composition of the body of activists changed during the life cycle of the movement. Some entered in the Peace Week period, others in the era of mass action; some left when the movement was geared to political action, others left when the action was over. These changes can be related to transformations in collective identity.

The Changing Composition of Peace Movement Activists

The changes in the composition of the body of activists of the peace movement are investigated in three different ways. First, I compare core activists from 1970, the beginning of the cycle, with core activists from 1985, the year of the People's Petition, the last mass action of the movement. Then, I investigate turnover among activists between June 1985 and June 1987. Applying a panel design, I describe which core activists left the movement between June 1985, the beginning of the petition campaign, and June 1987, a year and a half after the decision of the Dutch government to deploy cruise missiles and half a year after the start of the negotiations between Ronald Reagan and Mikhail Gorbachev, which rendered the government's decision obsolete. Finally, I discuss results of in-depth interviews with core activists, which were conducted in 1989. Based on their accounts, I reconstruct the changing configuration of core activists in the Dutch peace movement and review the possible consequences in terms of the transitions in collective identity.

A Comparison of Core Activists in 1970 and 1985

Schennink draws the following portrait of the core activist from the Peace Week era (1967–1977): "Almost all core activists are active church members. . . . The daily work of the core activist illustrates the consciousness raising characteristics of the network; 41 percent did pastoral work, 18 percent taught, 5 percent worked in adult education, 12 percent studied, 21 percent had other work" (1988, 255). Indeed, consciousness raising is the main goal of two-thirds of the core activists and almost 90 percent were engaged in such consciousness-raising activities as sermons (47 percent), discussion groups (50 percent), writing articles in parish newsletters (32 percent), and teaching at schools or local Peace Week manifestations (59 percent). Schennink observes that gradually a new category of core activists entered the local Peace Week groups, namely, people who were participants of other movement organizations. Unlike the early core activists, who preferred Christian Democratic parties, the new core activists preferred radical or pacifist left-wing parties. In the period of consciousness-raising, the peace movement could count on both categories. In fact, the IKV had hoped to bring the two together and to win support from Christian Democratic constituencies for views and policies normally advocated by radical, pacifist constituencies. According to Schennink, many of the activists from the first category dropped out when the movement moved in the direction of action mobilization.

A comparison of core activists of IKV in 1970 and 1985 confirms this assumption (Tables 7–1 and 7–2). In 1970, one-third of

Table 7-1	Political Party Preferences among Core Activists		
	Core Activists IKV 1970 (%)	Core Activists IKV 1985 (%)	Core Activists Peace Movement 1985 (%)
Conservatives	2	—	—
Christian Democrats	35	—	1
Democrats '66	10	1	1
Social Democrats	13	43	46
Radical Left	39	56	49
N	**479**	**119**	**149**

Sources: IKV 1970: Schennink 1988; IKV 1985: Panel study; Peace Movement 1985: Kriesi and van Praag 1988.

Table 7-2	Church Membership among Core Activists	
	IKV 1970	94%
	IKV 1985	80%
	Peace movement organizations 1985	55%
	General population 1985	54%

Sources: IKV 1970: Schennink 1988; IKV 1985: Panel study; Peace movement and general population 1985: Kriesi and van Praag 1988

the core activists of IKV preferred a Christian Democratic party and half of the activists preferred left-wing parties. In 1985, Christian Democrats are virtually replaced by left-wingers. At that time, the political preferences of core activists of IKV were similar to those of peace movement activists in general. This is not to say that all church members quit. Although the proportion of church members dropped from 1970 to 1985, 80 percent of the core IKV activists represents a substantial number. Church membership among activists of the peace movement in general was 55 percent in 1985, which is comparable to the proportion of church members in Dutch society.

From a church-oriented, consciousness-raising organization, the movement turned between 1970 and 1985 into an action-oriented movement against cruise missiles. Consequently, the composition of the body of activists in 1985 differed significantly from that in 1970: concerned Christians were overruled or replaced by pacifists; radical socialists and social democrats shaped the IKV into a more militant configuration.

Turnover among Activists

In November 1985, the Dutch government decided to deploy cruise missiles. In June 1987, we interviewed our sample of IKV activists for the third time. At that point 28 percent of the people interviewed had left their group since our previous interview in December 1985, many in reaction to the government's decision. The failure of the petition campaign was a blow to the movement, and even among those who stayed, 43 percent considered leaving at that time. Three questions come to mind regarding the composition of the body of activists: Who were the people who left? Who considered leaving? And finally, what can we say about their motivations?

Our panel study of 119 IKV activists contained several items that collected responses pertinent to the above questions. Because we had measures at three times—before the petition campaign, immediately after the campaign and the government's decision to deploy, and eighteen months later—we were able to trace changing patterns in who left, who stayed, and who considered leaving. We asked whether those who in 1987 had quit or considered doing so were already considering to leave in the years before. We also asked whether they were marginal members of their groups.

We found that those who left the movement in 1987 were more often already considering leaving in December 1985, immediately after the petition failed. We arrived at this assessment by conducting a number of regression analyses on the relationships between having left the movement in June 1987 and having considered leaving with whether they considered leaving in December 1985. The analysis revealed a strong positive beta coefficient (.36). Furthermore, by two measures, we were able to assess marginality of those who left. We found that those who left tended to be members of the movement for a shorter time; also, they tended to be less active members in their IKV groups. While their level of activity increased during the petition campaign, their marginality at its start was apparent. We found that those who left were less active members in relatively active groups. In other words, within the context of their own group, they were more marginal members.

What can we say about those activists who decided to stay in the movement? First, they were not the stereotypical "true believers." Many harbored doubts about the movement. Of those activists who were still members in 1987 (but who were considering leaving), most had first thought of leaving a year and a half earlier in December 1985. Their doubts did not necessarily translate into marginality. By the same measures used above (time spent in the movement and average time spent in group activities) we found that these members were *more* active in relatively *more* active groups, although the levels of activity declined dramatically in subsequent years. Given their levels of incorporation into local IKV groups and despite doubts about the movement, which integration into local groups apparently helped dispell, it makes sense that if these activists were to leave at all it would be a collective phenomenon. A locally based, collective identity as Christian peace activists seems to have carried them through the cycle of growth and decline.

For many activists, defection and the intention to defect had their roots in the period immediately after the end of the petition campaign. While all members experienced the campaign's failure, there are several shadings of attitudes and actions that warrant examination. For example, what made some activists consider withdrawing in December 1985 while others held steadfast? Also, what made some of them resign whereas others stayed, even as they harbored thoughts of leaving?

We asked a number of questions of our panelists that could provide insight into these differences, and we found a very strong relationship between considering to leave after the failure of the petition and having considered to leave six months earlier (in June 1985). This lends support to our contention that at least some of those who considered leaving were more marginal members in their groups. This was confirmed by the results of a regression analysis with the consideration to resign in June 1985 as a dependent variable. We found that activists who had considered leaving then were less committed to their group, felt less kinship with the people in the movement, and were less motivated to participate in the movement. Six months later, we found the tendency of being more estranged and less motivated was even more apparent.

In addition to the feelings of marginality that predated the petition drive, we found two important changes in opinion that seem to have contributed to the intention to leave in December 1985. Those who considered leaving in December 1985 were in June 1985 still relatively optimistic about the movement's future; they became pessimistic in December. We found a strengthening negative relationship between those who considered leaving in December and ratings on the statement "the movement is declining." Negative beta coefficients dropped from $-.12$ in June to $-.32$ in December 1985. Certainly, the failure of the petition campaign made these people lose their faith in the movement.

In addition to being marginal and becoming more pessimistic about the movement's future, those who intended to leave the movement in December 1985 were younger, and more often not members of a church. Not surprisingly, they did not have high expectations of the petition campaign in June, before it got under way. All these point to a shared set of characteristics that defined a subgroup of IKV adherents as early as June 1985. This observation is supported by our in-depth interviews, which I discuss below.

The second question asks, What made some of those who were considering leaving to take action and quit their IKV group, while others remained in the movement despite their ambivalent feelings? The interviews showed that a combination of even more pessimistic expectations about the future of the movement and a even stronger estrangement from other participants influenced the decision to leave. Based on interviews, we constructed a profile of those who left the movement in June.

1. These people left because they felt much more pessimistic about the chances that the movement would survive. It is obvious that the government's decision to deploy was an important factor. Interestingly, many of those who left moved on to other movements; perhaps these measures reflect a tendency to post-hoc self-justification.

2. Those who were outside the movement organization in December felt much less akin to the people in the movement than they did in June. This response was certainly influenced by the failure of the campaign.

3. Those who left were from the beginning less political. We measured this characteristic by evaluating their reasons for why being a core activist matters. We asked them to rate such items as "to mobilize the people in my community," or "to put pressure on authorities."

4. They were more expressively motivated. This was measured by their answers to such items as "to demonstrate my indignation" as a reason for being an activist.

5. Their own individual contribution was felt to be nonessential, as measured by the statement, "There is no need for me to participate since the action will be a success anyway."

6. They perceived the costs of participation to be higher, as gauged by the time spent in the movement and the negative reactions of significant others. These last two characteristics suggest that, as a group, those who left in June were less motivated initially to engage in the petition campaign.

7. Those who left had become much more militant in December 1985 as compared to June 1985. Again, this reflects the failure of the petition campaign, but it also suggests increasingly strained relations between moderate and radical segments of the movement.

Those who stayed, although they continued to consider leaving, may be profiled as follows:

1. They still evaluated the movement positively in December, even though the petition drive had failed.

2. They still felt akin to the other people in the movement in December; they remained that way with no appreciable change when we interviewed them again in June 1987.

3. They abided by the official IKV policy of refraining from more militant action.

The decisive factor about staying seems to be the participant's perspective about the future of the movement. Those who stayed were still optimistic about the movement's future in December even though their belief in the efficacy of the movement had waned. By June 1987, however, we found that this optimism had completely reversed. A highly significant positive beta coefficient for the "movement is declining" in December 1985 (.21) was replaced by an even more significant negative one in June 1987 ($-.49$). In other words, initial optimism was replaced by pessimism about the movement's future. In view of our earlier findings that pessimism contributed to the explanation of quitting, one needs little imagination to expect that these activists would be the next to leave.

These findings shape our views on the changing composition of the body of core activists. After the failure of the petition drive to influence governmental policy, many activists considered abandoning the movement. They were the more marginal group members, the younger activists who were not affiliated with a church, and those who were not very enthusiastic about the petition in the first place. Not all of them left. Those who stayed were still committed to the movement, still believed in its future, and abided by IKV's policy of refraining from militant action. Those, however, who doubted whether the movement would survive, who were more expressively motivated, and who had become more militant resigned in the months following. A specific type of core activist distanced himself from the movement after the campaign against cruise missiles had failed: the more marginal, the younger, the more militant, the more sensitive to the movement's failure, the more opposed to the petition, and the less affiliated to a church. This left behind a more moderate, church-oriented configuration of activists.

Persisters, Shifters, and Terminators

We observed the same patterns in the in-depth interviews with twenty-one people who had been very active in the peace movement's heyday. Nine were, at the time of the interview, still active in the movement (persisters), six shifted to other movements (shifters), and six stopped being politically active (terminators). We were interested in the question of whether persisters differed from terminators. In addition, we investigated whether shifters were different from terminators.

Although the three groups were similar in many ways—all had been a core activist—they differed in four highly significant dimensions.

1. More often than terminators and persisters, the shifters had been active in other movements before they engaged in the peace movement. These included the anti–nuclear power movement, anti–Vietnam War movement, environmental movement, student movement, third world support groups, and women's movement. Moreover, shifters had participated in militant protests like blockades and site-occupations more than the other two groups.

2. Persisters tended to occupy formal positions in the peace groups; shifters were more often informal leaders; terminators were neither of the two. Terminators spent the fewest hours per week on the movement; shifters spent the most; persisters occupied an intermediate position.

3. At the time of the interview (summer 1989), persisters and shifters were still spending considerable proportions of their time in movement activities. However, shifters were active on a much broader range of societal issues than persisters. The interviews left us with the impression that being an activist was a much more central part of shifters' identities than persisters'. For terminators, activism was a more external affair. Though they were more active than the average citizen, activism did not occupy their lives completely.

4. Commitment to a church was stronger among persisters than among shifters and terminators.

In sum, persisters have no personal history of social movement participation. The peace movement often was the first movement they had ever joined. They spent relatively large amounts of time in the movement, they occupied formal positions in the movement, and they continued to be active. They were more likely to be committed to a church. Of the three types, they identified most strongly with the peace movement. Shifters, on the other hand, had a lifelong history as activists. They were active in other movements before they entered the peace movement, and they continued to be active in other movements after they left the peace movement. They spent the most time on movement activities in the past and at the time of the interview. They participated in a broad range of activities, which adds to the image of committed activists. Terminators had a more marginal position in their groups. They spent less time, they assumed less responsibility, and they identified less with the movement.

The following picture emerges. Some of the peace movement activists joined a movement for the first time in their lives. They were and still are completely committed to the peace movement. They were the people who stayed in the movement. Some of the activists were less committed to the peace movement as such, but were activists in heart and soul. They participated in the peace movement when there was action, and they left it for another movement when the action was over. Other activists were both less committed to the peace movement per se and less committed to activism. They left the movement without attaching themselves to a new movement.

These findings suggest a solution for the somewhat paradoxical result of the panel study that dropouts were both more marginal and militant members. Two different sets of activists left the movement for different reasons and with different destinations.

On one hand are the relatively less active activists, who, after the disappointing results of the actions against cruise missiles, decided to give up activism. On the other hand are the activists who joined the movement to stage collective action, who responded to the movement's failure with increasing militancy, and who turned to other movements when the peace movement did not radicalize.

Conclusion

Different cohorts of participants carried the movement at different points in time. It started with the early church groups, who might not even have conceived of themselves as movement activists. Yet, they were to a large extent responsible for the establishment of an organizational network that later functioned as the backbone of the movement. This first generation of activists was oriented toward consciousness-raising; it had difficulties when more radical activists—often experienced in unconventional political action—came aboard. Some of them left the movement, others stayed. At the other end of the cycle, in 1989, those who stayed took precedence again when the radical activists left the movement to join action elsewhere. In the middle period, roughly between 1980 and 1985, the moderate activists who stayed joined forces with the more radical activists and shared with them the burden of organizing the movement. Yet, the latter seem to have put their stamp on the public image of the movement. In those days, the movement turned into an action-oriented, antigovernment coalition. One might suppose that, with regret, the original moderate activists witnessed direct action taking priority over reflection and discussion; antigovernment demonstrations were more important than consciousness raising within the churches. After the government decided to deploy cruise missiles, part of the activists radicalized; they left when the movement refrained from militant action. Others stayed, but when the movement declined rapidly they began to leave as well. A core of committed activists were left behind. They were not only more committed to the peace movement but also more committed church members and less militant. They lead the movement back to its origins: concerned church members.

The data on fifteen years of movement activity reveal considerable shifts in the composition of the body of activists. This brings us back to the question of the stability of collective identity. With such substantial changes in the configuration of activists, just how stable or transient will collective identity be? Collective identity has been described as the outcome of interpersonal interaction of movement participants. Although we were not able to document changes in collective identity, it is very likely that the three phases the peace movement went through not only brought considerable transitions in the body of activists but also brought transitions in the collective identity of core activists. Certainly, the corporate image of the movement changed considerably. Whether this was due to disparate sets of activists taking over at different times, and emphasizing some elements of collective identity and suppressing others, or whether it was a real shift in collective identity is difficult to assess on the basis of our investigations. The reappearance of church-oriented activists in the last period seems to suggest the former, but we may assume that the collective identity of these activists is formed by the previous action period just as by the initial consciousness-raising period. Whatever the dynamics may have been, shifts in the body of activists raise the question of how stable or transient collective identity is and underscore the importance of research into the formation and transformation of collective identity.

References

Gitlin, Todd. 1980. *The Whole World Is Watching: The Media in the Making and Unmaking of the New Left.* Berkeley: University of California Press.

Kriesi, Hanspeter. 1988. "Local Mobilization for the People's Petition of the Dutch Peace Movement." In *From Structure to Action: Comparing Social Movement Research across Cultures,* edited by Bert Klandermans, Hanspeter Kriesi, and Sidney Tarrow, pp. 41–83. Vol. 1 of *International Social Movement Research.* Greenwich, Conn.: JAI Press.

Kriesi, Hanspeter, and Philip van Praag, Jr. 1988. "De beweging en haar campagne." In *Tekenen voor de vrede. Portret van een campagne,* edited by Bert Klandermans, Dirk Oegema, Ben Schennink, Hanspeter Kriesi, and Philip van Praag, pp. 13–53. Assen: Van Gorcum.

McAdam, Doug. 1988. *Freedom Summer.* New York: Oxford University Press.

Melucci, Alberto. 1985. "The Symbolic Challenge of Contemporary Movements." *Social Research* 52 (Winter): 789–816.

———. 1989. *Nomads of the Present: Social Movements and Individual Needs in Contemporary Society.* Philadelphia: Temple University Press.

Morris, Aldon D., and Carol McClurg Mueller, eds. 1992. *Frontiers in Social Movement Theory.* New Haven: Yale University Press.

Oegema, Dirk. 1991. "The Dutch Peace Movement, 1977 to 1987." In *Peace Movements in Western Europe and the United States*, edited by Bert Klandermans. Greenwich, Conn.: JAI Press.

Rochon, Thomas R. 1988. *Mobilizing for Peace: The Antinuclear Movements in Western Europe*. Princeton: Princeton University Press.

Schennink, Ben. 1988. "From Peace Week to Peace Work: Dynamics of the Peace Movement in the Netherlands." In *From Structure to Action: Comparing Social Movement Research across Cultures*, edited by Bert Klandermans, Hanspeter Kriesi, and Sidney Tarrow, pp. 247–81. Vol. 1 of *International Social Movement Research*. Greenwich, Conn.: JAI Press.

Schennink, Ben, Marcel Becker, and Hans Bos en Cor Arends. 1988. *In Beweging voor de Vrede. Veertig Jaar Pax Christi: Geschiedenis, Werkwijze, Achterban en Invloed*. Nijmegen: Studiecentrum voor Vredesvraagstukken.

Taylor, Verta, and Nancy E. Whittier. 1992. "Collective Identity in Social Movement Communities." In *Frontiers in Social Movement Theory*, edited by Aldon D. Morris and Carol McClurg Mueller, pp. 104–29. New Haven: Yale University Press.

Chapter 8

Identity Fields: Framing Processes and the Social Construction of Movement Identities

Scott A. Hunt
Robert D. Benford
David A. Snow

Two related but theoretically unconnected sets of concepts have influenced recent social movement theory and research. One set focuses on framing processes that affect the interpretive schema movement participants construct as they make sense of their social worlds (Gamson, Fireman, and Rytina 1982; Snow et al. 1986; Snow and Benford 1988, 1992; Johnston 1991; Gerhards and Rucht 1992; Tarrow 1992; Benford 1993a, 1993b). The other set of concepts directs attention toward the personal and collective identities movement actors construct in their everyday accomplishment of collective action (Pizzorno 1978; Cohen 1985; Melucci 1989; Taylor 1989; Gamson 1992; Friedman and McAdam 1992; Hunt 1992, Taylor and Whittier 1992; Hunt and Benford, forthcoming). In this chapter we take a first step in elaborating the connections between framing processes and identity constructions, and we suggest how these linkages can facilitate our understanding of collective action mobilization.

Our orienting assumption is that identity constructions, whether intended or not, are inherent in all social movement framing activities. Not only do framing processes link individuals and groups ideologically but they proffer, buttress, and embellish identities that range from collaborative to conflictual. They do this by situating or placing relevant sets of actors in time and space and by attributing characteristics to them that suggest specifiable relationships and lines of action. Students of social interaction have long noted that interaction between two or more individuals or groups minimally requires that they be situated or placed as social objects (see Stone 1962; McCall and Simmons 1978; Snow and

Anderson 1987). In other words, situationally specific identities must be established. It is our contention that within the realm of collective action pertinent individual and collective identities are proffered and affirmed in two analytically distinct but interconnected ways: through engagement in collective action itself, such as protesting and celebrating, and through framing processes. In this chapter, we are concerned with the latter connection, that is, with the linkage between framing processes and the establishment or construction of identities relevant to collective action.

To elaborate the conceptual connections between framing and identity construction, we take as our focus social movement organization (SMO) actors' claims about relevant sets of actors within the contexts in which they operate. Based on research we had conducted on a variety of movements since the mid 1970s (Benford 1984, 1987; Hunt 1991; Snow 1993), and based on the conceptual observations of others regarding the categories of actors relevant to social movements (see Gamson 1990, 14–16; McCarthy and Zald 1977, 1221–22; Zurcher and Snow 1981, 472–77; Turner and Killian 1987, 216–17, 225–26, 255–58), we suggest that movement actors' claims about these relevant categories of actors cluster around three socially constructed sets of identities we conceptualize as identity fields. First, there are those individuals and collectivities who are identified as protagonists in that they advocate or sympathize with movement values, beliefs, goals, and practices, or are the beneficiaries of movement action. Second, there are other persons and collectivities who are seen as standing in opposition to the protagonists' efforts, and are thus identified as antagonists. Third, still others are perceived as audiences in the sense that they are neutral or uncommitted observers, even though some of them may respond to or report on the events they observe. We refer to these categories of identities as identity fields because the identities within each category overlap and hang together, and because the categories are elastic and expand and contract across time.

We explore the connections between these identity fields and framing processes with data drawn from our ethnographic studies of the Nichiren Shoshu Buddhist movement (Snow 1993); Nebraskans for Peace (Hunt 1991); and other local, regional, and national nuclear disarmament organizations (Benford 1984, 1987). But first we review extant treatments of identity, identity construction processes, and framing in the social movement literature. This overview provides a baseline for assessing the concepts we introduce and the theoretical extensions suggested by our analysis.

Identities and Social Movements

Although interest in the link between identities and movements has recently flourished, this link has been of long-standing interest to movement scholars. In tracing and critically assessing this interest, Hunt (1992) has discerned at least three tendencies in the way in which identity has been conceptualized and approached in the movement literature. One tendency is to treat identities as products of biological, psychological, or social structures. This tendency is evidenced in psychopathology models that suggest primitive instincts or inherent psychological structures produce violence, panics, riots, and other asocial behaviors (MacKay 1932; LeBon 1960; Trotter 1919; Freud 1922; McDougall 1928; Moscovici 1985). In this view, identities are manifestations of innate, asocial biological and psychological structures. These psychopathology perspectives are not the only ones that conceptualize identity as a product of underlying objective structures. Early thinking about ethnic identity, for instance, often treated it "as essentially 'primordial,' meaning some underlying and fundamental set of ascriptive characteristics" determines identities (Olzak 1983, 356). Along similar lines, "essentialist" approaches point to physiological characteristics, psychological predispositions, biological reproduction, and historical sexual divisions of labor as "determinants" of gendered, lesbian, and gay identities (Epstein 1987; Marshall 1991).

Strain theorists also suggest that identities are products of maladaptive social structures. For example, Klapp (1969), drawing from both symbolic interactionism and mass society theories, argues that modern social structures produce estrangement that pushes people toward collective searches for meaningful identities. Relative deprivation and status inconsistency approaches suggest similar arguments; they contend that movements emerge when a category of people experiences psychological dissonance stemming from discrepancies between real conditions and subjective expectations (see, e.g., Davies 1979; Wilson and Zurcher 1976). It is assumed that identities that are products of psychosocial structural strain render individuals particularly susceptible to collective action.

Inherent in this tendency to view identity as a product of objective structures are several shortcomings. Because identity is seen as a product or even a symptom, analytical attention is riveted on "discovering" the underlying structures that spawn identities. Thus, identity as such has not been the central subject of empirical investigations. There also is a tendency to reify identity concepts. Researchers frequently imply that entire categories of people possess uniform identities. Further, focusing on "determinant" structures implies that identities arise from a single dimension, for example, pathological instinct or psychosocial structural strain. Unidimensional arguments overlook a variety of identity components and complexities, especially how actors interpret, construct, and articulate identities (Blumer 1969).

A second tendency is to conceptualize identity concerns and changes in identity as manifestations of macro social change. This line of argument has recently been advanced by New Social Movement (NSM) theorists, who contend that changes in industrial societies reflect the advent of a new historical epoch that has given rise to a new set of identities (Pizzorno 1978; Habermas 1984, 1987; Cohen 1985; Gamson 1989; Kriesi 1989; Dalton and Kuechler 1990). According to Melucci (1989), there are a number of differences between previous forms of class conflict and today's emerging forms of collective action. In other words, NSMs are said to transcend traditional class divisions and corresponding struggles for control of state and economic institutions. Instead, they concentrate on transformations of civil society and life worlds.

Despite notable contributions to the study of contemporary movements, NSM theorists' tendency to view identities as manifestations of macro social change has several limitations. For one thing, this focus is perhaps overly narrow, examining only a "subset of social movements that happen to be predominantly white, middle class, and located in Western Europe and North America" (Gamson 1992, 58). Second, NSM theory examines only political-cultural movements with progressive agendas, thereby ignoring other kinds of movements (for example, religious, consensus, right-wing). Additionally, Melucci (1989), among others, argues against NSM theorists' reification of the "newness" of contemporary movements. Further, in the light of Weber's (1978) analyses of status conflicts, charismatic leaders, religious movements, and military orders, the assumption that all "old" movements were class-based seems unwarranted. To soften the assumption by maintaining that the only significant "old" movements were class-based would be simply self-serving. The tendency of NSM theorists to assert that the pivotal role of collective identity is new is suspect, because by definition any self-identified group makes a collective identity claim. Finally, some articulations of NSM theory imply a tautology: NSMs, defined in terms of self-limiting radicalism, identity politics, and transformations of civil society and life worlds, are manifestations of a new, emerging historical epoch, which is characterized by nonrevolutionary radicalism, valorization of devalued identities, and alterations of civil society and life worlds. The implication of these conceptual tendencies, with the exception of Melucci's work (1989), is that movement identities are viewed as being more or less historically determined rather than interactionally accomplished.

The third approach to conceptualizing identities treats them as interactional accomplishments. Joane Nagel (1986), for instance, conceptualizes ethnic identity as political constructions. Constructionist perspectives have countered essentialist arguments as well, by contending that gendered, lesbian, and gay identities are perpetually (re)constructed through social interaction (Ponse 1978; Gerson and Peiss 1985; Margolis 1985; Smith 1990; West and Zimmerman 1987; Marshall 1991). Melucci (1989) also stresses the interactional accomplishment of identity, arguing that "collective identity is an interactive and shared definition" (34). Borrowing from NSM, feminist, and symbolic interactionist theories, Verta Taylor and Nancy Whittier (1992) examine the interactional accomplishment of collective identity in terms of boundaries, consciousness, and negotiation.

Symbolic interactionist movement scholars have also had a long-standing, albeit mainly implicit, interest in the construction of identities. Blumer's (1939) emphasis on esprit de corps, morale, solidarity, and ideology points directly to identity construction issues. This focus is echoed by Turner and Killian (1987), who state that the "continuity of group identity" is a key aspect of collective action (224). And recent interactionist studies examine the discourse of personal identity construction in a variety of contexts (Snow and Machalek 1984; Snow and Anderson 1987). According to these works, personal identity, regardless of its objective constitution, is an interactional accomplishment that is socially (re)constructed. The discourse of personal identity is understood as a rhetoric "constructed in accordance with group-specific guidelines" and "redefined continuously in light of new experiences" (Snow and Machalek 1984, 175–77). At the organizational level of analysis, SMO actors provide "appropriate" vocabularies and stories for participants and sympathizers to (re)construct their personal identities in ways that link or further commit them to the movement or SMO (Benford 1993b; Hunt and Benford, forthcoming).

This interactionist emphasis on identity and universes of discourse is relevant to understanding the construction, establishment, and transformation of collective identities. If collective identity is conceptualized in terms of the range of salient characteristics an SMO avows and imputes to other sets of actors, then the construction and affirmation of identities clearly can be linked to framing processes.

Frames and Framing Processes

Attempting to elucidate ideational aspects of collective action, Snow, Benford, their colleagues, and others (Snow et al. 1986; Snow and Benford 1988, 1992; Johnston 1991; Gerhards and Rucht 1992; Tarrow 1992; Benford 1993a, 1993b) adapted Goffman's (1974) *Frame Analysis* to illuminate how movement actors make sense of their social worlds. A frame is "an interpretive schemata that simplifies and condenses the 'world out there' by selectively punctuating and encoding objects, situations, events, experiences, and sequences of actions within one's present or past environments" (Snow and Benford 1992, 137). In the context of social movements, collective action frames not only focus and punctuate "reality" they also serve as modes of attribution and articulation. So conceived, collective action frames focus attention on a particular situation considered problematic, make attributions regarding who or what is to blame, and articulate an alternative set of arrangements including what the movement actors need to do in order to affect the desired change. Snow and Benford (1988) suggest that the foregoing functions of collective action frames constitute three core framing tasks SMOs must accomplish in order to affect consensus and action mobilization: diagnostic framing, and prognostic framing, and motivational framing.

Diagnostic framing identifies some event or condition as problematic and in need of amelioration, and thereby designates culpable agents. The attributional function of diagnostic framing involves imputing traits and motives for those who are viewed as having "caused" or exacerbated the problem. In other words, it involves casting others into the role identities of villain, culprit, or antagonist. Prognostic framing outlines a plan for redress, specifying what should be done by whom, including an elaboration of specific targets, strategies, and tactics. While diagnostic and prognostic framing are required to affect consensus mobilization, agreement on these definitions of the situation does not automatically yield collective action. For people to take action to overcome a collectively perceived problem or "injustice," they must develop a set of compelling reasons for doing so. Motivational framing addresses this need by keynoting appropriate vocabularies of motive or rationales for doing something for the cause (Benford 1993b; see also Mills 1940). Thus, while diagnoses involve the imputation of motives and identities regarding antagonists or targets of change, motivational framing entails the social construction and avowal of motives and identities of protagonists. These shared identities and motives in turn serve as an impetus for collective action.

In consideration of these processes at the SMO level, Snow et al. (1986) identify and elaborate a set of frame alignment strategies. These are micromobilization processes whereby SMO actors seek to affect various audiences' interpretations regarding the extent to which the SMO's ideology and goals are congruent with targeted individuals' interests, values, and beliefs. In the context of this chapter, these frame alignment processes can be conceived as rhetorical strategies to affect the alignment of collective and personal identities.

As used by Snow, Benford, and their associates, framing concepts capture two interrelated qualities of movement actors' interpretive work. One is that ideology or belief systems are interactional accomplishments that emerge from framing processes; the other is that frames are cognitive structures that guide collective action, including subsequent framing processes. This suggests a key recursive relationship: framing processes produce frames which then condition ensuing framing processes. Framing concepts thus underscore the dynamic quality of movement participants' belief systems by fixing attention on the dialectical interplay between interpretive processes and cognitive structures. Personal and collective identities are, in part, a product or outcome of this dialectical interplay.

Identity Fields and Framing Processes

A central aspect of the framing process is the avowal or imputation of characteristics to relevant sets of actors within a movement's orbit of operation. Their avowed or imputed characteristics tend to be of two kinds: they assert something about a group's consciousness, or they make claims about aspects of a group's character. In the case of the former, levels or kinds of knowledge or awareness are attributed, values are highlighted, and changes in consciousness are noted or encouraged. The alignment processes of frame bridging, amplification, and transformation are the discursive vehicles through which attributions about consciousness are made. In the case of character attributions, specific claims are made about a group's strategic, moral, and cathectic or relational character. Adversaries, for example, are often personified as irrational, immoral, and devoid of compassion and feeling (Shibutani 1970).

Such attributions or claims are not only constitutive of collective identity but they are a necessary aspect of the collective action process inasmuch as they situate and place other categories of actors as targets of strategic action. As noted earlier, most such placements or constructions cluster into one of three generic categories we refer to as identity fields: protagonists, antagonists, and audiences. Each identity field typically consists of a multiplicity of imputed or avowed identities.

To date, interest in collective identity has focused primarily on what we call the protagonist field. From our vantage point, this focus is too narrow because it glosses the extent to which collective identities are social constructions, the extent to which the constitution of targets of action is contingent on the establishment of their identity, and the extent to which the flow of collective action itself is based on the kinds of identities imputed to the various sets of relevant actors. We argue that the identities associated with the antagonist and audience fields are as fundamental to the dynamic of collective action as those that define the protagonists. It is in the construction of these identity fields that framing processes are particularly relevant.

Protagonist Identity Field

Protagonist identity fields are constellations of identity attributions about individuals and collectivities taken to be advocates of movement causes. These usually include collective identity claims about "the movement" and allied aggregations and organizations. They also involve a variety of personal identity attributions such as movement heroes and heroines, paid and unpaid staffers, leaders, rank-and-file followers, and star supporters (for example, celebrities and politicians). Also included are collective and personal identity attributions about constituents, such as "innocent victims," aggrieved populations, "future generations," and "the silent majority." SMO actors also make personal and collective protagonist identity avowals. In this section we illustrate how the construction of numerous identities in a protagonist identity field is contingent on framing processes.

Protagonist identity attributions are intricately related to several framing processes. Through backstage negotiations and interactions, SMO actors engage in diagnostic framing, attempting to find the "best" ways, from their point of view, to convey to themselves and others their interpretations of what is wrong with extant conditions. SMO actors also construct prognostic and motivational frames that specify what needs to be done to rectify identified problems and why corrective actions are necessary. These framing processes represent emergent ideologies that advance implicit or explicit identity claims. As Downey (1986) contends, "Social action that implicitly conveys an ideology also communicates a public identity" (360).

In the course of framing diagnoses, prognoses, and motives, SMO actors locate their organization and its views within a collective action field or context. This entails making in-group/out-group distinctions and assigning other organizations to ideological, geographical, and tactical "turfs" (Blumer 1939; Melucci 1989; Benford and Zurcher 1990; Taylor and Whittier 1992). Such attempts to situate one's own organization in time and space in relation to other groups can be thought of as boundary framing. Taylor's (1989) work suggests the importance of boundary framing when she argues that boundary maintenance is a key component of abeyance structures and movement continuity. To illustrate boundary framing, leaders of the Nichiren Shoshu Buddhist movement would constantly make "us" and "them" kinds of distinctions. As explained in one editorial in the movement's newspaper, "No matter how prosperous some people may appear or how peaceful their family and personal life may be, it is like a fantasy that can disappear without even a trace remaining behind. As cold as it sounds, that is a fact of life without faith in the Gohonzon (the all-powerful scroll to which members chant)." Similarly, another leader's editorial explained, when referring to the rich, that, "they are lucky and live affluently, seeming unburdened by problems, but these are only superficial appearances. . . . Fortune is not only financial wealth, but most important, it is a wealth of true happiness gained only from the consistent practice of true Buddhism (the movement's brand of Buddhism)." In these and other such instances, members are continuously reminded of the myriad ways in which they differ from nonmembers, thus constituting and affirming simultaneously the markers bounding adherents from others.

The need for and reference to boundary markers is also a common feature of the other movements we studied. In the case of Nebraskans for Peace (NFP), for instance, a nineteen-year-old male Youth for Peace leader in Omaha relied on a boundary frame to explain his organization's decision to engage in guerrilla theater tactics at a planned demonstration at U.S. Air Force Strategic Air Command's (SAC) headquarters in Bellevue, Nebraska.

> There's a real need for our group here. We fill a much needed niche I think. We can go to SAC and burn a SAC flag to show in a powerful symbolic way what we think of their so-called peace mission. Whoever does that will probably get arrested. So what? What have any of us got to lose? Other groups around here, I won't mention any names, just can't do that kind of stuff. They're just too hooked into the system with jobs, reputations, and B.S. like that.

This statement articulates a boundary frame; it draws a distinction between Youth for Peace as a group that can make unadulterated political statements because its members have not gotten "hooked into the system" and other SMOs that take fewer "risks" because their members are part of "the system." Such boundary framing differentiates between the "truly committed" and those unwilling or unable to make personal sacrifices for the cause.

Boundary frames do not emerge ex nihilo, however. Rather, such framings are conditioned and constrained by SMO actors' interpretations of world, local, movement, and organizational histories. Indeed, a central feature of much diagnostic, prognostic, and motivational framing is the embellishment and reconstitution of relevant aspects of the past. For example, Nichiren Shoshu, not unlike most religious movements, claims that its mission was both preordained and divinely given. As one rank-and-file member, parroting movement leaders and literature, explained: "There is a whole history and theory going back 3000 years that points to Nichiren Shoshu as both the orthodox practice of Buddhism and the correct philosophy and practice for this time period [referring to the present]." This and other comparable statements suggest that Nichiren Shoshu sees itself not as some fly-by-night fad or cult but as contributing, instead, to the realization of a kind of cosmic plan that was divinely prophesized years ago. Not only do such claims situate and justify the movement historically, but they also proffer and affirm identities that confer special status on adherents.

While the link to some grand prophesy or moment in the past may be particularly characteristic of religious movements, such framings are also evident in more secular, political movements. During the 1991 Persian Gulf War, for example, a male NFP leader attempted, at a quarterly board meeting, to inspire and justify current action in terms of past organizational linkages and campaigns. "For many people out there, NFP, if it's anything at all, is an anti-war organization. For them, NFP from the beginning was anti-war, against the War in Vietnam. We really need to remember that. We need to be there now for them again. So what I'm saying is we need to really take the lead and make it clear we're still anti-war."

The foregoing suggests that framings that mark and bound a movement and its activities in space and time are central to the construction and maintenance of SMO actors' collective and personal identities. This process can be seen even more clearly when we consider the avowal or imputation of aspects of consciousness and/or character. As noted earlier, consciousness claims attribute an "awareness" and also specify those things collectivities and individuals possess awareness about. To illustrate, in the fall of 1990, NFP staff met to decide what the organization's response should be to the U.S. military buildup in Saudi Arabia. After the meeting, one of the staffers explained:

> This has caught us off-guard, completely off-guard. We knew about the Iran-Iraq war, we knew about Iraq's use of chemical weapons, but we really don't know much about that region, really. All the centuries of conflicts, religious tensions, political tensions, we only know the surface of these things. We know enough to know we don't know enough. We don't know enough to make dependable statements on the issue as an organization. We don't even know enough how to act in the best ways to promote peace. We just have a sort of knee-jerk response. Our military's involved so we must be against it. Before we can take definitive action we need to educate ourselves.

As a result of this meeting, NFP at the state, regional, and chapter levels began a series of forums on the Persian Gulf and the Middle East, relying on knowledgeable members and outside organizations, such as the American Friends Service Committee, to provide lectures and educational materials. The NFP staffer's response above suggests that the organization needed to have greater awareness of the history in the region. In other words, NFPers recognized the importance of consciousness expansion with respect to the issue, thus suggesting a collective identity that included an awareness of ignorance. Notice how this consciousness framing led to a preliminary prognostic frame. To overcome the organization's ignorance, NFPers called for educational forums. Before further diagnostic, prognostic, and motivational framings could take place, NFP needed to be educated, to have its consciousness enhanced.

In addition to consciousness claims, SMO actors attribute character to individuals and collectivities in protagonist identity fields. In doing this, movement participants interpret individual and collective actions as manifestations of particular cognitive or strategic, affective, and moral dispositions and propensities. SMO members typically point to their framings as "evidence" of their individual or collective characters. Similarly, SMO actors usually do not want to frame situations in ways that might be perceived as incompatible with individual and collective character avowals. The complex relationship between frames and character attribution is exemplified in the following field notes excerpt from the NFP study (Hunt 1991). During an informal conversation, a state-level NFP leader discussed the organization's position on the Israeli and Palestinian conflict.

> There's been atrocities on both sides. I have good friends in NFP on both sides of the issue. People passionately committed to their convictions. All of them are good people. People who are committed to fairness and justice. If we took a stance on this as an organization we'd in effect just be asking some members to leave. We know this wouldn't make sense. We have more in common then we have differences. There's so much work we can do together here in Nebraska and there's so few people working on issues of peace and justice here. To do something that would knowingly reduce our numbers would be damn foolish. So NFP as an organization takes no stand on the issue. We agree to disagree among ourselves and not to take a public stance. . . . I don't think this is a prostitution of our commitment to peace. I think it's just a practical response to a difficult situation. I think this stance of no stance speaks to our commitment to encourage diversity of opinion within our organization.

Several character attributions are made here at both the individual and organizational levels. Individuals (within NFP) "on both sides of the issue" were imputed to be "passionate" and "good people" "committed to fairness and justice." Similarly, NFP's decision to not offer a public framing regarding this issue was characterized as "practical" and ostensibly predicated on NFP's commitment to the tolerance of "diversity." Such post hoc avowals of motive or framings and reframings serve to foster a sense of shared identity among NFP protagonists.

Antagonist Identity Fields

Antagonist identity fields are constellations of identity attributions about individuals and collectivities imputed to be opponents of movement causes. These include claims about countermovements, countermovement organizations, hostile institutions, inimical publics, and social control agents. Additionally, numerous personal identity typifications are socially constructed and imputed for specific villains, oppositional leaders, rank-and-file opponents, and star adversaries. Collective and personal identity attributions are also made about antagonists' constituents such as "big business," "closet bigots," "cultural elites," and a host of others imputed to be secret supporters or "conspirators" of "liberal," "conservative," or "radical" causes.

SMO actors use a variety of frames and framing processes in making identity claims about antagonists. The most obvious way SMO participants impute antagonist identities is by identifying and defining individuals, collectivities, beliefs, values, and practices as being in conflict with protagonist identities and causes (Benford and Hunt 1992; Morris 1992). Such framing fosters the imputation of personal and collective identities, consisting of consciousness and character attributions.

To illustrate, from its inception in 1977, Mobilization for Survival (MFS) blamed a host of social problems—environmental degradation, third world poverty, the threat of nuclear Armageddon—on "unscrupulous capitalists." One MFS brochure asserted, for instance, that the U.S. projection of military might has been at the behest of U.S.-based multinational corporations. "Since World War II, American foreign policy has revolved around developing its sphere of influence and maintaining an environment conducive to investment for American corporations. The central focus has been in the underdeveloped—or Third World—countries. Third World nations provide natural resources, cheap, non-unionized labor, and easy markets for large multinational corporations." Following MFS's lead, activists of the Texas Mobilization for Survival (TM) and University Mobilization for Survival (UM) harped on the same themes: "When Ronald Reagan talks about 'national defense,' he is really talking about defending profits," a TM activist contended before a campus audience. Similarly, at an anti–draft registration rally, a UM leader asked rhetorically, "Do you wanna die and possibly precipitate nuclear war to protect the interests of multinational corporations?"

We suggest that such diagnostic framings not only serve the obvious function of attributing blame, they also facilitate the construction of both protagonist and antagonist identity fields. By specifying who is responsible for particular social ills, movement actors make implicit character claims about themselves, their organization, and others. For example, they, unlike their "immoral opponents," are not willing to tolerate injustice, human suffering, and the like.

Antagonist identity constructions are also important because they guide SMO actors' deliberations about an opponent's vulnerabilities and strengths and are therefore key in planning strategies and tactics. To illustrate, prior to national discussions in early 1990 of a peace dividend derived from the thawing of the cold war, NFP had devised a petition campaign modeled after the Freeze initiative to persuade Nebraska senator James J. Exon to vote for reductions in defense spending. An NFP staffer explained the development of this particular tactic:

> Exon, Mr. SAC, has not had an outstanding voting record on peace issues. But we figured he'd go for modest reductions in defense spending. . . . Why? Because of currents in the Democratic Party, because calls for reductions in defense spending by the Democrats will be used to discredit the Republicans by linking them to Reagan's outrageous increases in defense spending which was a big contributor to our current budget problems. We felt Exon would follow party line. . . . We've tried to guess what level of cuts Exon would support and use figures slightly above that as a basis for our "modest proposal" petition drive. The plan was to then present Exon with large numbers of signatures and organizational endorsements to apply some pressure on him to make sure he carries through with reductions.

This account of tactical development illustrates several aspects of oppositional identity framing. An antagonist identity field is referred to by equating Senator Exon with SAC. Alluding to a less than "outstanding voting record on peace issues" is an oppositional framing that portrays the senator's actions as being in conflict with peace movement goals. These claims also impute a particular identity to the senator, one that depicts him as a proponent of military spending but a loyal Democrat. The antagonist identity frame shaped NFP's "modest proposal" campaign.

Audience Identity Fields

Audience identity fields are constellations of identity attributions about individuals and collectivities imputed to be neutral or uncommitted observers who may react to or report on movement activities. For example, allied SMOs, the media, powerful elites, marginal supporters, sympathizers, and bystander publics can be the subjects of audience identity claims. A common characteristic of all imputed audience identities is that they are capable of receiving and evaluating protagonist messages in a favorable light. The construction of audience identities involves audience framing, defined as the imputation of observer role to individuals and collectivities. To illustrate, explaining her involvement in a Omaha coalition against racism, an NFPer discussed a need for the organization to link peace politics to struggles against racial prejudice and discrimination. "African Americans understand injustice. They have experienced first hand the inequalities brought about by the system. We [NFP] need to work against racism and make connections between militarism, economic injustice, and racism." The audience framing in this example imputes a consciousness of "injustice" to African Americans. This claim implies that such a consciousness makes African Americans a potential audience for traditional peace movement concerns about militarism. Moreover, the claim advanced here suggests that African Americans would be a receptive and supportive audience because they understand that inequalities are not mere misfortunes but manifestations of an extant social system. In other words, African Americans are imputed to be potential mobilization targets because they share a general diagnostic frame with NFP.

Audience framing is particularly important because SMO actors use these frames to determine what kinds of other frames will resonate, what kinds of "evidence" need to be marshaled to support movement claims, and how audiences' cultural symbols and narratives can be used in advancing movement claims (Snow and Benford 1988). Imputed audience identities influence the development of particular strategies and tactics. In a formal interview, an NFP male explained the organization's approach to communicating with elected officials.

> You have got to talk their [elected officials'] language. You can't tell them we should do x because x is the right thing to do. X is the right thing to do but they won't listen to that. You have to go in there and give them figures and statistics that support your position. And, when dealing with politicians, you have to show them the bottom line. You have to talk policies and programs in terms of dollars or they just won't listen.

In this case, it is imputed that quantitative data and financial expediency resonate with elected officials. Based on this understanding of politician identities, NFP's arguments were often carefully made with "figures and statistics," typically translated into "bottom-line" dollars.

Framing Outsiders' Identity Imputations

In the course of attributing identities to the relevant sets of actors within their environment, SMO actors are also confronted with interpreting outsiders' claims about them or other allied individual or group protagonist identities. There are at least four ways in which outsiders' identity imputations are responded to and framed. One way is to interpret imputations as incorrect. This kind of framing, or "keying" in Goffman's terminology (1974, 43–45), was clearly evidenced during the 1991 Persian Gulf War. Upon reading a letter to the editor in the *Omaha World Herald*, an NFP female commented:

> This letter says that those demonstrating for peace are unpatriotic. It says we should be grateful that men were willing to die to guarantee our rights of free speech. It suggests that since we protest for peace, we aren't grateful and we shouldn't be allowed to exercise our right of free speech that those men died for. Make sense to you? Even though this idea of patriotism has some limits, we are patriotic. We love our country and want it to do the right thing. I can't think of anything more patriotic than taking a despised position and making your voice heard so that your country will do the right thing.

The imputed identity of "unpatriotic" group was framed as an incorrect assessment. Indeed, this person reframed the meaning of the outsider's conception of patriotism to underscore the virtuous, principled character of NFP.

A second way to frame outsiders' identity imputations is to view them as a reinforcement of identity avowals. By this we refer to SMO actors' interpretations that external imputations are accurate positive portrayals of collective and individual protagonist identities. The following discussion of a charismatic NFP leader in Scottsbluff exemplifies this kind of framing.

> The *Star Herald* did a series, I think it was called community leadership series, and X was chosen of 1 of 20 people as community leaders. And I think that that's remarkable because he has only been

> here 5 or 6 years. He has touched that many people to have himself
> in that kind of a position. That is really really remarkable. And X
> is a perfect manifestation of all our best energy, our best selves. He
> says what we would all say if we had those words, you know?

Claiming that the NFP leader is a personification of the organization—he "is a perfect manifestation of all our best energy, our
best selves"—this NFPer frames the *Star Herald* personal identity
imputation as a reinforcement of the Scottsbluff chapter's collective identity.

A third way of framing outsiders' identity imputations is to
interpret them as misunderstandings based on flawed impression
management by the SMO and its adherents. In another words, the
imputed identities are not due so much to a faulty reading of the
movement but to adherent behavior that lends itself to such a
reading and is therefore indicative of poor impression management. The resulting framing thus defines outsiders' imputations
as reflections of image problems and, in turn, specifies corrective
action to remedy the flawed image. Snow's (1979) discussion of
building idiosyncratic credit as an impression management strategy speaks to this issue. His examination of Nichiren Shoshu
revealed that the movement's leadership was particularly sensitive
to its public image, as reflected in the comments of a leader at a
movement meeting. "The point to keep in mind is that many nonmembers judge NSA by the way each member presents himself.
If any one of us conducts himself in an obnoxious and disrespectful
manner, all who come in contact with us are going to think everyone in NSA is like that one person. We should therefore be aware
of how we look and sound to the general public and make a
good impression." Snow also found that the movement countered
outsiders' claims about the organization's "deviant" qualities by
pursuing public activities that would alter the group's public identity. Such activities are constitutive of attempts to build idiosyncrasy credit and thereby secure a more respectable identity in the
public's eye. Idiosyncratic credit accentuates "positive" character
attributes and thus can be understood as a frame amplification.

Finally, a fourth way to frame outsiders' identity imputations
is to perceive the characterizations as accurate depictions of "actual" flawed identities. Such framings revolve around SMO actors'
interpretations that outsiders' negative identity imputations are
accurate accounts of serious identity defects. This kind of framing

usually calls for radical identity or frame transformations. In the NFP study, this kind of response to outsiders' imputations was never widely shared. However, one member's dissatisfaction with NFP's support of the blockade of Iraq prior to the 1991 Persian Gulf War illustrates this framing process. "I know other groups around here must be surprised at our support for the [blockade]. I know I am. By international law [the blockade] is an act of war and NFP is supporting it. Unbelievable, just unbelievable. We're not Nebraskans for Peace, we're Nebraskans for a Little War." While this member continued to take an active part in NFP, his interpretation suggests that the group's support of the blockade represented a serious identity flaw that was reflected in his tongue-in-cheek renaming of the organization.

Conclusion

In this chapter we have attempted to link framing and identity construction processes. Both have received increasing attention in recent years by social movement scholars, but discussion and research has proceeded as if these processes referred to different orders of phenomena and therefore were essentially unrelated. Clearly that is not the case. As our observations suggest, framing and identity construction processes are interconnected in a dynamic, almost recursive fashion. The linkages between framing and identity construction processes direct attention to SMO actors' efforts to interpret and operate within collective action arenas. Making sense of collective action arenas entails framing situations and attributing identities to individuals and collectivities. We have suggested that identity attributions are claims about consciousness and character that cluster around protagonist, antagonist, and audience identity fields. Further, diagnostic, prognostic, motivational, boundary, history, oppositional, and audience framing tasks as well as frame alignment processes are central in attributing identities and communicating relationships between and among identity fields.

Moreover, our discussion has suggested how framing and identity construction processes condition micro and mesomobilization activities. For movement participants, frames and identities are part of an obdurate "reality" that conditions, constrains, and enables collective action (see Blumer 1969). That is, SMO actors follow certain lines of collective action rather than others based, in part, on their perceptions of the parameters implied by particular framing and identity constructions. Although we understand framing and identity construction as emergent processes, our approach does not assume that SMO actors operate in a vacuum. Indeed, as our observations show, key factors and events occur that are beyond the control of SMO actors (for example, the 1991 Persian Gulf War). History, social structures, and cultural arrangements constrain SMO actors' interpretive work. How these "realities" condition interpretive work, however, depends on how SMO actors' perceive history, social structures, and cultural arrangements. Particular lines of collective action emerge or fail to emerge not because objective conditions allow or prohibit them, but rather because SMO actors perceive "objective" conditions as allowing or prohibiting them. In short, to understand the emergence of particular expressions of collective action, analysts need to attend to SMO actors' intersubjective definitions of "reality." Identifying and elaborating the relationships between and among framing and identity construction processes promises to make advances along these lines.

Acknowledgments: Earlier versions of this chapter were presented at the annual meetings of the Midwest Sociological Society, Chicago, April 1993, and the International Institute of Sociology, Paris, June 1993. We are grateful to Hank Johnston and Enrique Laraña for their insightful comments on previous versions.

References

Benford, Robert D. 1984. "The Interorganizational Dynamics of the Austin Peace Movement." Master's thesis, University of Texas.

———. 1987. "Framing Activity, Meaning, and Social Movement Participation: The Nuclear Disarmament Movement." Ph.D. diss., University of Texas.

———. 1993a. "Frame Disputes within the Nuclear Disarmament Movement." *Social Forces* 71:677–70.

———. 1993b. " 'You Could Be the Hundredth Monkey': Collective Action Frames and Vocabularies of Motive within the Nuclear Disarmament Movement." *Sociological Quarterly* 34:195–216.

Benford, Robert D., and Scott A. Hunt. 1992. "Dramaturgy and Social Movements: The Social Construction and Communication of Power." *Sociological Inquiry* 62:36–55.

Benford, Robert D., and Louis A. Zurcher. 1990. "Instrumental and Symbolic Competition among Peace Movement Organizations." In *Peace Action in the Eighties: Social Science Perspectives*, edited by Sam Marullo and John Lofland, pp. 125–39. New Brunswick, N.J.: Rutgers University Press.

Blumer, Herbert. 1939. "Collective Behavior." In *An Outline of the Principles of Sociology*, edited by Robert E. Park, pp. 221–80. New York: Barnes and Noble.

———. 1969. *Symbolic Interactionism*. Englewood Cliffs, N.J.: Transaction Books.

Cohen, Jean L. 1985. "Strategy or Identity: New Theoretical Paradigms and Contemporary Social Movements." *Social Research* 52:663–716.

Dalton, Russell J., and Manfred Kuechler, eds. 1990. *Challenging the Political Order: New Social and Political Movements in Western Democracies*. New York: Oxford University Press.

Davies, James Chowning. 1979. "The J-Curve of Rising and Declining Satisfactions as a Cause of Rebellion and Revolution." In *Violence in America: Historical and Comparative Perspectives*, edited by Hugh Davis Graham and Ted Robert Gurr, pp. 415–36. Washington, D.C.: U.S. Government Printing Office.

Downey, Gary L. 1986. "Ideology and the Clamshell Identity: Organizational Dilemmas in the Anti-Nuclear Power Movement." *Social Problems* 33:357–73.

Epstein, Steven. 1987. "Gay Politics, Ethnic Identity: The Limits of Social Constructionism." *Socialist Review* 17:9–54.

Freud, Sigmund. 1922. *Group Psychology and the Analysis of the Ego*. Translated by James Strachey. London: Hogarth Press.

Friedman, Debra, and Doug McAdam. 1992. "Collective Identity and Activism: Networks, Choices, and the Life of a Social Movement." In *Frontiers in Social Movement Theory*, edited by Aldon D. Morris and Carol McClurg Mueller, pp. 156–73. New Haven: Yale University Press.

Gamson, Josh. 1989. "Silence, Death, and the Invisible Enemy: AIDS Activism and Social Movement 'Newness.' " *Social Problems* 36:351–67.

Gamson, William A. 1990. *The Strategy of Social Protest*. Belmont, Calif.: Wadsworth.

———. 1992. "The Social Psychology of Collective Action." In *Frontiers in Social Movement Theory*, edited by Aldon D. Morris and Carol McClurg Mueller, pp. 53–76. New Haven: Yale University Press.

Gamson, William A., Bruce Fireman, and Steven Rytina. 1982. *Encounters with Unjust Authority*. Homewood, Ill.: Dorsey.

Gerhards, Jürgen, and Dieter Rucht. 1992. "Mesomobilization: Organizing and Framing in Two Protest Campaigns in West Germany." *American Journal of Sociology* 98:555–95.

Gerson, Judith M., and Kathy Peiss. 1985. "Boundaries, Negotiation, Consciousness: Reconceptualizing Gender Relations." *Social Problems* 32:317–31.

Goffman, Erving. 1974. *Frame Analysis: An Essay on the Organization of Experience*. Boston: Northeastern University Press.

Habermas, Jürgen. 1984. *Reason and the Rationalization of Society*. Vol. 1 of *The Theory of Communicative Action*. Boston: Beacon Press.

———. 1987. *Lifeworld and System: A Critique of Functionalist Reason*. Vol. 2 of *The Theory of Communicative Action*. Boston: Beacon Press.

Hunt, Scott A. 1991. "Constructing Collective Identity in a Peace Movement Organization." Ph.D. diss., University of Nebraska.

———. 1992. "Social Movements and Collective Identity." Presented at the Annual Meetings of the Southern Sociological Society, New Orleans.

Hunt, Scott A., and Robert D. Benford. Forthcoming. "Identity Talk in the Peace and Justice Movement." *Journal of Contemporary Ethnography*.

Johnston, Hank. 1991. *Tales of Nationalism: Catalonia, 1939–1979*. New Brunswick, N.J.: Rutgers University Press.

Klapp, Orrin E. 1969. *Collective Search for Identity*. New York: Holt, Rinehart, and Winston.

Kriesi, Hanspeter. 1989. "New Social Movements and the New Class in the Netherlands." *American Journal of Sociology* 94:1078–1116.

LeBon, Gustave. 1960. *The Crowd: A Study of the Popular Mind*. New York: Viking.

McCall, George J., and J. L. Simmons. 1978. *Identities and Interactions*. New York: Free Press.

McCarthy, John D., and Mayer N. Zald. 1977. "Resource Mobilization and Social Movements: A Partial Theory." *American Journal of Sociology* 82:1212–41.

McDougall, William. 1928. *The Group Mind*. New York: G. P. Putnam's Sons.

Mackay, Charles. 1932. *Extraordinary Delusions and the Madness of Crowds*. Boston: L. C. Page.

Margolis, Diane Rothbard. 1985. "Redefining the Situation: Negotiations on the Meaning of 'Woman'." *Social Problems* 32:332–47.

Marshall, Barbara L. 1991. "Re-Producing the Gendered Subject." *Current Perspectives in Social Theory* 11:169–95.

Melucci, Alberto. 1989. *Nomads of the Present: Social Movements and Individual Needs in Contemporary Society*. Philadelphia: Temple University Press.

Mills, C. Wright. 1940. "Situated Actions and Vocabularies of Motive." *American Sociological Review* 5:404–13.

Morris, Aldon D. 1992. "Political Consciousness and Collective Action." In *Frontiers in Social Movement Theory*, edited by Aldon D. Morris and Carol McClurg Mueller, pp. 351–73. New Haven: Yale University Press.

Moscovici, Serge. 1985. *The Age of the Crowd: A Historical Treatise on Mass Psychology*. Cambridge: Cambridge University Press.

Nagel, Joane. 1986. "The Political Construction of Ethnicity." In *Competitive Ethnic Relations*, edited by Susan Olzak and Joane Nagel, pp. 93–111. Orlando, Fla.: Academic Press.

Olzak, Susan. 1983. "Contemporary Ethnic Mobilization." *Annual Review of Sociology* 9:355–74.

Pizzorno, Alessandro. 1978. "Political Exchange and Collective Identity in Industrial Conflict." In *The Resurgence of Class Conflict in Western Europe since 1968*, edited by Colin Crouch and Alessandro Pizzorno, 2:277–98. New York: Holmes and Meier.

Ponse, Barbara. 1978. *Identities in the Lesbian World: The Social Construction of Self*. Westport, Conn.: Greenwood Press.

Shibutani, Tamotsu. 1970. "On the Personification of Adversaries." In *Human Nature and Collective Behavior: Papers in Honor of Herbert Blumer*, edited by Tamotsu Shibutani, pp. 223–33. Englewood Cliffs, N.J.: Prentice-Hall.

Smith, Dorothy E. 1990. *The Conceptual Practices of Power: A Feminist Sociology of Knowledge*. Boston: Northeastern University Press.

Snow, David A. 1979. "A Dramaturgical Analysis of Movement Accommodation: Building Idiosyncrasy Credit as a Movement Mobilization Strategy." *Symbolic Interaction* 2:23–44.

———. 1993. *Shakubuku: Study of the Nichiren Shoshu Buddhist Movement in America, 1960–1975*. New York: Garland.

Snow, David A., and Leon Anderson. 1987. "Identity Work among the Homeless: The Verbal Construction and Avowal of Personal Identities." *American Journal of Sociology* 92:1336–71.

Snow, David A., and Robert D. Benford. 1988. "Ideology, Frame Resonance, and Participant Mobilization." In *From Structure to Action,* edited by Bert Klandermans, Hanspeter Kriesi, and Sidney Tarrow. Vol. 1 of *International Social Movement Research*. Greenwich, Conn.: JAI Press.

———. 1992. "Master Frames and Cycles of Protest." In *Frontiers in Social Movement Theory,* edited by Aldon D. Morris and Carol McClurg Mueller, pp. 133–55. New Haven: Yale University Press.

Snow, David A., and Richard Machalek. 1984. "The Sociology of Conversion." *Annual Review of Sociology* 10:367–80.

Snow, David A., E. Burke Rochford, Jr., Steven K. Worden, and Robert D. Benford. 1986. "Frame Alignment Processes, Micromobilization, and Movement Participation." *American Sociological Review* 51:464–81.

Stone, Gregory P. 1962. "Appearance and the Self." In *Human Behavior and Social Processes*, edited by Arnold M. Rose, pp. 86–118. Boston: Houghton Mifflin.

Tarrow, Sidney. 1992. "Mentalities, Political Cultures, and Collective Action Frames: Constructing Meanings through Action." In *Frontiers in Social Movement Theory*, edited by Aldon D. Morris and Carol McClurg Mueller, pp. 174–202. New Haven: Yale University Press.

Taylor, Verta. 1989. "Social Movement Continuity: The Women's Movement in Abeyance." *American Sociological Review* 54:761–75.

Taylor, Verta, and Nancy E. Whittier. 1992. "Collective Identity in Social Movement Communities: Lesbian Feminist Mobilization." In *Frontiers in Social Movement Theory*, edited by Aldon D. Morris and Carol McClurg Mueller, pp. 104–29. New Haven: Yale University Press.

Trotter, Wilfred. 1919. *Instincts of the Herd in Peace and War: 1916–1919*. London: Oxford University Press.

Turner, Ralph H., and Lewis M. Killian. 1987. *Collective Behavior*. 3d ed. Englewood Cliffs, N.J.: Prentice-Hall.

Weber, Max. 1978. *Economy and Society: An Outline of Interpretive Sociology*. Edited by Guenther Roth and Claus Wittich. 2 vols. Berkeley: University of California Press.

West, Candace, and Don H. Zimmerman. 1987. "Doing Gender." *Gender and Society* 1:125–51.

Wilson, Kenneth L., and Louis A. Zurcher. 1976. "Status Inconsistency and Participation in Social Movements: An Application of Goodman's Hierarchical Modeling." *Sociological Quarterly* 17:520–33.

Zurcher, Louis A., and David A. Snow. 1981. "Collective Behavior: Social Movements." In *Social Psychology: Sociological Perspectives*, edited by Morris Rosenberg and Ralph H. Turner, pp. 447–82. New York: Basic Books.

Chapter 9

Continuity and Unity in New Forms of Collective Action: A Comparative Analysis of Student Movements

Enrique Laraña

This chapter reviews an old and central issue in social movements research that focuses on their origins and evolution in order to understand the reasons for their emergence, the events and organizations that made them possible, their resulting processes, and their permanence and impact in society. This also was the object of my first empirical research on the Free Speech Movement (FSM) at the University of California, Berkeley (Laraña 1975). My goal was to explore the discontinuity of the student movement of that campus, one of the centers of student activism in the second half of the 1960s, ten years after the FSM. The same topic underlies my study of the student mobilizations that took place in Spain during 1986 and 1987. This nationwide movement acquired remarkable strength and played a role in one of the major conflicts of the decade. It emerged from "nowhere," without any historical or organizational antecedents and in an educational sector different from the student mobilizations of the 1960s. Student demands focused on the system that regulates the access to college education in Spain. The movement challenged the entrance exams that the Department of Education requires of all applicants to a public university. The relevance of this conflict for the analysis of contemporary social movements relates not only to its contribution to the knowledge of their emergence but also to the complexity of its constituency (high school students who acted independently from political parties), and the peculiar relationship they established with another section of the movement, integrated by university students.

In spite of those features, this movement presents some characteristics similar to other student movements that emerged in different social contexts and decades. I draw a comparative analysis below. Two premises of this chapter are that contemporary social movements in complex societies can be better understood through cross-cultural analysis, and that the concept of "new social movements" is useful for the interpretation of current forms of collective action in complex societies that cannot be explained by classical perspectives. Although I am aware of the debate about the validity of this concept (Tarrow 1989; Taylor 1989; Melucci 1989; see also Chapter 5), I use this term as a means to develop analytical tools to interpret contemporary social movements and as a relative concept that stems from comparisons with the forms of class conflict that were prevalent in European industrial societies. I draw two ideas from one of its founders, Alberto Melucci (1989). First, the novelty of these movements refers to morphological changes in their structure and action as well as in the social context in which they arise. Second, in order to avoid an epistemological problem intrinsic to the growing popularization of the term—its ontologization as an abstract generalization that prevents deeper analysis—research should focus on the distinctive features and the specific elements of contemporary movements. Research should stress what is new and its social implications.

Although the origins of this approach have been located in European scholarship (Melucci 1980, 1985, 1989; Klandermans and Tarrow 1988; Offe 1985, 1988; Dalton and Kuelchner 1992), important contributions came from such American sociologists as Ralph Turner (1969, see also Chapter 4) and Jean Cohen (1985). As this approach emphasizes the role of ideas and cultural processes in the emergence of contemporary movements, the contribution of frame analysis (Snow et al. 1986; Snow and Benford 1988, 1992; see also Hunt, Benford, and Snow, Chapter 8) enhances the bridge between the American and European traditions in this field. This bridge takes the form of a tendency toward synthesis manifest in the growing interest in research on identity by American scholars and an increasing interest in frame analysis by their European counterparts (Stompka 1992; Mueller 1993; Ibarra and Rivas 1993; Laraña 1993b, 1993c; see also Hunt, Benford, and Snow, Chapter 8).

The Issue of Continuity in Social Movements

In this chapter, I review some assumptions from collective behavior theory about continuities that contrast with my research on student movements; then I focus on some insights from the new social movements (NSM) approach that help to interpret that research and document the need to revise classical assumptions on continuity and unity of social movements. I analyze the relationship between both aspects in the last section of this chapter.

The NSM and resource mobilization approaches must address several problems of interpretation that are related to their emphasis on the external, structural factors of movements' emergence and their tendency to neglect cognitive and ideological factors (Snow and Benford 1988; see also McAdam, Chapter 2). I argue that these factors are crucial for the analysis of the formation and decline of contemporary movements. These factors are difficult to investigate using conventional research methods that try to get "hard data." I also argue that the traditions of ethnomethodology and cognitive sociology contain key insights for research on cultural factors. They may enable analysts to grasp a movement's symbolic functions, as well as to understand interaction as a source of collective beliefs. These symbolic functions, or "dimensions," consist of the ways by which movements achieve or construct their identities: new codes of interpretation and interpersonal relations. I also refer to the "ethnography of speaking" approach that focuses on the actors' discourse and pays special attention to its social context (Cicourel 1964, 1980, 1982; Briggs 1986; Johnston 1991). The integration of this approach within the field of social movements closes the distance between the macrosociological discourse prevailing in this field and the microsociological analysis that is needed for a better understanding of social movements and their identity dimensions. A step forward in that direction is the growing use of the term "micromobilization" in the literature on social movements since the late 1980s.

A similar process of integration is already taking place in social movement theory through the diffusion of frame analysis; this integration clarifies the process by which the value orientations of the individual become linked to those of the social movement organization (SMO) (Goffman 1974; Snow et al. 1986; Snow and Benford 1988). The integration of these approaches enables the analyst to ground useful macrosociological assumptions about NSMs in cultural analysis of participation through the observations of everyday interaction in social movements (Johnston 1991, 1992).

The collective behavior perspective considers the existence of organizational and temporal continuities as a defining characteristic of social movements. A social movement is "a collectivity acting with certain continuity to promote or resist changes in the society or in the group it is part of" (Turner and Killian 1987, 222). Continuity refers to the activities as a social movement develops to achieve its goals and lies in strategy and organization, in leadership and role structure, and in collective identity. The amount of time necessary to consider a collective mobilization as a social movement seems to depend on variable and common-sense criteria, which exclude such events as an organized demonstration that lasts a few hours or a three-week occupation of a building. A special collective dimension and continuity over time are considered intrinsic attributes of these phenomena that allow us to distinguish them from other forms of collective action such as migrations, strikes, or protest demonstrations (Gusfield 1970). Although both are collective events, protest demonstrations are spontaneous and ephemeral, and migrations lack a symbolic element that provides actors with a certain homogeneity in values and beliefs. This unifying component is expressed not only in a movement's orientation toward goals but also in its coercive capacity over individual behavior (Durkheim 1978).

Some conceptual problems arise if we apply those criteria to the investigation of student mobilizations in complex societies. Those taking place during the 1960s were categorized as "rebellions," "revolts," and "uprisings" in order to highlight their spontaneous and unpredictable nature. These terms accentuate difficulties in establishing continuities among them and in conceptualizing them as social movements (Draper 1965; Lipset 1965; Wollin and Schaar 1970). Two decades later (1986–1987) "mobilization" was the most common term used by the Spanish media to refer to protests against the official educational policy. The meaning of the later term enhances the idea of their spontaneous and unpredictable character, as well as the perception of them as more normal or everyday phenomena. However, the student movements of the 1960s were the first cases of new social movements and had crucial implications not only for the theories of collective action but also for sociological theory because they contributed to the questioning of Marxist and functionalist theories of order and conflict (Flacks 1967; Giddens 1979; Laraña 1982, 1993a). In the 1980s, important assumptions about collective action were revised in part because of the proliferation of new social movements in complex societies during the preceding three decades and the need to use more precise criteria in analysis. The current trend in sociology is to move from the construction of broad theories to detailed knowledge of the social mechanisms that lead to the emergence of collective phenomena (Elster 1989). This seems related to investigations that highlight the role of nonvisible networks, where movements "incubate" before they emerge into the public (McAdam 1988; Melucci 1989, see also Chapter 5; Johnston 1991, see also Chapter 11; Perez Agote 1987).[1]

In his well-documented study of student activism in Mississippi during the summer of 1964, McAdam (1988) locates the starting point of the 1960s student movements in this collective experience; it was the source of social relations between future leaders and activists as well as the source of feelings of solidarity and collective identity. McAdam credits white racial prejudice for the emergence of these movements on the white university campus and locates it in the main organizational structure of the civil rights movement, the Student Nonviolent Coordinating Committee (SNCC). His work shows the need to distinguish between the discovery of the movement by the mass media and its organizational and cultural origins (SNCC and the white students' program called Freedom Summer). McAdam asserts that an organization of black students gave way to the student movements of the 1960s; his research poses an important question about the emergence of social movements. Researchers distinguish between "latent" and visible phases in the formation of NSMs (Melucci 1989). That distinction makes problematic the issue of the origins of social movements as defined by conventional criteria in classical theories;[2] it shows the need to explore the social networks that exist before the public appearance of an NSM (McAdam 1988). The need to differentiate both phases of a contemporary social movement and the investigation of social networks in periods of "latency" becomes an essential tool in identifying continuities in collective action. The difficulties involved in studying student movements makes them a strategic platform for research on continuities because the very condition of being a student is transitory and because recent movement histories present important discontinuities.

Verta Taylor (1989) has researched the women's movement in the United States during a period of absence of mobilizations (1940–1960). She uses the notion of "abeyance structures" to explain sustained activism in nonreceptive political environments. This approach is a useful tool for explaining organizational and cultural aspects of movements. I use it to look at the student mobilizations at Berkeley. A current problem is that the professional interpretation of social movements usually focuses on the visible phases of social movements, neglecting the cycles of decline in activism (Taylor 1989; Melucci 1989). This emphasis led to a superimposition of the political over cultural meanings of a movement. This tendency is also manifest in the superimposition of the analyst's rational categories over those of the movement's actors, which I address in the following section. The "political-professional point of view" is the dominant view for describing social conflicts; it is spread by the mass media and is responsible for shaping the public image of movements (Baudrillard 1974). However, distinguishing between that image and the image the movement has for its members (or between the collective and the public identity) is an initial methodological premise for sociological research on new social movements.

McAdam argues (see Chapter 2) that the analysis of social networks has a tradition in the investigation of collective action since the 1970s in the United States. Unfortunately, it presents a "structural bias" because the analysis centers on the explanation of preexisting organizations and their resources. This bias is related both to the influence of approaches that focus on the visible aspects and political meanings of movements and to the lack of emphasis on their cognitive and symbolic elements. William Gamson (1988) considers this bias an important factor in the "underdevelopment" of research tools in this field.

My research on the continuity of student movements indicates that its existence cannot be an assumption prior to empirical investigation, nor can the researcher focus on organizational resources or determine continuity according to common-sense notions. Continuity is produced not only by the persistence over time of organizations but also through the endurance of some cultures that allow protest movements to reemerge (see McAdam, Chapter 2). Melucci's work (1989, 1990, see also Chapter 5) develops the theoretical relationship that exists between organizational and cognitive aspects of continuities in social movements, expanding the analysis by stressing the impact of changes in social movements in complex societies. He suggests that contemporary social movements are becoming centered in social networks that are established between persons and groups without public visibility in everyday life, and where their collective identity is produced (see also Mueller, Chapter 10). This is a helpful contribution to the knowledge of the sociocultural mechanisms that lead to the formation of collective action.[3] However, in this field we need more empirical, microsociological research documenting the emergent processes that occur in the daily life of the movements.

In the spring of 1974, student mobilizations emerged in order to protect a radical School of Criminology at the Berkeley campus of the University of California. They provide evidence of the relationship between latency and continuity of a social movement that was supposed to have disappeared at the beginning of the decade. At a period characterized by the absence of mobilizations, we witnessed large demonstrations and the occupation of two university buildings in response to the chancellor's decision to suppress the school. Student action was the result of daily work in nonvisible networks during the academic year. These networks created both the SMO and its alternative frame of reference.[4] This frame provided a radical interpretation of current political and university issues and was produced by several groups through weekly meetings and noncredited lectures by New Left intellectuals. They involved diverse topics, from the social sources of crime to the U.S. role in the world to the energy crisis. These student groups are also an example of the "abeyance structures" of the New Left that account for its continuity in the period of this movement's decline since 1969. In addition to this organizational continuity, the goal to "save the school" constitutes the movement's cultural counterpart because it corresponds to the demand for student control through participation in decision making in the university. These mobilizations documented how the nonvisible interaction within submerged networks produced new codes of interpretation as well as the social relations (Melucci 1989) that gave way to the mobilizations against institutional decisions.

The tendency of student movements toward discontinuity anticipates a frequent feature of new social movements that has been related to two factors: (1) the means by which personal identification among social actors emerges and the goals of the movement constantly change, and (2) the fact that their actors do not belong to a single social category, nor do they maintain the same attitudes for all their lives (Melucci 1989). I draw from Melucci the idea that the changes in contemporary movements demand the revision of traditional assumptions and research categories. The emphasis of more recent approaches on visible, structural, and organizational aspects might neglect research of earlier periods of developmental and cultural aspects of movement formation, which are crucial to our understanding of what has been going on in the social networks where movements are produced. Classical theories assume that continuity and unity are intimately related aspects of a social movement because the latter explains its persistence in time. Although the unity among the different elements of a movement is a puzzle to be solved, the tendency to presuppose unity as soon as a movement exists and to focus on external causes may have produced simplified interpretations.[5] In the following section I refer to an epistemological question that I consider related to these problems of interpretation, and which shows the need for an expansion of this field's boundaries.

Rational Assumptions in the Explanation of Collective Action

Since the mid 1980s, the growing interest in the symbolic and cognitive aspects of social movements has been developed within the perspective of symbolic interactionism through frame analysis. This tradition has provided a consistent analysis of the emergence of personal identity as a product of social interaction, which enables some of its authors to link frames and collective identity (see Hunt, Benford, and Snow, Chapter 8; and Johnston, Laraña, and Gusfield, Chapter 1). Both are essential concepts for the research developed from a social constructivist perspective that may overcome some of the problems of interpretation mentioned above. I suggest that a further step to understand the cognitive processes underlying social movement formation will come from the analysis of the discourse employed by movement actors. Although there is a rich material on the theoretical grounds and the methods of discourse analysis, it is hard to find studies using sociolinguistic techniques in this field.[6]

Discourse analysis is a fashionable concept in sociology today and it is employed from different perspectives, but the one I am referring to here places special emphasis in the context of speech and stems from ethnomethodology (Cicourel 1964, 1982). The points of convergence between ethnomethodology and social constructionism may be found in their conceptions about the nature of social movements and in the way to study them. They both consider social movements not as a "thing" or an integrated whole, nor the result of the characteristics of their social contexts, but as social processes that emerge and develop, though in periods with different degrees of visibility. We must investigate these processes in such a way that we can grasp the exchanges, negotiations, and conflicts going on inside them that generate collective definitions about limits and opportunities for action (Johnston, Laraña, and Gusfield, see Chapter 1). In order to study a movement's collective identity, and the webs of meaning where it develops, the analysis of the discourse used by actors to describe their experiences and motivations becomes a strategic tool that completes and enhances the qualitative methods traditionally used by symbolic interactionist scholars. A premise of the ethnography-of-speaking approach is that social discourse is always framed in a larger social context and its analysis provides substantive clues about the structure of the social interaction within the networks in which collective identity is constructed.

A central assumption of the ethnomethodology approach is that a social movement is not an object to be categorized by analysts' frameworks. Instead, it is a temporal event, a process self-ordered on the basis of the members' knowledge and know-how, a collective and gradual production not only of the actors but also of receivers and observers. Its organizational capacity lies in the ordinary practices of its members, and it reveals an internal order that provides identity and meaning for the participants (Quéré 1987). This element of internal rationality highlights the role of the human agency that tends to be neglected in structural approaches; this element originates in the "structures of meaning" that emerge in daily interactions (Cicourel 1964), within the social networks where collective action is built.

A problem for the interpretation of social movements lies in the tendency to explain them without exploring these cognitive structures and applying standard measures and patterns of rationality commonly used by scientific discourse. This problem is related to the goal of analysts to make social movements intelligible by using the prevalent categories in the rational explanations of the social order. Conformity with traditional norms is taken for granted, despite the fact that the will to transform some of these norms is often a central characteristic of social movements (Turner 1969; Gusfield 1970, 1973). This problem is also manifest in the tendency of "political-professional" perspectives to focus only on the visible aspects of mobilizations and their inability to perceive events from the actors' point of view. These perspectives are grounded in the social movements that emerged in European societies since the Industrial Revolution, whose main reference was the working-class movement (Melucci 1989). But the existence of continuities in the past does not prove their occurrence in the present, and assuming continuity might lead to interpretations that take for granted stability in the forms of collective action. When these forms change and continuity becomes more problematic, the search for the latter becomes a byproduct of the sociologist's rational expectations. This is related to the sociologist's traditional role as interpreter of collective phenomena, that is, one who must render them meaningful by showing the logical order underlying their apparent incoherence.[7] But from the ethnomethodological perspective, movements are neither organized structures arranged according to common scientific assumptions, nor are they the consequence of certain features of the social organization; instead, they constitute temporal social processes, self-generated on the basis of the daily practices of actors both among themselves and within the context (Quéré 1987).

Another problem in the study of social movements comes from taking for granted that social movements have an internal unity, which is manifested in the homogeneity of beliefs and values of actors, their consensus on demands, and the role of organizations where strategic decisions are made. This assumption was also present in the Marxist theory of ideology as a unifying force for the working-class movement (Turner and Killian 1987). Carol Mueller (1993) points out that modern perspectives have often ignored conflicts between the organizations and groups that constitute a movement. More recent research does not share the assumption of unity and stresses the relevance of internal conflict as an important factor in the emergence of, or a crisis in, a movement's collective identity (Melucci 1989; Mueller 1993; Laraña 1993a). The recent history of the women's movement in the United States provides very interesting information on the relationship between internal conflict and collective identity. This conflict has been related to the discriminatory practices toward women by their male colleagues in the New Left. Sara Evans (1980) provides an in-depth account of the impact that this conflict had in the development of a feminist identity and the radicalization of the younger branch of the women's movement (see also Mueller, Chapter 10).

In order to document this argument and my previous analysis, I now refer to the student mobilizations in Spain (1986–1987) and to the discontinuity of the student movement in the United States during the 1970s. These cases provide empirical information on the relationship between ideology and identity in a social movement, and they allow the study of the implications of the conflict between public and collective identities.

The Public and Collective Identities in the Movement against *Selectividad*

The mobilizations against *Selectividad*[8] were characterized by the heterogeneity of their demands, forms of action, and organizational structures, as well as the diversity of attitudes and ideas of the actors in high schools and universities. The first mobilizations in high schools provided the social base of the movement, and few university students supported them or were attracted to the events.[9] However, this was not only a "high school movement." An important role was performed by some college students in shaping the public image of the movement through the mass media. The organizational structures of the high school and university students were autonomous. The role of college students did not go beyond a representative function, nor did they provide the movement's master frame or its discourse.[10]

These mobilizations showed the strength of the media and the power of the public over the collective identity (see Johnston, Laraña, and Gusfield, Chapter 1). By shaping the movement's public image, university students fulfilled the role of "epistemological leaders" and spokesmen of a movement whose social base was not yet in the universities but was characterized by the expectation of entering them. This is one of the defining characteristics of this movement: its public image was produced by a politicized group of university students that had a different status than the movement's constituency, that did not adequately express the movement's motives or its demands, that did not use the same language, and that had a different ideology. My research shows a sharp contrast between the public image of the movement and the meaning it had for its participants. This contrast was manifest in the language, goals, and opinions of students in both sectors.

The peculiar division of labor among ages and social status in this movement created a double leadership: "de facto" and symbolic. While a group of university students played the role of spokesperson, high school leaders performed daily organizational activities with less notoriety and public visibility. This was not the only factor explaining the divergences between the way the movement was framed by public opinion and by high school supporters. The most widespread images showed the violence of students and depicted the movement as irrational and destructive,[11] but those images did not reflect the nature of the movement according to my data and direct observations. Although there were demonstrations of considerable violence (Gonzalez Blasco 1987), those actions came from small groups of ultra-rightist ideology and hooligans that were not representative of the movement.

If we draw from Max Weber's conception of social action as something that depends on the meanings individuals reciprocally attribute to it, the distance between the meanings this movement had for its actors and those assigned by the mass media illustrates the nature of the media and the stereotypes it tends to generate in public opinion. Although this distorting function has long been considered intrinsic to the intervention of the mass media (Baudrillard 1974), in this case it was exacerbated by the plurality of intervening elements in this conflict and by the delegation of the spokesman function to some university students. This case also highlights the complexity of contemporary movements and the need to analyze the divergences and conflicts among its constituent elements (Melucci 1989). In my view, the contrast between "identity confusion" and the collective identities of this student movement produced a "confusion" that was a decisive factor for its discontinuity in high schools three months later, together with the success it had through governmental acceptance of the need to change the exams of *Selectividad* and increase the educational budget. My analysis is based on data on the sharp differences in the discourse used by university and high school students, the negative conception of politics among the high school students and their reactions to the increasing politicization of the conflict, and the presence of trade union leaders in the demonstrations. A widespread feeling of being manipulated by political, nonstudent interests and organizations played an important role in the discontinuity of the movement, as did signs of good will toward some grievances by the Ministry of Education.

If we consider the strong differences in discourse, social positions, organizational structures, values, and goals of each sector, the questions are: Why did they ally? What factors made their collective action possible? These features might prevent treating those mobilizations as if their main actor were a single social movement.[12]

One of the problems in understanding the nature of current movements is that we tend to think in terms of old assumptions that may misguide the perception of those movements. In this sense, Melucci (1989) argues the need to abandon the conception of social movements as characters who play their roles on the stage of history, an idea inspired by the analogy between social life and dramatic representation. Movements were traditionally studied taking for granted that they constitute a "unified empirical datum," a homogeneous collective phenomenon that has its roots in the social conditions of the context where they arise. Environmentalist, peace, women's, and youth movements are thus vaguely described and often studied as if they were composed of individuals who share goals, values, meanings, and attitudes. However, the changes that are taking place in contemporary social movements demand abandoning this conception and approaching them as a system of action and social relations to be explored. Instead of assuming the existence of an external social dynamic, rooted in the mode of production or in the value system shared by members and promoting unity of action, Melucci proposes a different, social constructionist approach in which the causality of collective action is situated inside the movements and in their interaction with the environment. If the social movement does not constitute an entity whose elements are related by an external logic, the question is to know how and why they are united. Unity is not a prior condition to the existence of the movement but is the result of the negotiation, interaction, and conflict among different elements (Melucci 1989, 1990; see also Mueller, Chapter 10).

The case of student mobilizations mentioned above is better understood with the help of some concepts from frame analysis. "Frame bridging" refers to the process by which emerges "the linkage of two or more ideologically congruent but structurally unconnected frames on a particular issue" (Snow et al. 1986, 467). The mass media is a characteristic instrument for this reframing. The reasons for the "convergence in action" between the two sectors of this movement are found in the diffusion of a cognitive frame that provided a link between dissimilar goals and ideas in high school and university students that allowed them to overcome their differences. This ongoing cognitive process justifies the use of the term "movement" to refer to mobilizations in both sectors; it had its roots in the widespread unrest about the quality of public educational institutions and in the importance attributed to these institutions for future occupational opportunities. This unrest was the main motivational factor of the conflict. Its detonator was a diagnostic frame that had a high resonance in high schools and universities. In a country where 96 percent of all university students are registered in state educational institutions, the government was considered responsible for their low quality and for the arbitrary nature of the exams to enter them. The delegitimation of official authorities was grounded in the everyday life of students in those institutions. The emergence of the main grievance, the rejection of these exams, and the conviction about the need to act collectively was a result of framing processes similar to the ones that have characterized Catalan nationalism since the 1960s (Johnston 1991).[13]

Frame bridging took place through a cognitive relationship

between the issue of efficacy in educational institutions and the principles of social justice establishing equal opportunities for all citizens. Student mobilizations related to demands for more efficient educational institutions have been taking place in other Western countries as well (see Melucci, Chapter 5). But the difference with the ones analyzed here lies in a process of frame bridging and frame extension that produced the generalization of the movement throughout the country by linking the dissatisfaction with education, with its importance in contemporary societies, and with the sociopolitical implications of the selection system to enter universities. The rejection of this system became an issue of social justice that propelled the transformation of a specific demand—for more efficiency in the educational institutions—and a restricted frame into a broader one that had important political implications and generated widespread support in high schools, at some universities, and among parents of students.

This reframing process had a dual impact in the movement: Initially, it extended its social support, but later it become a factor of "identity confusion" (Erikson 1972) among high school adherents as a result of a conflict between the public and the collective identities. This process can be better understood through the concept of "frame extension," which refers to the expansion of the boundaries of the movement's primary framework "to incorporate interests and points of view that were incidental to its primary objectives, but of considerable salience for potential adherents" (Snow et al. 1986, 472). High school students were initially mobilized against what they perceived as a particular problem of efficiency in the selection system, that is, its arbitrary, lotterylike character that had dramatic consequences for those who were not selected. This sector's grievances did not oppose any selection exams per se, just the existing ones, whose nature was the object of daily experiences in the preparatory courses. However, the rejection of any required exams to enter institutions of higher learning became part of the movement's program and a defining characteristic of its public identity. This was a result of the role played by university spokespersons, who extended the movement's frame demanding a university "public, free, and open to every one."

These "media leaders" attributed a political meaning to an "antipoliticist" movement and acted as an instrument of apparent ideological unity between both sectors. But, according to my data, this unity did not exist. I use the term "convergence in action" to refer to the pragmatic alignment of two movement sectors with different frames and discourses. If pragmatism and a search for democratic reforms are central characteristics of new social movements (see Johnston, Laraña, and Gusfield, Chapter 1), this concept might be more useful than the usual meaning of "unity" because the latter can become a self-explanatory concept that takes for granted internal consensus.

In this case, the consequences of the imposition of a "politicist public identity" from above promoted its rejection by the younger sectors. This imposition was crucial in the breakdown of the convergence in action between the different status groups and the discontinuity of the movement in high schools three months earlier than in the universities. Instead of consensus around the movement's public identity, there was an initial pragmatic alignment with a political frame that did not respond to the motives for mobilization in high school students who soon came to feel manipulated by nonstudent organizations and interests. These feelings were related to the role played by some political organizations and trade unions that used their access to the mass media to exploit the students' dissatisfaction as an opposition instrument to the government (Gonzalez Blasco 1987).

This case documents the conflictive relations that can arise between collective and public identity and their impact on the movement. Student leaders from the university defined the movement's frame and its discourse with explicit terms that did not reflect the symbolic and often nonverbalized elements of the movement's collective identity in high schools. They also provided information on the delegitimation of conventional political institutions and the distrust toward politics in the younger constituency, a widespread feature of new social movements (Offe 1985; Laraña 1992). It is not by chance that the concept of "antipoliticism" also defined the workers' movement frame during the premodern period of social movements in Spain (from the 1850s to the Civil War of 1936; see Alvarez-Junco, Chapter 13; Laraña 1993b). The revival of this frame in a milder fashion among the younger constituency might account for applying the theory of postmodernism to new social movements, to the extent that they question some elements of contemporary societies through a return to older, premodern meanings and ideas. The contempt for parliamentary politics, the hostility toward political power, and the indifference toward the political form of the state are central characteristics of the old frame that reemerged in the high school student movement of 1986 and 1987. This is another reason to study movement continuities beyond visible phases of mobilization and locate the search in a larger historical context (Laraña 1993b). The existence of these kinds of continuities cannot fit in the theoretical perspective of the apocalyptic analysis of new social movements as a "revolt against modernity," a perspective that rules out their novelty by distorting the essence of the dialectical process involved in the historical evolution of social movements (Mannheim 1936).

Ideology and Pluralism in Student Movements

Comparative research on other student movements is useful to further understand the reasons for convergence between the different sectors that support a social movement (Melucci 1989; Turner 1969, see also Chapter 4). This consensus often resembles Erving Goffman's notion of "working consensus" (1959).[14] Instead of taking for granted the existence of shared values and ideas among participants, "consensus mobilization" (Klandermans and Oegema 1987) is a social construction of each group. It tends to emerge in relation to the movement's pluralism, its capacity to integrate very different political orientations, and its ability to produce new definitions of the situation that account for individuals' alignment with the proposed frame of reference. Those elements are very different from traditional ideologies of mobilization. To the extent that this potential is associated with the group's collective identity, it tends to be stronger when it is based on symbols and linguistic categories that constitute the group's boundaries; and it is amplified to the maximum in those ethnic communities with their own language, as is the case of the Basque or Catalan nationalist movement (Linz 1980; Perez Agote 1987; Johnston 1991). As shown in research on the recent evolution of women's movements in the United States and new social movements in Milan during the 1980s (Melucci 1989; see also Mueller, Chapter 10), this mobilization potential arises through daily interaction in social networks where movements are incubated; it is expressed in the meanings, symbols, and collective beliefs that emerge from participation in the movement and allow members to put aside their ideological differences (Laraña 1993a).

The wide support given to the Free Speech Movement in Berkeley or to SDS, the main student SMO of the 1960s, was related to their capacity to integrate front groups and individuals with different ideologies (Draper 1965; Sale 1974; Wollin and Schaar 1970, Laraña 1975). As in the 1987 student mobilizations in Spain, their collective action was possible because internal debates centered on strategic and not ideological issues, on which consensus mobilization would have been extremely difficult. A similar pragmatic orientation made possible the emergence of a unitary master frame among the oppositional movements to Franco's dictatorship in Spain (Johnston 1991). This frame's characteristic "politicism," and its associated pattern of movement subordination to political parties, stands in contrast with the antipoliticist frame of the earlier period and with the features of contemporary new social movements. The historical stages in the evolution of social movements in Spain present sharp discontinuities because of reframing processes that cannot be explained only by changes in the political conditions of the country (Laraña 1993b; Johnston 1991; see also Alvarez-Junco, Chapter 13).

The student movements I have studied not only show important weakness in functionalist social theories but also question the validity of Marxist assumptions that were very influential in many European movements until the end of the 1960s. They question the notion of class consciousness as a precondition for unity of the social movement that is considered the "agency of history." That uniform element rarely emerges in new social movements, and classes are no longer the social basis for the majority of the mobilizations; instead of an obstacle, the ideological pluralism of these movements becomes decisive for their convergence in action (Draper 1965; Laraña 1975, 1993a). The presence of this pluralism in many contemporary movements since the 1960s confirms the role of student movements as precursors of new social movements. It also supports the use of the NSM concept as a tool to identify common features in contemporary movements and points to the changes these movements imply in reference to the worker's movement (see Johnston, Laraña, and Gusfield, Chapter 1; Laraña, 1993c; Melucci 1989; Offe 1985).

The Spanish student movement of 1986–1987 provides us with an example of the need to revise both traditional and modern assumptions on the unity of social movements. It addresses a central question in ongoing research: How are collective identities related to the movement's frame and to the role that traditional ideologies of mobilization may play (Melucci 1985, 1989; see also Mueller, Chapter 10)? The absence of the traditional leftist ideology among high school students strengthened the movement and enabled it to integrate different tendencies, in spite of the fact that university student leaders promoted a political frame based on Marxist assumptions. This process was already emerging in the student movements of the 1960s. Although they presented a peculiar version of the traditional revolutionary ideology and the socialist utopia, these elements had an essentially symbolic meaning as an alternative worldview and social project for the younger generation. Marxism and its socialist utopia were mainly self-affirmation symbols used by students to express their rejection of the adult order and impel democratic reforms and their own participation in social institutions. This ideology was only part of the alternative cognitive structures from which the young New Left tried to build its collective identity.

This analysis is reinforced if it is formulated in the opposite way. A fundamental factor for discontinuity in the U.S. student movement in the 1960s was the internal conflict arising around what model of society the movement was striving for. This ideological issue was related to the identity of students as an agency of radical social change and to what strategies should be used to achieve this goal (Ashley et al. 1970; Sale 1974). This conflict had a turning point in the SDS national convention of June 1969, when several groups advocated profound ideological and strategic changes; the abandonment of some basic New Left ideological and organizational principles such as ideological pluralism, autonomous and decentralized organization, and faith in democratic principles; and a turn toward traditional Marxist assumptions (Jacobs 1970; Sale 1974; Laraña 1982, 1993a). Those elements, which anticipated some of the main features of new social movements, constituted the "identity resources" of this movement (see Johnston, Laraña, and Gusfield, Chapter 1; Melucci 1989). The triumph of the proposal of some Marxist groups produced a shift in the politics of the New Left and the withdrawal of the wide support this movement had among college students. This shift was intimately associated with the distinctive character of the "new politics" and had strong cultural and generational elements (Laraña 1982).

The 1969 SDS convention exemplified the depth of the disintegrative process in the collective identity of the movement. The crisis was a result of four interrelated factors: repression, lack of legitimation of political institutions and democratic ideals, growing radicalization, and separation between the political and cultural sectors of the student movement (Laraña 1992). For one movement sector close to the New Left ideas, the crisis affected the available means to achieve the democratic principles, not the principles themselves or the values supporting them. For the contending groups, the crisis included those principles and the prevailing social model as a whole. That debate triggered the disintegration of the movement after New Left groups abandoned SDS and the Weatherman group went underground, becoming the "suicidal vanguard" whose mission was to bring the liberation wars in the Third World to the United States (Jacobs 1970; Sale 1974). This group was one of the first to engage in the widespread terrorism of the 1970s and 1980s in European countries, which arose from the breakdown of student movements (Laraña 1993a). They constituted a bloody expression of the kind of continuities that can emerge in movements that were initially motivated by liberal-democratic ideas and later followed totalitarian ideologies.

Notes

Acknowledgments: This chapter's findings are the result of research funded by the Centro de Investigaciones Sociológicas and the Comité Conjunto para la Cooperación Cultural entre Estados Unidos y España. I thank Aaron Cicourel and Hank Johnston for their insightful comments on the early versions of this chapter.

1. This tendency could be a consequence of more moderate analytical ambitions on the part of researchers after recognizing the limits of social science. This scaling down has been considered necessary for the development of the field (Cicourel 1964; Shibutani 1960).

2. This term is used here to refer to Marxist and collective behavior theories of social movements and conflict.

3. According to Melucci (1989), these networks function as laboratories

for the development of alternative codes of behavior, interpretation, and interpersonal relations. Produced through daily interaction, these codes are the "cognitive resources" of the movement for maintaining unity and allowing confrontation with structures of political and institutional power. They are the source of a collective identity that is the fundamental factor of unity and continuity in new movements. It substitutes in the role of "ideology," which was the unifying factor of collective action in Marxist theory, and gives the movement a large part of its mobilization potential (Laraña 1993a). The daily construction of alternative cultural codes nurtures the antagonistic character of the movement (Melucci 1989, see also Chapter 5).

4. The Criminology School Defense Committee was an ad hoc group of criminology students and members of several neo-Marxist organizations stemming from SDS, such as the Radical Student Union, the New American Movement, and the Young Socialist Alliance.

5. This is another reason why the validity of these assumptions is being revised by current research. This process follows the historical path for the development of science (Cicourel 1964).

6. A relevant exception to the neglect of discourse analysis in this field is Hank Johnston's (1991) research on the nationalist movement in Catalonia.

7. This argument could be applied to my research in the mid 1970s of the student movement in Berkeley, where the lack of visible action contrasted with its intense public presence during the second half of the 1960s (Laraña 1975).

8. *Selectividad* refers to the required exams to enter Spanish universities. They have a twofold function: to insure that all university students have a certain competence, and to redirect students with poor results to other studies that do not have high registration enrollments.

9. In the high schools, the demonstrations started in November 1986, almost simultaneous with similar ones in France, and ended in the last weeks of February 1987. In some universities, demonstrations started in January 1987 and ended on different dates, even as late as May.

10. Part of my research was conducted in a popular, middle-class high school located in the center of Madrid. I observed a considerable lack of knowledge about the role of university students in the demonstrations; a noncongruent situation with the possibility of a shared leadership.

11. The best known are the pictures of an individual the media called *cojo Mantecas*, a handicapped student who was transformed into the symbol of the demonstrations after a photo showing him breaking a street lamp with his crutches was widely displayed, and those of young people who covered their faces with scarves to protect their identity when committing violent acts against the police or public property.

12. As happens with the analysis of continuities in collective action, this is not simply a formal question but a substantive one that concerns which theoretical model is used to analyze a social movement.

13. In his work on the Catalan nationalist movement, Johnston (1991) shows how a similar process of frame extension integrated a new social sector (immigrants) in the original movement constituency and has had parallel implications for the spread of the nationalist frame in Catalonia since the 1960s.

14. This concept is an important contribution to counterbalance the functionalist and Marxist theories on social conflict. It refers to the process in social interaction by which individuals adapt their definition of the situations to that of the group, through a pragmatic agreement considered essential for the construction and continuity of social groups (Goffman 1959).

References

Ashley, Karin, et al. 1970. "You Don't Need a Weatherman to Know Which Way the Wind Blows." In *Weatherman*, edited by Harold Jacobs. Berkeley, Calif.: Ramparts.

Baudrillard, Jean. 1974. *Crítica de la economía política del signo*. Madrid: Siglo Veintiuno.

Briggs, Charles L. 1986. *Learning How to Ask*. Cambridge: Cambridge University Press.

Cicourel, Aaron. 1964. *Method and Measurement in Sociology*. New York: Free Press.

———. 1980. "Three Models of Discourse Analysis: The Role of Social Structure." *Discourse Processes* 3:101–32.

———. 1982. "Interviews, Surveys, and the Problem of Ecological Validity." *American Sociologist* 17:11–20.

Cohen, Jean. 1985. "Strategy or Identity: New Theoretical Paradigms and Contemporary Social Movements." *Social Research* 52, 4:663–716.

Coneim, Bernard, et al. 1987. "Comment comprendre le movement?" *Raison Présente* 82:9–16.

Dalton, Russell, and Manfred Kuelchner. 1992. *Los nuevos movimientos sociales*. Valencia: Edicions Alfons el Magnanim.

Draper, Hall. 1965. *La revuelta de Berkeley*. Barcelona: Anagrama.

Durkheim, Émile. 1978. *Las reglas del método sociológico*. Madrid: Akal.

Elster, Jon. 1989. *The Cement of Society: A Study of the Social Order*. Cambridge: Cambridge University Press.

Erikson, Erik. 1972. *Sociedad y adolescencia*. Madrid: Siglo XXI.

Evans, Sara. 1980. *Personal Politics*. New York: Vintage Books.

Flacks, Richard. 1967. "The Liberated Generation: An Exploration of the Roots of Student Protest." *Social Issues* 13, 3:52–76.

Gamson, William. 1988. "Political Discourse and Collective Action." In *From Structure to Action*, edited by Bert Klandermans, Hanspeter Kriesi, and Sidney Tarrow. Vol. 1 of *International Social Movement Research*. Greenwich, Conn.: JAI Press.

Giddins, Anthony. 1979. *La estructura de las clases sociales avanzadas*. Madrid: Alianza Edit.

Goffman, Erving. 1959. *The Presentation of Self in Everyday Life*. New York: Anchor Books.

———. 1974. *Frame Analysis*. Boston: Northeastern University Press.

Gonzalez Blasco, Pedro. 1987. "Reflexiones en torno al malestar estudiantil." *Razón y Fe*.

Gusfield, Joseph. 1970. *Protest, Reform, and Revolt: A Reader on Social Movements*. New York: John Wiley and Sons.

――――. 1973. *Utopian Myths and Movements in Modern Society*. University Program Modular Studies. Morristown, N.J.: General Learning Press.

Ibarra, Pedro, and Antonio Rivas. 1993. "Environmental Public Discourse in the Basque Country." Paper presented at the 21st Congress of the International Institute of Sociology, Paris, June 21–25.

Jacobs, Harold. 1970. *Weatherman*. Berkeley, Calif.: Ramparts.

Johnston, Hank. 1991. *Tales of Nationalism: Catalonia, 1939–1979*. New Brunswick, N.J.: Rutgers University Press.

――――. 1992. "Fightin' Words: Discourse, Frames, and Cultural Analysis of Social Movements." Paper presented at the Conference on Culture and Social Movements, University of California, San Diego, June 17–20.

Klandermans, Bert, and Dirk Oegema. 1987. "Potentials, Networks, Motivations, and Barriers: Steps toward Participation in Social Movements." *American Sociological Review* 52, 4:519–31.

Klandermans, Bert, and Sidney Tarrow. 1988. "Mobilization into Social Movements: Synthesizing European and American Approaches." In *From Structure to Action*, edited by Bert Klandermans, Hanspeter Kriesi, and Sidney Tarrow. Vol. 1 of *International Social Movement Research*. Greenwich, Conn.: JAI Press.

Laraña, Enrique. 1975. "A Study of Student Political Activism at the University of California, Berkeley." Master's thesis, University of California, Santa Barbara.

――――. 1979. "La Constitución y el derecho a la resistencia." In *Revista de la Facultad de Derecho de la Universidad Complutense de Madrid*. Monograph on the Spanish Constitution, no. 2: 183–203.

――――. 1982. "La juventud contemporánea y el conflicto intergeneracional." *Revista de Juventud* 3:41–62.

――――. 1992. "Student Movements in the U.S. and Spain: Ideology and the Crisis of Legitimacy in Post-Industrial Society." Paper presented at the Conference on Culture and Social Movements, University of California, San Diego, June 17–20.

――――. 1993a. "Ideología, conflicto social y movimientos sociales contemporáneos." In *Escritos de teoría sociológica en homenaje a Luis Rodríguez Zúñiga*. Madrid: Centro de Investigaciones Sociológicas.

――――. 1993b. "History and Frames in the Construction of New Social Movements in Spain: A Model of Tendencies." Paper presented at the 21st Congress of the International Institute of Sociology, Paris, June 21–25.

――――. 1993c. "Los movimientos sociales en España (1960–1990): Análisis de tendencias." In *Tendencias sociales en España de hoy*, edited by Salustiano del Campo. Madrid: Centro de Investigaciones Sociológicas.

Linz, Juan. 1980. "The Basques in Spain: Nationalism and Political Conflict in a New Democracy." In *Resolving Nationality Conflicts: The Role of Public Opinion Research*, edited by W. Phillips Davison and Leon Gordeneker. New York: Praeger.

Lipset, Seymour. 1965. "Student Politics." In *The Berkeley Student Revolt*. Garden City, N.Y.: Anchor Books.

McAdam, Doug. 1988. *Freedom Summer*. New York: Oxford University Press.

Mannheim, Karl. 1936. *Ideology and Utopia*. New York: Harvest Books.

Melucci, Alberto. 1980. "The New Social Movements: A Theoretical Approach." *Social Science Information* 19, 2:199–226.

———. 1985. "The Symbolic Challenge of Contemporary Movements." *Social Research* 52:789–816.

———. 1989. *Nomads of the Present: Social Movements and Individual Needs in Contemporary Society*. Philadelphia: Temple University Press.

———. 1990. "Collective Action as Social Construction." Paper presented at the World Congress of Sociology, Madrid, July 9–15.

Mueller, Carol. 1993. "The Organizational Basis of Conflict and Identity in Contemporary Feminism." Paper presented at the 21st Congress of the International Institute of Sociology, Paris, June 21–25.

Offe, Claus. 1985. "New Social Movements Challenging the Boundaries of Institutional Politics." *Social Research* 52, 4:817–68.

———. 1988. *Partidos políticos y nuevos movimientos socials*. Madrid: Sistema.

Perez Agote, Alfonso. 1987. *El nacionalismo vasco a la salida del franquismo*. Madrid: Centro de Investigaciones Sociológicas.

Quéré, Louis, et al. 1987. "Comment comprendre le movement?" *Raison Présente* 82: 9–16.

Sale, Kirkpatrick. 1974. *SDS*. New York: Vintage Books.

Shibutani, Tamotu. 1960. *Sociedad y personalidad*. Buenos Aires: Paidós.

Snow, David A., and Robert D. Benford. 1988. "Ideology, Frame Resonance, and Participant Mobilization." In *From Structure to Action*, edited by Bert Klandermans, Hanspeter Kriesi, and Sidney Tarrow. Vol. 1 of *International Social Movement Research*. Greenwich, Conn.: JAI Press.

———. 1992. "Master Frames and Cycles of Protest." In *Frontiers in Social Movement Theory*, edited by Aldon D. Morris and Carol McClurg Mueller. New Haven: Yale University Press.

Snow, David A., E. Burke Rochford, Jr., Steven K. Worden, and Robert D. Benford. 1986. "Frame Alignment Processes, Micromobilization, and Movement Participation." *American Sociological Review* 51:464–81.

Stompka, Piotr. 1992. "Toward a 'Third Sociology' of Social Movements." Paper presented at the First European Conference on Social Movements, Wissenschaftszentrum Berlin für Socialforschung, Berlin, October 29–31.

Tarrow, Sidney. 1989. *Struggle, Politics, and Reform: Collective Action, Social Movements, and Cycles of Protest*. Ithaca: Cornell University, Center for International Studies.

Taylor, Verta. 1989. "Social Movement Continuity: The Women's Movement in Abeyance." *American Sociological Review* 54, 5:761–75.

Turner, Ralph H. 1969. "The Theme of Contemporary Social Movements." *British Journal of Sociology* 20:390–405.

Turner, Ralph H., and Lewis M. Killian. 1987. *Collective Behavior*. 3d ed. Englewood Cliffs, N.J.: Prentice-Hall.

Weber, Max. 1944. *Economía y Sociedad*. Mexico City: Fondo de Cultura Económica.

Wollin, Sheldon, and John Schaar. 1970. *The Berkeley Rebellion and Beyond*. New York: Vintage Books.

Zald, Mayer N., and John D. McCarthy, eds. 1987. "Social Movement Industries: Competition and Conflict among SMOs," and "Religious Groups as Crucibles of Social Movements." In *Social Movements in an Organizational Society*. New Brunswick, N.J.: Transaction Books.

Chapter 10

Conflict Networks and the Origins of Women's Liberation

Carol Mueller

Increasing cross-fertilization of social movement theory has occurred from both sides of the Atlantic over the last five years. The European "new social movements theory" and the North American theory of "resource mobilization," developed since the tumultuous 1960s, have been the major contributors.[1] Resource mobilization theory is based in a strategic approach to the study of social movements; it emphasizes the mobilization and allocation of resources by movement actors in the context of opportunities and constraints imposed by the social and political environment. Particular attention focuses on the role of formal social movement organizations as the key social actors planning strategies and mobilizing resources. Grievances are treated as a given preference structure in some of the most powerful statements of the theory.

New social movement theory has, strangely, emphasized issues that are largely ignored by resource mobilization. Instead of being taken as given, grievances are at the center a theory that locates their source in both social structure and the social psychological processes underlying their identification and development as part of movement culture. For many North American scholars, the strength of new social movement theory lies at the intermediate and the macro levels of analysis. New social movement theory has pointed to the need for a social psychology based in the social interaction of movement actors as well as the need to identify the source of grievances and collective actors for particular social movements in their historically variable structural context, particularly the changing class structure and symbolic environment of postindustrial, capitalist societies. While the latter contribution has been largely ignored,[2] interest in the intermediate level of analysis where social conditions are defined as grievances and personal misfortunes are translated into a collective sense of injustice has coincided with a developing focus on the creation of meaning by social movement actors among those who seek to expand the resource mobilization paradigm.[3]

As contributions to social movement theory increasingly merge into a more comprehensive whole it is important to explore the components of each theory more carefully and to "test" it against empirical studies on both sides of the Atlantic. Particularly important to scholars interested in developing the new emphasis on social construction processes has been the work of the Italian new social movement theorist Alberto Melucci. Melucci's (1989) theory develops the role of "submerged networks" in the process of creating collective identities, interpreting grievances, and evaluating the potential effectiveness of collective action. Despite this interest (see works by Gamson 1992; by Klandermans 1986, 1990, 1992; and by Taylor and Whittier 1992) and the publication of Melucci's book *Nomads of the Present*, Melucci's theory of "collective identity" and "submerged networks" has not been systematically evaluated in the context of North American social movements. This chapter rectifies this omission through a critical examination of Melucci's theory as applied to the origins of women's mobilization in the United States during the period from 1960 to 1970. It will then be possible to assess its role in a broader theory of the social construction of social movements. Of primary interest is Melucci's contribution to the intermediate level of analysis where social movement culture is generated and dominant cultural codes are challenged.

Melucci's Theory of Socially Constructed Collective Identities

Melucci's point of departure is what he characterizes as the false unity attributed by observers to collective action. He argues:

> The collective phenomenon—whether a panic, a social movement, or a revolutionary process—is treated as a *unified empirical datum,* which, supposedly, can be perceived and interpreted by observers. It is supposed that, first, individuals' behaviour forms *a unitary character* or *gestalt.* Second, this assumption is then transferred from the phenomenological to the conceptual level and acquires ontological consistency: the collective reality is seen to exist as a thing. (1989, 18)[4]

Melucci attributes the error of false unity to a model of analysis that grew out of the class struggles of the nineteenth century and the actions of the supposedly unitary working class as it [*sic*] demanded the expansion of citizenship rights to encompass suffrage, political association, free speech, and so forth (1989, 19). The working-class movement, in this historic context, was tied to the idea of social movements "as historical agents marching toward a destiny of liberation" (1988, 330).

It is this perception of a social movement as ossified in a unitary "collective identity" that Melucci seeks to correct with his own theoretical model. He attempts to explain social movements at an intermediate level of social processes that occur in face-to-face interactions. These processes connect the sense of personal misfortune that people experience in their everyday lives with a collective interpretation of these conditions as injustice or grievances that justify collective action. He seeks to identify those groups processes "by which individuals evaluate and recognize what they have in common and decide to act together" (1988, 339). Thus, he seeks to create a theory that links the structured practices of social life with the collective action of a social movement through the intermediate steps of face-to-face interaction and meaning construction.

There are three key features of his theory: (1) the content or outcome of the process of social construction, the "collective identity" of the movement that comes to exist as a part of the movement culture; (2) the social processes by which the collective identity is created in "submerged networks" of small groups concerned with the ongoing routines of everyday life; and (3) the emotional investments that enable individuals to recognize themselves as the "we" in a collective identity.

The first feature of Melucci's theory is his conception of the collective identity, which he defines as "nothing else than a shared definition of the field of opportunities and constraints offered to collective action: 'shared' means constructed and negotiated through a repeated process of 'activation' of social relationships connecting the actors" (1985, 793). For Melucci, the content of the collective identity or sense of "we" consists of a social resolution of three orders of orientation: "the *ends* of actions (i.e., the sense the action has for the actor); those relating to the *means* (i.e., the possibilities and the limits of action); and finally those relating to relationships with the *environment* (i.e., the field in which the action takes place)" (1988, 33). In other words, people will interact in "submerged networks" where they will arrive at a new definition of their situation. This definition is different from the ordinary outcomes of daily social interaction in that it is action oriented, and it includes a goal, tactics, and a strategy for collective action on behalf of shared grievances.

The incubation period during which new collective identities are formed occurs in submerged social networks out of view of the public eye. Melucci argues that by the 1980s when he conducted his research on three different movement groups in Milan, collective actions were created within networks composed of many groups that were dispersed throughout the urban landscape. They are fragmented in terms of their relationships with each other and they were invisible because of their immersion in everyday life. Not only are the networks submerged in the sense that their cultural experimentation is not readily visible to the wider public but they are transitory in that individuals have multiple memberships with temporary and limited involvement (1989, 60). The submerged network is a system of small, separate groups engaging in cultural experimentation, and it is also a system of exchange in which persons and information circulate freely within the network. These networks act as "cultural laboratories" submerged within civil society (1989, 60). Some agencies, such as local free radios, bookshops, and magazines provide sources of unity (1985, 800).

In these cultural laboratories, new collective identities are constructed from the expressive interactions of individuals experimenting with new cultural codes, forms of relationships, and alternative perceptions of the world. The creation of the collective identity occurs in the midst of tensions created by the inadequacy of the means currently available for reaching personal and collective goals. From these tensions, as well as the close face-to-face interaction, develops a heavy emotional investment that encourages the individual to share in the collective identity. As the collective identity is created to address these tensions, both leadership and organization attempt to give permanence through their tentative resolution. This process involves the negotiation of the three orientations given the constraints of resources and political opportunities within emotionally enriched relationships.

For Melucci, the hidden networks become visible only when collective actors "confront or come into conflict with a public policy," that is, when they confront the state (1989, 90). This confrontation adds to a state of tension and enhanced emotional investment. Melucci argues, for instance, that the massive peace mobilizations of the 1980s were based in the submerged networks of women, young people, ecologists, and alternative cultures. Thus, Melucci's submerged networks point to what he calls the relationship between the latency and visibility poles of collective action.[5]

While Melucci associates the submerged networks in which collective identities are formed with the relatively quiescent period of the 1980s in both Europe and the United States, other scholars have identified similar incubation networks in periods prior to mass mobilization. Aldon Morris (1984), for instance, describes the "halfway houses" throughout the southern United States that served as laboratories for working out a collective identity of ends (civil rights and racial integration), means (nonviolence), and environmental relations (the development of a network of alliance systems linking North and South) prior to the public phase of the civil rights movement that began in the mid 1950s. Doug McAdam's (1982) political process theory also posits a stage of "cognitive liberation" that precedes mass mobilization. Similarly, Verta Taylor (1989) describes the "abeyance processes" that link the periods of feminist activism in the United States from the suffrage movement of the early twentieth century to the contemporary movement.

Although Melucci argues that this process of constructing collective identities is a unique characteristic of highly complex societies, he may also underestimate how universal the process of cultural transformation has been as a prelude to previous periods of mass mobilization. The development of a collective identity centered on class consciousness among the working class in England (1780–1830), France (1830–1833), and Russia (1900–1914) point to a similar combination of social analysis contained within a new collective identity and institution building within submerged networks as prelude to collective action (see this analysis and a comparison with political consciousness of African Americans by Morris in Morris and Mueller 1992).

The basic thrust of Melucci's conception of submerged networks is the proposition that the initial challenge to the prevailing order takes place principally on symbolic grounds. That is, the status quo must be challenged at the cultural level in terms of its claims to legitimacy before mass collective action is feasible. Thus, Melucci argues that submerged networks "challenge and overturn the dominant codes upon which social relationships are founded. These symbolic challenges are a method of unmasking the dominant codes, a different way of perceiving and naming the world" (1989, 75). By concentrating only on the visible, public signs of a social movement's challenge to the existing order, previous theories of social movements have failed to appreciate the contribution of these cultural transformations. Melucci argues, for instance, that our concept of success should be expanded to encompass these cultural changes. This is the investment of the nascent movement in what he calls a "latency phase" as dominant cultural codes are unmasked and overturned.

Melucci contributes to a growing interest among students of social movements in the way that cultural codes are challenged; in the connection of social structure to culture through a social psychology that identifies face-to-face patterns of interaction and their location in submerged networks where cultural experimentation actually occurs; and in the new cultural codes that can serve as the basis of collective action. These are important contributions that have been too little appreciated. In addition, it has been too little realized that the tensions and emotional investments associated with the process of generating collective identities and initiating collective actions is often accompanied by internal dissension and organizational segmentation.

Nevertheless, there are unresolved issues in Melucci's theory that must also be identified before it can be successfully applied to a case study. While Melucci is unique in pointing to the role of externally derived tension in the development of new cultural configurations within social movements, his focus on resource and environmental constraints as the major source of tension fails to consider the important role of internal conflict and competition as an additional dynamic contributing to the generation of new collective identities (see, as examples, Mueller 1987; Tarrow 1989; Taylor and Whittier 1992). There are other unresolved issues in Melucci's theory as well, but the most important for present purposes is his disavowal of the role of the collective identity as historic actor. In his focus on an intermediate level of analysis, the face-to-face interactions where collective identities are forged, he unnecessarily abandons the cultural level of analysis at which the product of the submerged networks enters political culture. It is at this point that the social movement emerges as historic actor and agent of political change. These two concerns—the role of internal conflict in shaping the collective identity and the level of analysis—are brought together here in the course of applying his theory to a specific case, the origins of the contemporary women's movement in the United States. This application may also suggest the utility of Melucci's theory for readers who do not have access to his Italian case materials (see an evaluation of these materials in Johnston 1991).

Collective Identity and the Mass Mobilization of Women

To demonstrate the importance of submerged networks in challenging dominant codes and creating new collective identities that facilitate mass mobilizations, it is necessary to document that this configuration of the new identity was not already widely available. This seemingly simple condition is often ignored in empirical demonstrations of cultural innovations but is essential for the current case study of the creation of a new collective identity for women.

In the United States, the decade after World War II was characterized by later feminists as the "decade of domesticity" because of its high birthrates and its emphasis on home, family, and women's traditional roles. So pervasive was the dominant cultural code prescribing a narrow set of roles for women that few social scientists recognized its existence. To characterize women's condition as one of inequality much less as oppression would have been regarded as heresy. Yet, in 1951, an article appeared in an American sociological journal strangely titled, "Women as a Minority Group" (Hacker [1951] 1979). The author, Helen Hacker, took the lonely position that women's characteristic behavior and position of social inferiority paralleled that of Jews and Negroes, groups well recognized as "minorities" in U.S. culture. Hacker's article can be taken as a benchmark for its characterization of women according to the dominant cultural code of the United

States in the 1950s. Despite its poor reception at the time, it brought to consciousness a set of cultural assumptions that were largely taken for granted.

After itemizing discriminatory patterns against women in economic, political, and social life, Hacker noted that, although women showed no conscious self-awareness of their inferior status, other aspects of their behavior supported the analogy. She cited data from the World War II period indicating high levels of self-hatred associated with the status of being a woman. In surveys, women showed high levels of dislike for other women, women expressed a preference for working under the direction of men, women had misgivings concerning the value of participation in public life, and high proportions of women, compared to men, wished they had been born in the opposite sex. Hacker showed parallels in the castelike behavior and treatment of women and Negroes. She noted, for instance, high social visibility and frequent attributions of an inferior intelligence, a smaller brain, irresponsibility, emotional instability, and moral weakness (514). Like the Negro, the woman accommodated to her inferior status with smiles, laughter, rising inflection in conversation, and downward glances. She cultivated an appearance of helplessness and pursued her goals with a flattering manner and "feminine wiles." Yet, after Hacker identified a deeply repressed sense of inferiority, she issued no call for women to overcome their condition and seemed to see little possibility for change. Instead, she pointed out that there were a few women, like those in nontraditional, professional occupations, who broke the dominant cultural code and recommended that these should be studied (520). Although there were other women who had long challenged the assumptions of the dominant code among minority women (Hooks 1981) and among a small group of feminists who had pursued the Equal Rights Amendment since 1922 (Rupp and Taylor 1987), both groups were largely invisible because the challenge they represented had been marginalized and assimilated.

Hacker was not the only one who saw little potential for a change in women's collective identity. More than ten years later, at a conference called by the prestigious American Academy of Arts and Sciences, a dozen of America's leading intellectuals contemplated women's condition (Lifton 1967). Many of the leading male scholars celebrated women's traditional virtues. Erik Erikson noted that women inhabit a special "inner space," while Robert J. Lifton praised women's possession of insight and wisdom. David Riesman noted that the greater resourcefulness of the contemporary generation of young women was possible "without storming the barricades at home or abroad" (Riesman 1964, 97). Carl Degler, a historian, pointed to the revolutionary changes taking place in women's growing paid employment, but he noted that women would probably remain in segregated and low-paying jobs because there was no strong feminist push to improve their condition. He was pessimistic about any such change because, "The whole truth is that American society in general, which includes women, shuns like a disease any feminist ideology" (Degler 1967, 203). That is, in Melucci's terms, the male scholars either saw no need for a collective identity for women or, like Degler, found it impossible to imagine the conditions under which such a profound cultural transformation might be brought about.

There was one member of this august gathering, however, who was soon to achieve a certain notoriety for her paper, "Equality between the Sexes: An Immodest Proposal." The author, Alice Rossi, drew on Helen Hacker's paper from the 1950s to call for uncompromising equality in the socialization, schooling, and adult responsibilities of men and women (Rossi 1967, 98–143). Her paper was received with little enthusiasm by either male or female participants at the conference. Degler (1967) responded to Rossi's "immodest proposal" by asserting that, "in America the soil is thin and the climate uncongenial for the growth of any seedlings of ideology" (210).

Although this conference indicated the increasing concern with women's status in society, at this level of discourse where scholars and intellectuals bring issues to public awareness, only Rossi's paper suggests a potential for cultural reconstruction and a new collective identity. Clearly, some of the best informed leaders of American intellectual life were unaware that they were sitting on the brink of a massive shift of consciousness in the culturally prescribed roles for women and an unprecedented mass mobilization. How did it happen? Did scholarly discourse on the plight of women escalate from papers like that given by Rossi at the Academy of Arts and Sciences conference? Did women's organizations disseminate persuasive communications on what should be done?

Did young women defy the advice of their elders and take to the barricades? Did small groups of women get together in submerged networks removed from the public eye and renegotiate their identities as women and consider tactics and strategies that would challenge the dominant cultural code? Clearly, all of these things happened, but paramount place must go to the submerged networks where a transformed collective identity developed in the tense atmosphere of disagreement and conflict over the nature of the collective identity that would become the basis of a new set of goals and programs for change. Once this collective identity had been created, however, it would take on a life of its own as historic actor and source of political influence. The process by which the collective identity is created demonstrates the basic value of Melucci's theory.

The Origins of the Women's Movement

While the origins of women's mobilization in the United States are well documented,[6] two different explanations have been proposed to account for the beginning of the movement. The first explanation corresponds to the structural theories of the European new social movements literature that attempt to link changes in the objective condition of the mobilized group with changes in consciousness. Survey research is the tool usually employed with the goal of correlating clusters of attitudes reflecting a new collective consciousness with the subgroup defined by the objective condition. The key proponents of this approach for the U.S. women's movement have been Joan Huber (1976) and Ethel Klein (1984).[7] The second explanation corresponds in many ways to Melucci's emphasis on the generative role of submerged networks. Major contributors to this approach are Jo Freeman (1973) and Sara Evans (1980). A review of these theories suggests both the strengths and the weaknesses of Melucci's conceptions of submerged networks and collective identities in an understanding of the origins of the U.S. women's movement. To make these theories accessible to a European audience, I characterize them as the structural and the submerged network theories.

Structural Theories

Explanations based on changes in technology and the division of labor argue that "the decline in fertility and the shift of productive work from home to factory in the past two centuries has upset the equilibrium of sex stratification in industrial societies," thus paving the way for a shift of consciousness and the mobilization of women (Huber 1976, 372). Based on a historic analysis of women's work and child-care responsibilities, Huber documents that, after 1940, the female work force was increasingly composed of married women with children. She argues that the double burden of paid work and domestic work was so onerous that women were compelled to see that they were treated unjustly by society (1976, 372). From Huber's perspective, the contemporary women's movement is the "unplanned result" of the technological changes that transformed women's work and child-care responsibilities. She predicts that the movement will continue as long as women bear this double burden.

Although Huber describes objective conditions that might logically lead women to develop an "injustice frame," she does not demonstrate empirically that the women experiencing these changes were, in fact, developing a new consciousness (or collective identity). For this kind of data, it is necessary to turn to Klein (1984) who has made this connection between structural position and changed consciousness. Looking at three different dimensions of women's traditional roles—domestic employment, motherhood, and marriage—she, like Huber, describes changes brought about through mature industrialization. She links these objective, structural changes to shifts over time in public opinion toward greater tolerance for women's work outside the home, for reduced fertility and family size, and for the social acceptability of either single status or divorce. Despite the momentous changes occurring in women's lives throughout the century, she notes, it was not until the 1960s that public opinion polls indicated large numbers of women were endorsing a nontraditional role.

Klein's (1984) analysis is based on the overtime data from the National Election Studies, which have been gathered since the 1950s by the Survey Research Center at the University of Michigan. They indicate that, by the end of the 1960s, the majority of women were in favor of nontraditional roles for women based on social equality, and an increasing number felt that women faced discrimination (91). Klein characterizes this cluster of attitudes as a "feminist consciousness." Her data indicated that, by 1972, women who were psychologically more likely to support nontraditional roles for women were themselves found in structural positions where they were more likely to work outside the home, to have a job with high occupational status, to achieve more than a high school education, to be single, divorced, or separated, to live in a large metropolitan area, to have a mother who had worked, to be politically liberal, and to be little involved in organized religion (106–19). The more of these characteristics a woman possessed, the more likely she was to have a highly developed feminist consciousness.

Klein's data reveal a paradoxical finding, however. Despite the sharp increase in feminist consciousness among women, it was even higher among men. By 1972, men were even more likely than women to believe that society rather than nature or biology was responsible for women's roles; to support an equal role for women in business and industry; and to endorse equal employment treatment (100). Yet, needless to say, men did not create the women's movement nor did they encourage women's mass mobilization. This anomalous finding points to the limitations of the structural explanation of the origins of the women's movement. Despite Klein's careful connection of structural changes in women's roles to changes in public consciousness, to some extent, changes in social structure affected the consciousness of men and women similarly.

The structural theories and Klein's careful documentation of the rise of a feminist consciousness help to account for the large public support for the women's movement during the 1970s and, also, its considerable political influence after the period of mass mobilization beginning in 1970, but it cannot explain the origins of the movement for two simple reasons: (1) a new consciousness that is shared equally by men and women cannot explain why women rather than men formed a movement; and (2) widespread support among women for greater equality does not explain why some few specific individuals of the millions of American women affected by structural changes did, in fact, create a movement. To try to explain the origins of the movement with a structural analysis alone faces the same limitations that Melucci has identified in some of the European literature on new social movements:

"Approaches based on the *structure/motivation* dualism . . . view collective action either as a product of the logic of the system or as a result of personal beliefs" (1989, 21). The basic problem is that "both the macrostructural factors and the individual variables imply an unbridgeable gap between the level of explanation proposed and the concrete process that allows a certain number of individuals to act together" (1988, 332).

Melucci's proposed solution is an intermediate level of analysis in which submerged networks are studied as the source of new collective identities that encompass the definition of specific possibilities and limits of action. At the same time, relationships are activated within localized, submerged networks and particular individuals make commitments to act together in pursuit of specific goals (1988, 332). Applied to the origins of women's liberation, a generally diffuse feminist consciousness, while perhaps necessary, is not enough. To explain origins, specific individuals must be identified who have formed emotional bonds from their interaction, negotiated a sense of group membership, and made a plan for change (or series of plans), however tentative, with goals, means, and a consideration of environmental constraints: a collective identity.

The Submerged Networks

Previous scholarship on the women's movement has provided many of the pieces necessary for the kind of analysis that Melucci proposes. Freeman's (1973) and Evans's (1980) work on the origins of the U.S. women's movement are best known in this tradition. As Freeman indicates, the movement originated simultaneously in two different social locations in the mid to late 1960s from their respective sources among, first, the "older branch" of women active in national politics who were involved in the new State Commissions on the Status of Women, and a, second, "younger branch" of women who had been participants in the civil rights movement and the New Left. Freeman (1973) argues that the origins of the movement in these two branches can be explained by the availability of compatible communications networks, a series of "crises" that focused each branch of women on feminist issues, and experienced organizers in the younger branch who could weld together local groups into a national movement. It was the older branch that created the

National Organization for Women (NOW), which eventually became the major social movement organization for the movement. The younger branch developed the small groups, consciousness-raising, and the less conventional tactics of the movement. Evans (1980) provides an in-depth study of how the younger women were radicalized by the humiliations they experienced from their male colleagues in the social movements of the 1960s. In the course of describing what Melucci would characterize as "submerged networks," Evans also indicates the degree to which conflict and struggle played a role in developing collective identities in the submerged networks of both branches of the movement. It was in part the struggle over the notion of the emerging collective identity that led to cultural innovation, organizational segmentation, and the spread of movement groups in the five years preceding the Women's Strike. This event, in August 1970, marked the symbolic beginning, the public "coming out," of the movement.

The processes of negotiation and identity construction in the two branches reflected the very different political cultures of electoral and movement politics in the mid 1960s. The older branch, or what came to be called "equal rights feminism," was based in the policy debates, organized interests, and campaign obligations of political actors in state and federal governments. The conflicts that led to changes in women's consciousness arose from policy debates regarding women's rights. In this context, the collective identity that developed followed the model of the civil rights movement in emphasizing the source of women's problems in systematic patterns of discrimination that could be eliminated or mitigated primarily through appropriate legislation, regulations, litigation, and enforcements but not excluding marches and demonstrations. Through conflict with Commission members, congressional representatives, officials, and the media over the Equal Rights Amendment, the interpretation of Title VII of the Civil Rights Act, employment policy, the enforcement practices of the Equal Employment Opportunities Commission, and a host of other policies, a relatively small network of politically well-connected women developed a conception of gender equality or collective identity that was thoroughly radical in its implications[8] (see Hole and Levine 1971, 15–107; Carden 1974, 103–47; Freeman 1975, 44–102).

The conflict that occurred over the formulation of this identity among equal rights women led to a proliferation of organizations devoted to efforts on behalf of specific constituencies, issues, or policies. In 1967, for instance, women from the United Auto Workers were forced to withdraw from NOW because their union opposed inclusion of the Equal Rights Amendment in the NOW Bill of Rights (they formed the Congress of Labor Union Women). Further segmentation occurred with inclusion of abortion in the NOW Bill of Rights, which led women more concerned with issues of economic discrimination to leave and form the Women's Equity Action League (WEAL). Further division occurred when younger women from the New York NOW chapter charged the national organization with an elitist decision making structure and formed the October 17 Movement (later known as The Feminists). In 1968, two of NOW's lawyers walked out in disgust over the inefficiency of the organization, taking two of its most important cases. They then formed other social movement organizations—first, Human Rights for Women and, later, the Legal Defense Fund—to support sex discrimination cases (Freeman 1975, 80–81). The proliferation of equal rights organizations reflected not only important differences of emphasis among women searching for political solutions to multiple sources of discrimination but also the pursuit of an area of action where individual women could create a highly personal interpretation of their collective identity. Unfortunately, for present purposes, accounts of these conflicts are devoted almost exclusively to the policy provisions involved in the debates and tell us little about the face-to-face process of collective identity construction as it occurred.

In contrast, there is a rich literature on the evolution of collective identity in the submerged networks of younger women who came to constitute the women's liberation branch of the movement. Whereas the older branch identified what they came to understand as the "overt" discrimination against women that appeared in employment, politics, credit, and educational opportunities, the younger branch turned to the personal politics that Helen Hacker ([1951] 1979) had associated with women's status as a minority. The collective identity that emerged had no precursor in the liberal politics of the early civil rights movement. It came to be identified as "women's liberation."

Prior to 1970, women's liberation had been a "movement of friends" in the submerged networks of civil rights and the New Left. Several detailed historical accounts indicate the intensity of the social interactions and the high level of emotional investment of the young people who were experimenting with the creation of new social forms of living as well as the means of achieving political goals. From 1964 to 1967, isolated pairs or small groups of activist women began to voice a sense of uneasiness to each other about what they perceived as a different and unequal role for women in the actual day-to-day activities of these movements. As Evans (1980) points out, attempts to articulate this uneasiness about women's assignment to the mundane and routine activities of kitchen work, mimeographing, typing, and cleaning evoked reactions of scorn and fury from the male radicals—first in the Student Nonviolent Coordinating Committee (SNCC), the major youth organization of the civil rights movement, and soon after in Students for a Democratic Society (SDS), the leading student organization of the New Left in the United States throughout the 1960s. The younger women were rebuffed time after time as they tried to discuss their concerns regarding gender differences within the limits of debate prescribed by the leaders of the civil rights and New Left movements. Conflict, ridicule, and exclusion greeted their attempts to extend the emotional bonds forged during the early 1960s to the sense of injustice and grievances arising from women's personal experiences within the movements.

As they continued to receive rebukes and scorn from the male radicals—at a SNCC staff meeting in the summer of 1964; at the SNCC Waveland Retreat in November 1964; at an SDS conference in December 1965; at a 1966 SDS convention; and, finally and most dramatically, at the first nationwide gathering of New Left groups in Chicago, the National Conference for a New Politics (NCNP), in September 1967—women's confusion and search for a new identity turned to rage and alienation (Evans 1980; Hole and Levine 1971, 109–16). The submerged networks of women that had developed within the New Left organizations moved outside to begin an autonomous existence in major cities in the East Coast and the Midwest.

The transitory processes that Melucci describes of conflict, segmentation, and dissolution of organizations is illustrated in Figure 10–1, which represents one year in the life of the New York

RADICAL WOMEN /
NEW YORK
RADICAL WOMEN

Recruits from Princeton
SDS Meeting ————▶

Action: "Burial of Traditional Womanhood" at Washington, D.C., antiwar
demonstration Spring 1968 directed
at Jeanette Rankin Brigade.
"Sisterhood Is Powerful" first used.

Defection of 300–
500 women in ————▶
Washington, D.C.,
from Jeanette
Rankin Brigade

Action: published mimeographed
journal, "Notes from the First Year," ———▶
June 1968
• article "The Myth of the Vaginal
   Orgasm"
• dialogue "Women Rap about Sex"

read throughout
the country

Joint action with
women from ————▶
New Jersey,
Washington, D.C.,
and Florida

Action: Miss America Contest
Demonstration, September 1968 ———▶
• live sheep crowned
• bras, girdles, high heels, curlers
   dumped into Freedom Trashcan.

first national
media coverage

WITCH
fall 1968
Women's International
Conspiracy from Hell

San   Covens   NYC
Francisco

disintegration

THANKSGIVING MEETING IN CHICAGO
November 1968
200 women/37 states

GROUP I	REDSTOCKINGS	FEMINISTS	NY RADICAL FEMINISTS
Counter-Inaugural Action, January 1969	• Wide use of con-sciousness-raising • "Pro Women Line" • "Woman as a Political Class"	• Ti-Grace Atkinson • Theory Action • "Radical Feminism" • Attack on sex roles • Rotation of leadership • Anti-male • Anti-"star-making"	Three-stage structure: • Consciousness-raising • Brigade membership • Mass organization
	disintegration 1969	disintegration 1969	disintegration 1970

Source: Hole and Levine 1971, 115–58.

women's liberation groups after they separated from the New Left in 1968. The collective identity that came to be associated with "women's liberation" in the early 1970s developed out of this process of conflict and negotiation. Figure 10–1 illustrates schematically how this process occurred in one location. The upper left-hand column indicates the processes of repeated conflict and segmentation of the New York radical feminists which, at the same time, gave rise to a series of collective actions that symbolically depicted the common understandings developing within the network. In contrast to the older branch of equal rights feminists, the radicals challenged the personal characteristics and patterns of social interaction assigned to women by the dominant cultural code through public actions and confrontations that increasingly gained national media coverage and public attention. By fall 1968, the Atlantic City demonstrations against the image of women portrayed in the Miss America bathing suit contests brought front page coverage throughout the country. A live sheep was crowned Miss America and bras, girdles, and other "instruments of torture" were dumped into a Freedom Trashcan. Young women, with their open disrespect for "Miss America" and the image of women it celebrates, were soon dubbed "bra burners" by the mass media. Despite this distortion of their collective actions (or because of it), their numbers continued to grow. By November, a national meeting gave a sense of common purpose while contributing to the formation of additional radical groups that continued the process of conflict, segmentation, and dissolution throughout 1969. At the same time, the rudiments of a new collective identity were taking shape.

Although New York drew on an unusually large constituency of radical women, their experiences reflected a microcosm of centers of mobilization around the country. Throughout the year, an understanding of women's oppression (in contrast to discrimination) developed among the New York women that emphasized a politics of interpersonal relations; the bonding of women as an oppressed class; the use of rapping (later, "consciousness raising") to bring out the emotional pain of women's lives; a fear of leadership and hierarchy; and the creation of novel and innovative tactics to voice women's anger against the symbols of conventional femininity. These common understandings grew in an emotional atmosphere of tension and conflict over major points of disagreement within the emerging identity of radical feminists. Every action and every organizational split reflected both a conflict over identity and the emergence of a new basis of understanding.

Through the processes associated with identity construction, the movement experienced extraordinary growth between 1969 and 1970. By mid 1970, *Notes from the Second Year*, a feminist journal of 126 pages, sold over forty thousand copies (Hole and Levine 1971, 158). The number of movement periodicals increased from two in 1968 to sixty-one in 1972. Small groups proliferated throughout the country, and regional conferences to coordinate their activities had become commonplace by 1970 (Carden 1974). By August 1970, the highly diverse submerged networks of equal rights feminists and women's liberation were ready to emerge as womanhood united, the historic actor.

The Women's Movement as "Historic Actor"

Melucci has rightfully pointed to the origins of social movements at an intermediate level of analysis: the submerged networks of face-to-face interactions like those of the New York radical feminists who created the basis of a new collective identity during a short period of cultural experimentation. In the process of testing new representations through collective actions, experiences of conflict, internal dissension, and organizational segmentation and dissolution, new understandings were developed that became the basis for challenging the dominant cultural code at its roots. As this identity developed, however, it gathered increasing support from the structural changes that had altered the lives of U.S. women throughout the twentieth century and led to a massive shift in consciousness among both men and women. As the two branches of the movement increasingly engaged in common actions during the summer of 1970, they found that the collective identity they represented has massive appeal.

Like other new movements, the women's movement in the United States first achieved widespread national recognition and political influence at its point of initial mass mobilization. Women's Strike for Equality Day, August 26, 1970, marked the symbolic starting point for the contemporary women's movement in the United States. Sponsored by a broad coalition of women's movement organizations and coordinated by the National Organization for Women (NOW) to commemorate the fiftieth anniversary of the Suffrage Amendment, tens of thousands of women went "on strike" for equality. It was the largest protest on behalf of women in U.S. history (Hole and Levine 1971, 420). Women across the country marched and picketed, held rallies and attended teach-ins. In New York, women set up a child-care center in City Hall Park; in Chicago, sit-ins were held at restaurants barring women (Deckard 1975, 343); in New York, feminists went to the editor of the *New York Times* to protest an editorial titled "Henpecked House," against the Equal Rights Amendment (ERA); and in Minneapolis, a guerrilla theater group portrayed the parts of key figures in the universal abortion drama for downtown audiences (Hole and Levine 1971, 263, 299). The most memorable event in media coverage, however, was the unprecedented outpouring of tens of thousands of women who marched down Fifth Avenue in New York carrying signs that read, "Don't Cook Dinner—Starve a Rat Today!" "Eve Was Framed," and "End Human Sacrifice! Don't Get Married!!" (Hole and Levine 1971, 78; Deckard 1975, 343). Despite its label as "Equality Day," the protests, demonstrations, guerrilla theater, chants, and banners that marked the day represented not only the discrimination issues of equal rights feminists but also the personal politics of women's liberation.

Equality Day marked a turning point in terms of women's political influence and the nature of the women's movement. The size of the mobilization made it clear that the movement would now have to be taken seriously (Freeman 1973, 84). Only after Equality Day did Congress act on behalf of women. During the 1960s, Congress had considered 844 bills concerned with women's issues and passed only 10 (Klein 1984, 22). The Ninety-second Congress passed more women's right legislation than the total of all previous legislation combined (see Freeman 1975, 202–5). By 1980, 71 bills had been passed on behalf of women (Costain 1988, 161). In addition to political influence in Congress, media interest in women began a sharp upward trend after Equality Day as well (Cancian and Ross 1981). Public awareness of the new movement almost immediately reached 80 percent of adult Americans (Hole and Levine 1971, 269), and public opinion polls began to show a marked increase in support for improvements in the status of women. Women began to win elections to local, state, and federal office in unprecedented numbers (Mueller 1987).

The movement itself was transformed by the publicity associated with the Strike. New members had been recruited primarily through personal networks of activists in the period from 1965 to 1970, but after the Strike, contact with the movement through the media played an increasing role (Carden 1974, 32–33). Because of its greater visibility and respectability, the new recruits flooded the modest NOW offices in major cities. Chapters often expanded by as much as 50 to 70 percent in a few months (Freeman 1975, 85). The National Organization for Women mushroomed from a membership of several thousand in 1969 to fifteen thousand by 1972 (Carden 1974, 194). By the end of the decade, it had become a mass membership organization of several hundred thousand (Costain and Costain 1987).

For three years after the Equality Day Strike, the Women's Movement acquired the character of that mythical, historical actor that Melucci has typified as a "unified empirical datum" or collective reality that is seen to exist as a "thing" (Melucci 1988, 330; 1989, 18). This "thingness" of the movement's collective identity in the eyes of the national media, Congress, the state legislators, and, probably, the general public is anathama to Melucci because it denies the diversity and the tentativeness of the "real" social movement that he has observed in submerged networks. Yet, there is considerable evidence to suggest that The Movement as historical actor was thought to represent an aroused and angry womanhood. Congress yielded to its demand for equality in their passage of legislation on behalf of women.[9] For a brief moment, a very brief moment, women emerged as historic actor with a seemingly homogeneous identity centered on a wide-ranging quest for equality.

Despite the impressive evidence that a homogeneous and unitary movement was demonstrated by the Equality Day marches, both feminist activists at the core of the movement then and scholars who have studied the movement since have realized that The Movement was a highly diverse aggregation of women with many different grievances, programs of action, and visions of the future. As Melucci has claimed for the European "new social movements," at the level of interpersonal, face-to-face relationships, the movement was not then, nor has it ever been, a unified whole.[10]

Yet, a more comprehensive analysis would encompass not only the interactions and meanings of the core actors who created the movement or even those who were recruited to it but also its contributions to public discourse and political culture. To understand the political influence of the movement would require consideration of the impression of unity created by the Equality Strike and its media coverage as a major datum to be explained. Such an analysis would draw from much of the new work on social construction that seeks to explain the consequences as well as the origins of social movements. To address this level of public discourse and political influence is not to deny that origins of movements lie in submerged networks and must be analyzed with a different set of conceptual and empirical tools. Nevertheless, it requires an analysis that includes but extends beyond Melucci's important contributions.

Conclusion

This case study focuses on two moments in the life of the contemporary women's movement—the first mass mobilization of U.S. women in the Women's Equality Day Strike of August 1970, and the five-year period preceding the Strike—when the two branches of contemporary U.S. feminism were constructing a new identity through a process of internal conflict and organizational segmentation. These two stages in the development of the movement point to both the strengths and the weaknesses of Melucci's intermediate level of analysis for a comprehensive theory of social construction.

Melucci's theory is most telling when it calls attention to that level of face-to-face interaction where collective identities are developed in submerged networks through a process of social negotiation. It is at this point that structural sources of personal injury—such as the contradiction that younger branch women felt between their high levels of education and the low status they experienced in the personal politics of the 1960s movements—are translated into a shared sense of injustice focused on grievances that are articulated as part of a program for change. The case study also demonstrates, however, that the creative tensions that fuel these negotiations spring as much from internal competition and conflict within movement networks as from the inadequacy of means for realizing goals. Although the new collective identity of women continued to change in the submerged networks of the movement and to be challenged by countermovements such as those that arose in the mid 1970s to oppose early feminist victories in abortion rights and the Equal Rights Amendment, the collective identity soon took on a life of its own.

The independent existence or "thingness" of the identity of "women" that existed in the early 1970s suggests that a comprehensive theory of social movement construction cannot restrict its attention to the intermediate level of submerged networks if it is concerned with the political influence and cultural changes achieved by the movement. The collective identities created within submerged networks achieve an independent existence once they become public through the movement's explanatory apparatus of manifestos, programs, press conferences, banners, slogans, insignia, costumes, and guerrilla theater that attempt to account for the movement and its collective actions. Through these devices, a collective identity becomes public that has a potential for political influence. It is then subject to attempts at distortion and marginalization of state, media, and countermovements. (See Gitlin's [1980] description in his excellent study of media treatment of Students for a Democratic Society [SDS] during the 1960s.) At this public stage of movement development, when the collective identity becomes a historic actor, it would be an empirical as well as a theoretical mistake to equate the public persona of this collective identity (an object of political culture and public discourse) with the collective identity of Melucci's submerged networks (an object of continuing negotiation and renegotiation amid fluid but intense face-to-face interactions).

The distinction between these two levels of analysis is important not only for our appreciation of Melucci's strengths and weaknesses but also for locating his contribution within the developing work on the social movement of social movements. As this work has proliferated, it has become increasingly important to identify theoretical contributions in terms of appropriate levels of analysis.

The most comprehensive attempt to specify these levels is Klandermans's (1992) essay in which he distinguishes three levels of social construction: (1) public discourse and the formation and transformation of collective identities; (2) persuasive communication during mobilization campaigns by movement organizations, their opponents, and countermovement organizations; and (3) what he terms "consciousness raising" during episodes of collective behavior. At the first level, he combines the two construction processes that have been distinguished here: public discourse such as William Gamson's (1988) work on "issue packaging" by the media and Melucci's (1989) conception of the construction of collective identities in submerged networks. The second level of persuasive communication by social movement organizations and their opponents encompasses Klandermans's (1984) own work on consensus mobilization and the work of David Snow and his associates (1986) on frame alignment. At the third level, Klandermans includes the changes of meanings and perception that occur during the course of experiencing collective action as described, for instance, in the work of Rick Fantasia (1988) on industrial strikes.

Klandermans distinguishes these three levels in terms of two implicit criteria: the number of people involved and the degree to which social construction is purposive or spontaneous. Public discourse is a diffuse process encompassing major media of communication for a society or sector of society. Social constructions created by social movement organizations are purposive and reach a more limited audience than public discourse. Finally, construction processes involving the participants and spectators at a collective action event are even more limited by the situational opportunities for direct participation or observation.

While Klandermans's typological distinctions are extremely useful in ordering this growing field of research, our lengthy consideration of Melucci's theory of collective identity suggests several modifications. After Melucci has so carefully indicated that the submerged networks are part of the latency phase of social movements, an "invisible process" out of the public eye, it is inappropriate that this process should be considered a part of public discourse. In fact, as Melucci argues, it is partly the freedom from public scrutiny that permits people to interact in small groups where experimentation and negotiation of identities can result in the development of new social codes and goals for action. Thus, when selecting groups for study in Milan, Melucci deliberately chose the most grass-roots level of participation because, he noted, leaders were more likely to present, what was to him, a falsely unified version of the collective identity if they had to interact frequently with public actors such as media representatives or officials (1989, 242). It was only at the grass-roots level, he felt, that such false presentations (which should properly be considered part of public discourse) could be avoided and maximum heterogeneity in experimentation and negotiation be observed.

On the other hand, our case study of the public phase, or "coming out," of the women's movement at the Women's Strike for Equality Day indicates that collective identities do become a part of public discourse and, potentially, historic actors if the movement attempts to bring about social or political change. At this public level of analysis, a different set of social and political actors, particularly the representatives of formal organizations, will attempt to influence the nature of the collective identity and fit it to their own interests and systems of meaning.

These observations suggest the utility of four rather than three levels of analysis: public discourse, persuasive communication initiated by movement organizations, "consciousness raising" from participation in episodes of collective action, and the creation of collective identities in submerged networks. To the extent that the four levels of analysis have a natural sequencing in a cycle of protest, it seems likely that social movements based on a major reconstruction of collective identities will require either a lengthy or an intensive period for the gestation of the new identity. An ideal typical sequence would progress from least to most public awareness (and, undoubtedly, back again). Groups of individuals in submerged networks would experiment with new collective identities and action proposals, increasingly taking their new social constructions into conflict with targets of change or potential converts outside their own small circle just as the New York radical feminists crowned a sheep "Miss America." As a collective identity takes shape, potential activists may come together and create a social movement organization with a public declaration announcing their new collective identity like the women from the State Commissions on the Status of Women who formed the National Organization for Women and drew up a Bill of Rights for women in the mid 1960s. Collective actions such as those associated with women's Strike for Equality Day offer opportunities for direct experience of action and perceptual change based on the newly revealed collective identity. Finally, the national media may be attracted by the newsworthiness of the confrontation or the importance of the values at stake, and the social reconstruction represented by the new collective identity may become a part of public discourse. (See Freeman on the "grand press blitz" of the women's movement, January through March 1970 [1975, 148–51].) Over the course of any social movement, these processes of social construction will cycle back and forth between levels in increasingly complex patterns depending on the degree to which all sectors of society become involved and how quickly the movement is controlled.

Yet, the search for stages is somewhat premature in a field that is only now beginning to distinguish one level of analysis from another. In this chapter, I have attempted to distinguish two of these levels and to suggest that Melucci's contribution lies in highlighting an intermediate level of analysis in a latency phase that may precede the creation of formal organizations. His work suggests the importance of the opening skirmishes between members of submerged networks and symbolic representations of the dominant cultural code through collective actions that begin a more public phase of the movement.

Although the political fortunes of any subordinate group, such as women, demand that it enter a public phase to challenge the cultural order directly and to influence public affairs, such an analysis would not explain how women came to develop and identify with an analysis of women as a minority group and to share what Gamson and his colleagues (1982) call an "injustice frame" and McAdam (1982) terms "cognitive liberation." To understand how several hundred women throughout the United States constructed the new identity of women as historic actor that became an influential political force for change in the status of women, it is necessary to understand the origins of the women's movement in the preceding decade. It is here that Melucci's theory is most convincing.

Notes

1. Increased awareness began with the New School volume, edited by Jean Cohen in 1985, which was followed by a series of papers by Bert Klandermans and Sidney Tarrow (see Klandermans 1986; Klandermans and Tarrow 1988; Klandermans 1990).

2. But see *From Structure to Action,* in which Klandermans, Kriesi, and Tarrow attempt to connect social structure to collective action. In the introduction, Klandermans and Tarrow (1988) indicate that the volume seeks to "bridge that gap between structure and participation" (10).

3. Important representations of this developing interest in social movement culture and processes of social construction as applied to social movements are found in contributions to *Frontiers in Social Movement Theory*, edited by Aldon Morris and Carol Mueller (1992).

4. Later, I argue that the "unified empirical datum" is not necessarily a false reification but is instead a cultural artifact that serves to enhance or detract from the movement's political influence. A similar perception of unity in crowd behavior by observers is also a starting point for recent theories of collective behavior (see the first edition of *Collective Behavior* [Turner and Killian 1957]).

5. The latent/manifest distinction refers to the difference between the private, "submerged" life of the movement in groups and communities that experiment and negotiate challenges to the dominant cultural code and the visible, public challenges to that code that usually begin in collective action events or in symbolic insignia of dress or behavior (see also Taylor and Whittier 1992).

6. The most authoritative accounts are those by Hole and Levine (1971); Carden (1974); Freeman (1973, 1975); Deckard (1975); Cassell (1977); Evans (1980); and Ferree and Hess (1985).

7. Corresponding examples for the new social movement approach in Europe are Inglehart 1977 and Barnes, Kaase, and Allerbeck 1979.

8. Just how radically different their collective identity had become from women outside the movement could not be appreciated until it was incorporated into the Congressional hearings that became the basis for interpreting the implications of the Equal Rights Amendment (see Brown et al. 1971). These implications, including the obligation of women to perform military service and to surrender their (largely inoperative) support prerogatives in divorce proceedings, became the target of attack in a ferocious campaign in the mid 1970s by conservative women that undermined the impression of the women's movement as united womanhood, a historic actor (see Mansbridge 1986).

9. Margaret Heckler was Republican leader of the Congressional Women's Caucus throughout much of the 1970s. She was one of two women first appointed to the Cabinet by President Ronald Reagan in an attempt to woo the women's vote.

10. Nevertheless, the power of the unitary image is revealed in comments by Freeman (1975), who notes, "The pluralistic nature of the women's liberation movement is a characteristic that has not been adequately appreciated either by the movement's participants or by its critics" (150).

References

Barnes, Samuel H., Max Kaase, and Klause R. Allerbeck. 1979. *Political Action: Mass Participation in Five Western Democracies.* London: Sage.

Brown, Barbara A., Thomas I. Emerson, Gail Falk, and Ann E. Freedman.

1971. "The Equal Rights Amendment: A Constitutional Basis of Equal Rights for Women." *Yale Law Journal* 80:955–62.

Cancian, Francesca M., and Bonnie L. Ross. 1981. "Mass Media and the Women's Movement: 1900–1977." *Journal of Applied Behavioral Science* 17:9–26.

Carden, Maren Lockwood. 1974. *The New Feminist Movement*. New York: Russell Sage Foundation.

Cassell, Joan. 1977. *A Group Called Women*. New York: David McKay.

Cohen, Jean, ed. 1985. "Social Movements." *Social Research* 52 (Winter).

Costain, Anne N. 1988. "Women's Claims as a Special Interest." In *The Politics of the Gender Gap*, edited by Carol M. Mueller, pp. 150–72. Beverly Hills: Sage.

Costain, Anne N., and Douglas Costain. 1987. Unpublished calculations on feminist memberships made available to the author. Department of Political Science, University of Colorado, Boulder.

Deckard, Barbara. 1975. *The Women's Movement*. New York: Harper and Row.

Degler, Carl. 1967. "Revolution without Ideology: The Changing Place of Women in America." *The Woman in America*, edited by Robert Jay Lifton, pp. 193–210. Boston: Beacon Press.

Evans, Sara. 1980. *Personal Politics*. New York: Vintage Books.

Fantasia, Rick. 1988. *Cultures of Solidarity: Consciousness, Action, and Contemporary American Workers*. Berkeley: University of California Press.

Ferree, Myra Marx, and Beth B. Hess. 1985. *Controversy and Coalition: The New Feminist Movement*. Boston: Twayne.

Freeman, Jo. 1973. "The Origins of the Women's Liberation Movement." *American Journal of Sociology* 78:792–811.

———. 1975. *The Politics of Women's Liberation*. New York: David McKay.

———. 1979. "The Women's Liberation Movement: Its Origins, Organizations, Activities, and Ideas." In *Women: A Feminist Perspective*, edited by Jo Freeman, 2d ed., pp. 557–74. Palo Alto, Calif.: Mayfield.

Gamson, William A. 1988. "Political Discourse and Collective Action." *From Structure to Action: Comparing Social Movement Research across Cultures*, edited by Bert Klandermans, Hanspeter Kriesi, and Sidney Tarrow, pp. 219–47. Vol. 1 of *International Social Movement Research*. Greenwich, Conn.: JAI Press.

———. 1992. "The Social Psychology of Social Movements." In *Frontiers in Social Movement Theory*, edited by Aldon D. Morris and Carol McClurg Mueller, pp. 53–76. New Haven: Yale University Press.

Gamson, William A., Bruce Fireman, and Steve Rytina. 1982. *Encounters with Unjust Authority*. Homewood, Ill.: Dorsey.

Gitlin, Todd. 1980. *The Whole World Is Watching: Mass Media in the Making and the Unmaking of the New Left*. Berkeley: University of California Press.

Hacker, Helen Mayer. (1951) 1979. "Women as a Minority Group." In *Women: A Feminist Perspective*, edited by Jo Freeman, 2d ed., pp. 505–20. Originally published in *Social Forces* 30 (1951): 60–69.

Heckler, Margaret. 1977. Talk at Wellesley College. Wellesley, Mass.

Hole, Judith, and Ellen Levine. 1971. *Rebirth of Feminism*. New York: Quadrangle.

Hooks, Bell. 1981. *Ain't I a Woman?* Boston: South End Press.

Huber, Joan. 1976. "Toward a Socio-Technological Theory of the Women's Movement." *Social Problems* 23:371–88.

Inglehart, Ronald. 1977. *The Silent Revolution: Changing Values and Political Styles among Western Publics.* Princeton: Princeton University Press.

Johnston, Hank. 1991. "Movements, Methods, and Melucci." Paper presented at the annual meeting of the Pacific Sociological Association, Irvine, California, April 14–17.

Klandermans, Bert. 1984. "Mobilization and Participation: Social Psychological Expansions of Resource Mobilization Theory." *American Sociological Review* 49:583–600.

———. 1986. "New Social Movements and Resource Mobilization: The European and the American Approach." *International Journal of Mass Emergencies and Disasters* 4:13–39.

———. 1990. "New Social Movements and Resource Mobilization: The European and the American Approach Revisited." Department of Social Psychology. Vrije Universiteit, Amsterdam.

———. 1992. "The Social Construction of Protest and Multiorganizational Fields." In *Frontiers in Social Movement Theory*, edited by Aldon D. Morris and Carol McClurg Mueller. New Haven: Yale University Press.

Klandermans, Bert, and Sidney Tarrow. 1988. "Mobilization into Social Movements: Synthesizing European and American Approaches." In *From Structure to Action: Comparing Social Movement Research across Cultures,* edited by Bert Klandermans, Hanspeter Kriesi, and Sidney Tarrow, pp. 1–38. Vol. 1 of *International Social Movement Research.* Greenwich, Conn.: JAI Press.

Klein, Ethel. 1984. *Gender Politics: From Consciousness to Mass Politics.* Cambridge: Harvard University Press.

Lifton, Robert J., ed. 1967. *The Woman in America.* Boston: Beacon Press. Originally published as a special issue of *Daedalus: The Journal of the American Academy of Arts and Sciences* (Spring 1964).

McAdam, Douglas. 1982. *Political Process and the Development of Black Insurgency, 1930–1970.* Chicago: University of Chicago Press.

Mansbridge, Jane. 1986. *Why We Lost the ERA.* Chicago: University of Chicago Press.

Melucci, Alberto. 1985. "The Symbolic Challenge of Contemporary Movements." *Social Research* 52:789–816.

———. 1988. "Getting Involved: Identity and Mobilization in Social Movements." In *From Structure to Action: Comparing Social Movement Research across Cultures,* edited by Bert Klandermans, Hanspeter Kriesi, and Sidney Tarrow, pp. 329–48. Vol. 1 of *International Social Movement Research.* Greenwich, Conn.: JAI Press.

———. 1989. *Nomads of the Present: Social Movements and Individual Needs in Contemporary Society.* Philadelphia: Temple University Press.

Morris, Aldon. 1984. *The Origins of the Civil Rights Movement: Black Communities Organizing for Change.* New York: Free Press.

Morris, Aldon D., and Carol McClurg Mueller, eds. 1992. In *Frontiers in Social Movement Theory.* New Haven: Yale University Press.

Mueller, Carol McClurg. 1987. "Collective Consciousness, Identity Transformation, and the Rise of Women in Public Office in the United States." In *The Women's Movements of the United States and Western Europe*, edited by Mary Fainsod Katzenstein and Carol McClurg Mueller, pp. 89–108. Philadelphia: Temple University Press.

Reisman, David. 1964. "Two Generations." In *The Woman in America*, edited by Robert Jay Lifton, pp. 72–97. Boston: Beacon Press.

Rossi, Alice. 1967. "Equality between the Sexes: An Immodest Proposal." In *The Woman in America*, edited by Robert Jay Lifton, pp. 98–143. Boston: Beacon Press.

Rupp, Leila J., and Verta Taylor. 1987. *Survival in the Doldrums: The American Women's Rights Movement, 1945 to the 1960s.* New York: Oxford University Press.

Snow, David A., E. Burke Rochford, Jr., Steven K. Worden, and Robert D. Benford. 1986. "Frame Alignment Processes, Micromobilization, and Movement Participation." *American Sociological Review* 51:464–81.

Tarrow, Sidney. 1989. *Democracy and Disorder.* New York: Oxford University Press.

Taylor, Verta. 1989. "Social Movement Continuity." *American Sociological Review* 54:761–75.

Taylor, Verta, and Nancy Whittier. 1992. "Collective Identity in Social Movement Communities: Lesbian Feminist Mobilization." In *Frontiers in Social Movement Theory*, edited by Aldon D. Morris and Carol McClurg Mueller, pp. 104–29. New Haven: Yale University Press.

Turner, Ralph H., and Lewis M. Killian. 1957. *Collective Behavior.* Englewood Cliffs, N.J.: Prentice-Hall.

Part III

Collective Action and Identity in Changing Political Contexts

Chapter 11

New Social Movements and Old Regional Nationalisms

Hank Johnston

Alongside the growth of New Social Movements (NSMs) in the 1970s and 1980s, there has also been a proliferation of ethnic nationalist movements. In Spain and Canada, ethnic nationalisms challenge the integrity of the state; in what was Yugoslavia, they have destroyed it; and in several former Soviet republics, nationalism has become the fundamental principle of state power. Sometimes nationalist sentiments are so strong and pervasive that they subsume feminist, ecological, and peace agendas under the banner of the nation, as occurred in Quebec, the Basque region, Catalonia, Estonia, Latvia, and Lithuania. Although ethnic nationalisms do not constitute a new social force by any means, it would be incorrect to say that they are characteristic only of less developed social structures. Ethnic movements have flourished in highly industrialized regions such as Catalonia, Euzkadi, Quebec, Flanders, and in the Baltic states where industrial development and standards of living were superior to those in other Soviet regions.

The substantive goals of NSMs and ethnic nationalisms are widely divergent: NSMs focus on the individual search for identity in the context of global programs for social change, while nationalist movements reflect political and cultural aspirations of communities that are subordinated by a core region. Nevertheless, there exists an unexpected convergence of emphasis concerning two key points. First, regarding motivations to participate, the goals and activities of ethnic nationalist movements are thoroughly embedded in the identity of their proponents, although the emphasis is on ascribed characteristics such as culture and language rather than life-style. Second, patterns of participation are anchored in the everyday lives of their adherents.

Insofar as theorists of NSMs discuss their ethnic movements, the concept of identity-search is appended to conventional explanations, such as unequal nation-state development, without much empirical support. Alberto Melucci and Mario Diani (1983) observe that ethnic movements are a combination of both residues of communal identity from the nation-building process and a reflection of identity needs arising from the demands of a complex social system. Melucci (1989, 90–92) also suggests that they in part reflect the need for an integrating identity that arises in response to the disparate role constellations that confront the individual today. "Ethnic solidarity also responds to a need for identity of an eminently symbolic nature. It gives roots" (93). This perspective, he suggests, must be added to the better known explanations of ethnic nationalisms: age-old communal conflict, competition for scarce resources, and political contention in multinational states.

The student of contemporary social movements is left with something of a dilemma. "Old" ethnic nationalisms proliferate alongside "new" movements that are conceptualized as unique products of postindustrial social structure. This could be easily explained if these two types of movements occur among groups occupying different positions in society, but this is not always the case since, as mentioned above, it is common that NSM issues are "nested" within nationalist agendas. As an initial attempt at conceptual refinement, I take a comparative approach to the ethnic movements in both Spain and the several former Soviet republics. I focus on two areas of similarity: identity formation and the role of everyday life experiences in participation. I conclude by relating my tentative findings to the NSM model.

In Spain, I refer to Catalonia and Euzkadi under the Franco regime, leaving aside the weaker Galician nationalist opposition. The newly independent states of Ukraine, Estonia, Latvia, and Lithuania and the Transcaucasian states of Armenia, and Georgia are the comparative foci. Each of these nations maintains a strong cultural and linguistic heritage that has survived alongside (and competed with) more extensive, world-status languages and cultures: Spanish and Russian. These regions also share memories of independence or autonomy, passed from one generation to another, which combine with remembrances of war, repression, and exile to foster among the minority populations antipathy toward either Russians or "Spaniards."

What makes the movements in Spain and the former Soviet Union especially interesting is the force with which they were reasserted after long periods of state repression. In both cases, latent sentiments of nationalism were reawakened by cautious attempts at liberalization by the state. After 1985, *perestroika* and *glasnost* provided opportunities for nationalist expression that were unfathomable a decade earlier. Spain's tentative *apertura* (opening) in the 1960s under Manuel Fraga Iribarne precipitated the growth of nationalist groups and several important mobilizations. Once rekindled, the force of protest gathered momentum in both countries. It continues in the former Soviet republics, while in Spain, it has been for the most part channeled by democratic competition and regional decentralization. In both cases, questions about identity and everyday life were played out under conditions of considerable personal risk. That nationalist sentiments survived in virtual dormancy to burst forth once repression was eased suggests an analytical focus on those aspects of social life where ethnic identity can be nurtured out of the view of the state, namely, the inner recesses of primary relations with family and friends.

Identity Received: Socialization in Nationalist Subcultures

Leaving aside biological influences on personality, a person's identity can be conceived as a thoroughly social construct. In analyzing its social components, it is useful to distinguish between primary and secondary socialization, between identity formation based on intimate relations—family and close friends—and that which is based on impersonal relations outside the orbit of parents and ascribed social ties. Primary ties are characteristic of Gemeinschaft, secondary ties of Gesellschaft; and it is generally agreed that as societies develop and differentiate, the relative emphasis shifts from primary to secondary socialization as the fundamental inputs to adult social identity.

The NSM perspective implicitly extends this dichotomy to postindustrial society by locating key identity-formation processes in temporary groups of erstwhile strangers. NSMs are said to reflect system incongruities that appear as society develops, and which are experienced on the individual level as conflicting role alternatives (Melucci 1985, see also Chapter 5). Attempts to forge new identities therefore comprise a "bottom-up" mechanism whereby the need for structural adjustments in the social system are pointed out by the coalescence and collective action of like-minded folk in NSMs. Social identity is forged in the context of participation in groups united by shared but nevertheless ill-defined answers to identity conflicts. In these groups new life-styles and new identities are forged, radically deracinated—at least for the time being—from antecedents of family and primary ties.

It is on this point that my own thinking about identity in nationalist movements takes a sharp detour. Although there is considerable debate about the actual strength of ethnic identity in modern society (for example, Nagel and Olzak 1982; Nagel 1986; and See 1986 argue they are attenuated), the Spanish and Soviet cases indicate that primary ties comprise important channels in keeping nationalist sentiments alive, and for some participants, strong factors in their participation.

Data for Catalonia and Euzkadi strongly point to the exis-tence of articulated subcultures where ethnic identification and nationalist sentiments were passed from one generation to an-other.[1] While the data are still sketchy and preliminary, the sur-vival of nationalist sentiments in the former Soviet Republics over forty years of severe repression, and their rebirth in the form of National Fronts, strongly suggest the presence of these sorts of subcultural patterns and integrated social relationships, especially in the Baltic and Transcaucasian regions.

Nationalist subcultures are based on relatively permanent so-cial ties and a well-developed system of symbols, values, and be-liefs derived from the minority culture. Because they embody an alternative to the official reality endorsed and promoted by the state, these subcultures convey the illegitimacy of the state at a very basic level. While many people may carry antiregime and nationalist sentiments, not all are integrated into these subcultures. For those on the outside, the main difference lies in the absence of interpersonal and organizational linkages by which a more devel-oped set of oppositional symbols are maintained, and, more im-portant, by which they are passed to new generations.

These subcultures can be analyzed in terms of their cultural content and of the relations that sustain them. On the one hand, the cultural content typically is a mix of religious, political, and national ideas and symbols. Much of it reflects ideological continu-ity with a time prior to the current regime when many of the values and symbols of the subculture were public and widely practiced. In Catalonia and the Basque region, the Statutes of Autonomy under the Second Spanish Republic (1932–1939) served as guideposts for political debate. Religious traditions, holidays, and shrines took on subliminal oppositional and political significance. The Monastery of Montserrat in Catalonia and the Marian cult located there were prominent oppositional symbols, just as the Hill of Crosses at Siauliai, Lithuania, and the Cathedral at Etchmiadzen in Armenia are symbolic of their respective national traditions. The church also played an organizational role in both the Catalan and Basque nationalist opposition (Johnston and Figa 1988; Johnston 1989), as it did the Catholic church in Lithuania, the underground Uniate church in the Ukraine, and to a lesser extent, the Lutheran church in Estonia and Latvia.

A second aspect of the nationalist subculture is the way this cultural content is passed and refined between generations. A key locus of this process is the primary socialization that occurs in the family. This is especially true with respect to family religious practice and traditions whereby antiregime attitudes were fused with religious symbols and beliefs are passed from one generation to another. In Catalonia, nationalist militants frequently came from religious homes in which nationalist symbolism was closely tied to the Montserrat Monastery (Johnston 1989, 1991). The subculture was further articulated in the context of youth activities such as schools, catechism classes, and even boy scout troops that took place under church auspices and away from the scrutiny of the regime. In the Basque region, the religious link was also strong. Schools called *ikastolas* that clandestinely taught the Basque language were frequently located in churches. Through these processes, a small but important proportion of the population was schooled in antiregime values, assuring generational continuity of nationalist and oppositional sentiments. Although there are important differences between the Basque and Catalan cases, especially concerning the direction that Basque youth took their nationalism (see Pérez-Agote 1986; Zulaika 1988), national subcultures can be identified in both regions. In Catalonia, there are indications that a disproportionate number of future political leaders emerged from this group.

Concerning Soviet nationalisms, a good starting place is Lithuania, where a close identification of nationalism with Catholicism dates to the nineteenth century and suggests a subculture in the Basque and Catalan mold. Lithuanian *samizdat* publications during the 1970s were almost wholly from Catholic sectors. Despite the severe repression of the church under the Soviets, estimates of the Catholic faithful range between 50 percent and 80 percent, even among Lithuanian youth (see Bourdeaux 1979; Vardys 1978, 217). The persistence of Catholicism among the younger generation who had not only never experienced religious freedom but also had been subject to intensive antireligious propaganda and sanctions raises the question of how it was accomplished. The answer, I suggest, is to be found in the primary socialization accomplished by the family and closest friends. For the most part, this interaction was beyond penetration by the KGB and the Communist party.

If we can draw parallels from the Basque and Catalan cases, some families not only passed religious traditions but also secular accounts of civil society prior to the loss of independence or autonomy. This was reported by some Catalan militants, although other respondents spoke of frustrating quiescence in their own families about civil war politics. Alfonso Pérez-Agote (1986, 88–92) holds that silence on these matters was especially characteristic in the Basque region and can partly explain the singular extreme course of Basque nationalism. In the Baltics, little was said officially about the period of "bourgeois independence" although, privately, the secret Molotov-Ribbentrop accords that robbed the Baltics of their independence were well known. Beginning in the late 1960s, Lithuanian students began to form "ethnographic study groups" in order to explore the muted—or officially distorted—aspects of recent history. These groups functioned as cover organizations for nationalist activities, much like excursionist groups (hiking and outing clubs) in Catalonia and Euzkadi. In Catalonia, *excursionisme* displayed a strong nationalist orientation prior to the Civil War. After the war, most were closed, but the ones that were able to remain (either by duplicitous assent to Francoist ideology or the patronage of well-placed individuals) often promoted the clandestine study of history, literature, and the Catalan tongue under the innocuous cover of map-making, geography, or archaeology classes (Johnston 1985). To a lesser extent, similar strategies were followed by the Basque outing groups called *mendigortzales*. In Lithuania, student ethnographic groups, in addition to the "bourgeois" promotion of national culture, collected documentation on the period of independence and on the anti-Soviet resistance. Eventually their covers were penetrated by the secret police, and they were suppressed (Vardys 1978, 173).

There is also evidence of a subculture in the western Ukraine that persisted despite the most intense repression. The Ukrainian Uniate church, a Catholic church of the Greek rite, was outlawed by Stalin after World War II, but rather than acquiesce to its mandated incorporation into Russian Orthodoxy, Uniate rites were adminstered in the deepest secrecy by priests—at great personal risk—for forty years. Only in the late 1980s have their clandestine practices become widely known. With neither buildings nor formal organization, the central locus of the Uniate church was the family and close circles of friends (Markus 1975, 108).

Like Lithuania, Ukrainian nationalists see the Uniate church both as a symbol of national subordination and national resiliency. Even nonbelieving nationalists and dissidents have adopted the Uniate cause because of its close identification with the people of the region (Bociurkiw 1975, 73). While the intense repression directed at the Uniate church distinguishes it from Euzkadi and Catalonia (where the church enjoyed privileges under the Franco regime), and from Lithuania (where repression, while severe at times, was generally less blatant), in all cases church-based groups carried strong oppositional credentials, and there were linkages between the religious and secular oppositions.

In Latvia and Estonia, the merger of Lutheranism and nationalism is indicated by the presence of Lutheran clergy and human rights groups at nationalist rallies. While the nationalist-religious link was evident prior to Gorbachev (Parming 1977, 30–31), it seems weaker than in Catalonia, Euzkadi, or Lithuania. This may be due to its more recent origin, dating the period of independence between 1923 and 1939. Prior to independence, German clerics were common in Estonian and Latvian Lutheranism, and they held positions of power in the ecclesiastical hierarchy.[2]

German influence in the Lutheran church parallels the subordination of the Autocephalous Georgian Orthodox church under the Russian Patriarchy between 1810 and 1917 and may account for a weaker religionationalist linkage there as well (Zeigler 1987, 27; Melia 1971, 237). Nevertheless, like Estonia and Latvia, a degree of symbiosis does seem to be present. One description of Georgian nationalism states that many of the intelligentsia have been baptized and display religious icons in their homes. Also, religious rites are commonly administered at burials. The report characterizes these vestiges of Georgian Orthodoxy as reflections of national consciousness (Kolack 1987:40), rather than measures of fealty to church doctrine.[3] There were strong religious overtones in a 1981 nationalist protest commemorating the restoration of Georgian as an official language.

In Armenia, the independence of Armeno-Gregorian Christianity from both Rome and Orthodoxy has fostered a strong linkage between church and nation. This has been reinforced by centuries of religious and national persecution by the Ottoman Turks. Communal pride is fostered by the knowledge that Armenia's conversion to Christianity in A.D. 301 predated Constantine's conversion of Rome by fifteen years. Despite the strength of the religious-nationalist link, and—paradoxically—because of it, the Communist party apparently held Armenian Christianity to be less of a threat than Islam, Catholicism, Lutheranism, or Judaism because it did not imply allegiances beyond Soviet borders. Also, the Armenian church had traditionally been pro-Russian in response to the Islamic threat to the south and east. Thus, the Armenian church was not only tolerated but supported within limits that were liberal by Soviet standards.

Church-state relations in Armenia present a pattern much closer to the Catalan and Basque Spanish cases during the Franco regime. In August 1953, Spain signed a Concordat with the Vatican whereby the church was granted virtual freedom from state control. At the national level, these liberties were purchased by the church's legitimizing blessing on Francoism, but in Euzkadi and Catalonia it had the delegitimizing effect of freeing local churches to more openly promote national culture and to serve as one of the few places where the nascent opposition could escape police surveillance. In Armenia, subordination of the church to the state was greater, and it has been noted that most Armenians were reconciled to subordination to Moscow as long as their church survived in one form or another (Dadrian 1977, 328; see also Wixman 1982, 150). But like Catalonia and Euzkadi, this allowed the church to serve as a crucible of national culture where elsewhere similar manifestations of "bourgeois nationalism" were prohibited. Activities at Montserrat provided opportunities for nationalist expression during the severest years of Francoist repression, such as the anniversary celebrations of Virgin of Montserrat in 1947, the Eucharistic Conference in 1952, and the "rutas de Montserrat" pilgrimages. In a similar manner, Armenian pilgrimages to Etchmiadzin, Caesarea, and Tcharchaban combined religious practice and ethnicity, and no doubt a modicum of secular discussion in the atmosphere of discontent that prevailed in the 1980s.

This brief review strongly suggests patterns of ethnic identification in several republics of the former Soviet Union that parallel those in Catalonia and Euzkadi. It presents a picture of ethnic identity that derives from primary socialization in national, cultural, and religious values. In the words of one Lithuanian observer, "Preschool education, generally accomplished in the home, is done in such a way as to nurture and develop a national consciousness: to teach the language, the customs, and the national character" (Finklestein 1977, 64). These are the social processes by which nationalist movements maintain continuity with the past. While they were not found in all families, and while there were variations in what was passed on, it makes sense that, in the East as well as the West, this kind of socialization played an important role among young adults who were particularly adamant about their national identity, and who demonstrated a propensity to some form of militancy.

The key point concerning the new social movement perspective is that here, a central aspect of identity is ascribed by virtue of the web of social relations one is born into instead of defined in the course of participation in the movement. Nationalist subcultures provide networks of association that can serve as vehicles of recruitment and often persist into adult life. Insofar as nationalist movements remain social forces in modern societies, the cultural and social media of primary socialization must be factored into the theoretical equation. While it lies beyond the scope of this discussion to specify how variations in the organization and substance of these subcultures might affect mobilization, this is an important area for further study.

Group Identity, Grievances, and Everyday Life

Within NSMs, the definition of identity within dense networks of adherents is a key motivation for participation. NSMs provide "new social spaces" where (predominantely young) like-minded persons seek their own individuality in a complex and often contradictory world. They experiment in new life-styles as assertions of their individuality that lie outside accepted models. These activities combine into a way of life that, although typically involving only a short-term commitment, nevertheless provides a social arena where many are able to define who they are.

This is a view that stands in sharp contrast to the model of social movement participation based on rational choice. Briefly, the rationalist model proposes that an individual chooses to participate in a movement if the perceived benefits of action outweigh the costs. Olson (1965) predicted that in large movements, most people would not participate if not for "selective incentives" such as ancillary benefits of association and camaraderie. The rational actor understands that the addition of one other person to the movement often has little effect on the movement's success. Furthermore, many people will withhold participation because they will enjoy the fruits of the movement's success anyway; they become "free-riders" on the backs of active movement participants. This is an approach that does not really deal with questions of identity, although selective incentives of solidarity and camaraderie imply the salience of social aspects of identity based on participation. By the same token, the self-interested individualism of the rational-choice model suggests that participation would be quickly terminated if the group failed to meet one's identity needs.

Both these approaches deemphasize the notion of injustice as a force behind group formation and solidarity. Research by Gamson, Fireman, and Rytina (1982) demonstrates the close affinity between an emergent sense of injustice and group cohesiveness. Based on a series of ingenious experimental situations, they show that an emergent "injustice frame" provides a vehicle by which previously unconnected individuals can coalesce to act collectively. In this section, I argue that the strong quotidian basis of nationalist grievances imparts a high degree of commonality that easily translates into nationalist solidarity and that establishes a strong association between national consciousness and one's social identity. This stands in contrast to the NSM model that, despite an emphasis on everyday organization and participant identity, does not accord much weight to collective grievances. In the Spanish and Soviet cases, nationalist movements exhibit fundamental grass-roots qualities that reflect definitions of injustice based in everyday life rather than in abstract political or historic claims to autonomy. This is not to say that historically based political programs are absent or that strategic and individualizing motivations (characteristic of rational choice and NSM models) never play a role. Rather, based on preliminary comparisons, and in the aggregate, they seem to play secondary and sometimes symbolic functions in mobilization.

Fundamental to nationalist grievances is the way minority status renders the national culture a problematic feature of daily life. In the context of economic and political subordination, daily activities in the local language, predicated on shared cultural values and norms of behavior, are subject to conflict with the majority culture. Encounters with the state, typically in the persona of a representative of the core region, cause numerous quotidian molestations that are easily interpreted in the context of national subordination. To put it another way, everyday life is the arena where the shared injustice frame is maintained and articulated. Not only because grievances are so widely shared but also because these little injustices pertain in a most immediate fashion to one's way of life, nationalist movements are characterized by a high level of solidarity. Indeed, defense of a way of life may in part explain the high level of emotionality typical of nationalist movements.

The empirical basis of these propositions lies in my own Catalan interview data and is supported by Pérez-Agote's interviews in Euzkadi (1986, 158–80). In Catalonia and the Basque region, prohibitions against the language and culture caused innumerable situations where what was typically unproblematic on an everyday basis suddenly becomes an experience of discrimination. In the course of interviews with Catalan militants, I was struck by the frequent mention of apparently insignificant experiences in the context of explaining one's nationalism. One respondent opened his interview with a description of how, immediately after the Civil War, he was forced to retake exams in Castilian while all his previous secondary education had been in Catalan. For a youth, this was no doubt a particularly onerous policy. He also described the traditional, Catholic, and politically rightist background of his family, and how they welcomed Franco's victory. But the regime's anti-Catalan policies rendered problematic what for him had previously been unproblematic. This was his justification for taking up nationalist militancy, in spite of a social background that would otherwise place him among stalwart Francoists.

Another representative account describes how activities of the respondent's boy scout troop were broken up by Falangist bullies. Like many other described events, these seem unimportant in the sweep of history that includes civil war, class conflict, and severe state repression, but their importance is suggested by the fact that they were presented as explanations of why one pursued nationalist militancy.

> For example, uh . . . the Spanish state had its own youth organization, which was Falangist. When Falangists and Scouts met on the train, there always were fights. When in the year 1952, the Boy Scouts organized for the first time a rather important camp-out, members of Franco's guardia came to break it up with clubs. All this created a reaction with the kids, who never had any political discourses. We reacted against, that is, we got to be in favor of a situation and against the official regime. It was, let's say, a very natural form of this phenomenon being produced.

The respondent reports that many ex-scouts became leaders in the nationalist opposition; during the democratic transition, they became political leaders in Catalonia.

Other respondents recounted similarly mundane and personal occurrences: the arrogance of a petty official, a railroad clerk who refused to answer if addressed in Catalan, insulting remarks to one's mother or father, or a shove from a Falangist bully. Often remembered were several anti-Catalan epithets of those years, "Speak Christian, Catalan Dog," or "Speak the language of the Empire." These everyday encounters, seemingly minor but perhaps traumatic for a youth, accumulated over time to tax the patience of Catalans. It is also significant that although the postwar years were difficult economic times for the middle class and working class alike, it is comments such as these rather than memories of hardship and deprivation that are invoked during interviews. Similarly, in Pérez-Agote's study of Basque militancy, many of his respondents described repression by the state apparatus. Some of his interviews contain vivid and emotional descriptions of how the state penetrated their everyday lives (1986, esp. 173, 180).

In the Soviet Republics, similar mundane grievances were often at the heart of nationalist outbursts, even in a time prior to *glasnost*. In 1978, there were violent riots at Alma Ata university in Kazakstan over admissions policies. Similarly in Tblisi, Georgia, students reacted violently to a 1980 law that made Russian the official language. It would be incorrect to interpret these outbursts simply as explosions of pent-up nationalism. Rather, as with the Catalan respondent whose exams were nullified, nationalist grievances were synonymous with everyday grievances: language and admissions policies directly affected the daily lives of the participants.

The everyday basis of linguistic conflict is especially apparent when high immigration increases the likelihood of interethnic contact. Centralized economic planning stimulated Russian and other Slavic immigration into peripheral republics (Zaslavsky 1980, 57–64) and has drastically increased contact between locals and immigrants since 1980. In Lithuania, immigrants comprise 20 percent of the total population, and the proportion is close to 50 percent in the capital, Vilnius. This pattern is similar to Catalonia and Euzkadi, where immigrants to urban areas constitute almost half the population and about 30 percent in the region as a whole. In Estonia and Larvia, the proportion of immigrants is higher, 34 percent and 46 percent, respectively. In June 1986, ten thousand Ukrainian and Belorussian refugees from the Chernobyl disaster worsened already severe housing shortages and aroused resentment among locals who feared further deterioration of their standard of living.

Karklins's (1986, 67, 112) respondents reported considerable ethnic tension on the everyday level, especially in the Baltics (epithets hurled on the street and in public transportation, for example), and a high level of ethnic tension in the Soviet Army, particularly in the linguistic domain. This is aggravated by the superordinate status of the Russian nationality as the "big brother" among the "little brother" minority nationalities. Kathryn Woolard (1989) demonstrates with respect to Catalonia that unequal status relationships are easily transferred to bilingual speech situations by immigrants. Prior to independence, the Estonian parliament passed laws requiring Russians to learn Estonian and mandated the use of Estonian on stamps, signs, reports, and advertisements intended for the public. Russian text can also appear, but it cannot be larger (Fisher 1989, 8). It was also reported that in Tallinn, public signs in Russian were obliterated with spray paint (Keller 1988, 6). The passage of similar language laws in Moldavia, Georgia, and other national republics suggests that resentment of linguistic subordination to Russian was widespread. With independence, vindictive linguistic policies can poison relations between locals and immigrants.

Finally, deteriorating economic conditions can aggravate communal conflict on the everyday level. In Riga, the capital of Latvia, Smith (1979, 61) observes that shortages of housing and consumer amenities and lack of services caused conflict with Russian immigrants. Similarly, prior to Estonian independence, shortages of food and consumer goods were blamed on Russian tourists attracted by the relatively high standard of living and Western ambience. Signs appeared in stores requiring buyers to show proof of Estonian residency in order to make purchases.

While these are all secondary accounts, they nevertheless suggest how communal conflict is played out on an everyday level. They also suggest the possibility of a relationship between everyday grievances and two distinguishing features of nationalist mobilization. If the degree to which national subordination penetrates quotidian life is conceptualized as a variable, it may be associated with the emotionality of nationalism the breadth of nationalist oppositions.

First, scholars have for a long time noted that the nationalist pantheon houses symbols that are capable of invoking emotional and often violent responses from the faithful. This is typically explained by reference to the collective history and shared experiences of suffering that these symbols represent. While historical memories are certainly present, passed through the subcultural networks discussed earlier, I also suggest that cultural and political legacies are further animated by everyday repression. Indeed, without the kind of mundane reinforcement I have been describing, it is likely that the power of these symbols would dissipate over time. On the other hand, the destabilization of everyday life reinforces historical symbols and interpretations. The emotionalism of nationalist movements is more comprehensible when one recognizes that interruption of everyday business represents a threat to one's way of life: it is a disruption of all that is taken for granted. Besides family and daily bread, it makes sense that this will be defended more vigorously than anything else.

Second, by breadth of nationalist opposition, I refer to the ability of nationalist movements to subsume other movements under the nationalist banner. Although the "grievance of preference" among adherents may differ, varying between economic discrimination, cultural preservation, ecology, or even feminist and peace agendas, because the medium of debate and solidarity is the minority culture, a strong affinity between nationalist and other grievances exists. This is often reinforced by the relationship between certain grievances and immigration, such as when large atomic power projects (in Ignalina, Lithuania, for example) will require a large immigrant labor force, or the association of the Soviet military with the presence of nonindigenous personnel (hence the peace movement's proposal to make the Baltic region a nuclear free zone). In a minority national context, almost any problem can be defined as resulting from the policies of the core region; its just resolution can be found in the devolution of political power to the region.

Examples are numerous. While the Ukrainian Republic party demanded an independent Ukrainian state, it also called for the establishment of a private market economy and the closure of nuclear power stations (*Los Angeles Times,* May 1, 1990, A6). Similarly, the Lithuanian Sajudis movement subsumed several smaller dissident movements such as the Greens and feminists. Basque nationalist Herri Batasuna received the support of antinuclear groups, homosexual rights activists, and women's groups (Douglass and Zulaika 1990, 250). Because the national culture is the media through which contact between groups takes place, and cultural preservation and promotion goals of the larger movement, there is a tendency to mute conflict between different sectors, and to accentuate points of agreement.

Final Thoughts on Identity, Grievances, and NSMs

These comparisons between minority nationalisms in Spain and the former Soviet
Union help to draw two important distinctions between nationalist
movements and NSMs. First, nationalist movements seem to
share a strong ascribed component in the form of a subcultural
base. This is a source of continuity with the past that is absent
in contemporary analyses of most NSMs. Second, while both
nationalisms and NSMs have their foundation in the everyday life
of their adherents, the key difference is that there is a strong sense
of injustice at this level among nationalist militants that is absent
in many NSMs.

The shared issues of identity and mundanity have justified
the use of the NSM model as a conceptual counterpoint in these
comparisons. But because the preceding pages have focused more
attention on nationalist mobilization than on NSMs, I close by
compensating for the relative neglect. Specifically, I have in mind
how these two issues, ascribed aspects of identity and the mundanity of grievances, suggest new directions for NSM research.

First, like nationalist movements, the choice to advocate
peace, women's issues, or ecology takes place within a historical
context where the meanings of these choices and the parameters
of the action they entail are already partially established in the
prevailing cultural milieu. While in part received and constrained
through various cultural media, these identities are further elaborated within the dense networks of membership that NSM analysts have identified. The NSM model emphasizes elaboration
within the context of the group but deemphasizes the historical
and cultural contexts of these movements.

Much may be gained by reconsidering the cultural and historical legacies of many NSMs. It has been demonstrated, for example, that the women's movement in the United States has drawn
heavily on the work of its predecessors and that this continuity has
been obscured by the waxing and waning of political and cultural
opportunities (Rupp and Taylor 1987). Similarly, the roots of the
environmental movement lie in the anti-industrial romanticism of
the nineteenth century. Nor is the notion of pacifism anything
new: it has strong roots in religious sects like the Quakers and

Mennonites. In a different light, many NSM repertoires of contention draw on different and New Left protests of the 1960s, and on the civil rights movement in the United States.

These links are particularly apparent when there is intergenerational continuity, as demonstrated with the 1960s Free Speech Movement and the New Left in the United States, many of whose militants came from families of the "Old Left." While familial socialization and historical continuity tend to soften the "newness" of the NSM model, researchers in the future should look closely into the social backgrounds of NSM participants for patterns of family influence and for the mechanisms of organizational and cultural maintenance.

Second, NSMs emphasize everyday life within the movement as the locus of identity formation, whereas nationalist movements grow out of discrimination and repression regularly played out in mundane affairs. These grievances give rise to a sense of commonality based on national identity that is general and widely shared but not in itself sufficient to account for participation in the movement organization. They must be distinguished from the social processes that occur within the militant group whereby everyday grievances are defined and amplified in the context of interaction—strategy sessions and militant actions, for example. Indeed, it makes sense that, being so widely shared, mundane grievances of national subordination are placed in the background in favor of more immediate, intense, and interactionally based experiences that comprise participation in the movement organization. Under these situations, like NSMs, social identities of nationalist militants are based on interaction within the group.

Clearly there is a strong association between the intensity of interaction among participants and the degree to which their social identity derives from those activities. What distinguishes the NSM model is the disjuncture between movement adherence and the background of participation embedded in grievances. Rather than an emerging collectivity defined by shared definitions of injustice, NSM participants come as individuals (and apparently leave that way, too) in search of solidarity qua social identity among erstwhile strangers. This is what makes the NSM model so interesting and provocative, but I suggest that the place of collective grievances has perhaps been too easily dismissed.

Despite the emphasis on identity, it is important to note that the NSMs most frequently mentioned have some grievance base. Furthermore, a question remains about the degree to which, experienced at the everyday level, these grievances provide motivations for participation. In the women's movement, for example, the gospels of feminism according to de Beauvoir and Friedan had such a wide resonance among women that surely they articulated grievances that were widely felt. Similarly, the connection between the stresses and congestion of modern urban life and participation in the environmental movement suggests an injustice frame in which a wide range of everyday experience fits. Perhaps the link is more symbolic, as with antinuclear mobilizations representing a focused point of protest for the innumerable molestations of modern urban life.

The general point is that quotidian grievances may be fundamental to processes of group formation and solidarity. Especially in early stages of movement formation, the collective expression of grievances represents the emergence of collectivity-cum-movement and a primary source of initial coordination. To put it another way, grievances are a part of the social media that conveys organization while the interactional base of identity formation and solidarity are still being forged. Future NSM research might focus on the period prior to when the individual is fully integrated into interpersonal networks to see what keeps him or her there. It may be that at this crucial juncture, when the movement itself is most vulnerable, "old-time" concepts like grievances and a sense of injustice are decisive.

Notes

1. Data for Catalonia was collected as part of a larger study reported in Johnston 1991. Eighty-two interviews with nationalist and working-class militants were conducted in 1981, when Spanish democracy was not yet firmly established and debates concerning regional autonomy for minority nationalities were still raging. Chapter 2 in that work provides a detailed description of methodological procedures and interviewing strategies.

2. While it makes sense that the linkage of religion and nation deepens and strengthens the oppositional subculture, the religious factor may not be necessary. In Catalonia, the importance of the church partly resided in its provision of organizational resources and ready-made networks for recruitment and action (Johnston 1991, chap. 4). Similar organizational resources can come from other sources, such as community structure, cultural patterns of friendship and acquaintance, and informal professional and intellectual groups, as found in Estonia

(see Taagepera 1983, 78). Also in Estonia, the role of choral groups was significant, hence the "Singing Revolution" of 1989.

3. It should be noted that this study focused on the intelligentsia, a group that one might expect to have attentuated religious beliefs. It may be that even deeper religious sentiments would be found among less cosmopolitan social classes.

References

Bociurkiw, Bhodan R. 1975. "Religious Dissent and the Soviet State." In *Religion and Atheism in the USSR and Eastern Europe,* edited by Bohdan R. Bociurkiw and John W. Strong, pp. 58–90. London: Macmillan.

Bourdeaux, Michael. 1979. *Land of Crosses: The Struggle for Religious Freedom in Lithuania, 1939–78.* Devon, England: Augustine.

Dadrian, Vahakn N. 1977. "Nationalism in Soviet Armenia—A Case Study of Ethnocentrism." In *Nationalism in the USSR and Eastern Europe in the Era of Brezhnev and Kosygin,* edited by George W. Simmonds, pp. 202–58. Detroit: University of Detroit Press.

Douglass, William A., and Joseba Zulaika. 1990. "On the Interpretation of Terrorist Violence: ETA and the Basque Political Process." *Comparative Studies in Society and History* 32:238–57.

Finklestein, Etian. 1977. "Old Hopes and New Currents in Present-Day Lithuania." In *The Violations of Human Rights in Soviet Occupied Lithuania,* edited by Thomas Remeikis, pp. 58–66. Glenside, Pa.: Lithuanian American Community.

Fisher, Dan. 1989. "New Law in Estonia Requires Russians There to Learn Native Language." *Los Angeles Times,* January 19, p. 8.

Gamson, William A., Bruce Fireman, and Steven Rytina. 1982. *Encounters with Unjust Authority.* Homewood, Ill.: Dorsey.

Johnston, Hank. 1985. "Catalan Ethnic Mobilization: Some 'Primordial' Modifications of the Ethnic Competition Model." In *Current Perspectives in Social Theory,* edited by Scott McNall, vol. 6. Greenwich, Conn.: JAI Press.

———. 1989. "Toward an Explanation of Church Opposition to Authoritarian Regimes: Religio-Oppositional Subcultures in Poland and Catalonia." *Journal for the Scientific Study of Religion* 28:493–508.

———. 1991. *Tales of Nationalism: Catalonia, 1939–1979.* New Brunswick, N.J.: Rutgers University Press.

Johnston, Hank, and Jozef Figa. 1988. "The Church and Political Opposition: Comparative Perspectives on Mobilization against Authoritarian Regimes." *Journal for the Scientific Study of Religion* 27, 1:32–47.

Karklins, Rasma. 1986. *Ethnic Relations in the USSR: The Perspective from Below.* Boston: Unwin Hyman.

Keller, Bill. 1988. "When It Comes to Russians, the Estonians Say Go." *New York Times,* October 9, p. 6.

Kolack, Shirley. 1987. "Ethnic Minorities in the Soviet Union: The Unfinished Revolution." *Journal of Intercultural Studies* 8, 1:38–44.

Markus, Vasyl. 1975. "Religion and Nationality: The Uniates of the Ukraine."

In *Religion and Atheism in the USSR and Eastern Europe,* edited by Bohdan R. Bociurkiw and John W. Strong, pp. 101–22. London: Macmillan.

Melia, Elie. 1971. "The Georgian Orthodox Church." In *Aspects of Religion in the Soviet Union, 1917–1967,* edited by Richard H. Marshall, pp. 223–38. Chicago: University of Chicago Press.

Melucci, Alberto. 1985. "The Symbolic Challenge of Contemporary Movements." *Social Research* 52:789–816.

———. 1989. *Nomads of the Present: Social Movements and Individual Needs in Contemporary Society.* Philadelphia: Temple University Press.

Melucci, Alberto, and Mario Diani. 1983. *Nazioni senza stato.* Turin: Loescher editore.

Nagel, Joane. 1986. "The Political Construction of Ethnicity." In *Competitive Ethnic Relations,* edited by Susan Olzak and Joane Nagel, pp. 93–112. Orlando, Fla.: Academic Press.

Nagel, Joane, and Susan Olzak. 1982. "Ethnic Mobilization in New and Old States: An Extension of the Competition Model." *Social Problems* 30:127–43.

Olson, Mancur. 1965. *The Logic of Collective Action.* Cambridge: Harvard University Press.

Parming, Tonu. 1977. "Roots of Nationality Differences." In *Nationality Group Survival in Multi-Ethnic States: Shifting Support Patterns in the Soviet Baltic Region,* edited by Edward Allworth, pp. 24–57. New York: Praeger.

Pérez-Agote, Alfonso. 1986. *La reproducción del nacionalismo. El caso vasco.* Madrid: Centro de Investigaciones Sociológicas and Siglo XXI.

Rupp, Leila J., and Verta Taylor. 1987. *Survival in the Doldrums: The American Women's Rights Movement, 1945 to the 1960s.* New York: Oxford University Press.

See, Katherine O'Sullivan. 1986. *First World Nationalisms.* Chicago: University of Chicago Press.

Smith, Graham E. 1979. "The Impact of Modernization on the Latvian Soviet Republic." *Co-existence* 16, 1:45–64.

Taagepera, Rein. 1983. "Nationalism, Collaborationism, and New-Leftism." In *The Baltic States: Years of Dependence, 1940–1980,* edited by Romuald J. Misiunas and Rein Taagepera. Berkeley: University of California Press.

Vardys, V. Stanley. 1978. *The Catholic Church, Dissent, and Nationality in Soviet Lithuania.* Boulder, Colo.: East European Quarterly.

Wixman, Ronald. 1982. "Ethnic Nationalism in the Caucasus." *Nationality Papers* 10, 2:137–56.

Woolard, Kathryn A. 1989. *Double Talk: Bilingualism and the Politics of Ethnicity in Catalonia.* Stanford: Stanford University Press.

Zaslavsky, Victor. 1980. "The Ethnic Question in the USSR." *Telos* 45(Fall): 45–76.

Ziegler, Charles E. 1987. "Nationalism, Religion, and Equality among Ethnic Minorities: Some Observations on the Soviet Case." *Journal of Ethnic Studies* 13, 2: 19–32.

Zulaika, Joseba. 1988. *Basque Violence: Metaphor and Sacrament.* Reno: University of Nevada Press.

Chapter 12

Greens, Cabbies, and Anti-Communists: Collective Action during Regime Transition in Hungary

Máté Szabó

Social movements under authoritarian systems have mobilization patterns and policy outcomes that are very different from movements in pluralist democracies. On the one hand, social forces have "unlimited possibilities" for articulating new issues because the inertia of official politics recasts any challenge in terms of the broader drama of democracy versus authoritarianism. In Eastern Europe, the result was the existence of some very limited initiatives that had public and intellectual significance disproportionate to the small number of supporters. These small groups set an example: they showed how small, powerless groups could become capable of articulating very important—even crucial—but neglected sociopolitical issues.

On the other hand, mobilization under authoritarian systems is hampered by the administrative-bureaucratic environment and the use of legal and illegal means of social control. Otthein Rammstedt (1978) observes that movements can fail to develop at all stages of their "life-cycles." In East Central Europe, it was common that social mobilizations were often stopped and dispersed before reaching the phase of fully developed movements. Movement "initiatives" and "quasi" movements that could not expand because of political pressure were often transformed into isolated, self-contained subcultures, sects, and political-social groups.

In East Central Europe, the transformation of the sociopolitical system posed challenges to former "oppositional" movements. Their very identity, existence, and strategic-ideological character were rooted in the ancien régime, and they had to change to keep up with new sociopolitical environments. The result was that not all oppositional movements of the state socialist past survived. The free flow of the ideas and opinions relegated some of the earlier movements to marginal positions. New, and even old, precommunist social movements emerged and reemerged, challenging the former "challengers." Between 1988 and 1990, all movements rearranged themselves according to changing political opportunity structures (McAdam 1982; Tilly 1978; Neidhardt and Rucht 1991).

Some social movements have undoubtedly benefited from the extension of their mobilization possibilities, but this does not automatically mean a growth in their resource capacities. On the basis of the "equality of the opportunities," they now must fight for their "real" political space within a new political system. There is consensus among the new political forces that urgent social problems be dealt with efficiently. Survival in an environment of pluralist political competition is a hard task for many former movements. There is no longer a special reward for "heroic dissidence." Moreover, there is a "scarcity of support," and sharp competition for the limited amount of supporters. In this chapter, I compare two important social mobilizations in Hungary, one under the communists and one after system transition, to demonstrate the effects of changing political opportunity structures on protest mobilization, and conversely, the variable effects mobilization can have on the process of political transition.

Stages of Regime Transition

In general, the process of system transformation in East Central Europe had a similar overall dynamic, although there were important national differences (Szabó 1991). Three characteristic steps can be identified. The first is the *time of crisis,* when the destabilization of the old political institutions and elites and the emergence of new political forces occurred. In this phase, elite strategies interacted with the dynamics of the protest. The opening up of new political spaces, agreements on a framework of transition, and division within the old elite between conservatives and reformers were the distinctive features of this phase. Elite reaction was an important factor in the unity of new political forces. There was some kind of cooperation between all the new, noncommunist political forces, but the organizational and strategic unity of these groups was usually temporary.

The next phase was the *breakthrough period* when the dissolution of the communist monopoly on political and administrative power was completed. With the exception of Romania, this occurred typically through negotiation and nonviolent mobilization, although there were differences between countries about whether mass mobilizations were necessary to push the communists to bargain and to accept compromise. National unity was represented in "umbrella organizations," in all-embracing "national fronts," and in roundtable talks by all national political forces. Traditional institutions and nationally recognized dissident figures were accepted as symbolic and integrative forces of the new political community. These functioned as temporary arrangements, however. With the advent of free elections, former movements of "national unity" dissolved, and the organization of "national fronts" began their transformation into to multiparty systems.

Institutionalization of a new political system also followed similar patterns: constitutional change, free elections, and differentiation of the new political forces between the poles of the government and the opposition. The distribution of power occurred according to the recently established "rules of the game" in constitutional-liberal democracies. Emergence of party systems was an important step in the institutionalization process. With free elections, the distribution of power and the formulation of national policy concluded in new institutional structures that represented "national" interests within pluralistic, conflict-based modern societies. It was a long and precarious journey from the "national unity" embodied in the "umbrella organizations" and "roundtables" of the breakthrough phase; completion of the institutionalization process remains distant for most Eastern European countries. Interest articulation must occur along the lines of political cleavages, political ideologies, and institutionalized political structures, but this has often been a highly unstable and volatile process. Stabilization of new institutions and acceptance and internalization of the rules of the game by the emerging political culture are long-term processes.

Regime Transition in Hungary

Since 1956 there has been considerable political stability in Hungary. Elsewhere, a scarcity of food and consumer goods provoked discontent and protest, but in Hungary a type of "consumer socialism" had emerged since the 1960s. Kadarist economic policy secured a regular supply of the consumer goods and acceptable levels of welfare and health services; compared to other socialist countries, living standards in Hungary were high. This "paternalist" orientation of the welfare state stabilized communist Hungary for decades (Bruszt 1988, 23–47); but stability was secured by extremely high foreign debt. Openness to the West provoked "rising expectations" that were eventually disappointed by the inevitable turn of economic fortunes.

Kadarist policies also aided the development of a limited civil society (Frentzel–Zagorska 1990). The structure of the Hungarian oppositional subculture (Johnston 1991, 49–54) was more fragmented, more intellectual, and less tied to churches or workers' groups. This impeded the creation of "umbrella organizations" (like Solidarity in Poland) to represent national consciousness and mitigated the intensity of the crisis stage considerably. It also condemned the Hungarian opposition to only temporary unity of oppositional groupings for bargaining with the Hungarian Socialist Workers party (Körösényi 1991).

Despite the absence of strong national unity organizations, symbolic issues of a national scope played an important role in the transformation to democracy. There were several large mobilizations during 1988 and 1989: commemoration of the Hungarian revolution of 1956, a demonstration during the reburial of its leader Imre Nagy, anti-Ceaucescu protests, and a demonstration on the anniversary of the Hungarian revolution of 1848 (Muravchik 1990). During the breakthrough phase, joint action of relevant oppositional groups was established, and their divisions were held in abeyance in the common anticommunist struggle. However, as the new Hungarian government became institutionalized, the unity of these various oppositional groups dissolved. Division first occurred during the roundtable talks in the summer of 1989 when conflict over a strong presidency (in the Polish pattern) emerged. Radical liberal democrats organized a successful plebiscite against a bargain between populists and reform communists on a strong and directly elected presidency.

Compared with other former socialist countries, the Hungarian breakthrough was more a change of elites and less a mass movement (Tökés 1990). This had the advantage that violent conflicts between the police and masses were avoided; on the other hand, no affective loyalty toward new leaders and institutions was developed. Compared with other former socialist countries, where mass protests and violent conflicts raised a new democratic consciousness, Hungarians in 1990 felt more alienated from the new politics.

The institutionalization phase was impeded in Hungary by the differentiation of oppositional movements (Schöpflin 1979) and the emergence of a fragmented party system (Körösényi 1991). The electoral campaign was already under way when disagreements about the presidency and sharp conflicts between the nationalists, liberals, and socialists were taking place. While the Hungarian party system is an adequate and relatively stable representation of plurality within civil society, the rather weak presidency and the absence of national unity organs on the level of party system have impeded the institutionalization of a stable democratic government (Körösényi 1991).

The existence of democratic institutions does not necessarily insure a political culture that regulates pluralist competition. At first, mobilization against the old regime united all new political forces. But during the process of democratization, competition in elections and, later, in Parliament made it clear that compromise and tolerance were in short supply. A high degree of "ideologization" that recycled political conflicts from the interwar years occurred in the parliamentary debates (Schöpflin 1991, 60–68). Efforts at holding consultative meetings between all parliamentary parties were blocked by sharp tensions between liberals and Christian nationalists. The "camp mentality" of conflicting parties hindered any cooperation in the public sphere. When programs to rationalize the economy and reduce domestic consumption were combined with the shocks of marketization and privatization/reprivatization and with the collapse of the communist trade bloc, COMECON, social stability was severely challenged (see Burszt 1988, 716–29). It was not possible to organize concerted action among the political parties when the new regime encountered its first major crisis: the taxi driver blockade.

The changing political opportunity structure in Hungary redefined the political space for social movements in a very short period of time. Political possibilities and mobilization capacities changed through the three stages of system transformation, and new movements emerged alongside or took the place of former opposition groups. This was demonstrated in the evolution of a major ecology protest, the Danube movement, that occurred during the crisis period in Hungary. Its rapid mobilization and success can be attributed to the peculiar shape of the crisis stage in Hungary, while its rapid demobilization derives from radically changing political opportunities during the breakthrough stage.

The Danube Protest: Mobilization during System Transition

The Hungarian ecology movement was born in the mid 1980s (Sólyom 1988), but, given the constraints of mobilizing under the one-party state, it never attained an integrated organization. Rather, it existed in the form of unconnected local citizens' initiatives, single-issue groups, and alternative life-style communities. Unlike ecology movements in France and West Germany in the 1970s, there was no unifying antinuclear group in Hungary, despite Chernobyl and the scandals surrounding the only Hungarian atomic power plant in Paks.

The biggest citizens' initiative during these years was mobilization against the Hungarian-Czech Danube power plant at Bos-Nagymaros, which was financed on the Hungarian side with credit from the Austrian government and built by Austrian firms. Here, too, political integration under the broad canopy of an organized ecology movement was not achieved. Beginning in 1984, plans for the power station were challenged by a variety of groups: The Blues, Friends of the Danube, Alliance for the Danube, and the Danube Circle. The Danube Circle disputed the project's economic viability, questioned the state's arguments that the project was indispensable to the power supply, and criticized the immense squandering of energy within the Hungarian economy. Above all, the project was opposed for its catastrophic ecological consequences. Unique flora and fauna were endangered, and the supply of drinking water was threatened.

The opposition to the Danube power station originated among a group of specialists who went public after they criticized the project within the scientific community. In 1984, a Committee for the Danube collected ten thousand signatures on a protest letter to the communist government. Officials reacted with an array of repressive measures that ranged from hindering the collection of signatures and forbidding demonstrations and publications to firing individual activists. The official press barely covered challenges to the power station; it did so only through indirect allusion. As a result, the Danube Circle published an unauthorized magazine, and otherwise had to rely on reports in the underground press of the democratic opposition. All attempts by civilian environmentalists to form some sort of legal organization were blocked, which had the effect of closing off sources of funding from international environmental groups. Demonstrations were forcefully dissolved by the police. Signed petitions for a referendum were regularly confiscated by the police. Finally, when the Hungarian government received massive financial assistance for the project from Austria, the movement was weakened to the point of marginalization.

Both analysts and activists have realized that in an authoritarian system there is but scant political space for single-issue movements challenging the state (Haraszti 1990, 71–88). Yet, mobilization in an authoritarian context paradoxically gives rise to an unanticipated but often quite powerful symbolic resource. Because activists must fight restrictions on freedom of association, press, information, and limitations on other basic civic rights, the assertion of a particular grievance can be recast as part of the more general democratic opposition. This was first apparent with respect to the Danube Circle in 1985 when, prior to parliamentary elections, several movement activists joined with other dissidents and for the first time presented themselves as independent candidates. This paired the environmental movement with the broader oppositional forces, and placed it in the avant-garde of the re-emerging civil society in Hungary. It provided a forum for political decision-making, participation, and public criticism of the regime. This process gathered further momentum in 1988 when, assisted by Kádár's fall from power and by a more liberal stance among the renewed political leadership, the hydroelectric project became largely congruent with the division between those who blocked and those who supported the process of democratization.

In May 1988, five thousand people demonstrated in front of the Austrian embassy in Budapest against Austrian participation in the building of the Danube power station. Reflecting the changing political environment, this was the first time that a mass demonstration was tolerated. Moreover, it was fully reported on Hungarian television; subsequently, the official press began to report the power project from a more critical perspective. In June, on the parliamentary initiative of an independent member of parliament, twenty-three votes were cast for the cessation of building on the Danube. In September, thirty-five thousand people demonstrated in Budapest when Austrian firms speeded up work on the project.

These mobilizations were rallying points for broader demands of democratization. Thematically specific grievances of the Danube citizens' initiatives merged over the years with a general rejection of the system by the democratic opposition; the demonstrations reinforced the self-confidence of the opposition. This occurred even in the absence of immediate concrete success, for just one month later Parliament once more backed continuation of the power project. For the time being, the campaign could not achieve its goal, but its activities speeded up the process by which the legitimacy of the parliament was challenged and the deficiencies of the prevailing constitutional framework were made abundantly clear.

During 1989, the structure of political opportunities changed rapidly in Hungary. The new reform-minded government of Miklós Németh halted construction of the Danube project in order to regain legitimacy for the new government. Party reformers tried to distance themselves from the conservative forces around the party secretary Grosz, but by then it was too little too late. The rehabilitation and reburial of Imre Nagy later that year indicated that the fall of the regime was under way. Already there was a rapidly growing opposition organized into parties that were about to push through democratization at roundtable negotiations.

This marked a turning point for the Hungarian ecology movement. After the decision to suspend new construction, the political debate was channeled in other directions. The main point of crystallization was the roundtable bargaining between the Hungarian Workers' party and the "United Opposition" during the summer of 1989, in which the ecology movement was not an active participant. Many former activists left the "umbrella" of the Danube protest for other "real" and "more relevant" political organizations and issues. Even the protest coordination offices were closed in the summer of 1989. All the new political parties that had supported the Danube protest before—explaining its spectacular victory—turned to other matters—explaining its subsequent dissolution as well.

Because the ecological movement largely took the form of small associations prior to the democratic transition, it was not well situated to make the transition to a party organization. These groups did not set up a broader network beyond protest coordination. Although they were united in opposition to the project, they were often divided on other issues. A small group of former activists set up a Green party, but after the "Danube battle" had been won, there were not many possibilities left for them in the election campaign. The Green party received only 3.7 percent of the votes on a national level in the elections of spring 1990, which was not sufficient to secure parliamentary representation.

Today there is a wide range of ecological groups that form a spectrum from loose local amalgams and temporary protest groups to institutionalized and stable organizations. Still, ecology remains on the margin of the new politics in Hungary, where problems of economic and public policy seem much more immediate. Problems of economic growth are urgent, and the so-called postindustrial tasks of the ecologists, reducing growth and consumption, are not likely to be mobilizing issues. The change of the political opportunity structure and of relevant sociopolitical issues, together with the dissolution of the protest issue as a "yes-no question," resulted in the marginalization of the Danube protest movement. It was one of oldest and most successful protest movements in Hungarian politics; it was a protest movement that survived Kadarism, realized its protest goal, and enjoyed temporary political support of all relevant oppositional forces, yet it no longer has a secure place in the new Hungarian democracy.

It was the changing political situation and not the organizational-strategic skill of the Danube Movement that was the primary determinant of success, that is, bringing an end to construction of the power plant. The dynamics of system transformation thrust the Danube issue into the oppositional consciousness, where it was an important theme uniting the extraparliamentary opposition against the party state. For the major opposition groups, the Danube project was a core symbol of democratization processes in their protest activities. The symbolic role of the Danube protests and, ultimately, the limited capacities of the ecology movement itself became very clear once success was achieved and transformation of the state brought other issues to political center stage.

The Taxi-Driver Blockade: Protest in a New Democracy

The declaration of the Hungarian republic on October 23, 1989, the thirty-third anniversary of the anti–Stalinist revolution of 1956, was an important event in the democratization of the former Soviet bloc. Just one year later, on October 26, 1990, the first crisis of the new Hungarian Republic occurred. It took the form of a blockade of streets and highways by taxi drivers and private truckers in protest against a large increase in fuel prices. The blockade paralyzed the new democracy for three days; it provoked an atmosphere of fear, tension, and aggression until an eleventh-hour compromise was worked out. Rather than an organized social movement along the lines of the Danube initiative, the blockade was a collective protest of relatively short duration. Its relevance derives from its occurrence during the institutionalization phase of the transition and the way that a relatively circumscribed event reverberated throughout Hungarian politics and posed a serious challenge to the government. There was a set of opportunity structures unique to the institutionalization phase, and they both influenced the course of mobilization and were altered in the resolution of the crisis.

The sudden and drastic raising of fuel prices on the night of October 24, 1990, provoked a spontaneous and illegal demonstration. Mass actions emerged from discussions between private drivers and entrepreneurs who were queuing up at stations late that night. Protesting drivers first drove to the parliament building hoping to open negotiations to restore prices to previous levels. When their appeal was rejected, they moved to block all main traffic routes in the country. The blockade developed quickly the next day and almost all traffic was stopped throughout the country, including all international transport. The blockade was maintained all of Friday, Saturday, and Sunday, with some breaks for medical and food supplies. During these three days the atmosphere was electrified: people bought the stores empty and feared violent conflict. Supporting protests were joined by masses of poor people who were generally protesting worsening living conditions.

The government, backed by a strong coalition of Christian-Democratic parties, at first rejected all bargaining with illegal protest groups and threatened them with police intervention and arrests. In the face of mounting protest, the police and army refused to intervene, and they sided with the protesters. In the streets, there was a solidarity between the protesters, the police, and the local population that reinforced discipline and order in the protests. No remarkable acts of violence were reported, despite provocation by a "countermovement" mobilized by the governing party, the Hungarian Democratic Forum (Magyar Demokrata Forum, or MDF). Where there were confrontations, the police prevented violence from erupting.

A compromise between the protest groups and the government was worked out on Sunday night in order to secure a normal start of the work week the next day. The rise in the fuel prices was reduced 35 percent. There was also an agreement to ease fuel prices in the future and connect them to prices on the world market. Protest groups promised to remove all traffic barricades by the morning, and a promise of an amnesty for all the protest groups was given, although it had to be approved by parliament. The compromise had been worked out in an extremely tense atmosphere while the social and political workings of the country were stalled for three days.

The taxi drivers, as the main activists of the protest, were commited to the single issue of fuel prices; but political organizations supporting the protest recast the mobilization into a more general criticism of state policy. They even demanded the resignation of the government. At the grass-roots level, too, in talks and discussions around the blockade points, participants voiced more generalized grievances against the government; they shifted the single issue of fuel prices to "social self-defense" against the "antisocial" economic policies of the government. Thus the blockade— wholly spontaneous and begun without any broader political objectives—became a serious delegitimizing threat to the new Hungarian government (see Table 12-1).

The taxi driver protest presents a very special form of political opportunity structure for the articulation of social-political protest. The political system had been very recently democratized, and the institutionalization process was not yet complete. Legitimacy of the new government derived in part from recent antiauthoritarian and anticommunist mobilizations, but the newly established political institutions were untested and unstable. Elites were less experienced in political problem-solving and crisis manage-

Table 12-1   Citizens' Evaluation of Taxi-Driver Blockade

| | Percentage | | |
Question	Yes	No	Don't Know
Do you think the majority of citizens supported the taxi drivers during the crisis?	78	7[a]	15[b]
Were the taxi drivers concerned only with their own interests?	12	84	4
Did the taxi drivers represent public opinion?	72	22	6

Note: These public opinion questions were posed to about one thousand citizens by telephone immediately after the crisis by Magyar Közvéleménykutató Intézet (1990, 597–98).
[a]Refers to those who felt the majority supported government.
[b]Refers to those who felt the "majority supported neither."

ment, and many evinced a political style rooted in the authoritarian past. There is virtually no tradition of democratic authority in Hungarian history (Völgyes 1987, 191–213); on the other hand, rebellion against the state is part of the political mythology, especially since 1956. The combination of these elements produced a certain ambivalence among some elites toward social protest, and among others, outright rigidity. Still others, drawing on past traditions and on recent experiences in the anticommunist opposition, especially opposition groups and parties, saw protest mobilization as a positive political force. The political opportunity structure in Hungary can be summed up in the following way:

- A certain degree of openness toward social protest among some sectors
- Unstable political alignments between parties
- Political volatility of support groups, trade unions, interest groups, small parties, and other social groups in the newly congealed civil society
- Division among the political elites
- Restricted possibilities of political-administrative control by the government

The existence of a differentiated/pluralized political opportunity structure is an innovation in Hungary, but it provided a highly restricted opportunity structure—albeit restricted in different ways from the authoritarian past—for protest movements. The result was a series of events surprisingly similar to the expansion of goals in the Danube protest movement even though the political context had radically changed.

Mobilization during regime transition can transform initial and specific themes of protest into "metaconflicts" that transcend the original aims of the movement and can be said to reflect the way the broader society interprets its "real" meaning. Significant actors in redefining a movement are the mass media; counter-movements; and agents of control such as the police, army, and quasi-official thugs and vigilante groups (Neidhardt and Rucht 1991, 459). In crisis and breakthrough phases, this kind of frame bridging and frame expansion (Snow and Benford 1988) was accomplished through the participation of broadly based umbrella and national unity organizations. Their central role was clearly demonstrated in the Danube movement by its rapid disintegration once these groups staked out their positions in the newly emerging political environment. In the institutionalization stage, the "meta-conflict" of the taxi-driver blockade was generated by the unresponsiveness of the government in the face of continued socioeconomic deterioration.

Mobilizations during the institutionalization phase challenge governments that are ill-equipped to deal with crisis. The taxi drivers initially wanted to reach their limited, single-issue goal through an aggressive protest, but inexperience and the unavailability of established channels for managing pluralist competition and protest embedded the narrow goal in a broader set of demands, which were articulated by the mobilized parties: interest organizations, mass media, and sectors of the public. The result was a government reaction that in many ways parodied the authoritarian past. Events were destabilized by initial refusals to negotiate and by calling out the police and army. They were further aggravated by the mobilization by the Christian Democrats of a countermovement that bordered on vigilantism. Finally, there were attacks on the media. Because the main parts of the talks were broadcast live by the mass media, they produced a situation that was highly challenging to the governing Christian-Democrats. Broadcasts of the negotiations led to charges of disloyalty, and the government attempted to control the media by administrative means. In the summer of 1991, the prime minister appointed new vice-presidents to the state-owned networks to counterbalance liberal influences, but the state president refused to authorize the appointments. Once again, in the precarious context of the institutionalization of democratic legality, the crisis was broadened—or rather detoured—to embrace intense political conflicts between the opposition Liberals and the Christian-Democrat government over the competence of the president and control of the media (*East European Reporter* 1992, 28–40).

The key difference between the late 1980s and post-transition 1990 was the tentative structure of adaptive, policy-making channels of political consultation that had emerged in the first stages of the institutionalization phase. Tentative as these were, they were employed to negotiate an end to the crisis. In contrast, mobilization during the crisis phase led to capitulation by the government that hastened the downfall of the regime, whereas resolution of the blockade, in some ways, can be said to have further institutionalized democratic institutions. After initial intransigence and almost reflexive recourse to authoritarian solutions of the past, the new Hungarian government utilized an established consultative organ, the Council of Interest Representation. Before the crisis the Council had functioned nominally as a forum for discussion about social and economic policy between employees, employers, and the government, but it had little political relevance. It became an acceptable venue because it was legal and institutionalized, and it therefore implicitly supported the legitimacy of the new state. By the same token, the Council was acceptable to protest groups because they could embed their particular demands in a broader framework of public economic and social criticism.

Summary

Consideration of these two protest campaigns in Hungary suggests that there are considerable differences in the dynamics of mobilization for different stages in regime transformation. Possibilities for mobilization were extended during the crisis and breakthrough periods as political institutions opened up and social and political protests spread throughout the country. Later, revitalization of the Hungarian state and political life in general—especially in local administration, trade unions, voluntary associations, parties, and representative groups—channeled mobilization into party competition in the local and national elections.

The Danube protest was significantly shaped by changing political opportunity structures. After long years of political suppression, the movement rapidly reached its peak in 1988 and 1989. The suspension of work on the dam and the pluralization of politics cut support for the issue, and, except for some networking and public relations activities, the mass campaigns did not last beyond regime transition.

The mobilization of the taxi-driver blockade occurred during the institutionalization period in Hungary. Unlike the Danube protests, the taxi drivers' protest was pursued and legitimized within the context of a constitutional democracy. This was the first time that Hungarian politicians and intellectuals had to deal with questions of loyalty and legitimacy in a civil protest. Although branded by many as an illegal challenge to the new regime, the taxi-driver protest was broadly supported by the Hungarian public.

Changing political opportunity structures also affected the articulation of issues. The Danube protest was a mixture of symbolic protests against the regime and genuine ecological concerns that echoed protests in the West against large energy projects. In the taxi-driver blockade, there was no need for antiregime symbolism. Rather, grievances developed within and were primarily concerned with the context of the emerging Hungarian democracy.

Changing political contexts prepared the way for new political actors. The Danube movement organized through a slightly differentiated network of informal groups and protest movements that were reminiscent of oppositional subcultures elsewhere (Johnston 1991). These social networks formed the basis of an emergent civil society that confronted a homogeneous, elite-dominated, authoritarian state. As the confrontation progressed, a differentiation process occurred on both sides, resulting in a broadened political spectrum on the one hand and a democratized political-administrative system on the other. The taxi-driver protest occurred within the context of political pluralism and a rapidly differentiating civil society. Rather than a confrontation pitting "society" against the "state," the conflict took the form of a three-way political division along the lines of "government," "opposition," and "extra-parliamentary opposition." In each of these three groups there were institutionalized and informal political subgroupings.

Although, on the surface, a single-issue movement backed by the anticommunist opposition would seem to have little in common with a protest of an organized professional subculture against the social costs of the market economy, the internal dynamics of these movements were surprisingly similar. Both lacked stable internal structures for mobilization; both suffered from a lack of material resources; and, from the point of view of collective behavior, both lacked strategic and organizational planning beyond the scope of their single issues. Nevertheless, both experienced "white-hot" mobilization and short-term successes; in the longer term, the lack of organization and resources led to an abrupt end of the mobilization dynamics and rapid dissolution.

Any assessment of the impact of these two campaigns must be placed in the context of how social movements in transitional regimes differ from those in Western democracies. These protests are benchmarks in the emergence of the new Hungarian democracy, and constitute learning processes for the political elite, protest organizers, and the public. No one has long-term experience with electoral effects of policy reactions to protest movements. The intermediary system of protest and the public feedback through electoral choice is still in the making in Eastern Europe. Political institutions have not yet stabilized, and political parties are still "mobilizing parties" with roots in mass mobilizations against communist systems. The cultural background for new political institutions is also emerging, and neither political institutions nor political cultures are experienced in conflict management. The result is a tendency for transitory, extrainstitutional forms of bargaining and crisis management.

References

Bruszt, László. 1988. "Political Orientation in Hungary." *Social Research* 55, 1–2:43–77.

———. 1989. "The Dilemmas of Economic Transition in Hungary." *Südosteuropa* 38, 11–12:716–29.

East European Reporter. 1992. 5, 1:28–40.

Frentzel-Zagorska, Janina. 1990. "Civil Society in Poland and Hungary." *Soviet Studies* 42, 4:759–77.

Haraszti, Miklós. 1990. "The Beginning of Civil Society: The Independent Peace Movement and the Danube Movement in Hungary." In *In Search of Civil Society*, edited by Vladimir Tismaneanu, pp. 71–88. New York and London: Routledge, Chapman, and Hall.

Johnston, Hank. 1991. *Tales of Nationalism*. New Brunswick, N.J.: Rutgers University Press.

Körösényi, András. 1991. "Revival of the Past or a New Beginning? The Nature of Post-Communist Politics." *Political Quarterly* 62, 19:52–75.

McAdam, Doug. 1982. *Political Process and the Development of Black Insurgency, 1930–1970*. Chicago: University of Chicago Press.

———. 1988. "MicroMobilization Contexts and Recruitment to Activism." In *From Structure to Action*, edited by Bert Klandermans, Hanspeter Kriesi, and Sidney Tarrow, pp. 125–55. Vol. 1 of *International Social Movement Research*. Greenwich, Conn.: JAI Press.

Magyar Közvéleménykutató Intézet. 1990. "A politikai közvélemény 1990-ben." In *Magyarország Politikai Evkönyve*, edited by Kurtán Sándor et al., pp. 597–98. Budapest: Economix. Rt.

Muravchik, Joshua, ed. 1990. "Democratic Transformation in Hungary." Special issue of *World Affairs* 151, 4.

Neidhardt, Friedhelm, and Dieter Rucht. 1991. "The Analysis of Social Movements: The State of the Art and Some Perspectives for Further Research." In *Research on Social Movements: The State of the Art in Western Europe and the USA*, edited by Dieter Rucht, pp. 421–65. Frankfurt am Main and Boulder, Colo.: Campus Verlag and Westview Press.

Rammstedt, Otthein. 1978. *Soziale Bewegung*. Frankfurt am Main: Suhrkamp Verlag.

Schöpflin, George. 1979. "Opposition and Para-Opposition: Critical Currents in Hungary, 1968–1978." In *Opposition in Eastern Europe*, edited by Rudolf Tökés, pp. 142–87. London: Macmillan.

———. 1991. "Conservatism and Hungary's Transition." *Problems of Communism* 40, 1:60–68.

Snow, David A., and Robert D. Benford. 1988. "Ideology, Frame Resonance, and Participant Mobilization." In *From Structure to Action*, edited by Bert Klandermans, Hanspeter Kriesi, and Sidney Tarrow, pp. 197–217. Vol. 1 of *International Social Movement Research*. Greenwich, Conn.: JAI Press.

Sólyom, László. 1988. "Citizen's Participation in the Environmental Movement." *Ifda-Dossier* 6, 64:23–35.

Szabó, Máté. 1991. "Die Rolle von sozialen Bewegungen im Systemwandel in Osteuropa: Ein Vergleich zwischen Ungarn, Polen und der DDR." *Österreichische Zeitschrift für Politikwissenschaft* 20, 3:275–89.

Tilly, Charles. 1978. *From Mobilization to Revolution*. Reading, Mass.: Addison-Wesley.

Tökés, Rudolf L. 1990. "Campaign 90: A Midterm Report on Party Politics and Elections in Hungary." *Südosteuropa* 39, 2:110–19.

Völgyes, Iván. 1987. "Political Culture." In *Ungarn. Südosteuropa-Handbuch*, edited by Klaus Detlef Grothusen, 5:191–213. Göttingen: Vandhoek and Ruprecht.

Chapter 13

Social Movements in Modern Spain: From the Pre–Civil War Model to Contemporary NSMs

José Alvarez-Junco

This chapter compares three basic stages in the development of forms of collective action in modern Spain. I call the first stage traditional or classic. Its beginning can be dated around 1890, the year that a universal suffrage law was enacted and the first May Day was celebrated. The inauguration of universal suffrage made massive political participation possible for the first time. May Day marked the beginning of mass mobilization practices among the Spanish working class.[1] The first stage culminates in the Civil War of 1936–1939. A modern stage comprises collective protest actions arising under late Francoism and the crucial years of the transition to multiparty liberal democracy. This stage developed after a "dormant" period during which repression by Franco's dictatorship made impossible any open political mobilization. Its beginning can be pinpointed in the 1961–1962 miners' strikes in Asturias.[2] Its end came with the first municipal elections in April 1979. The present stage can be called postmodern. It began in 1979 or, more clearly, in October 1982, with the resounding election victory of the Partido Socialista Obrero Español (PSOE). This stage followed a transitional period (1979–1982), in which "modern" and "postmodern" traits coexisted, but not without tension.

Contrary to the prevalent interpretation among historians of social movements, I believe the factor that genuinely marks and differentiates the history of collective protest in modern Spain has little to do with class makeup, the absolute or relative "deprivation" of the people mobilized, or with the socioeconomic goals put forward. Rather, it involves the organization and degree of development of the state, the participatory opportunities the political system provides, and, above all, the political culture and self-perception of leaders and participants in the social-political strug-gle that encourages them to avail themselves of such opportu-nities.[3]

Social Movements in "Classic" Spain

The use of the term "classic" to designate this stage is not without irony, for some of the more widely held stereotypes about this historical period in Spain were elaborated by non-Spanish romantic writers and art-ists. The image they rendered—of a heroic people struggling for freedom under brutal repression by medieval rulers—was so indel-ibly etched that it came to be accepted by many as the "typical" or "eternal" Spain. Forming an indispensable part of that depic-tion were the anarchist and socialist movements, Jerez and the *Mano Negra jacqueries,* Barcelona's Tragic Week and Ferrer Guard-ia's execution in 1909, the convent burnings of 1931, the October 1934 uprising in Asturias, and, above all, the Civil War.

Conversely, the most accepted perception among both Span-ish historians and leaders and ideologues of movements in this stage betrayed little romantic influence. This model was deeply influenced by Marxism, which was dominant in academic circles, which were largely hostile to Franco's regime, and among leaders of social protests. This view can be summarized as follows: The prime movers of collective protest actions are social classes, and their actions are driven by common material interests and oppres-sive labor conditions. Of the contesting classes, the revolutionary class is the industrial proletariat. The "natural" representatives of the proletarian movement are parties and trade unions, through which the social group's interests achieve clear and faithful expres-sion. Given that the ability to work is the only asset possessed by those rising up against the established social order, the preeminent tactic is, logically enough, the strike, which in confrontations of the highest order is widened into the general strike. The "con-scious" expression of the demands raised by the oppressed social group's protest movement, regardless of how limited those de-mands may be, form part of a globalizing "progressive" world outlook or ideology. This means that every victory won through popular protest is a step toward rooting out the cause of all social injustice and speeding up the arrival of the free and egalitarian ideal in which human history will culminate.

The last trait of this model is that the basic political reference in which this social struggle develops in modern societies is the bourgeois revolution, which is the the political translation—both consequence and agent at the same time—of the transition from a feudal to a capitalist mode of production. Spanish leaders and ideologues generally tended to agree that bourgeois revolution in Spain had been "incomplete" (Alvarez-Junco 1985); as a consequence, political struggle did not so clearly revolve around the bourgeoisie-proletariat binomial as in Europe's most advanced countries. Instead, complex alliances between the proletariat and modernizing sectors of the bourgeoisie arose against an oligarchic power bloc formed from industrial and finance capital's fusion with the old landed aristocracy.

Under the rubric of "history of the labor movement" or "history of Spanish social movements,"[4] this model generated such an enormous number of studies that it can be considered as the "inherited paradigm" in 1960s and 1970s Spanish historiography. The model has been the object of vigorous critique for at least a decade now (Alvarez-Junco and Pérez Ledesma 1982); I do not intend to add anything to that debate. Its problems are many and deep, but no more so than those ailing classic histories of labor movements in France or Italy.

What is surprising about the Spanish model, however, is its rather simplistic, mimetic regard for other European versions and its longevity. This longevity affected the development of social movements in the late Francoist and transition period. It became the most widely accepted self-image for the protagonists of the period's social protests, notwithstanding that, by then, ongoing social and political changes and the emergence of new movements were increasingly exposing the model's inadequacy.[5]

The historians and social scientists who most clearly perceived the peculiarities of the Iberian case were not Spanish. Even those who accepted Marxist social struggle as the basic theoretical framework fused it with the romantic notion of the uniqueness of Spanish history. Iberian uniqueness was demonstrated to them by, more than any other feature, the importance and persistence of anarchism.

Anarchism is, indeed, a singularly important feature of Spanish history; also important are popular protests or phenomena
that were not labeled as anarchist. I suggest that, instead of social
struggle as explained in the "inherited paradigm," *antipoliticism*
is the most characteristic and generic feature of labor and social
movements in Spain during the "classic" stage. As Santos Juliá
puts it, "Spanish workers—both those in the CNT and in the
UGT—were characterized by their indifference to the political
form of the state and their hostility to political power, which
naturally gave rise to an absence of debate about the state and
conquering power and to the belief the revolution's entire content
lay in the administration of society by labor organizations."[6]

Antipoliticism is defined here as the disdain for parliamentary
politics and reform. The goal of the Spanish workers' movements
was not to reform, nor even to take over the state, but to topple
it, or at least expose its weakness through blows aimed at the heart
of the system. Even the moderate Socialist party, led by Pablo
Iglesias for more than forty years, concentrated its efforts in union
organization and strike activities. It considered its participation in
local and parliamentary elections only as a means for improving
its propaganda forums and possibilities. And, in spite of their
constant defeats, they stubbornly refused all offers made by "left
bourgeois" Republicans to enter in electoral coalitions before
1910. By that year, enough pressure had been put on the old leader
to force him to accept the coalition, and thus enter the Spanish
Cortes for the first time. Yet, the antipolitical frame of reference
was preserved among his successors. As late as in 1925, Largo
Caballero, the secretary of the socialist union, accepted an official
position offered by the dictator, Primo de Rivera, on the grounds
that all "bourgeois" regimes were similar and that the labor movement should only be concerned with strengthening its organization and its influence on social legislation (Ben-Ami 1978, 101–
27). When the Republic was instituted in 1931, working-class
loyalties were very unclear. The Partido Comunista de España
(PCE) contemptuously rejected the new Republic as a "bourgeois
farce"; the anarchists repeatedly rose against Republican governments, pressing for faster and deeper land reform (Malefakis
1970); and even the moderate PSOE engaged in an armed rebellion
in Asturias against the legal government when electoral results

granted power to a conservative party in 1934 (Juliá 1977; Preston 1979).

This is not the place to discuss the complex causes of this antipolitical or anarchistic trend in Spanish labor movements. I only list here some of the divergent interpretations offered by the different historical schools on the matter, and I add a couple of remarks. The traditional and romantic historians rooted anarchistic tendencies in mysterious and indelible racial Iberian peculiarities (Díaz del Moral 1967; Brenan 1943; Castro 1954). Advocates of economic explanations tended to single out the country's irregular and insufficient industrial development as the causal factor. They focused on the "failure" of the industrial revolution, which was a result of the "absence" or "incomplete nature" of the bourgeois revolution.[7] Above all, antipoliticism has been attributed to the political structure of the Canovist Restoration, namely, the oligarchic and exclusionary character of the political system, the *cacique* clientele networks and their mockery of the recently achieved universal suffrage. In this view, these factors widened the alienation of laboring classes and generated radically antisystem forms of protests (Calero 1976; Balcells 1980; Alvarez-Junco 1986).

As for the supposed Spanish innate anarchistic tendency, anarchism was neither as constant a phenomenon nor as deeply rooted as is generally held. Before 1910, at the earliest, Spain does not present anarchist features any more pronounced than, say, France or Italy.[8] Nor should it be forgotten that other European labor movements did not shed their antipolitical origins until very late, basically on the eve of World War I. The question should thus be seen as one of pace, of lag, more than of any essential exceptionalism.

As for the attribution of labor antipoliticism to the political structure in which the movements developed, it is not as obvious as might first appear. Were it so, antipoliticism should have spread and strengthened under Francoism, a political system more closed to popular participation than any other. Yet, just the opposite occurred. Our assumption must therefore be that antipoliticism was rooted in the political culture developed by the Spanish Left itself, which, following old millenarian patterns and pervaded by mid–nineteenth century romantic revolutionism, constructed its identity as an enemy of *all* "authorities" and the liberator from *all* oppresions.

The Reemergence of Social Mobilization

The 1936–1939 Civil War marked the culmination and the end of the type of social strife that had dominated the previous tumultuous decades of Spanish history. General Franco's dictatorship broke that pattern and initiated a new historical stage of markedly different features.

Two phases of the long Franco era are usually distinguished; each has a crucial, though very different, bearing on our subject. In the first phase (1939–1959) the country lived through intense political repression and a totalitarian attempt at ideological reorientation on a fascist model. Taken together, they proved brutally effective in demolishing the inherited traditions of social rebellion. During the second period (1959–1975), after having failed in its effort to erect a new model of national "coexistence" on the ruins of liberal-democratic and working-class traditions, the regime poured its efforts into economic growth. Notable success in this realm, aided by a favorable European period of expansion, kicked off spectacular sociological changes in a few short years.

I do not attempt a detailed analysis or description of the changes in Spanish society from 1959 to 1975. Simply put, by 1975, the dramatic increases in Gross Domestic Product and per capita income, the geographical mobility of the population, the redistribution of labor force, and the urbanization process made Spanish society something altogether different from what it had been only fifteen or twenty years before.[9]

More important for our argument is that this social transformation was accompanied by major growth and increased efficiency of the political apparatus. The nationalist totalitarianism underpinning Francoism required a strong state capable of molding society along the lines demanded by the ideology. The combination of political repression and social paternalism required a police force; a large, centralized civil administration; public services; and a tax system with which to fund them. All this was done in despotic fashion and at great cost,[10] but the state succeeded in stamping its mark on society in an incomparably broader and deeper way than ever before in Spanish history. By the 1960s, oppositional forces aimed bitter criticisms at the economic policies of the *desarrollista* or "developmentalist" governments, but those very critiques implied acceptance of the necessity for the government to have an industrial or commercial policy. The quality of and waste in the public health-care system or the small retirement pensions could also be criticized, but it would have been difficult to convince Spaniards they could live without some type of government-administered welfare and social services system.

Thus, upon his death in November 1975, Franco left behind a country that had undergone a dual process of "modernization." Social modernization was brought about by industrialization and urbanization. Despite the lack of democracy, political modernization resulted in the growth of the state and its administrative efficiency.

Social change brought conflict. Initial conflicts were economically motivated; later they were more openly political. Opposition spokesmen and intellectuals tended to view conflicts as marking a resumption of interrupted history—the decades of dictatorship being a mere parenthesis—and believed that a return to the "classic" model of popular mobilization was under way. The labor movement, now captained by the Communist party and imbued with a strong Leninist sense of its leadership role, would be the antagonistic pole to the semi-feudal oligarchy that was victorious in the Civil War.

The development of the political struggles of the late 1960s and early 1970s supports such an interpretation. After a period of isolation due to the unhealed wounds of the Civil War, the Communist party had emerged as the dominant opposition force.[11] This was probably due to its influence on or open control of the clandestine trade union organization, Comisiones Obreras, which was overwhelmingly dominant among politically active workers, as was proven by syndical elections in 1966. Around the Communist party and the Workers' Commissions there gravitated the stormy student movement[12] and the most politically committed intellectuals. The most frequently used—almost the unique—method of action for confronting the regime, and the most destabilizing, was the industrial or university strike. Finally, the semi-clandestine anti-Francoist culture was dominated by a *progresista* ideology (to use the revealing term the opposition attributed to itself), which combined a defense of democratic liberties with an anticapitalist economic outlook (Preston 1976; Vilar 1984).

Another argument in favor of the return of the "traditional" model in this "modern" phase is that Spain had shed most of its anarchic singularity from the pre-1936 period. The CNT (Confederación Nacional del Trabajo) had not played any important role in the conflicts of the late Francoist era, nor, counter to many predictions, was the anarchist union reborn from its ashes when the dictator died. In 1976, the anarchists held a couple of massive, fervid assemblies and there were those who thought that anarchist Spain was indeed eternal.[13] What those fleeting explosions demonstrated was not the continuity but rather the distance separating 1936 from 1976. The old CNT trade unionists found themselves face to face with young, irreverent *ácratas* (libertarians), who were less interested in trade unionism that in "happenings," personal freedom, and transgressing social taboos—whether by free love, drugs, or outlandish aesthetic provocations. The elders replied in puritanical tones, unable to comprehend the new phenomenon.[14]

In fact, what was occurring in anarchist circles was, not a confirmation of the return to a traditional stage, but rather a symptom of the country's "modernization." In the prewar Spain one could hardly find the individualistic and aesthetic anarchism of the kind existing in radical intellectual circles north of the Pyrenees. In Spain, the dominant current was the militant and austere solidarity represented by the "lay saints" of the CNT. The situation changed radically in the 1950s and 1960s, and the newly re-emerged Spanish anarchist movement during late Francoism and the transition to democracy period answered to the individualistic model (Alvarez-Junco 1977). Spain was becoming "Europeanized" in this sense.

The importance of individualistic or *ácrata* anarchism was not the only new development. In the late 1960s and early 1970s, new types of conflicts and mobilizations appeared; they were very different from those preceding the Civil War and apparently identified with the new social movements springing up in industrial democracies after the institutional crisis suffered by political parties and representative mechanisms in the wake of 1968. Workers were not the only ones, indeed, perhaps not even the majority, rising up against Francoism. From the mid 1960s on, important social mobilizations were emerging; massively in student and nationalist circles, and more embryonically in such important arenas as neighborhood associations, feminist organizations, and environmental groups.

Student activism achieved a primordial importance among

political protests emerging in the late 1960s and early 1970s, and it became a genuine nightmare for the Franco regime in its later years.[15] It seemed that Spain was not an exception amid the world-wide university rebellion symbolized by the anti–Vietnam War protests in American colleges and by the May 1968 revolt in Paris. Although student unrest undoubtedly shared some common traits all over the world, Spanish events cannot be seen as simply more episodes in the general wave: The internal situation of the dictatorship stamped their development with very specific markings.

There were, to be sure, specific complaints against academic authorities and rigid norms of student conduct, as well as calls for modernizing academic institutions and subjects of study. Like everywhere else, these demands were mixed with—or a pretext for—more radical expressions of incompatibility with capitalism and industrial society. The student mobilization as a whole, however, cannot be properly understood only in terms of problems in the educational system, or the general revolutionary consciousness of student leaders, or the mimicking of the European and American models.

What set the Spanish case apart and endowed student actions with a distinctive meaning vis-à-vis those in advanced industrial democracies was the rigidity of the political system that they were confronting. For any dictatorship, all open conflict becomes an intolerable defiance of the principle of authority.[16] For Francoism, which had aspired to model an *espíritu nacional,* to exert totalitarian control on culture and ideas, the university rebellion was even worse: It was an attack on the fundamental values on which the authoritarian system was based and a demonstration of its failure. Thus, student protest—which also benefited from its characteristic knack for communicative impact—acquired an inordinately large "subversive" potential. Students were supported by faculty and by the mass media that did not identify with the regime; they became symbolic standard bearers for demands ranging far beyond the academic world.

Something similar could be said of social mobilizations inspired by or related to the reawakening of nationalist feelings, especially in Catalonia and the Basque region. I do not deal here with the regional nationalist agendas, since their clearly political goals and quick institutionalization make it difficult to consider them social movements in a strict sense. But under national banners there were many mobilizations that were not exactly driven by nationalistic goals. Some of the claims in favor of regional languages and local traditions were supported by patently conservative sectors of those local communities (Catalan bankers and Basque priests, to cite two clear examples), some of which had even supported Franco in the Civil War (Carlists). Yet, to the regime, any recognition of cultural diversity that went beyond local folkloric quaintness was subversive; it was seen as questioning the sacred principle of the "unity of Spain." Police repression—including beating and jailing young people from respectable social sectors—easily moved the entire "aggrieved" community into identifying with the persecuted.

After 1965–1966, nationalism galvanized much more than cultural and social elites in Catalonia and the Basque region.[17] It also gave rise to very significant mobilizations throughout Spain, as in 1970, when nine ETA (Euskadi Ta Askatasuna [Basque Homeland and Freedom]) militants were sentenced to death by a military court in Burgos, sentences which had to be commuted by Franco under strong national and international pressure (Tuñón de Lara 1980, 414–15; Payne 1987, 557–58). The fact that most of the outside support for peripheral nationalisms disappeared at the end of the transition seems to indicate that it was not inspired by truly sympathetic feelings for Basquism or Catalanism; rather, there were oppositional attitudes toward the regime that took advantage of any opportunity to express their dissent.

A weaker movement of the mid 1960s saw the birth of neighborhood associations, which protested against the problems stemming from the accelerated urbanization of the 1950s and 1960s (Castells 1983). By the end of the decade, some feminist and environmentalist organizations also became visible, and there even were some timid collective protests against the military service.[18]

From many standpoints, all these developments seriously modified the inherited working-class paradigm that anti-Francoist leaders and ideologues were busy extending and shoring. They did so at least in several fundamental ways, and in this sense seemed to be giving birth to what in European and American industrial societies was being called "new social movements."

These movements were defined by their belonging not to a particular social stratum or class but to a new urban world (neighborhood movements), generation (students, environmentalists), culture (nationalists), or gender (feminists), which were different from the dominant movements. Each stepped forward to demand recognition of new collective identities. The content of movement demands also placed these conflicts outside the traditional framework of class struggle. Calls for salary increases and improved working conditions, typical of the harshest stages of the first economic take-off, were complemented or supplanted by new, more sophisticated requirements relating to consumer matters, quality of life, democratization of the forms of everyday communication, control of the environment, and respect for cultural heritages. The organizational and mobilizing model of the movement was informal and discontinuous, far removed from the rigid and hierarchical underground calls that the militarized Francoist police was accustomed to battling. Finally, the strike continued to hold a preeminent importance but was now—both in the aims of the strikers and in the government plans for stifling them—more a matter of disrupting public order than of exerting economic pressure on employers. In fact, by the end of Francoism, strikes had lost importance in favor of demonstrations, occupations of public spaces, and a series of other "expressive" actions.

None of these characteristics, however, altered the fundamental self-perception and strategic approach of anti-Francoist leaders and ideologues. Although their daily practice contradicted many of the traditional class-struggle presuppositions, they continued to hold that all the new phenomena be subordinated to the undeniable centrality of the "workers' movement." Old militants could even think that student, citizen, and feminist protests were transitional phenomena, and wave them off as products of an "insufficient" understanding of historical reality attributable to the "petty bourgeois" background of the activists. Of course, they were considered useful to the movement if they fell in line behind the proletarian vanguard.

In fact, the traditional Left, notwithstanding apprehensions it felt over the novelties presented by these new movements, was using them politically. Their effectiveness in destabilizing the regime was outstanding. Although both the mass media and police—equally under the sway of the traditional paradigm—viewed workers' strikes as the gravest of confrontations, day-to-day protagonism was achieved by the new conflicts.

Many of the new activists held political allegiances different from orthodox communism and acknowledged difficulties in understanding the traditional Left parties—which they were beginning to dub as "stodgy," *"machista,"* and "centralist." Some even pondered the need to create their own organizations. Nonetheless, in the end most of the activists accepted the need to have a workers' vanguard and entrusted the PCE with symbolic representation and decision-making power for the movement as a whole or at least considered it the fundamental reference when discussing strategies.

The PCE's strategy—and this is key to understanding the new situation—was no longer to push the proletarian revolution, but rather to subordinate it to political reform. After summary analyses of the socioeconomic situation and none-too-polished strategic argumentations (in short, the bourgeois democratic revolution had not yet been consummated in Spain), the PCE concluded that the "workers' " movement needed to ally itself with the "reformist bourgeoisie" to impose democratic reform on the dictatorship. The pressing problem was therefore the state's democratization and its conversion into the main instrument of social reform. It was a symptom of the new situation that the rallying cry or watchword for mobilization was the "general political strike," to which was usually added, "aimed at reestablishing democratic liberties."

The acceptance of this strategy distorted the orientation and significance of the Spanish student, feminist, and citizen movements; they could not fit the characteristics of the new social movements as they developed in the 1970s in European and American industrial democracies. Citizens' movements, for instance, "fulfilled the political strategies of the Partido Comunista de España and of the Organización Revolucionaria de Trabajadores, the two main parties that had agreed to share power in the executive committee of the Federation" (Castells 1983, 229). The largest feminist organization, Mujeres Democráticas, was also controlled by the PCE and, naturally, submitted itself to the political necessities of the struggle against the regime. Similar, although oriented toward different political goals, was the distortion forced on environmentalism by Basque radicalism in its struggle against the nuclear plant of Lemóniz, when environmental concerns were the apparent cause for mobilizations in support of an armed organization characterized by anything except respect for human lives.

Thus, social mobilization in Spain in the last years of Franco-ism (1960–1975) and during the political transition (1975–1979) was born into a contradictory situation, in a complex mixture of old and new elements. On the one hand, the country's sociological modernization had given rise to an urban middle-class culture, which in turn generated new demands on the state and a remodel-ing of collective identities, all expressed through new forms of social mobilization. On the other hand, the obsolescence of the regime's structures jarred ever louder with Spanish society's mod-ernization and desire to integrate into its European setting, and, insofar as its repressive institutions were concerned, proved inca-pable of dealing with the new social mobilization phenomena. The opposition's political culture was a mixture of obsolescence and modernity. It was obsolete in that it failed to recognize the novelty of opposition demands and forms of action and interpre-ted itself in the language of working-class redemptionism. Much of the opposition was still weighed down by pre-1936 antipoli-ticism, that is, it was more disposed to confronting the state than to reforming it.[19] That working-class outlook, framed in the "in-herited paradigm" of anti-Francoist ideologues, led newer move-ments to accept subordination to class struggle, that is, to the PCE strategy of securing democratic rights that eventually absorbed all other strategic goals. In this sense, the movements finally become political.

Anti-Francoist political preoccupations dominated NSM concerns with objectives and modes of action; in this sense, there was no *newness* in Spanish social mobilization. At the same time, that political concern was a genuine novelty in Spain, especially in relation to the model from the pre–Civil War stage, which was characterized by antipoliticism. Anti-Francoist mobilizations were the first in the history of Spain to define their strategies in politi-cal terms.

All that is to beg the question: Why this turn? And why at that time? European working classes were integrated into their respective national political systems on the occasion of the First and Second World Wars, conflicts in which Spain was not involved (Payne 1987, 6–7). Spain did experience its own configuration, however, the Civil War of 1936–1939. It was then that the workers' movements first became identified with a political regime: the Republic. Recall the mistrust with which workers' movements received the Spanish Republic of 1931 and the strategy of confrontation they adopted during its first years. The PCE reversed this strategy in 1935 at Moscow's prompting; it became a stalwart defender of the Popular Front; and, when the war broke out, it defended a democratic republic as a positive response to fascism. The Socialists (Partido Socialista Obrero Español) likewise heeded the voices calling for collaboration with the republicans over the ones drawn to maximalist pretensions. Even the anarchist CNT-FAI (Consejo Nacional de Trabajo-Federación Anarquista Ibérica) accepted several ministerial portfolios (the height of contradiction) in republican wartime governments.

It was in that conscious identification with antifascism that the Spanish working-class framework of reference changed and became politicized; this development was eclipsed by subsequent defeat in the Civil War and shaded from public view until the Left's reappearance at the end of Francoism. The identification with parliamentary democracy was expressed in the programs of the PCE, the party that more fully than any other jettisoned all antipolitical ambiguity while at the same time conserving enough "revolutionary worker" legitimacy to be able to impose its political project on the whole of the Spanish Left in the 1960s and 1970s.

The Transition to Democracy and Postmodern Social Mobilization

The transition from Francoist institutions to a parliamentary democracy was at long last carried out, and with much less strife than had been foreseen.[20] With regard to social movements, certain peculiarities can be noted.

Although strikes, demonstrations, and labor conflicts unquestionably constituted anti-Francoist pressure tactics and continued to do so during the transition's first years,[21] the fact is that it was neither the unions nor the social movements but the political parties that piloted reform. Of the parties, the pace of events was not set by the proletarian vanguard or by any coalition under its leadership, but rather by a recent formation, the Unión de Centro Democrático, which was composed of reformists from within Francoism and leaders of the most moderate opposition. They were succeeded, in 1982, by a socialist party (PSOE) that had played a minor role in the opposition to Francoism. Despite its old name, this party could also be considered a new political organization, with small revolutionary proletarian engagement. The whole process was marked by fear of renewed political instability, which led to a constitutional and electoral framework that favored the concentration of power in the national leadership of the parties and a weakened role for rank-and-file activists, parliamentary groups, or local networks. Little room was left for participation and internal renewal. In the years of transition toward democracy, the social movements that had played such an important role in the battle against Francoism disappeared or were subjected to organizations that were more institutionalized and focused on specific political objectives.

The primary and most spectacular 1977 electoral collapse was that of the powerful and moderate Partido Comunista as well as of the revolutionary Left, which apparently had been behind so many of the anti-Francoist mobilizations. Communism's worldwide weakening was already obvious by the late 1970s, and it was especially lacking in appeal for a newly prosperous society such as Spain. These political organizations probably also suffered from the inconsistency between their institutional nature as Leninist parties at the same time as they were fostering the idea of being anti-institutional and grass-roots "movements." In any case, the numerous revolutionary organizations that had been considered prime movers of mobilizations simply disappeared at the first general elections of 1977. The possibility should not be dismissed that its strength had always been more apparent than real. The PCE, the main anti-Francoist force, which expected to gain 20 to 25 percent of the votes in 1977, obtained less than 10 percent that year and less than 5 percent in 1982. It was removed from the primary position it had occupied in Spanish politics during the transition years.

Trade unionism, contrary to expectations, also declined, in both strike activity and membership. The first sign was the fall from preeminence of the Comisiones Obreras. Its place was taken by the Unión General de Trabajadores (UGT), which was much more tightly institutionalized and politically controlled by the PSOE. The second symptom was the acceptance by both unions of the priority of political reform over labor demands. These agreements were codified in the Moncloa Pacts, which insured social peace in exchange for "consensus" agreement on political reform.[22] Comisiones Obreras finally ended the political transition as a political appendage of the PCE, as UGT was to the PSOE. None of them has raised the low level of union membership—about 13 percent of the labor force—which tightens their dependence on state budgets (Fishman 1990, 187).

As for the student movement, the transition led to its dissolution. Its demands were revealed to be too thin or too heterogeneous to sustain an organized front. By the time political reform was largely in place, radical revolutionary political lines were defended by small leftist groups with little influence over the student body. Those actively advocating positions close to the PCE subordinated their entire strategy to the regime's democratization, whose realization left them the sole alternative of becoming professional politicians in an electoral system. A certain degree of permanence was achieved in the early 1980s by the demands raised by unions and special collectives who, with the passing of time and their incorporation into the lower ranks of the teaching body, were no longer made up of students but of young professors (the so-called PNNs[23]). These demands eventually took the form of salary increases and job stability (achievement of civil servant status) and were basically satisfied by the successive reforms. University unrest as a chronic phenomenon disappeared.

After the 1977 general election, nationalist demands were reduced to socially conservative legal parties that used mobilizations in order to threaten Madrid and widen their decentralized domains and their share of the national budget. ETA, of course, remained alive, but, instead of getting the widespread support it had enjoyed among anti-Francoists, the reaction now tended to be bitter enmity. It was viewed by the rest of the political spectrum as jeopardizing a democratic edifice of whose solidity no one was entirely sure.

Citizens' movements, which once were labeled as "the largest and most significant urban movement in Europe since 1945,"[24] did not survive the first municipal elections of April 1979, when most of Spain's major cities elected nationalists, socialists, or socialist-led coalitions to power. Madrid's Federation of Neighborhood Associations demanded without success that the new Spanish constitution recognize the public interest of neighborhood associations, as was done with trade unions. The movement was unable to participate in the newly elected institutions of local government, and it was unable to survive as an organization independent from political parties (Castells 1983, 225, 236).

The social movements remaining at the end of the political reform process (about 1981–1982) were small groups of environmentalists, pacifists, and a few new voices defending sexual minorities. Only these really can be called new social movements. They were stripped of political colorings or dependence on political parties, and, notwithstanding how incompatible they deemed their values to be with respect to the dominant ones, they harbored no dreams of revolutionary conquests of power to propel sweeping social changes.[25] They were guided by pragmatism, and they centered their efforts on the reform or control of specific segments of social life or the recognition of new collective identities. From an organizational standpoint, they rejected both the social-democratic bureaucratic model and Jacobin-Leninist discipline; they idealized grass-roots politics and its segmented, decentralized, rank-and-file controlled organizations.

These characteristics made Spanish mobilizations of the 1980s comparable to the 1970s European NSM model.[26] Even so, Spanish NSMs have peculiar features. They are not just late, they are extremely weak. This weakness is derived, on the one hand, from Spanish society's traditional incapacity for civil organization and action away from the state, and, on the other, from the consolidation of a system of representation that is controlled by the top leadership of the political parties.

Between 1977 and 1982, public opinion poured its hopes into the political arena. Especially from February 1981, when the democratic system was threatened by an attempted military coup, all hopes were centered on a PSOE accession to power. In 1982, the new young rulers arrived, backed by their anti-Francoist credentials; there was peace and demobilization for some three years.

The "progressive" intelligentsia had by that time realized that the state of political affairs was completely controlled by party leaders. The term *desencanto* (disenchantment) was coined to describe their feelings of impotence as well as the destruction of millenarian-revolutionary expectations. The old revolutionary Left saw itself withering away, laminated between two worlds: politics, now the purview of professionalized parties and whose only road to power was by way of election victories; and social movements, weak, depoliticized, and focused on partial objectives.

Spain did not witness a peace mobilization of the kind that swept Europe in the early 1980s (Klandermans 1991). Toward the end of 1985, when the PSOE's reformist drive was ebbing and harsh recessionary measures were wearing thin, the government's decision to advocate remaining in NATO, counter to its implicit electoral promises, catalyzed discontent. In the spring of 1986 the NSMs, together with remnants from anti-Francoist social movements, mobilized in the campaign to vote no in the NATO referendum, which was nevertheless won by the government. The sense of impotence heightened, and there began a period marked by sporadic outbursts of angry collective protest actions. These are exemplified by the student movements of 1986 and 1987 that ousted Education Minister José María Maravall and by the general strike of December 14, 1988, that demanded less austere social and salary policies.

None of these protests, though, meant a reversal of the process at work in the previous phase. Student activism vanished and no viable organization survived in the 1986–1987 flare-up; union membership remained rutted at the previous low levels and no new phase of strike activity or social mobilization began. Nor did the rebukes of the PSOE signify confidence in other parties: the PSOE again obtained absolute majorities in the general elections called in 1986 (after the NATO referendum) and 1989 (after the general strike).

The occasional protest-mobilization capacity displayed by a collection of groups with such a tenuous base can only be explained if the demonstrations against government education and economic policies were vehicles for expressing other things: the frustration of youth in a society and power system overly controlled by a generation with much future still ahead of it; an ethical sanction of the ready rapport of new socialist leaders with the old oligarchies;[27] or popular aversion for their *prepotente* (arrogant, imperious) style of exercising power.[28]

Summary and Conclusions

In this chapter I emphasize the importance of the internal framework of reference and self-perception of social movements, following a comparison between different stages in Spanish modern history.

In the first, or traditional, period, an antipolitical culture dominated. The political system provided few possibilities for participation or social reform through legal channels. More important, social movements showed little interest in pushing for reform of the state. It would be difficult to assert that the first phenomenon caused the second, for in the next stage, despite the total absence of participatory possibilities provided by Francoism, social movements, guided by the realistic *posibilista* strategy of the principal underground opposition force, fully embraced the struggle to democratize the regime.

The most evident cause of this shift was the politicization of the working classes during the struggle against Francoism initiated during the Civil War. A quarter century of repression and silence was followed by the reemergence of protests, this time under new conditions. Unprecedented economic growth and social modernization was under way. The presence of the state in the life of society—in the form of police vigilance but also of administrative apparatus, social welfare programs, and public services—grew to an extent previously unthinkable.

The new strategy adopted by anti-Francoist mobilizations proved that the war had not been forgotten. The paramount objective was not social revolution but the replacement of the "regime of 18 July" with a democratic political structure.[29] This priority was defended by most opposition forces, but it was above all defended by the PCE, which was charged by the rest of the Left with leading the social mobilization. This involvement in political struggle marks the difference between Spanish social movements of the 1960s and 1970s and NSMs in European and American democracies of the same epoch. This politicization also differentiates pre–1936 Spanish mobilizations from those after 1960. Similar observations may be made about the most advanced countries in Europe in the pre–1914 and post–1945 periods. The process of political incorporation is similar, the timing is different.

The self-perception in working-class terms that drove the

social movements to become politicized eventually was their un-doing. Subsumed by the political parties, they relinquished leader-ship of the democratic transition to those who, out of fear of a return of the pre–1939 constitutional and governmental instability, organized a system in which social participation was much cir-cumscribed.

Once the political reform has finished, a third, postmodern, stage begins. Again, the Spanish situation can be likened to that in other advanced industrial societies. Yet, the predominantly po-litical orientation of social movements in the previous phase now makes them unable to organize and counterpoise the power exer-cised by political parties. Social mobilization loses its strength of the 1960s and early 1970s as its leaders either become part of the "political class" or are pushed off-stage.

There is then a resurgence, though only sporadic and incom-parably weaker than in the past, of the Spanish tradition of mis-trust of the state, the antipoliticism of pre–Civil War culture. The public feels disappointed and duped by *los políticos*. The govern-ment is used as an excuse for impotence or inaction and is blamed for all social ills. Social movements, though garnering little social support in their day-to-day doings, become occasional vehicles for sporadic criticisms of the government by society.

The combination of chronic weakness with a surprising rep-resentative capacity at certain junctures seems to be the model for social mobilization in the near future, unless there is a substantial shift in the society's capacity for self-organization and the political system's capacity for absorption and flexibility.[30] Either there arises in Spain a tradition of organized citizen activism and the institutional checks and impediments to citizen participation are eased, or social mobilizations will continue to be characterized by a somewhat schizophrenic duality. Incapable of achieving sus-tained social support, they will live through long periods of apa-thy, silence, and impotence, punctuated by heady moments of protagonism when issue, climate, and rallying call combine to bring forth popular outpourings of anger against the government.

Notes

1. Its antecedents can be traced to the 1830s, when the first workers' associations began to operate in the Catalan textile industry.

2. Again, some could argue that the real awakening began in 1956, a year

of students' protests and a transportation strike in Barcelona, but that was an isolated period of unrest. It is only since 1961 that confrontation with the regime became more or less continuous.

3. This suggestion partially draws from Tilly's approach (1990) to the relationship between social mobilization and the state's repressive ability and from Tarrow's (1991), according to which social mobilization traits depend on political opportunities.

4. Among the many possible examples, the most influential has been Tuñón de Lara 1971. Similar traits were shared by previous publications, such as Lambert 1953; specialized books on anarchism (Nettlau 1969; Gómez Casas 1977) or socialism (Gómez Llorente 1976); or general histories, such as Ramos Oliveira 1946 or the more recent Gil Novales 1985.

5. See, for example, the *Manifiesto-Programa* of the PCE, in 1975, especially part 2: "The struggle against the state power of the capitalist oligarchy; for social and political democracy; for socialism"; or Tamames 1973.

6. Juliá 1990, 183; see also Juliá 1988. CNT (Confederación Nacional del Trabajo) and UGT (Unión General de Trabajadores) were, respectively, the anarchosyndicalist and socialist trade unions.

7. See for instance, Vilar 1962. This was also the tendency of J. Vicens Vives in his various works on nineteenth-century Catalonia. Hobsbawm (1959) partially took up this interpretation.

8. The IWMA (International Working Men's Association) entered Spain slightly late, in 1868; Spaniards opted for Bakuninism, in the 1872 split between Marxists and Bakuninists, but so did all other southern European organizations. The decadence of the First International a year later was as sudden as everywhere else, only with the brief exception of an ephemeral resurgence in Andalusia (1881–1883). The 1890s witnessed anarchist terrorism in Barcelona, but to a lesser degree than in Italy, France, tsarist Russia, or the Austro-Hungarian empire (the detailed files kept by the French police from 1892 to 1894 show only 2 or 3 percent of suspected anarchists to be Spaniards). The assassination attempt on the Spanish prime minister, Antonio Cánovas, in 1897 was carried out by an Italian (see Alvarez-Junco 1992). The rise of revolutionary syndicalism in the first years of the twentieth century had also occurred in France in the previous decade. Spanish exceptionality really began in 1910, with the foundation of the anarchist union CNT (Confederación Nacional del Trabajo); and even then we should speak of brief flare-ups (1917–1920, 1931–1937), with a great chronological and geographical discontinuity. In industrial Catalonia, its traditional stronghold, anarchism lost strength in the 1930s, while it expanded among Castilian and Aragonese rural workers. The celebrated "anarchist collectives" existed mainly in Aragón. Many of them were merely a product of the presence of anarchist troops, located in villages where the CNT had no affiliates before the Civil War (Casanova 1985).

9. By 1950, 70 percent of the Spanish population was still living in localities of less than 50,000 inhabitants and 48 percent of the labor force was employed in agriculture (not very different from the beginning of the century, when the respective figures were 80 percent and 60 percent). By 1975, these ratios dropped to below 60 percent and 25 percent—signaling a crucial advance toward the

situation in 1990, when more than half the population lived in large cities and less than 15 percent of the active labor force was engaged in the primary sector. The total number of cars in the country, which in 1950 had not yet surpassed 100,000 vehicles, jumped to 5 million in 1975 and topped 12 million in 1990. The number of tourists, barely 1 million in 1955, surged to 6 million by 1960, and shot up to 14 million in 1965 and 30 million in 1975; it was more than 50 million in 1990. In 1975, after fifteen years of economic growth of about 7 percent each year, the country was the world's tenth largest industrial power. The illiteracy affecting 60 percent of Spaniards at the beginning of the century only survived in marginal clusters of the elderly and rural population. Birth rates fell below those of France (Linz 1981; Herr 1971, chap. 15; or *Anuarios* from Instituto Nacional de Estadística).

10. Gallo 1969; Tamames 1973; Tuñón de Lara 1980; Fusi 1985; Payne 1987.

11. The Communist party was excluded from the general opposition meeting held in Munich in 1962.

12. The student movement included other forces, which, for the most part, were weaker or, as in the case of the FLP (Frente de Liberación Popular), more ephemeral than the communists.

13. A rally in San Sebastián de los Reyes, Madrid, and the *jornadas libertarias* in Barcelona, in the summer of 1976.

14. See, for example, the article published in *L'Espoir,* the voice of the exiled Spanish anarchists in France, on "La droga" (Toulouse, June 24, 1973).

15. Maravall 1978; Peña 1966. Students protests had already been extremely important in the fall of Primo de Rivera's dictatorship in 1929–1930 (Ben-Ami 1983, 157, 344–55).

16. When unrest began to grow in the 1960s, Franco was obsessed with distinguishing between "labor-motivated" and "political" strikes. He could not understand that the very nature of his regime made all protests political (Tuñón de Lara 1980, 371).

17. A symptom of that support was the popularity of the Catalan *nova cançó* among the *progresista* youth all over Spain. The year 1965 was symbolic because of the repercussion of the intellectuals' sit-in at the Capuchin convent in Sarriá.

18. The magazine *Bicicleta,* in the late 1970s, was very informative on movements in defense of the environment in Spain. On pacifism, see Pérez Ledesma 1982.

19. A symptom of this could be the ironical rebukes to the PCE leader's moderate strategy so frequent among the *progresista* culture, as shown in the well-known *copla:* "Carrillo / ¿adónde vas tú, Carrillo / con la reconciliación? / Coge la hoz y el martillo / y haz la revolución / no sólo contra el Caudillo" (Why do you talk so much of reconciliation, Carrillo? Take the hammer and sickle and make revolution, not only against the *Caudillo* [Franco]).

20. Among the vast academic production on the Spanish political reform, the most helpful are Carr and Fusi 1981; Casanova 1983; Maravall 1984; Gilmour 1985; Gunther, Sani, and Shabad 1986; Preston 1986; Díaz 1987; Juliá 1988.

21. For example, the wave of strikes that the Arias-Fraga government

confronted in the first half of 1976; these strikes can be credited with thwarting the government's *proyecto continuista* (or the project of continuity, the plan to keep Francoist institutions with mild reforms).

22. The Moncloa Pacts were signed by the main parties (ranging from the Communist party to Alianza Popular, a new conservative force made up by former Francoist "reformers") seeking to insure stability after the general elections of 1977.

23. The Profesores No Numerarios, or PNNs, were college lecturers or teaching assistants who did most of the teaching at rapidly expanding public universities in the 1960s and 1970s. Qualifications and research requirements were low, but so was the salary; PNNs did not enjoy tenure guarantees. They became politicized quickly and they were an important factor of instability during late Francoism and transition years.

24. This is Castells's (1983, 216) somewhat idealized version; Touraine was influenced by it (1984, 6).

25. A telling evolution was in the environmental movement. At a stormy meeting in Cercedilla in 1977, *políticos* (controlled by the revolutionary group ORT) and genuine environmentalists split. I thank Enrique Laraña for this reference.

26. In the sense defined by Melucci (1989), for instance.

27. The marriage between the former minister of finance, Miguel Boyer, who was responsible for the austere policies of 1982 through 1985, and Isabel Preysler, a well-known figure of the Costa del Sol "jet-set," caused a great moral scandal in the summer prior to the general strike. On the strike, see Juliá 1989.

28. The result was the exclusive attribution of political power to those who had won the elections. This was considered a betrayal by protagonists of anti-Francoist mobilizations who had believed literally in "popular participation" rhetoric.

29. The Franco regime often used this name to refer to the date on which the military *pronunciamiento* against the Republic began in 1936.

30. In the sense in which Samuel Huntington has used these concepts in *Political Order in Changing Societies* (New Haven: Yale University Press, 1968), for instance. See their application to the Spanish case in Carnero 1988.

References

Alvarez-Junco, José. 1977. "Los dos anarquismos." *Cuadernos de Ruedo Ibérico* 55–57:139–56.

———. 1985. "A vueltas con la Revolución Burguesa." *Zona Abierta* 36–37:81–106.

———. 1986. "El anarquismo en la España contemporánea." *Anales de Historia contemporánea* 5:189–200.

———. 1992. "Pedro Vallina, un anarquista español el Paris de 1900." *Historia Social* 13:23–37.

Alvarez-Junco, José, Gloria Martinez Dorado, and María Luisa Sanchez Mejias. 1983. "Las alternativas revolucionarias en España. ¿Fracaso en la democracia?" *Nueva Sociedad* 69:123–33.

Alvarez-Junco, José, and Manuel Pérez Ledesma. 1982. "Historia del movimiento obrero. ¿Una segunda ruptura?" *Revista de Occidente* 12:19–41.

Balcells, Albert. 1980. *El arraigo del anarquismo en Cataluña: Textos de 1928–34.* Barcelona: Júcar.

Ben-Ami, Shlomo. 1978. *The Origins of the Second Republic in Spain.* New York: Oxford University Press.

———. 1983. *Fascism from Above: The Dictatorship of Primo de Rivera in Spain, 1923–1930.* New York: Oxford University Press.

Brenan, Gerald. 1943. *The Spanish Labyrinth.* New York: Oxford University Press.

Calero, Antonio M. 1976. *Movimientos sociales en Andalucía (1820–1936).* Madrid: Siglo XXI.

Carnero, Teresa. 1988. "Política sin democracia en España." *Revista de Occidente* 55–56: 43–70.

Carr, Raymond, and Juan Pablo Fusi. 1981. *Spain: Dictatorship to Democracy.* London: Allen and Unwin.

Casanova, José V. 1983. "Modernization and Democratization: Reflections on Spain's Transition to Democracy." *Social Research* 50:4.

Casanova, Julián. 1985. *Anarquismo y revolución en la sociedad rural aragonesa, 1936–1938.* Madrid: Siglo XXI.

Castells, Manuel. 1983. "The Making of an Urban Social Movement: The Citizen Movement in Madrid towards the End of the Franquist Era." In his *The City and the Grassroots: A Cross-Cultural Theory of Urban Social Movements.* Berkeley: University of California Press.

Castro, Américo. 1954. *La realidad histórica de España.* Mexico City: Porrúa.

Díaz, Elías. 1987. *La transición a la democracia. Claves ideológicas.* Madrid: Eudema.

Díaz del Moral, Juan. (1929) 1967. *Historia de las agitaciones campesinas andaluzas.* Madrid: Alianza.

Fishman, Robert. 1990. *Working-Class Organization and the Return to Democracy in Spain.* Ithaca: Cornell University Press.

Fusi, Juan Pablo. 1985. *Franco. Autoritarismo y poder personal.* Madrid: El Pais Editores.

Gallo, Max. 1969. *Histoire de l'Espagne franquiste.* Paris: Robert Laffont.

Gilmour, David. 1985. *The Transformation of Spain.* London: Quartet Books.

Gil Novales, Alberto, ed. 1985. *La Revolución Burguesa en España.* Madrid: Akal.

Gómez Casas, Juan. 1977. *Historia del anarcosindicalismo español.* Madrid: Editorial Aguilera.

Gómez Llorente, Luis. 1976. *Aproximación a la historia del socialismo español.* Madrid: Edicusa.

Gunther, Richard, Giacomo Sani, and Goldie Shabad. 1986. *Spain after Franco: The Making of a Competitive Party System.* Berkeley: University of California Press.

Herr, Richard. 1971. *An Historical Essay on Modern Spain.* Berkeley: University of California Press.

Hobsbawn, Eric. 1959. *Primitive Rebels.* Manchester: Manchester University Press.

Juliá, Santos. 1977. *La izquierda del PSOE (1934–36).* Madrid: Siglo XXI.

————. 1988. "Transiciones a la democracia en la España del siglo XX." *Sistema* 84: 25–40.

————. 1989. *La desavenencia. Partido, sindicatos y huelga general.* Madrid: El País and Aguilar.

————. 1990. "Poder y revolución en la cultura política del militante obrero español." In *Peuple, mouvement ouvrier, culture dans l'Espagne contemporaine,* edited by Jacques Maurice. Paris: Presses Universitaires de Vincennes.

Klandermans, Bert. 1991. "The Peace Movement and Social Movement Theory." In *Peace Movements in Western Europe and the United States,* edited by Bert Klandermans, pp. 1–39. Vol. 3 of *International Social Movement Research.* Greenwich, Conn.: JAI Press.

Lambert, Renée. 1953. *Mouvements ouvriers et socialistes (Chronologie et bibliographie): L'Espagne, 1750–1936.* Paris: Editions Sociales.

Linz, Juan, ed. 1981. *Informe FOESSA: Informe sociológico sobre el cambio político en España (1975–1981).* Madrid: Euramérica.

Malefakis, Edward. 1970. *Agrarian Reform and Peasant Revolution in Spain.* New Haven: Yale University Press.

Maravall, José María. 1978. *Dictadura y disentimiento político. Obreros y estudiantes bajo el franquismo.* Madrid: Alfaguara.

————. 1984. *The Transition to Democracy in Spain.* London: Croom Helm.

Melucci, Alberto. 1989. *Nomads of the Present: Social Movements and Individual Needs in Contemporary Society.* Philadelphia: Temple University Press.

Nettlau, Max. 1969. *La Première Internationale en Espagne, 1868–1888.* Dordrecht, Holland: D. Reidel.

Payne, Stanley. 1987. *The Franco Regime: 1936–1975.* Madison: University of Wisconsin Press.

Peña, Antonio. 1966. "Veinticinco años de luchas estudiantiles." In *Horizonte Español 1966,* 2:169–212. Paris: Ruedo Ibérico.

Pérez Ledesma, Manuel. 1982. Introduction to *Contra el hambre y la carrera de armamentos.* Madrid: Fundamentos.

Preston, Paul. 1979. "The Struggle against Fascism in Spain: *Leviatán* and the Contradictions of the Spanish Left, 1934–36." *European Studies Review* 9, 1:81–103.

————. 1986. *The Triumph of Democracy in Spain.* London: Methuen.

————, ed. 1976. *Spain in Crisis: The Evolution and Decline of the Franco Regime.* Hassocks, England: Harvester.

Ramos Oliveira, Antonio. 1946. *Politics, Economics, and Men of Modern Spain (1808–1946).* London: Gollancz.

Tamames, Ramón. 1973. *La República. La era de Franco.* Madrid: Alianza/Alfaguara.

Tarrow, Sidney. 1991. " 'Aiming at a Moving Target': Social Science and the Recent Rebellions in Eastern Europe." *Political Science and Politics* 29:12–20.

Tilly, Charles. 1990. *Coercion, Capital, and European States.* Oxford: Basil Blackwell.

Touraine, Alain. 1984. "Les mouvements sociaux: objet particulier ou problème central de l'analyse sociologique?" *Revue Française de Sociologie* 25, 1:3–19.

Tuñón de Lara, Manuel. 1971. *El movimiento obrero en la historia de España.* Madrid: Taurus.

————. 1980. *España bajo la dictadura franquista*. Barcelona: Labor.
Vicens Vives, Jaume. 1986 *Los catalanes en el siglo XIX*. Madrid: Alianza.
Vilar, Pierre. 1962. *Historie de l'Espagne*. Paris: P.U.F.
Vilar, Sergio. 1984. *Historia del anti-franquismo, 1939–1975*. Barcelona: Época.

Chapter 14

The Party's Over—So What Is to Be Done?

Richard Flacks

Two hundred years after the French Revolution, when the division between Left and Right began to be used to map political alignments, it seems obvious to many that such clear-cut political differentiation has lost any meaning. Certainly, it is argued, the Left no longer can be said to have reality in the light of the collapse of international communism, the decomposition of the Soviet bloc, the abandonment of socialism by those living under its "actually existing" form, and the recent conservative drift of politics in many Western countries. I argue, however, that we still need "Left" and "Right" to signify certain essential political and cultural differences. I propose that what is dying is a particular type of political mobilization. It is the Left as a "party" that has come to an end.

The Left as a Tradition

The Left is, first of all, a tradition—a relatively distinct body of belief and action that began to have a coherent character at the time of the American and French Revolutions. An enormous variety of ideological perspectives constitute that tradition. It is known by a host of labels: socialism, anarchism, communism, pacifism, radical democracy, feminism, and certain variants of libertarianism. In the United States, instead of these relatively specific labels, leftists typically refer to themselves by using such ideologically euphemistic terms as progressive, liberal, populist, and radical.

Left ideological perspectives have often been propelled by organizations created to advance them. The proliferation of ideological perspectives, of variants within these, and of organizations representing them competing for support has meant that the tradition of the Left has been deeply structured by internecine struggle. Given the ideological divisions and warfare on the Left, what warrants the assertion that there is nevertheless a shared tradition? What, if anything, do the Left fragments have in common?

One answer is that there is an essential idea that underlies these ideological differences. That idea can be captured best by a statement like this: Society should be organized so that the people make their own history. Here are some other ways of putting it: Social and economic life should be arranged so that every member of society has the chance to have some voice in shaping the conditions within which their lives are lived; Socioeconomic arrangements in which a few can decide the lives of the many should be replaced by arrangements based on collective self-government; or Social life should be structured as much as possible on the basis of reasoned discourse among society's members, rather than by the exercise of power or by chance (or the working of impersonal markets).[1]

In short, the Left tradition is the cumulative struggle to envision and practice a fully realized democracy. Most of the ideological differences within the tradition of the Left have revolved around issues of power and strategy. Disputes over what kinds of power—economic, political, military, sexual—are primary and over the agencies, levers, and processes of change have been so deeply divisive that they have frequently obscured the elements of agreement in these ideological fragments. Still, the factional strife of the past seems now overshadowed by a sense of commonality.

The Left as Identity

The Left tradition has provided rich material for the construction of personal identity. Indeed, it is crucial to understand that the tradition has been carried forward not only by formal organizations and literature but, more fundamentally, by individual human beings who share a personal identity based in that tradition. That identity is centered on a sense of responsibility to live one's life in relation to history and as an active contributor to social transformation. Conscious Leftists, I imagine, conceive of themselves as duty-bound to connect to public life, to speak out against injustice; they feel most fulfilled when they believe that they have made some difference in the world, hoping, at a minimum, that, as Brecht put it, "the butchers would have slept more easily without me." Current emphasis on identity as a central theme in "new" social movements ignores the fact that, for generations, commitment to the labor movement and other "traditional" movements has had much to do with self-expression and not just a pursuit of "rational" interest.

Social traditions and identities do not "succeed" or "fail"; they develop, renew, stagnate, and die. The Left, defined as tradition and identity, may well continue, even though many of its most potent symbols have been discredited. Such continuity will depend on a radical revision of the narratives that undergird the Left's self-understanding. Can the dissidents in Eastern Europe who took on the burdens of opposing communist authority come to be seen as reinforcing and enriching an identity that was shaped in earlier generations by communists? Will the moments in the streets of Prague and Leipzig and Peking when masses confronted the party dictatorships come to be viewed as episodes in a tradition of popular democratic struggle marked, in earlier generations, by the unfurling of red banners and socialist slogans? Such constructions may appear absurd until one recalls that the most profound critiques of communism have, for decades, been made from within the Left tradition. To a great extent, our understanding of the historical significance and cultural meanings of social movements depends on such constructions, that is, on a continuing contest about how particular episodes may be situated within long traditions of thought, action, and expression.

The Left as a Party

For one hundred years, most people on the Left throughout the world have shared elements of a vision and of an identity, and also a sense of common strategy. The key strategic idea during this century of struggle has been that social transformation depends on the development of the Left as a vehicle of power. Most particularly, it depends on the emergence of a party that is capable of winning power and using the machinery of the state to implement a program of change.

This mass party strategy was seen as necessary for several reasons. First, it was essential to unify the working class, articulate its shared grievances, and mobilize its collective energy. Ever since the mid-nineteenth century, Left activists and intellectuals have seen the working class as both the moral source and the practical resource for democratic and socialist transformation. If the working class could be united, its collective power, based in the production process, could eventually achieve revolutionary change; more immediately, the numerical strength of a politically unified working class would be central to the achievement of Left political power.

Second, workers and other subordinated groups needed a vehicle of representation; they needed the means to defend their interests in capitalist society without always having to be prepared to strike or engage in other direct action. A working-class party, together with labor unions, would give workers an institutionalized voice that would enable them to be politically defended while they, as individuals, could deal with the demands of personal life.

Third, the party provided the social framework within which an effective professional stratum that was capable of governing in the name of the working class could be created. The party was to be the institutional arena within which specific policies and programs could be formulated and the leadership cadre could be groomed and trained. Moreover, in addition to developing leadership, the party could also be the primary means to enable the political and cultural development of its mass constituency. All manner of educational, cultural, and self-help institutions would be created. Through its program and through its cultural practices, the mass party was built to be the embodiment of Left tradition and identity for its members and for ever-widening circles to whom it reached out.

Finally, once the party assumed government power, it would use the legal, economic, and military resources of the state to implement a program of social transformation. Since this program would be mightily resisted by the powers that be, the party in power would not only govern society in the name of the great majority but it would also be a framework for continuously mobilizing popular energy to sustain the momentum of reform in the face of various kinds of conservative resistance.[2]

Many of the weaknesses of this strategy have been known for decades. In the European parliamentary states, social democratic mass parties have never been able to win a majority by relying solely on a strategy of uniting the working class. The base of the working class has been too narrow to constitute a majority, and the class itself has been too variegated with respect to skill and sectoral difference to unite around a radical program. Accordingly, all social democratic parties have had to adopt moderate programs or otherwise reduce their ideological clarity and militancy in order to gain majority support (see Laclau and Mouffe 1985).

Robert Michels was the first—but hardly the last—to observe that the representational character of the party, and the professionalization of its leadership, created an almost inescapable tendency toward "oligarchy." The more that party leaders became career politicians, the more stake they had in maintaining their control of the party and using it as a vehicle for their own well-being. The result: bureaucratic, top-down control; the depoliticizing of the mass membership; the fostering of a privileged elite; corruptions of various kinds; and a growing tendency for the party to abandon its transformative goals. In the Soviet bloc, the communist parties, exercising a monopoly of power, made bureaucratic, oligarchical party dictatorship synonymous with communism. Michels, writing before World War I, had anticipated that the communists' social democratic antagonists in Western Europe would not be immune to similar—if far less brutally expressed—tendencies (Michels 1959).

The experience of parliamentary democracies has been that party control of government does not equal party control of the state, nor does it provide the power to bring about socialist restructuring. Every move toward radical reform of a capitalist society by a governing socialist party has tended to result in destabilization of the economy by capitalists seeking to protect their investments against the threat of encroachment. The main state functions—the military, the administrative bureaucracy—are not readily controllable by a party just because it happens to win an election. At this writing, one could hardly maintain that the election of an established socialist party in any of the Western European countries would have any chance of resulting in a "socialist" government. Disillusionment with these parties dates back to the World War I and the advent of Leninism as a supposed alternative.

The Leninist solution to the riddle of how socialists could use state power for socialist ends was to seize power through military means. Through the use of ruthless force, the state became the vehicle of the party's will and the party controlled the political discourse of the whole society. We have known for decades that such party dictatorship created the opposite of the socialist ideal, but for years, many Marxists assumed that, at least, something alternative to capitalism was being constructed. We now know that even this was not the case.

After one hundred years in which Left activists and intellectuals tried to embody their emancipatory hopes in one or another form of party, we are now at the point where virtually all can see that this strategy was doomed to failure. Today mass, "hegemonic" parties seem to be disintegrating everywhere. I refer here to the collapse of the Eastern European communist parties, and to the decline of such social democratic parties as Labour in England and Labor in Israel, as well as others as varied in form and ideology as PRI in Mexico, the Liberal Democrats of Japan, Congress of India, and the Democratic party in the United States. All of these have seemed hegemonic, all have contributed to modernizing their societies and to creating welfare-state supports for their mass constituencies. That they were not vehicles of emancipatory aspiration has long been understood. Today, they seem obsolete even as vehicles of power; they seem to have lost a good deal of their capacity to maintain their majority base. Indeed, to win back effective electoral majorities, such parties have tended to jettison even a semblance of their earlier programmatic emphasis on economic redistribution and social equality.

How might we account for the decomposition of the mass party? I think there are several clues:

1. The globalization of the world economy weakens the capacity of mass parties to use the state as an instrument for allocating resources to benefit their constituencies. Welfare states face intensifying fiscal crisis; capital flow is beyond state control; and Keynesian policies supporting high wages seem to conflict with the need to revitalize national competitiveness. The social democratic/welfare state program no longer seems sustainable, and promises made in its name lose credibility.

2. The very success of the mass parties is part of their undoing. Large numbers of workers seek now to protect relative advantage, resent taxation that supports the welfare state, and hope for more opportunity to own things. Against this, party appeals to traditional bases of solidarity and impulses to equality and the

common good seem stultifying. Class identity breaks apart into many fragments.

3. All the mass parties established their dominance not only by being a voice for disadvantaged mass constituencies but by maintaining the silence of some of these (women, ethnic minorities, the least skilled, for example). One of the primary reasons for the decline of these parties is that previously silent minorities are now mobilizing. As a result, the parties find themselves paralyzed, no longer able to offer a credible, majoritarian program that meets the needs of both the relatively advantaged and the newly emergent groups that constitute their base. Limited on the one hand by the conservatism of their more advantaged constituents and on the other hand by the fiscal constraints resulting from dependency on global capital flows, these once dominant parties appear mired in compromise and contradiction. Because state-based strategies of social reform—whether they are called socialist, capitalist, corporatist, or something else—appear to be politically and economically unviable, the parties whose programs were based on such strategies seem to have had their day as embodiments of popular hope.

All during the twentieth century, Americans leftists have hoped to see a party of the European type to represent their values and serve as a vehicle for working-class empowerment. For all these years, the fact that no such party formation was possible—the so-called American Exception—has been a source of deep feelings of failure among American leftists, who have typically measured their efforts against the achievements of various of the European Lefts. The main reason for the American Exception has been the enormous diversity of the American working class with respect to race and ethnicity. Because ethnic difference and competition became deeply intertwined with differences in life chances, American workers typically found Left calls for class solidarity hopelessly impractical. Instead of supporting a Left party, American workers joined political machines and unions based on ethnic solidarity and exclusion. These sources of empowerment, in turn, reinforced a conception of freedom, already culturally dominant in the United States, that was defined in terms of individual autonomy rather than participatory democracy, a culturally rooted definition of rationality based on short-run advantage rather than on the common good.[3] Having never experienced a multiethnic framework of political solidarity, Americans have regarded the good society as one in which they have the opportunity make their own lives, rather than to make their common history. The dominant culture encourages Americans to place their hopes for fulfillment, not on collective action in the public sphere, but on the results of their individual efforts within the spheres of work, education, and family. Rather than endorsing ideological appeals to overthrow the powers that be, Americans in the majority have preferred to live within what amounts to a contract with them—a contract that allows elites to rule in return for continuing provision of the material basis for a "normal life."

The privatism and accommodation of the American majority is, however, not simply the natural expression of American culture. Mass political apathy and conservatism has always been the result of a prior history of mass mobilization and militancy. The specific terms of the American social contract have changed fundamentally from generation to generation because our shared conception of the requirements of "normal life" has greatly expanded. American history has been shaped by the fact that groups disadvantaged by a given contract have, over time, struggled to rewrite the contract so that their rights will be taken into account.

Social Movements

The primary means for carrying on such struggles, however, has not been to support a party that inscribes these rights as its program. Instead, when disadvantaged and disenfranchised groups in America have sought change they have done so through social movements. The essence of such movements is direct action—action that often breaches political rules and conventional norms. Such action eventuates when people who share common life circumstances come to believe that their daily lives are not normal, or that they are threatened or unnecessarily disadvantaged. They discover also that through their collective action they have a reasonable chance to change the conditions and terms that disadvantage or threaten them.

In the United States, left-wing activists could not build a

mass party of the workers; instead the great majority of America's leftists—socialists, communists, Marxists, social democrats, radical democrats, feminists, pacifists, anarchists—helped build movements by serving in a variety of leadership, educative, and organizing roles. Such Left movement activists were often members of ideologically oriented organizations, yet the record suggests that they were most effective not when they took their cues from the party line or followed party discipline but when they responded to the experienced consciousness and needs of the people with whom they were sharing struggle. The ideological Left parties rarely provided useful strategic direction to their activist members (indeed the party lines were often exceedingly counterproductive); instead, the primary positive function of the Socialist party, the Communist party, and other ideological organizations was to nurture members' activism. These parties' main historical contribution was that they provided training, support, and a sense of moral purpose that enabled at least some of their members to become centers for initiative for grass-roots action quite separate from the party's orbit.

American leftists for generations have had a contradictory attitude toward their participation in movements. On the one hand, when they ask themselves what they have accomplished in their political lives, overwhelmingly they respond by taking satisfaction from the historic changes wrought by the movements they have helped: the rights that have been won, the entitlements achieved, the ways in which protest has opened up the culture to new voices and expanded the horizons of exploited and oppressed groups. But when conscious leftists try to interpret the long-term meaning of their activity, they have a tendency to view these movements as something less than the "real thing." The real thing, they cannot help but feel, is a unified, class-based movement whose center is a party capable of taking power. The fragmented, nonideological movements of the United States are seen as rehearsals for the revolution, that is, the base from which more "advanced" consciousness and action can be launched.[4]

This attitude toward movements, we can now more clearly see, was delusory. The global decomposition of the party strategy ought to persuade us of what, in fact, has always been the case: if the Left is understood as a cumulative struggle for the democratization of society, then social movements themselves are the real embodiment of the Left tradition.[5]

Movements rather than parties are more likely to be vehicles of popular voice. Because the party by its nature is set up to represent, it reinforces the passivity of most members, although it may also serve as a socializing and educative framework for large numbers. Because of their relatively spontaneous, uninstitutionalized character, because they are dependent on high levels of participation by large numbers, because they are implemented in manifold activities at a micro level, and because they are moments in which previously inarticulate actors find voice and public visibility, movements are the closest thing we have, in practice, to authentic democracy. It is in moments of collective defiance that the possibility for democracy achieves some concrete reality and lagging democratic faith gets renewed.

After decades in which the American Left looked to Europe for models of advanced action, the tables have turned. If we want to know what can fill the vacuum created by the decline of the popularly based party, we might look to the U.S. experience, where such a vacuum has been a permanent political reality. What we learn from that experience is that social movements, representing a range of distinct interests and identities, constitute the primary vehicle of dramatic expression. Indeed, such a shift is now taking place globally as the key to democratic transformation.

Movements and Electoral Politics

Movements act in the streets, in civil society. They are, by definition, extraparliamentary. They use means of expression and power other than those available within politics normally understood. The American experience shows that movements must also interact with the state not only as a source of pressure on elites from outside but as a vehicle for achieving representation. Movement demands have to be legislated; rights claimed have to be legitimated. Moreover, the high intensity of mass action is not sustainable indefinitely; movement members need to go home, they want to live in the space their actions have helped create. They need political representation in order to carry on daily life. As a result, American movements have sought entry into the electoral arena. After some decades of experimentation with efforts to create their own parties—of which the Populists, the Socialist party of Eugene Debs, and the La Follette Progressive party of the 1920s are prime examples on the national level—movements have, especially since the New Deal era, sought influence in the Democratic party.

The movement effort to influence and penetrate the Democratic party has been going on now for fifty years. It was spearheaded by the labor movement in the 1930s and 1940s; it was followed by the civil rights movement in the 1960s, the women's movement in the 1970s, and by gays, environmentalists, and antinuclear groups in the years since. Movement strategies have included a variety of elements: the construction of movement-controlled state and local organizations to back candidates especially favorable to movement interests; election of delegates to party conventions to directly influence candidate selection and platform planks; mobilization to demand change of party rules to reduce power of professional politicians and party machines, and to require representation in party decision-making of women, minorities, and other previously underrepresented constituencies; and formation of national movement-based structures, such as the National Women's Political Caucus or Jesse Jackson's Rainbow Coalition, parallel to the official party structures, to influence selection of candidates and party directions and to mobilize movement constituencies in behalf of endorsed candidates.

The Democratic party has been significantly reshaped by the strategies and claims of diverse movements demanding place. Labor leadership succeeded in gaining access to the New Deal administration; labor exercised considerable control over a few key state party structures in the 1950s; and labor forged some fruitful alliances with key Democratic politicians. The civil rights movement succeeded in compelling the party to break the power of white supremacist Dixiecrats and to open its internal procedures so that blacks and other minorities could gain direct access. Machine control over urban party organizations was broken under the pressure of civil rights and Left-liberal mobilizations. By the end of the 1970s, the party leadership both locally and, to some extent nationally, included sizable contingents drawn from the ranks of civil rights, women's, antiwar, and labor movements. The major democratic movements are both outside and inside the Democratic party; each has won some position and influence within it. From the perspective of party professionals and professional politicians, the pressures of the labor, black, women's, environmentalist, and other movements threaten the party's organizational efficacy, while alienating the support of millions of "moderate" voters (that is, middle- and working-class privatized voters who are predominantly white, male, and middle aged). From the perspective of the movements, the party's professional leadership appears increasingly rudderless, lacking in will and imagination, and often cynical in its use of movement symbols to avoid substantive change. Bill Clinton's presidential campaign resolved this deadlock in behalf of the professionals, but movement leadership actively supported him nevertheless. The professional perspective dominates media framing of the purposes and strategies of the Clintonites (movement pressures are attributed to "narrow special interests" and "old-fashioned liberalism," while Clinton is defined as a "new Democrat neoliberal"). The character of the Clinton presidency remains uncertain. Beneath the current media frame there continues to be a considerable contest between movement and professional perspectives on both policy and political reality.

The "Local Level"

Since the 1960s, movement activists have had substantial success in influencing electoral politics and governmental policy at the level of city and state politics. In the aftermath of the 1960s, considerable numbers of New Left activists came to see that the student movement as such was a limited vehicle for advancing far-reaching social change. The university campus, despite its significance in "post-industrial society," remained too isolated from the political and cultural mainstream; students, despite their capacity for dramatic and effective disruption, could not achieve their goals without substantial links to potential majorities. And, from a biographical perspective, students must graduate into a wider world, where the styles and perspectives of political activism are quite different.

These insights led many student activists into local communities. Since the United States lacked a national political party framework that could smoothly absorb postgraduate students, many embarked on efforts to "organize at the local level." They focused on issues rooted in the experienced threats and grievances found there. What we mean by "new social movements" has much to do with these post-1960s organizing efforts, for it is out of these that feminism, environmentalism, gay liberation, and the anti-nuclear movements emerged.

The localist emphasis of post-1960s activism resulted in part from the limited resources available—most particularly the absence of any central organizational authority that could have directed a national strategy. Localism derived also from the ideological perspectives that dominated the New Left: the emphasis on participatory democracy, on decentralization, on human scale. The feminist critique of patriarchal leadership encouraged both male and female activists to work in self-effacing, face-to-face ways rather than in the self-promoting, top-down manner that "national" politics requires.

The new movements have developed, accordingly, in highly decentralized ways. Although each of them contains national organizational structures, these have relatively little to do with directing the manifold movement activities that have evolved over the last twenty years, most of which revolve around issues that arise in particular regions, communities, neighborhoods, and workplaces. For example, the "environmental movement" is best understood as constructed out of a host of seemingly disparate local protests and projects: struggles over land use, urban development, population growth, toxic waste disposal, nuclear power, neighborhood preservation, defense of traditional culture, occupational hazards, and so forth. In each case, members of a local community act in response to a threat while, at times, making use of the resources (language, know-how, material support) made available by the formal organizations of the national movement. In the midst of such local struggles there may well be some veteran activists— people whose identities were shaped in the Old or New Left—but, increasingly, such veteran leadership may not be a necessary ingredient for enabling local protest to take off. After twenty years, many who do not consider themselves to be "activists" have acquired the consciousness and skills to act effectively in local protest.

These local protests have been successful in deflecting some of the particular threats that initially sparked them, or in achieving various sorts of accommodations and ameliorations. But locally based movement activity rather quickly developed a certain strategic thrust that went beyond the merely reactive. This thrust may be summarized by saying that the movements have been struggling for local institutional change that would enable them to exercise a direct voice in governmental and institutional policy making. Beginning in the early 1970s, new social movement activists, especially in towns with large university populations, embarked on a strategy of running for local office. This effort has widened, and to some degree has resulted in local "rainbow coalition" strategies. In some places, blacks have linked with feminist, environmentalist, gay, and peace constituencies. Today, progressive coalitions have come to local power in a variety of places rather different from the "progressive" university town. Indeed, such political development seems likely wherever minority, environmental, women's, or gay constituencies carry some strategic weight. In many parts of the United States, local elections are nonpartisan; these provide the greatest space for such formation. There is probably no major city in the country whose local politics has not been affected by the separate and combined efforts of movement activists to win at least a piece of local power.

This is not the place to detail the substantive programmatic reforms that such local efforts have attempted, or to try to evaluate the results. It is perhaps a fair generalization to say that the most successful achievements have been those involving symbolic and legal reform rather than material reallocations. These include: more "diversity" and "affirmative action" in governmental staff appointments (so that more minorities and women now occupy administrative and advisory positions); more community recognition of minority identity claims (the Martin Luther King holiday was an early success in this regard; extension of antidiscrimination principles to gays would be another); support for movement-based human service activities (city subsidies for a variety of medical, counseling, legal, and educational services, but as the 1980s wore on, budgetary crunches hit these particularly hard).[6]

Perhaps the most interesting types of reform, however, were those that compelled public accountability and voice with respect to decisions that were previously reserved for specialized or elite arenas. Perhaps the biggest local gain of the environmental movement in California has been the environmental quality legislation that requires that all local development be subject to environmental impact review. The EIR process requires a public weighing of social costs, provides an arena for public testimony, and supplies the opportunity for public negotiation of "mitigations" with respect to all changes of land use. This process is a prime example of the way in which governmental procedures such as mandatory public hearings can provide community movements with significant opportunities for mobilization, public education, the development of expertise, and the exercise of community leadership. From the perspective of public authority, the process is designed to get movements "off the streets" and into the bureaucratic structure; in practice, however, it provides a degree of information and opportunity for voice not previously available, especially if those administering the hearing processes were elected with the backing of the movement.

In general, a variety of mechanisms embodying principles of public review and participatory planning have emerged in American community and institutional life. In addition to land use and related environmental decisions, similar mechanisms exist in some locales with respect to job hiring and promotion policies, police practices, health service provision, provision of services for the aged, and public education. The development of these mechanisms has meant considerable change in the structure of power at the local level in the United States. This statement is a limited one; American communities are now places where social movements have some ability to veto to modify unwanted decisions. What eludes them are institutional mechanisms for promoting economic redistribution, for effectively controlling the flow of capital, or for effectively determining the planning processes that shape their community's future. These processes derive from sources beyond the locality—the megacorporation and the national state—and it is these sources that are beyond the reach of locally based mobilization.

Coalition

The national political stalemate and the limits of local initiative together define the political situation shared by all of the social movements that are related to the Left tradition. Each of the movements—both "new" and "old"—has succeeded in advancing parts of its particular agenda. Certain rights, certain kinds of political representation, and certain aspects of cultural recognition have been achieved. As a result, a society that earlier denied workers elementary rights to organize, denied blacks and women elementary rights to vote, and whose towns and cities were dominated by rather tight circles of the economically powerful now more closely approximates the model of a politicocultural pluralism.

The most evident failure of the movements, however, has been their ability to meet the material needs of their most disadvantaged constituents. The labor movement presents the most glaring inventory of recent failure. It lost much of its power to protect gains previously won for its members, and it cannot advance the claims of unorganized workers. The black movement's advances in local power and cultural recognition, and the improved material position of the black middle class has been accompanied by a frightening deterioration in the life chances of blacks in the "inner city." The women's movement's gains have not prevented the "feminization of poverty."

Each of the movements taken separately lacks the power in numbers and in leverage to advance a credible program that might lead toward economic redistribution. The most likely strategic solution, then, would be to find the basis for movement coalition, since it is only by making effective alliance that political resources for such change might be found. The political potential for movement coalition stems from the immediate need of each movement for allies. But there are deeper and more promising grounds for movement coalition. Beneath each of the major movements' particular sectoral agenda is an implicit demand for fundamental social restructuring. Despite their apparently nonideological and reformist character, each movement embodies a far-reaching social vision. Even when these movements have seemed narrowly focused on a single issue, the cumulative effect of their pressure on social institutions has broad implications for the way power is structured and authority is exercised.

It is currently fashionable to assert that we have passed the point in history where "common ground" can be found among social fragments. The value of this claim is that it has permanently delegitimated the notion that "class" is the primary political category and that class interest constitutes the basis for a unified and more "advanced" politics. But "common ground" as articulated by contemporary movement theorists does not require that discrete movements abandon their separate cultures and claims. Instead, what can be imagined are efforts to find programmatic ways to respond to the shared needs of movement constituencies. Such needs exist in large measure because "class" remains a fundamental measure of life chances, even if it is not a conscious framework for social identity. To give a concrete illustration, in the United States the socialization of health care is a programmatic direction desperately needed by large numbers of workers, by women of diverse backgrounds, by the gay community struggling with the scourge of AIDS, by minority communities, as well as by millions in the "middle class" and by many businesses whose private provisions for employees are inadequate to cope with spiraling health costs. Similar points can be made about other areas of social need such as housing and education. It is, in short, not enormously difficult to identify needs shared by black and white workers, by women and men, by the young and the old, and to imagine how these shared needs might form the basis of a common political agenda for a new political coalition.

An effort to construct such a coalition among the movements around such an agenda is the main hope for a revival of social reform in the United States. Movement-oriented intellectuals have been arguing this for a number of years. Jesse Jackson's presidential effort in 1988 tried to articulate these themes and to project the possibility of such a coalition. Despite expectations that the Jackson project would be attempted again during the 1992 campaign, Jackson and other movement leaderships chose instead to work actively but quietly for the Clinton campaign, whose strategy focused on winning over those working-class voters (white, male) who were most alienated from the movements. In other words, instead of trying to create a program that might serve to coalesce the movements and simultaneously appeal to the disaffected "middle class," movement leaders tacitly agreed to their tactical marginalization. The hope, of course, was that a Democratic presidency would reopen public space for a revival of social reform.

It seems possible that some significant reform measures will be enacted during the 1990s. In the next decade, some sort of comprehensive national health insurance seems likely to be adopted, some refunding of education will take place, and there will be some national effort to restore economic chances for some of those in the working class who have lost ground in the last decades. These are measures that are likely to have considerable corporate backing because they provide some public investment and socialization of costs that many corporate leaders have begun to identify as necessary for capital accumulation and national competitiveness. But such programs are likely to be an inadequate basis for common ground. For one thing, state fiscal constraints will limit their substantive value. Already we have been told that there will not be a "peace dividend" large enough to meet pressing social needs and that paying for the financial and environmental costs of the Reagan years will further exacerbate already threatening budget deficits. A new movement coalition is likely to discover that an effort to revitalize the New Deal during the Clinton years will not result in major change, although it may succeed in providing at least a brief period of state-sponsored reform.

Beyond the Welfare State

A movement coalition needs to be grounded in a vision that goes beyond the welfare state if it is to construct a viable politics in a time when the economy is globalized and society is decentered. I suggest that the heart of that vision is to be found in the largely unarticulated shared logic of each of the major movements—whether "new" or "old." What is shared by these movements is precisely the demand that society should be structured so that people can shape the conditions of their lives. The labor movement did not struggle simply for better wages and working conditions; it struggled for workers' voice, for their right to organize and to determine the terms of their employment. The black movement did not campaign simply for equal treatment; its central demand has always revolved around empowerment. Feminism is not just about gender equality; it aims at the fundamental restructuring of power relations between the sexes. Both the peace and environmental movements are fundamentally efforts to make public decision-making fully accountable to those affected by it and to give people in their communities the chance to control their own futures.

If we can no longer rely on the hope for a party to represent the people, or on a nation-state to embody the people's hopes, then we have to make concretely realizable a vision of a society organized so that people have some chance to directly express themselves as well as to hold those who speak for them account-able. Perhaps the answer to the domination of the megacorpora-tion and the disintegration of the national state is to enable people to find power in and through communities.

The logic of social movements suggests that the nature of the state needs to be fundamentally reconceived. If democratization were taken as the guiding principle of political action and the primary standard of political legitimation, then the state would be seen not as the center of rule making and the source of social welfare but as a vehicle for community empowerment and local control. We need to think of the national state not as the source of initiative and control, not as the vehicle for solutions of problems, but principally as the potential source of capital and law that would enable people to solve their problems at the level of the com-munity.

Indeed, such a function may be the only viable one remaining for the national state in a society that is both globalizing and decentering. It may seem absurd to reimagine the central state as a vehicle for decentralization. But the American experience, with its federal constitution and traditions of local control, provides some examples of how such a process could work. I briefly sketch some of the kinds of state policies that would support the logic of democratic decentralization.

1. Legal recognition of movement-based organization. An example in practice is the Wagner Act of 1936 that guaranteed workers' rights to form unions and to strike and established a machinery requiring collective bargaining between recognized unions and employers. Similar kinds of organizing and bargaining rights have been proposed for public utility consumers, neighbor-hood organizations, and tenant unions. A number of federal pro-grams have required "participation" in planning service delivery on the part of client groups. Such provisions have encouraged the growth of movement organizations among the urban poor and among senior citizens.

2. Federal subsidy for community organization. Again, there is precedent, in such programs as VISTA, and the 1960s War on Poverty, and a variety of other direct and indirect programs.

3. Legal and material support for locally based "impact review." On the model of the California Environmental Impact Review, communities could require a wide range of social accounting with respect to a variety of publicly relevant decisions, broadening the concept to include "economic" and "social" as well as "environmental" impacts. Such review could be federally mandated, and federal programs could assist community-based groups by providing technical expertise, research support, and the like.

4. Federal "block" grants. A necessary function of central authority is redistribution; decentralization is bound to result in manifold inequalities. Rather than administer such transfers, subsidies, and reallocations through centralized bureaucracies with elaborate rules and programmatic targets, a decentralizing approach is embodied in the idea of block grants—unencumbered funds provided to communities on need-based formulas with the use of these funds to be fought out politically at community or regional levels.

5. Federal allocation of capital. Community empowerment requires the ability to create community owned, locally based enterprises where "private," market-based investments do not meet community defined needs. Community ownership of public utilities can support local autonomy, provide an infrastructure for "soft" energy alternatives, and generate revenues for local use. Community investment in job-creating enterprises can be a response to the loss of private investment. Community provision of services can offset loss of services from cost-cutting private firms. The national government may be a necessary source for capital and expertise for the initiation of such enterprises. A national, public bank could be such a mechanism for social investment.[7]

I am not here putting forward specific proposals; my point, instead, is to illustrate how central government could provide the legal, material, and technical foundation for various forms of local, participatory democracy. The outcome of such a process of decentralization would be the institutionalization of social movements as frameworks of everyday, popular participation in institutional governance, community planning, and regional resource allocation. Such institutionalization seems to me to be inherent in the logic of the movements. The drive to transform the state in such a direction, I suggest, could be an effective basis for movement alliance. Now that the party is over, the people themselves are going to have to take responsibility for their collective futures. The movements—as social formations, as repositories of social vision, as training grounds for political competence—seem destined to be the vehicles for such responsibility.

Notes

1. Obviously in practice many leftists have fundamentally violated their radical democratic claims. As I discuss below, leftist struggles for state power, using professional political organization as a vehicle, were always contradicting their fundamental moral claims.

2. Note that I am deliberately—and I hope provocatively—glossing over the deep differences among the types of parties that emerged during this century. Certainly, there was a profound moral as well as practical gulf between the social democratic parties of Western Europe and Lenin's "party of a new type," between parties led by Marxists of various stripes and non-Marxist socialist or labor parties. Through all of their histories, these parties fought each other most bitterly, both within their own societies and in the arenas of international socialism. Yet, all of these party formations were grounded in certain shared strategic principles and, despite their deep differences, all shared certain key contradictions.

3. The interplay of class, race, and ethnicity is a topic of much research and discussion. I have been particularly influenced in my own thinking by Aronowitz (1992) and Bonacich (1976).

4. Again, despite current emphases on movement fragmentation and identity politics as "new" and "postmodern," the actual history of U.S. social movements suggests that these have always been characteristic.

5. For a fuller development of this argument, see Flacks 1988.

6. The rise of progressive electoral coalitions has been described in Clavel 1986. For studies of two key cases see Kann 1990 and Conroy 1990. See also Kling and Posner 1990.

7. One of the best sources of ideas and schemes—some derived from other societies—using government as a source of capital for twenty-seven communities is Carnoy and Shearer 1980. An important recent statement of a vision of a decentralizing national state appears in Alperovitz 1992.

References

Alperovitz, Gar. 1992. "Memo to Clinton." *Tikkun,* November, 13–19.
Aronowitz, Stanley. 1992. *False Promises.* Durham, N.C.: Duke University Press.

Bonacich, Edna. 1976. "Advanced Capitalism and Black-White Relations in the U.S.: A Split Labor Market Interpretation." *American Sociological Review* 41:34–51.

Carnoy, Martin, and Derek Shearer. 1980. *Economic Democracy.* Amonk, N.Y.: M. E. Sharpe.

Clavel, Pierre. 1986. *The Progressive City.* New Brunswick, N.J.: Rutgers University Press.

Conroy, W. J. 1990. *Challenging the Boundaries of Reform: Socialism in Burlington.* Philadelphia: Temple University Press.

Flacks, Richard. 1988. *Making History: The American Left and the American Mind.* New York: Columbia University Press.

Kann, Mark. 1990. *Middle Class Radicalism in Santa Monica.* Philadelphia: Temple University Press.

Kling, J. M., and P. S. Posner. 1990. *Dilemmas of Activism.* Philadelphia: Temple University Press.

Laclau, Ernesto, and Chantal Mouffe. 1985. *Hegemony and Socialist Strategy: Toward a Radical Democratic Politics.* London: Verso.

Michels, Robert. 1959. *Political Parties.* New York: Dover.

The Contributors

José Alvarez-Junco was professor of history of political ideas and social movements at the University of Madrid, and he currently holds the Prince of Asturias Chair in Spanish History and Civilization at Tufts University. He is the author of several books and numerous articles on cultural and social aspects of Spanish political life in the late nineteenth and early twentieth centuries.

Robert D. Benford is an associate professor of sociology at the University of Nebraska–Lincoln, where his teaching and research interests are in social movements, peace and war, and social constructionism. He has recently published articles in *American Sociological Review, Social Forces, Sociological Quarterly, International Social Movement Research, Journal of Contemporary Ethnography,* and *Sociological Inquiry*.

Richard Flacks is professor of sociology at the University of California, Santa Barbara. His most recent books include *Making History: The American Left and the American Mind* (New York: Columbia University Press, 1988); and, with Jack Whalen, *Beyond the Barricades: The Sixties Generation Grows Up* (Philadelphia: Temple University Press, 1989).

Joseph R. Gusfield is professor emeritus of sociology at the University of California, San Diego. He has written widely on developing nations, the sociology of education, and political sociology, but his major work has been in social movements, social problems, and the sociology of law, with focus on the legal and political controls on alcohol and other health behaviors. Among his books are *Symbolic Crusade: Status Politics and the American Temperance Movement* (Urbana: University of Illinois Press, 1963); *Protest, Reform, and Revolt* (New York: John Wiley and Sons, 1970); and *The Culture of Public Problems: Drinking-Driving and the Symbolic Order* (Chicago: University of Chicago Press, 1981). He has been president of the Society for the Study of Social Problems and of the

Pacific Sociological Association. He received the Charles Horton Cooley Award for outstanding book of 1981–1983 from the Society for the Study of Symbolic Interaction; he was also awarded their George Herbert Mead Award for lifetime achievement.

Scott A. Hunt is assistant professor of sociology at the University of Kentucky. He received his Ph.D. from the University of Nebraska-Lincoln in 1991. His publications include articles in *Perspectives on Social Problems, Sociological Inquiry, Journal of Contemporary Ethnography, Rural Sociology,* and *Mid-American Review of Sociology.* His areas of interest include social movements, identity, social problems, theory, symbolic interactionism, and the social construction of commonsense knowledge.

Hank Johnston is a lecturer in the Department of Sociology, San Diego State University. He has published research on nationalism and political opposition in *Journal for the Scientific Study of Religion, Sociological Analysis, Research in Social Movements, Conflict and Change, Journal of Baltic Studies,* among others. He is the author of *Tales of Nationalism: Catalonia, 1939–1979* (New Brunswick, N.J.: Rutgers University Press, 1991). He is conducting research on nationalism and the arts and on the sociolinguistic aspects of collective identity.

Bert Klandermans is professor in the Department of Social Psychology, Free University, Amsterdam. His research focuses on mobilization and participation in social movements. He is currently studying farmer's protests in the Netherlands and Spain and, with John Olivier, the responses of movement and countermovement supporters to the social and political transitions in South Africa. He is the editor of a new series of monographs on social movements and protest published by University of Minnesota Press. His *Social Construction of Protest: Social Psychological Principles of Movement Participation* is forthcoming from Basil Blackwell. He is the editor with Craig Jenkins of *The Politics of Social Protest: Comparative Perspectives on States and Social Movements* (University of Minnesota Press, 1993).

Enrique Laraña is titular professor of sociology and coordinator of the doctoral program at the University of Madrid, Somosaguas

Campus. He is currently studying the organization and development of new social movements in Spain. He is the author of numerous articles and chapters in edited volumes. He organized the seminar "New Social Movements and the End of Ideology" in August 1990 at the Menédez Pelayo International University, Santander, Spain, where several of the essays in this volume were first presented.

Doug McAdam is professor of sociology at the University of Arizona. He is the author of *Political Process and the Development of Black Insurgency, 1930–1970* (Chicago: University of Chicago Press, 1982), and *Freedom Summer* (New York: Oxford University Press, 1988), which was honored as the cowinner of the C. Wright Mills Award. His current research interests in social movements include the cross-national diffusion of movement ideas and the relationship between social movements/revolutions and demographic processes.

John D. McCarthy is professor of sociology and a member of the Life Cycle Institute at the Catholic University of America, Washington, D.C. He has served as president of the Collective Behavior and Social Movements Section of ASA. He has published numerous articles and chapters, over the past two decades, that have helped set the agenda for research in the field of social movements. Many of these are collected in *Social Movements in an Organizational Society,* which he edited with Mayer N. Zald (New Brunswick, N.J.: Transaction Books, 1987).

Alberto Melucci is professor of sociology and clinical psychology at the University of Milano, and he is a practicing psychotherapist. Through numerous books and articles, his contributions to the field of social movements and collective and personal identity are internationally recognized. His recent books include *Nomads of the Present: Social Movements and Individual Needs in Contemporary Society* (Philadelphia: Temple University Press, 1989), and *Il gioco dell'io* (Milan: Feltrinelli, 1991).

Carol Mueller is associate professor of sociology in the Social and Behavioral Sciences Program of Arizona State University West. She has served as president of the Collective Behavior and

Social Movements Section of the ASA. She is editor, with Aldon D. Morris, of *Frontiers in Social Movement Theory* (New Haven: Yale University Press, 1992), and, with Mary Katzenstein, *The Women's Movements of the United States and Western Europe* (Philadelphia: Temple University Press, 1987).

David A. Snow is professor of sociology and head of the Department of Sociology at the University of Arizona in Tucson. He is coauthor, with Leon Anderson, of *Down on Their Luck: A Study of Homeless Street People* (Berkeley: University of California Press, 1993), and he is currently conducting research on social movement mobilization among the homeless across eighteen of the nation's largest cities. He has published widely on social movement micromobilization, on framing processes in relation to social movements, and on conversion processes, particularly in relation to religious cults and movements.

Máté Szabó is assistant professor of political science at the Eötvös Loránd University, Budapest, and he has written numerous articles in English and German. He was a guest lecturer at the University of Hamburg and a research fellow at the Alexander von Humboldt Foundation at the University of Hamburg Institute of Political Science. He has served as the secretary general of the Hungarian Political Science Association, and he is currently editor of the *Hungarian Political Science Review*.

Ralph H. Turner is professor of sociology emeritus at the University of California, Los Angeles. He has been president of the American Sociological Association and chair of the Collective Behavior and Social Movements Section. He is author, with Lewis M. Killian, of *Collective Behavior* (Engelwood Cliffs, N.J.: Prentice-Hall, 1957, 1962, 1987), and he has written numerous articles in the field of collective behavior and social movements.

Index

Abeyance processes, 214, 215, 238
Abolitionist movement, 40, 79, 95
Abortion rights movement, 8, 63, 69, 70, 256 (*see also* Antiabortion movement); framing in, 69
ACLU. *See* American Civil Liberties Union
Activists, 93–94, 95, 186, 216, 221; discourse of, 211, 217; intergenerational relationship among, 27–28, 29, 283; in political office, 343; structural roles of, 6, 8, 226; subcultures of, 43–45
African American movement, 341; common ground shared by other new social movements and, 88, 96, 98n6, 347; failures of, 345
African Americans, 200, 241
Aiken, Doris, 144
Alcohol industry: and the anti–drunk driving movement, 160–61n7, 161–62n16, 163n18; and the public health frame, 159
Alcohol Safety Action Programs (ASAPs), 140–41, 149, 161–62n16
Alternative medicine. *See* Health movements
Altri Codici (Melucci), 14
"America First" movement, 98n8
American Academy of Arts and Sciences, 241–42
American Civil Liberties Union, 161–62n16
American Constitution, 95, 98n9
American Friends Service Committee, 44, 196
American Indian movement. *See* Native American movement
American Revolution, 49, 82, 98n9, 330
Anabaptists, 81
Anarchism: and the Left, 330, 338; in Spain, 307, 308, 311, 324n8
Animal rights movement, 3, 6, 49, 59, 65

Antiabortion movement, 63, 69, 74. *See also* Abortion rights movement
Anti–drunk driving movement, 52, 139 (*see also* Drunk driving); activists' role in, 146–50, 154–55, 156–57, 158–59, 161n11, 161–62n16; constituents of, 144–45; federal and state facilitation of, 138–41, 155–57, 158, 159, 160n5, 161–62n16, 163n19; mobilization in, atypical, 155–56; organizations in, 143–46, 161–62n16
Antinuclear movement, 3, 59, 186; British, 93; and the Democratic party, 340; grievances in, 40, 284; and identity issues, 94; as linear movement, 65; roots of, 342; structural roles of participants in, 6
Antipornography movement, 98n5
Anti-Semitism, 91, 98n8
Antismoking movement, 8
Antiwar movement. *See* Peace movements
Armenia, 274; nationalism in, 268, 271, 272–73, 274–75. *See also* Soviet Union, nationalism in
ASAPs. *See* Alcohol Safety Action Programs
Asian movement (United States), 7
Asturias miners' strikes, 304, 305
Atkinson, Ti-Grace, 250
Austria, 3, 293, 294
Automobile crashes, 133, 135
Automobile safety, 140, 160n5; frames for, 135, 136–38, 142, 157, 160n2, 160n3, 160n4, 160n5, 163n20; public attention to, 142, 146
Aveni, Adrian, 24

Baltic states, 267, 272, 279, 281
Basque nationalist movement, 315 (*see also* Spain, nationalism in); activist subcultures in, 44, 270, 271, 272–73; consensus mobilization in, 225;